"This is an important and provocative book historical roots and contemporary twists i Reese forcefully reveals how politics really sometimes murky prehistory to the 'welfare repeal' of 1996, just as politics will surely matter again in this ostensibly post-welfare era."

JAMIE PECK, author of *Workfare States*

"Reese provides a powerful analysis of the reasons why America's poorest families are increasingly being left to struggle on their own. This book authoritatively exposes the politics that have undermined the economic human rights of this nation's impoverished mothers and children. Reese's careful scholarship probes deeply into the forces fueling America's hostility toward welfare and those forced to rely upon it."

KENNETH J. NEUBECK, coauthor of *Welfare Racism: Playing the Race Card Against America's Poor*

"This is an exhaustively researched book about changing U.S. attitudes and policies toward welfare mothers in the second half of the twentieth century. Reese richly conveys the profound human costs of the backlash against welfare for the women, children, and families who are bearing the brunt of these attacks. This is a book on a vitally important topic of great public interest. Reese breathes humanity into both the political players and the victimized welfare mothers."

DAVID A. SMITH, Professor of Sociology at the University of California, Irvine, and former editor of *Social Problems*

"Thoughtful and extremely well researched, this book reexamines and sheds new light on the origins of the current welfare 'crisis.' Reese shows the tragic consequences for welfare families and calls for a New Deal for working families. This book could not be more timely."

JOEL F. HANDLER, author of *The Poverty of Welfare Reform*

"Comprehensive, with insightful analysis. Reese provides thoughtful policy suggestions for a New Deal for working families. This book is a must-read for anyone concerned with the plight of poor women and their families."

JILL QUADAGNO, author of *One Nation, Uninsured: Why the U.S. Has No National Health Insurance*

Backlash against Welfare Mothers

Backlash against Welfare Mothers

Past and Present

ELLEN REESE

University of California Press

BERKELEY   LOS ANGELES   LONDON

Ideas discussed in chapters 1–6 and chapter 11, and data appearing in tables 3, 4, 6, 7, and the appendices, appeared previously in Ellen Reese, "The Politics of Motherhood: The Restriction of Poor Mothers' Welfare Rights in the United States, 1949–1960," *Social Politics: International Studies in Gender, State, and Society* 2001, vol. 8 (1): 65–112, and appear by permission of Oxford University Press.

Similar ideas to those discussed across the book appear in Ellen Reese, "Patriarchy, Racism, and Business Interests: Cross-Class Support for Welfare Retrenchment in the United States," in *Looking Forward/ Looking Back: An Introduction to U.S. Women's Studies*, ed. Carol Berkin, Carole Appel, and Judith Pinch (Upper Saddle River, NJ: Prentice Hall, forthcoming).

University of California Press
Berkeley and Los Angeles, California

University of California Press, Ltd.
London, England

Library of Congress Cataloging-in-Publication Data
Reese, Ellen, 1969–.
   Backlash against welfare mothers : past and present / Ellen Reese.
      p.   cm.
   Includes bibliographical references and index.
   ISBN 0-520-24461-3 (cloth : alk. paper) — ISBN 0-520-24462-1 (pbk. : alk. paper)
      1. Public welfare—United States—History.   2. Welfare recipients—Employment—United States.   3. Aid to families with dependent children programs.   4. Single mothers—Government policy—United States.   5. United States—Social policy.   I. Title.
HV91.R4225   2005
362.5'568'0973—dc22   2004019546

Manufactured in the United States of America

13   12   11   10   09   08   07   06   05
10   9   8   7   6   5   4   3   2   1

Printed on Ecobook 50 containing a minimum 50% post-consumer waste, processed chlorine free. The balance contains virgin pulp, including 25% Forest Stewardship Council Certified for no old growth tree cutting, processed either TCF or ECF. The sheet is acid-free and meets the minimum requirements of ANSI/NISO Z39.48–1992 (R 1997) *(Permanence of Paper)*.

For all those forced to cope with the shortcomings of the current welfare system, and all those fighting for a better one

Contents

Illustrations

Acknowledgments

This book began as a dissertation focusing on the 1950s welfare backlash, which I wrote while a graduate student at the University of California, Los Angeles. The chair of my dissertation committee, Ruth Milkman, generously supported my research, and her insistence on the connections between labor and welfare politics helped to shape it. Other members of my dissertation committee, Michael Mann, Rebecca Emigh, Joel Handler, and Vilma Ortiz, also provided invaluable feedback on my dissertation, as did my dissertation support group, Susan Markens, Eva Fodor, Manali Desai, and Julie Press. Susan Markens and Joel Handler read subsequent drafts of the book, providing critical feedback and support in later years.

My editor at the University of California Press, Naomi Schneider, and my reviewers at the Press, Fred Block and Jamie Peck, challenged me to examine the present period of welfare politics in more depth and make it more central to the book. This task sometimes seemed daunting, but I believe this book has more to say as a result of their advice. Thoughtful feedback from these reviewers, David A. Smith, and Elizabeth Berg improved the manuscript considerably.

As I transformed my dissertation into a book, I was warmly supported by colleagues at my first two jobs, at the University of Missouri, Columbia, and California State University at San Bernardino, as well as my current position at the University of California, Riverside. Many scholars, both at these institutions and outside of them, read and commented on various parts of my book, providing invaluable feedback and support. These include Edna Bonacich, Scott Coltrane, Gary Dymski, Tracy Fisher, Joya Misra, Felicia Kornbluh, Clarence Lo, Peter M. Hall, Masako Ishii-Kuntz, Kenneth Neubeck, Ann Orloff, Karen Pyke, Tom Reifer, and Marguerite Waller. Edna Bonacich and Scott Coltrane provided considerable advice and support on the project.

My participation in the welfare rights movement in Los Angeles began in 1998 and eventually grew into a multi-state research project on political struggles over welfare reform. Though not my original intention, insights I gained from this movement eventually made their way into this book, especially chapter 1. I am very grateful to all the activists who welcomed me into their world, answered my questions, and spoke at protest events and public hearings. I learned a great deal from them. In many great conversations, Nancy Berlin, Bob Erlenbusch, Shawn Goldsmith, John Jackson, Dennis Kao, Alicia Lepe, Abdullah Mohammed, Matt Sharp, Frank Tamborello, and Amy Schur kept me informed on welfare issues. While I was teaching, a number of students, who had experienced welfare reform as recipients or case managers, shared their personal stories with me. They helped open my eyes and inspired me to write.

I am particularly grateful to my husband, Ernest Savage, for providing feedback on many of the ideas contained in this book and generously sharing his own research on welfare issues for his documentary film *The Price of Poverty* and news reports for KPFK. He also provided loving support during both the high and the low points of writing this book, as well as my moves in and out of four different universities. My family and many other friends, colleagues, and housemates were important sources of support, advice, and feedback at various stages of this project. These include Aldaberto Aguirre Jr., Terri Anderson, Eileen Boris, Linda Brewster-Stearns, Chris Chase Dunn, Piya Chatterjee, Amy Denison, Alan Emery, Manali Desai, G. William Domhoff, Gabriella Fried, Christine Gailey, Bill Gallegos, John Galliher, Elham Gheytanchi, Mary Grigsby, Pat Gowens, Joan Hermsen, Jennifer Jordan, John Krinsky, Eric Magnuson, David S. Meyer, Mike Miller, Mary Jo Neitz, Francesca Palik, Frances Fox Piven, Eyal Rabinovitch, Cynthia Reed, Dylan Riley, Connie Santos, Michele Sartell, Jacob Savin, Sara Shostak, Max Stevens, Aaron Thomas, Delores Trevizo, Jonathan Turner, Zulema Valdez, Nicholas Wolfinger, Dianne Wright, and Maurice Zeitlin.

Finally, I wish to thank Erin Ladd, Shoon Lio, Acela Ojeda, Katrina Paxton, Elvia Ramirez, and Fannie Siu for their research assistance. I owe special thanks to Shoon Lio, who provided the most assistance for this project and often went beyond his assigned duties. Conversations with Elvia Ramirez, Shoon Lio, and Acela Ojeda and articles they gave me helped shape my ideas for this book. My research would not have been possible without the skills and generosity of many librarians and archivists. I am grateful to the UCLA Center for the Study of Women, UCLA Department of Sociology, UCR Division of the Academic Senate, UCR Center for Ideas and

Society, and the Woodrow Wilson Foundation for financial support for this project. My cross-country visits to libraries and archives would not have been financially possible, or as enjoyable, without the hospitality of many people who welcomed me into their homes, including the Hull family, the Markens family, Michael Lloyd, Francesca Palik, my sister, and my parents.

Abbreviations

ADC	Aid to Dependent Children
AEI	American Enterprise Institute
AFBF	American Farm Bureau Federation
AFDC	Aid to Families with Dependent Children
BPA	Bureau of Public Assistance
CED	Committee for Economic Development
CISW	California Institute for Social Welfare
CWA	Concerned Women of America
CWT	Community Work and Training
EITC	Earned Income Tax Credit
FAIR	Federation of American Immigration Reform
FAP	Family Assistance Plan
FRC	Family Research Council
GAI	guaranteed annual income
HEW	Department of Health, Education, and Welfare
IAV	Institute for American Values
INS	Immigration and Naturalization Service
JOBS	Job Opportunities and Basic Skills
MDTA	Manpower Development and Training Act
NAM	National Association of Manufacturers
NIT	negative income tax
NOLEO	"Notice to Law Enforcement Officials"
NWRO	National Welfare Rights Organization

OAA	Old Age Assistance
OASI	Old Age and Survivors Insurance
OBRA	Omnibus Budget Reconciliation Act
OEO	Office of Economic Opportunity
PBJI	Program for Better Jobs and Income
PRWORA	Personal Responsibility and Work Opportunity Reconciliation Act
SOS	Save Our State
SSI	Supplemental Security Income
TANF	Temporary Aid to Needy Families
TVC	Traditional Values Coalition
W-2	Wisconsin Works
WET	Work Experience and Training
WIN	Work Incentive Program
WTW	welfare-to-work

PART I

Welfare Opposition

Causes and Consequences

1. Deferred Dreams, Broken Families, and Hardship

The Impact of Welfare Reform

Welfare reform is supposed to help people, but instead it is causing me hardship. . . . Welfare reform is nothing more than reducing caseloads, cutting people off [of] welfare, pushing us into greater poverty.

ANONYMOUS WELFARE MOTHER

[Welfare reform] was portrayed initially as a program that would result in people moving out of poverty . . . Let's just say what it actually is, which is a program that puts people to work and stops public assistance, and it doesn't matter what the work is.

ACTIVIST FROM 9TO5, an organization for working women

A lot of people are not able to attain their dreams and goals because they've had to cut everything short to get a minimum wage job at Wendy's or McDonald's. Working in those places, no one is going to be able to become independent and support a family.

ANONYMOUS WELFARE MOTHER struggling to stay in college

GETTING PAST THE DOGMA

In 1996, following mounting attacks on Aid to Families with Dependent Children (AFDC), Congress passed the Personal Responsibility and Work Opportunity Reconciliation Act, which significantly restricted poor families' rights to income and social services. It ended their federal entitlements to welfare, froze welfare expenditures, and replaced AFDC with a more decentralized and selective program called Temporary Aid to Needy Families (TANF). A central aim of the new welfare law was to promote self-sufficiency, through work and marriage, among low-income mothers, who make up about 90 percent of adult TANF recipients.[1] To do so, it imposed two-year consecutive and five-year lifetime limits on receiving welfare, significantly expanded welfare-to-work programs, and provided funds for programs promoting marriage and sexual abstinence. PRWORA targeted legal immigrants for the most drastic cuts, denying most of them access to federal public assistance during their first five years in the country. Encouraged to experiment with new rules and regulations, many states further restricted welfare. Twenty states adopted time limits shorter than the federal government's lifetime limits,[2] and twenty-three adopted a "family cap" or "child exclusion" policy that denies additional benefits for children conceived during welfare receipt.[3] After PRWORA's passage, congressional politicians continued to attack poor mothers' welfare rights. They are now poised to impose even tougher work requirements on welfare mothers and expand schemes to promote marriage and sexual abstinence. Welfare for low-income families, already far more restrictive in the United States than in other Western industrialized countries, is likely to become even more so.

Supporters of welfare reform policies claim that tough rules and regulations are necessary for disciplining the poor and encouraging self-sufficiency. Praising the success of welfare reform, politicians tell "success stories" about individual recipients who managed to make the transition from welfare to work,[4] and note the dramatic decline in welfare cases, from 4.5 million families in 1996 to 2.1 million families in 2002.[5] They also highlight research showing that in the late 1990s, between one-half and two-thirds of former recipients were employed one or two years after leaving welfare,[6] while employment rates among adult TANF recipients rose from 8 to 28 percent between 1994 and 1999.[7]

Caseload reductions and rising labor force participation rates, however, are problematic indicators of welfare reform's success. First, some researchers contend that they are just as much, if not more, the product of the employment boom of the 1990s, than of welfare reform.[8] Indeed, the employment rate among current and former welfare recipients began to rise *before* federal reforms were implemented, increasing from 20 to 27 percent between 1992 and 1996. Likewise, the number of families receiving welfare began declining in 1994, from 5 million to 4.4 million in 1996.[9] Moreover, when labor market conditions worsened after 1999, welfare caseloads in many states began to rise, while current and former recipients' employment rates declined.[10]

Second, caseload reductions are not always something to celebrate. Not all women who leave welfare do so voluntarily or because they have found a job. National studies of mothers who left welfare between 1995 and 1999 found that between 40 and 50 percent of these women were not working, and 12 to 20 percent had no apparent source of income.[11] Nationally, more than five hundred thousand families were sanctioned off welfare for not complying with regulations between 1997 and 1999, and many others were discouraged from applying for welfare.[12] By 2000, only 50 percent of those people who were eligible for welfare were receiving it, down from 84 percent in 1995.[13] Even during the employment boom of the late 1990s, homelessness and hunger increased after PRWORA's implementation and worsened after the onset of the recession in 2001 when many recipients reached the end of their time limits.[14]

Most recipients who managed to leave welfare for work also remained poor. Most were earning poverty wages, and between one-fifth and one-third continued to cycle between welfare and work.[15] Some employed mothers were even worse off financially than they had been before leaving welfare because of the loss of subsidized child care and health care and other work-related expenses.[16] As a result, although welfare caseloads declined dramatically, child poverty rates did not. By 2002, the official U.S. child poverty rate was 17 percent, compared to 18 percent in 1990; the poverty rates of single, working mothers remained stagnant in the late 1990s.[17] More disturbing, as the social safety net shrank, the depth of poverty increased sharply between 1996 and 2002.[18]

Of course, poor families' experiences with welfare reform are not uniformly negative. Some recipients—such as grandmothers, women on Native American reservations where more than 50 percent of the population is unemployed, and mothers in two-parent households when the father works—are exempt from new welfare-to-work (WTW) rules, time limits, or both.[19] Other recipients find WTW programs helpful in finding employment and leaving welfare. This experience is more common among women who have higher educational attainment, more job skills and work experience, speak English, live outside job-poor inner cities and rural areas, have older and healthier children, and are white (and so are less vulnerable to employment discrimination).[20] Transitions from welfare to work that significantly increase income do improve family well-being and boost elementary school children's educational achievement.[21]

On the other hand, many recipients are not so fortunate. Recipients' negative experiences with, and criticisms of, welfare reform are seldom included in public policy debates. Indeed, whereas more than a hundred business representatives testified in welfare reform hearings before the 104th Congress, only seventeen former or current welfare recipients did.[22] As one service provider observed, "Some of these mothers are having hardships and no one is listening."[23] Many mothers, ashamed of their poverty, remain in "the welfare closet," silent about their daily battles for survival and upward mobility.[24] When they do speak, they often recount tales of frustration and suffering. This chapter shares some of these stories and puts them in the context of national and local studies of the impact of welfare reform.

FROM THE AMERICAN DREAM
TO THE AMERICAN NIGHTMARE

A central goal of welfare reform is to increase employment among low-income mothers. Many are unable to obtain employment because they lack education and training. About 44 percent of adults receiving TANF lack a high school diploma or GED, which significantly lowers their employment prospects.[25] National studies suggest that welfare-to-work (WTW) programs that emphasize job quality lead to better employment outcomes than those based on a "work first" approach, which encourages participants to take the first job offered.[26] Despite such research, most states implement "work first" policies that prioritize paid employment over job training, education, and supportive services.[27] The "work first" philosophy presumes, often wrongly, that "a job, any job, is better than no job."[28]

Welfare regulations and the "work first" philosophy create many obstacles for welfare mothers who want to pursue the American dream by obtaining more education and training. WTW participants are often limited in terms of the number of hours that they can spend in classes, and social workers frequently pressure students to accept employment and quit school. For example, when Wisconsin Works (or W-2) was first implemented, many teen parents were encouraged to find work rather than graduate from high school. In that state, participants in subsidized employment there were allowed to devote only ten to twelve of their required forty hours of work activity per week to education and training. Research suggests that caseworkers also tend to discriminate against racial minorities, giving them less encouragement to go to school and finish their high school degrees.[29]

Time limits and the "work first" approach also hinder the efforts of welfare mothers to complete vocational training programs or obtain higher education. As one student, enrolled in an employment training program, described, "The time limits . . . [are] stopping [me] from succeeding. . . . I want a career for myself. I want a better life for my kids. I don't want my kids to grow up without hope. I want my kids to live in a home. How am I supposed to give them a home and a healthy future when they're cutting me off? . . . I want an education . . . that will help lift me out of poverty."[30] Similarly, a welfare mother pursuing a master's degree in social work described the problems she faced:

> I'm in my last year and I'm hoping to be able to finish in the fall. But I'm being pressured by [the] welfare [department] to leave my school program . . . and go to work. And I keep asking them, "Please let me finish my program. I'll be off welfare forever, for good." And they just

keep harassing me, "No you need to go to work. Your time is up. You already have a B.A." And they've even offered me jobs at Krispy Kreme doughnuts, which I don't think is right. I'm trying to be a social worker so I can help people and they won't let me finish my program . . . I was sanctioned for three months and they're trying to sanction me again.

Her grant was reduced through this sanction, making it difficult for her family to make ends meet. Her daughter, standing beside her, commented, "I think it's really sad. My mom has come a really long way, she's trying to get her master's degree, which I think is a really big accomplishment, and they're trying to make her quit school to work at a Krispy Kreme doughnuts. It's ridiculous."[31]

Another welfare mother, who finished her social work degree within eighteen months, expressed her concerns that two-year time limits would prevent other poor mothers from completing a four-year bachelor's degree: "My concern [is] the other single parents who want to attain college education, who have that dream in their mind and their heart. . . . Because of time limits and because they're forced to turn towards low-wage employment, they will not be able to attain the dream that I did. . . . Because [I received welfare], I stand here today as a tax-paying citizen who is middle-class and able to contribute to society."[32] The problems in attaining a four-year college degree because of the two-year time limits were described first-hand by another Los Angeles welfare mother:

During my first semester at [college] I got pregnant. . . . The world was suddenly a very dark and scary place. After months of agonizing with my husband on how we were supposed to support our new family and still stay in school, we decided to apply for aid. The day we went to apply for welfare was a very sad day in my life. . . . I felt so ashamed. I felt like such a failure. I was embarrassed to hold my head up. It was a rude awakening to my new reality. This was now my life. We knew that the decision we were going to make before my daughter was born would shape the kind of life we would lead. It was so important for us to stay in school. I could not give up that dream of a degree. We knew that was the only way to ensure that our family wouldn't live in poverty forever.

I had been receiving aid for about a year when somebody finally told me I only had eighteen months to get my degree. I was in shock, disbelief, I was so angry because this was the whole reason why we did it, to stay in school, to get that degree. This August I will be transferring to a [four-year university]. I have my applications [in] and I am so proud of myself, I got my plan back, I'm still doing college, I'm still going to get that great job. I'm very excited, bring on the work, bring on those college essays, I'm going to do it. Unfortunately, when I'll be starting my fall semester my two-year time limit expires, and my worker has told me that I have to quit school and get a job in order to receive benefits. Nothing has made me so angry in my life than for somebody to sit there and tell me that I cannot accomplish my goals. Everyone should have a right to education and I am no exception. I have such potential to . . . succeed in life and we all do.[33]

Other WTW regulations also prevent welfare mothers from attending school. For example, one recipient had to drop out of college because she was told she qualified for subsidized child care only if she worked.[34] Another recipient dropped out of technical school after she was told that she could not qualify for welfare while receiving financial aid.[35]

These were not isolated cases. In 1994, there were about 7,000 welfare recipients in training programs at the Milwaukee Area Technical College, but only 274 by 1997.[36] Similarly, City University of New York's enrollment declined from 27,000 to 17,000 between 1994 and 1997. Massachusetts community colleges experienced nearly a 50 percent decline in enrollment over the same period. The number of public assistance recipients in Illinois associate and bachelor's degree programs declined from 4,281 in 1996 to 1,889 in 1998.[37] These trends are disturbing, given that 88 percent of former welfare recipients who earn associate degrees and nearly all of those who earn bachelor degrees remain economically independent.[38] As one welfare mother explained, education "give[s] us a real chance towards self-sufficiency . . . so we can rise up far beyond the poverty level and be the examples that our children need."[39] Pat Gowens, a former welfare mother and founder of Milwaukee's Welfare Warriors, echoed her sentiment, claiming that welfare mothers deserve "education, not training—we're not dogs."[40]

Time limits and the "work first" approach also pose considerable obstacles for immigrants, many of whom are not proficient in English.[41] As a Cambodian-American welfare mother explains: "When I got welfare, I wanted to get a job, but I didn't know English. At the welfare office, no one would help me learn English. . . . I learned [English] from my kid. I want to learn to read and write English, but it is very hard with four kids and my job."[42] Without language skills, many immigrants have difficulty finding good jobs that pay a living wage, especially since so few are given the same level of job training as English speakers. A Los Angeles County study, for example, found that recipients with limited English proficiency earned, on average, $355 per month, compared to $545 per month for English speakers.[43] In this area, many Asian immigrants are pressured into taking jobs in the garment industry, notorious for its sweatshop conditions, because these jobs do not require English proficiency.[44]

Many WTW programs provide only minimal training. For example, a 1998 survey of 670 participants in Milwaukee found that most respondents were doing nothing beyond their job assignments and were receiving no training or education. Most were menial, low wage jobs, including food service, cleaning, and packing and sorting.[45] Hundreds of WTW participants in Milwaukee were placed in jobs, mainly light industrial, assembly, and warehouse positions, through temporary employment agencies.[46] Although Milwaukee's welfare department claimed that these assignments provided on-the-job training, it was often very minimal. As one participant explained, "At regular jobs, I have done factory work, packing, and cashiering. Through welfare, I have done the same type of work. Even though they call it training, I am already experienced in this work."[47] Similarly, a local welfare rights advocate told me, "One of the things they used to have them do was count hangers, in order to get a grant, which is ridiculous. [What they consider being "job ready"] is getting up in the morning and getting somewhere. They're not giving them any skills. . . . These [welfare] agencies don't have any real commitment to pulling people out of poverty."[48] In large cities, such as Los Angeles and New York City, welfare mothers were commonly assigned to all kinds of menial jobs for municipal governments, such as picking up trash, scrubbing toilets, routine paperwork, and providing security in parking garages.[49]

When welfare mothers do find a job, they often have difficulty keeping it because they lack supportive services. Describing her WTW trials and tribulations, one welfare mother said, "I moved from one job to the next job because . . . [there] wasn't enough assistance [and it] was delayed. Transportation was delayed. Childcare was delayed . . . . I haven't got any help."[50] A Milwaukee child care provider similarly described problems of Wisconsin Works (W-2) participants:

> With a few families I can see that the children are not getting enough food or they are wearing the same clothes every day. One poor baby didn't have a winter jacket, so we bought him one. . . . Because of W-2, these mothers are barely able to get by and provide for their children. They want their children to be in daycare, but can barely pay. Another problem is transportation. With W-2 there was supposed to be money for transportation, but the county said they don't have any money left for that. They want to get their kids to my center, but can't afford the bus fare. . . . The mothers complain because they have no time or money to get their kids to the center and to work on time.[51]

Welfare departments' failure to provide adequate, affordable child care for WTW participants has tragic, even fatal, consequences for children. For example, a thirteen-year old child with cerebral palsy, DeAndre Reeves, accidentally scalded himself to death in a bathtub after his mother, a WTW participant without access to affordable child care, left him in the care of her teenage son. The teenager was downstairs making lunch when DeAndre, unable to call for help, turned on the hot water faucet. Even though Yvette Reeves, a single mother, had previously been exempt from work so that she could take care of her disabled son during the summer months, her case worker, following Wisconsin's tough new WTW regulations, required her to work for Pizza Hut.[52] Another WTW participant, who could not find child care for her six-month-old baby, decided to stay at home with him. After being sanctioned for not cooperating with her work requirements, she was eventually left homeless.[53]

After leaving the welfare system, mothers frequently experience even greater problems obtaining support services, making it difficult for them to make ends meet and remain off of welfare. Participation in Food Stamps and Medicaid declines dramatically after families leave TANF, because of program rules, confusion over eligibility, and faulty administrative practices. At most, only about one-third of former recipients with jobs receive child care subsidies.[54] As one former client, now employed in a garment factory, described:

> Now I have a job, but I still have problems. . . . After I bring all the kids to school, I go to work. I work on an assembly line. I have a one-hour break at four o'clock. At this time, I have to pick up my son from child care and bring him home. Then I have to return to work. I have to work until seven o'clock at night. During this time, I leave my kid at home alone until his brother comes back from school. While I am working, my mind is still with my kid, I worry about my kid at home alone. [Choking up.] I am scared that someone will find out they are home alone and take them away.[55]

Compounding work and family conflicts, many of the low-wage service jobs that employ former welfare mothers have inflexible schedules and few benefits, such as sick leave. As a result, many lose their jobs when child care problems arise or a child gets sick.[56] Such problems help to explain why, according to one survey, nearly half of former welfare mothers with jobs are employed only part of the year.[57]

Many of the low-wage jobs available to recipients, mostly in service or retail trade, also have high job turnover rates or are seasonal or temporary.[58] For example, a Milwaukee study shows that about 42 percent of

42,120 jobs held by former welfare recipients were found through temporary agencies.[59] New WTW requirements and competition between private and public agencies for government contracts create intense pressure on case managers and job developers to place recipients in the first job they find, regardless of its potential for stable employment. For example, former employees of a private welfare contractor in Southern California claimed that if they did not make five job placements in a week, they would be fired. Under pressure, some employees made their quota by funneling WTW participants into temporary or part-time jobs. In fact, employees had an incentive to do this because the more temporary or part-time jobs a participant had, the more job placements they could claim: "It was pointed out in a couple of our meetings that if we really wanted the [job placement] statistics to go up to maybe use the temporary agencies. . . . Let's say they worked one week in a temporary assignment. Well technically, if they worked another week in another assignment, that would be two job tallies. . . . They just wanted them hired. They weren't concerned about keeping them in that employment as long as we met our quota for the month."[60] According to my informant, even if a participant was given a four-hour job assignment, this would count as a job placement. Similarly, a former employee of Maximus Inc., a private welfare contractor, claimed that "they don't care how long people keep the job." He recalled that at one job fair organized for WTW participants the only employer present was a temporary agency.[61]

Problems with child care, insecure employment, and making ends meet contribute to frequent cycling between welfare and work and reliance on welfare to supplement low earnings.[62] A national survey of those who left welfare between 1997 and 1999 found that 22 percent had returned to welfare, while another 16 percent were working at a part-time job.[63] "Leaver studies," which examine the outcomes for recipients who left welfare in the late 1990s, found that most of those employed were earning between $7.00 and $7.50 per hour. If these wages were consistent, this would mean that most would be living at or near the poverty line. However, because most former recipients do not work full-time and year round, it is estimated that their average annual earnings could be $10,800 or less.[64]

A study of long-term employment outcomes among "welfare leavers" found that five years after they left the welfare rolls, only 25 percent were consistently employed in a full-time job, and 33 percent were not working. The remaining 42 percent were working, but most of these were in part-time or temporary jobs. Only five percent of the women worked full-time for the whole year during the entire five-year period. While their earnings tended to increase over time, 42 percent of those still employed had incomes below the poverty line five years after leaving welfare.[65] Other researchers estimate that at most only 10 to 20 percent of former recipients are able to permanently leave poverty.[66] As one welfare mother explained, "We need more than a just a job. We need a career."[67]

When mothers leave welfare for work, they incur added expenses, such as child care, transportation, and work clothes. About 80 percent of former recipients lose their access to health insurance when they leave welfare.[68] As a result, low-wage mothers often experience as much material hardship as welfare mothers.[69] As a childcare provider serving former welfare recipients in Los Angeles described to me, "They're struggling to make ends meet . . . . I see them struggling just to keep their phone on, their utilities on, and just to get medicine for their kids."[70] National surveys from the late 1990s indicate that more than one-third of current and former recipients experienced a time in the previous year when they were unable to pay their mortgage, rent, or utility bills,[71] while about 25 percent of mothers who had left welfare in the past six months had had their heat cut off.[72] Other surveys found that equal portions—about one-third—of former and current recipients had to skip or reduce the size of meals because they ran out of food.[73] Some surveys even show that former recipients with jobs experienced greater housing or food hardship than current recipients.[74]

WTW programs thus frequently serve to recruit workers into low-wage jobs, while new regulations create added barriers for poor mothers to receive additional education and training. Far from experiencing the "American dream," many welfare mothers are living the "American nightmare," stuck in low-wage, insecure, menial jobs that provide no benefits. Lacking access to health care and publicly subsidized child care, many experience even greater material hardship than before they made the transition from welfare to work. When Congress restricted welfare and adopted tough WTW policies, it did little to provide single mothers with sufficient jobs, wages, education, training, or services to pull them out of poverty.

LIFE AFTER WELFARE: BROKEN FAMILIES, MEAN STREETS, AND HUNGRY BELLIES

With the implementation of welfare reform's tough new eligibility rules, many poor families were denied or discouraged from using welfare. For example, PRWORA denied public assistance to most legal immigrants for their first five years in the country. The new rules had a "chilling effect" on immigrant welfare applications. Confusion over the new rules and fear that welfare receipt would interfere with their ability to obtain citizenship discouraged qualified immigrants from obtaining welfare.[75] As a result, the number of immigrant welfare applications approved dropped sharply—71 percent between January 1996 and January 1998, while their use of TANF declined 60 percent between 1994 and 1999.[76] A number of immigrants, fearful about their loss of benefits, contemplated or actually committed suicide.[77]

Poor families were also discouraged from seeking aid through "diversion programs," adopted in twenty states, that encourage prospective welfare clients to seek work or other sources of help before completing a welfare application.[78] Many families also lost benefits through other diversionary tactics. For example, welfare applicants were discouraged from filling out welfare applications in Alabama and encouraged to go "dumpster diving" in Washington.[79] In Milwaukee, where TANF was administered by five private agencies,[80] there were especially strong financial incentives to divert welfare applicants off the rolls. Employees made bigger bonuses if they denied benefits, while agencies were allowed to keep the money they did not spend on recipients.[81] As a result, agencies encouraged prospective welfare clients to ask friends, relatives, and churches for help before completing their applications and denied benefits to those deemed "job ready," even if there was no job waiting for them. They also practiced a "light touch policy," informing clients about supportive services only when asked about them.[82]

Nationally, it is estimated that at any point in time, about one-quarter of recipients are sanctioned for failing to comply with program rules, more than double the rate prior to PRWORA's adoption. Recipients are often sanctioned because they miss appointments, lack required documentation, or because of administrative problems, such as bureaucratic errors, lost paperwork, delays in program implementation, lack of coordination between welfare departments and employers, or a lack of translation services.[83] Across states, sanction rates vary, from 5 to 60 percent, as do their meaning. In some states, sanctioned recipients experience temporary and partial benefit cuts, while in other states they are permanently banned from using welfare.[84] Proponents of sanctions claim that they instill work discipline in recipients. However, one survey found that only 6 percent of sanctioned recipients were working after they lost their benefits. It also found that sanctioned recipients were significantly more likely to experience hardships such as going without food, medicine, or heat compared to those who left welfare voluntarily.[85]

By June 2000, 60,000 people had lost TANF benefits because they reached the end of their time limits.[86] Structural employment barriers, such as inner-city job shortages and employment discrimination, keep many women, especially women of color, from finding a job within required time limits. Such employment barriers help explain why unemployment rates are twice as high for blacks than whites. Many welfare mothers also face a variety of other obstacles—such as substance abuse problems, extreme depression, learning disabilities, men who stalk them, or homelessness—that make it difficult for them to find or keep a job.[87] Recipients are often not given additional time to cope with such crises, leaving them even less time to receive employment counseling or job training.[88] Although thirty-one states exempt domestic violence victims from WTW requirements so that they can seek counseling, researchers estimate that only 1 or 2 percent of domestic violence victims are actually identified by social workers.[89]

Many of these employment barriers are quite common among welfare mothers. Recent national surveys found that between 36 and 44 percent of adult recipients report problems with their physical or mental health, while one-fifth reported problems with insecure housing. A multi-city survey found that about one-third of adult TANF recipients had a moderate or high risk of depression, while three state-level surveys indicate that between one-fifth and one-third of adult TANF recipients have learning disabilities. Surveys suggest that 60 percent of welfare mothers experienced sexual or physical abuse at some time in their lives, while the U.S. Department of Health and Human Services estimates that as many as 34 percent are current victims of domestic violence. Multiple barriers to employment are also common. According to the Urban Institute, nearly half of TANF recipients report more than one barrier to employment, such as their own or their child's physical or mental health problems, limited skills or work experience, transportation problems, or language barriers.[90] Multiple barriers make it especially difficult for recipients to comply with program rules and find work.[91]

Welfare mothers are also sanctioned because of inflexible program rules. As one child care provider put it, welfare departments are so strict that "even if [clients] have a sick child, they cannot miss work or be late."[92] One WTW participant in Los Angeles was sanctioned after one of the two buses she took to get to her required class was late:

> I was sanctioned off welfare for being ten minutes late for [my WTW class]. . . . I wasn't able to afford to keep up [my] rent. It was horrible. . . . [From where I lived], it took me an hour and twenty minutes to get there. I said, "I did show, you don't think you could squeeze me in a class?" and they said, "No, we'll reschedule you." And a couple of months later I got something in the mail that said they were sanctioning

me off [welfare]. . . . I lost a grant of about $140 and that made it impossible for me to continue to pay rent and bills.

Like many other sanctioned recipients, she became homeless.[93]

The dramatic rise in rents, especially in urban areas, creates considerable housing insecurity for former recipients and other low-wage workers. In no metropolitan area in the nation can those earning less than 30 percent of the local median income afford a two-bedroom home at fair market rent.[94] As a result, about one-fifth of former welfare recipients have difficulties paying rent, significantly higher than the portion of comparable families still receiving welfare, while one in ten former recipients have been evicted or become homeless.[95] Housing insecurity for low-income people has been especially acute in California and the Northeast, where the housing markets are least affordable.[96] In New Jersey, for example, about half of former recipients surveyed experienced serious housing problems or were evicted in 1997.[97]

Since PRWORA's passage, hunger and homelessness has risen in cities throughout the nation, even during the economic boom of the late 1990s.[98] Homelessness, increasingly common among working families,[99] plagues many former welfare mothers. A six-state survey found that 8 percent of former recipients were forced to rely on a homeless shelter. An Illinois survey found that about equal proportions (between 5 and 7 percent) of employed and unemployed former recipients became homeless.[100] With the onset of the 2001 recession, homelessness increased.[101] Homelessness is likely to rise even more as additional welfare mothers hit the end of their time limits. Becoming homeless puts women and children in physical danger, is emotionally traumatic, disrupts schooling, and creates additional barriers to employment.[102] Describing her experience with becoming homeless, one mother said:

> The most painful thing that I remember is running out of money. That was my biggest fear, staying in a hotel and no more money. [I paid] my last $40 one night and . . . I couldn't sleep, I didn't know where I was going to go. . . . I felt like I had lost all hope. I was very discouraged. I cried a lot. I just didn't think that I would be able to make it. I prayed and things started coming along, people started helping me. . . . From the hotel I started living with a couple of friends. From one friend to the next friend to the next friend, I lived with three friends who also had kids. . . . It's very shameful being in that situation with three kids, running from pillar to post, in and out of hotels. It was hard and I lost everything—clothes, the whole nine yards, even shoes. My kids lost a whole lot; it took a lot from them and it took a lot from me. My kids were devastated. . . . They couldn't play right, couldn't adjust right. The

kids were always fussing and fighting with each other and homework got misplaced.[103]

While this homeless mother was able to stay with friends and keep custody of her children, many former welfare mothers have not been so fortunate.

Many of these poor families are now at the mercy of private charities, emergency shelters, soup kitchens, and food pantries, which experienced rising demand for their services.[104] A 2003 survey of twenty-five cities found that most did not have sufficient resources to meet the demand for emergency food and shelter. Chicago's food banks turn away about one million people each year.[105] As a Milwaukee shelter worker explained to me, "From the beginning of [welfare reform], the overnight shelters for women have been full . . . . All the services to poor people, all the food pantries, . . . everything has been really over-burdened."[106] Similarly, a New Orleans shelter worker reported, "When I started here three years ago, we had plenty of family space. Since welfare reform, I don't have a bed."[107] In Los Angeles, surveys revealed that 40 percent of the city's downtown female homeless population in 2001 had a child under eighteen. Many of these destitute women, forced to give up custody of their children, were sleeping in tents and cardboard boxes on the trash-filled, urine-smelling streets of downtown's Skid Row. The local women's shelter, out of space, gave priority to the rising number of women still accompanied by their children.[108] Nationally, families with children make up about 40 percent of the homeless population and about 59 percent of people who request emergency food.[109]

Throughout the nation, many former welfare mothers were forced to give up custody of their children to friends, family, or the foster care system. Partly as a result of this, the nation's foster care population and the share of TANF cases that were "child-only" rose dramatically.[110] "Child-only" grants are given to parents or guardians who do not qualify for welfare themselves but care for a child who does. More than half, or 54 percent, of these children live separately from their parents, often with a relative who is not legally required to support them.[111] There are no national estimates of the number of mothers who lost custody of their children because of welfare reform, but state and local studies are suggestive. In Wisconsin, an estimated 5 percent of former welfare recipients were forced to abandon their children. In a 2000 survey of current and former welfare recipients in Salt Lake City, Utah, 10 percent of respondents reported losing their children to state agencies.[112] According to a national law passed in 1997, if children stay in the foster care system for fifteen out of twenty-two months, their mothers permanently lose custody.[113]

A shelter worker who has observed these trends firsthand reported that as a result of welfare sanctions, "Women were plunged into serious destitution and poverty. . . . [They] couldn't pay their rent and became homeless either with their children or losing their children in the process. . . . [Some women] have had their children taken from them. [They were] found, in their destitution and poverty, guilty of neglect of their children. They've had their children removed from them to foster care or even to adoption."[114] Other clients gave custody of their children to friends or family after losing their welfare benefits:

> In the overnight shelters, what we have is a growing population of single women. . . . That does not mean that they don't have children. . . . When the women lost their housing, a lot of times they would move into [homes of] relatives or friends. . . . In those very crowded conditions . . . where everybody is all jammed in there, after a while things become so tough that somebody has got to go. A lot of times, the women are the sacrificial lambs. They have left their children with their relatives or with their friends and hit the streets. . . . If you're jammed into an apartment that's made for six to eight people at the most and you've got twenty-one people living there, it's crazy. You're stressed out and people don't eat right. . . . People can't afford to eat. In that kind of scenario, we have women saying, "Okay, I'll go." Or else the fighting gets so bad, or the sexual stuff. . . . These single women would be put up at whatever church was taking a turn.[115]

In another interview I conducted at this shelter, three former welfare mothers shared stories about giving up custody of their children. One said, "My daughter? She's in foster care. I asked them to put her in foster care because I didn't want her to be in this homeless situation with me like this. This ain't right for no child." The second told me, "My life has been going up and down and I don't want her going through all of that because she's only three. If her life goes up and down with mine, she won't be stable." The third said, "My daughter is eight, she's in the third grade. Ain't no way I would have my baby out on the streets. It's too rough for me as it is and it would be even worse for her."[116] Even if welfare families arrive at a homeless shelter as an intact family, they are forced to separate because of shelter rules. Fathers and older boys are often forced to go to a single men's shelter, while mothers and younger children are given space in a women's shelter.[117] Far from promoting "family values," welfare reform has torn many poor families apart.

Furthermore, PRWORA failed to attain one of its primary stated goals: reducing the rate of out-of-wedlock childbearing. Upholding heterosexual married households as the ideal, Congress included a number of measures that were designed to encourage marriage and reduce the rate of out-of-wedlock births. For example, PRWORA authorized funds for marriage counseling among poor couples and abstinence education among teens, despite little evidence of the effectiveness of such programs.[118] As explained in the law, abstinence education was supposed to teach "that sex outside marriage is psychologically 'harmful,' that abstaining from sex outside marriage is 'the only certain way to avoid out-of-wedlock pregnancy, sexually transmitted diseases, and other associated health problems,' and that 'a mutually faithful monogamous relationship in the context of marriage is the expected standard of human sexual activity.'"[119]

Congress also offered states an "illegitimacy bonus": $20 million for each of the top five states in reducing out-of-wedlock birth rates without raising the abortion rate.[120] In 2001, only three states qualified for this bonus. In each case, the reduction of their extramarital birth rate was minimal—4 percent in the District of Columbia and less than 1 percent in Alabama and Michigan—and was mainly attributed to broader demographic trends. Meanwhile, the national extramarital birth rate rose by almost 2 percent.[121] Ethnographic research from two cities suggests that welfare reform policies did not change welfare mothers' views on marriage and that a large majority are not planning to marry in the near future.[122] Such findings are consistent with research that suggests that the rise of single motherhood is due not to welfare policies, but instead to broader economic and social changes, such as declining labor market conditions for working-class men, women's rising labor force participation, and greater tolerance for premarital sexual activity and single motherhood.[123]

While welfare reform proponents claim that they want to help welfare recipients get out of poverty, the tough regulations they advocate create tremendous hardship and obstacles for poor families. Supporters of "get tough" welfare regulations defend them with "culture of poverty" arguments, which assume that people are poor primarily because they lack a work ethic and traditional "family values," and are unable to delay gratification. Such views and policies fail to address the structural barriers that prevent employment, discourage family formation, and keep people poor: the lack of steady, full-time, living-wage jobs and the shortage of child care, health care, transportation, affordable housing, and educational opportunities. As a result, even when recipients find employment, most remain in poverty. Some poor families who lose access to welfare are left homeless and hungry. As more recipients reach the end of their time limits, even more poor families are likely to be pushed into the streets and experience serious hardships. If restrictive welfare policies cause such misery, why is political support for them so strong? The rest of this book, which traces the ebb and flow of welfare opposition since the late 1940s, addresses this question.

2. Attacking Welfare, Promoting Work and Marriage
Continuity and Change in Welfare Opposition

Many Americans were injured by the helping hand. The welfare
system became an enemy of individual effort and responsibility,
with dependence passed from one generation to the next. . . . We
will strengthen work requirements for those on welfare. Work is
the pathway to independence and self-respect. . . . We will work
to strengthen marriage. As we reduce welfare caseloads, we must
improve the lives of children. And the most effective, direct way
to improve the lives of children is to encourage the stability of the
American family.

PRESIDENT GEORGE W. BUSH

The propaganda is probably one of the most crucial things for them
to be able to carry out this attack on the poor . . . . Everyone from
middle class to working class truly believes that everyone's better
off without welfare.

PAT GOWENS, founder of Welfare Warriors

Why does the United States, one of the richest nations on earth, have such
an obsession with purging the "undeserving poor" from the welfare rolls?
How did AFDC, considered to be the least controversial welfare program
when it was created, become the most controversial?[1] How did a program
that was originally designed to keep poor mothers at home with their children become transformed into a draconian workfare program forcing poor
mothers to accept "a job, any job"?[2] This book addresses these questions by
examining the political forces generating attacks on welfare mothers' rights
from the end of World War II until the present. I examine how a state-level
revolt against welfare developed into a national-level assault that ultimately
shredded a critical part of our nation's safety net. In doing so, my study adds
historical perspective to recent research on welfare state retrenchment. While
insightful, this literature tends to suffer from historical amnesia, with some
scholars even suggesting that retrenchment is "the *new* politics of welfare."[3]

Welfare state retrenchment involves various kinds of policy changes, including those "that either cut social expenditures, restructure welfare state programs to conform more closely to the residual welfare state model, or alter the political environment in ways that enhance the probability of such outcomes in the future."[4] In this book, I am mainly concerned with efforts to restrict eligibility for AFDC. For that reason, I will use the term *welfare* or *welfare system* to refer to this program, despite the fact that there are many forms of public assistance, including assistance for upper- and middle-class families, provided by our welfare state.[5] This chapter provides an overview of my analysis and puts it into the context of both the early history of government aid for poor mothers and other perspectives on U.S. welfare retrenchment.

Since World War II, there have been several waves of attacks on welfare mothers. The first major backlash against Aid to Dependent Children (ADC, later renamed AFDC) emerged in the late 1940s in response to the postwar expansion of welfare and its rising use among unwed mothers and racial minorities.[6] This backlash was very similar to the contemporary one but happened only at the state level. Between 1949 and 1960, almost half the states, mainly in the South and Southwest, restricted welfare eligibility through work requirements or "suitable home" policies. This early welfare backlash represented an important prologue to the contemporary one, leaving two important legacies for welfare politics. First, it produced the first formal work requirements for welfare mothers, providing a precedent for contemporary workfare policies. Second, politicians created and popularized racist images of black and brown welfare mothers to justify welfare cutbacks, images that have since become pervasive. Despite its importance, scholars have neglected this early welfare backlash. Most studies of it are brief accounts in academic journal articles or book chapters that focus almost exclusively on the South.[7] My book aims to shed greater light on this state-level revolt against welfare, carefully examining the conditions under which it became ascendant and providing detailed case studies of these antiwelfare campaigns.

As welfare caseloads rose, this first welfare backlash swept across the country, reaching the national level in the late 1960s. This first welfare backlash culminated in several failed attempts to replace AFDC with a guaranteed income program. Liberal reformers' failure to create a popular alternative to AFDC in the 1960s and 1970s paved the way for a second backlash against welfare mothers that rose to new heights in the 1980s and is still under way. This time, reformers sought to replace AFDC with a far more restrictive welfare program and, with the passage of PRWORA in 1996, were successful in achieving their aims. Congressional politicians are currently poised to further restrict poor families' welfare rights through the reauthorization of this legislation. By comparing these two welfare backlashes and their outcomes, I hope to cast new light on the continuities and changes in welfare politics.

I argue that opposition to welfare in the United States has mainly come from conservative and low-wage employers and the white working and middle classes, who become more closely allied and powerful during politically conservative periods. Whereas business leaders mainly pursued welfare cutbacks to protect the supply of cheap labor and minimize their taxes, white voters' support for them was deeply tied to broader shifts in racial and gender politics. Popular opposition to welfare, strongest among conservative white voters, has historically been fueled by a broader white backlash against civil rights gains and the in-migration of racial minorities, political efforts to reinforce patriarchal family values, and expectations that poor mothers should work. Despite these broad historical continuities, both popular and elite support for welfare retrenchment broadened and deepened over time. On the one hand, business leaders' interest in welfare cutbacks increased in response to the rise of neoliberalism, economic globalization, and economic restructuring. On the other hand, popular support for welfare declined as women of color and unwed mothers became the main recipients and maternal participation in the labor force increased. While the current welfare backlash is a mighty force in American politics, it is not unstoppable. I argue that a bold alternative to the current welfare system could turn the current era of welfare retrenchment into one of welfare expansion.

THE EARLY HISTORY OF MOTHERS' AID

Welfare programs for poor families—from state and local mothers' pensions to federal A(F)DC—were originally based on the widely held maternalist belief that children received the best care from full-time mothers. Maternalist reformers, mainly white upper-class and middle-class women, hoped that these programs would ensure that poor mothers could stay at home with their children, and portrayed aid as compensation for the work of raising good citizens.[8] These programs were extremely limited in their reach and generosity before the late 1940s, however. Recipients were forced to work because of inadequate benefits, while unwed mothers and racial and ethnic minorities were routinely denied welfare.

Forty states enacted mothers' pension laws between 1911 and 1920, despite opposition from private charities, which argued that welfare should remain voluntary.[9] The passage of these laws can largely be attributed to the campaigns of women's associations, such as the General Federation of Women's Clubs, Mothers' Congresses, and Consumers' Leagues.[10] These campaigns drew strategically on maternalist rhetoric but also had classist, racist, and ethnocentric overtones, as reformers sought to use mothers' pensions to improve "the race" and assimilate immigrants and working-class women.[11] To appease conservative and business interests by keeping expenditures low, mothers' pensions were adopted as enabling legislation, authorizing but not requiring counties to provide aid.[12] As a result, large inequities in pension coverage developed across counties. Contrary to reformers' intentions, local administrators considered the mother's "ability to earn" and encouraged applicants to accept employment.[13] Because few rural areas authorized mothers' pensions, they interfered little with farmers' labor supply. In addition, mothers' pensions were so poorly funded that many recipients had to continue wage work to survive.[14] A 1923 study of nine locations, including urban and rural areas, revealed that more than half (52 percent) of mothers receiving aid were employed.[15]

Mothers' pensions were almost exclusively given to "deserving" white widows. Juvenile court judges and social workers commonly required beneficiaries to regularly attend Protestant churches and refrain from tobacco, alcohol, and extramarital sex and used "suitable home" and "fit mother" rules to deny aid to unwed, divorced, and separated mothers. Such policies reinforced the "marriage ethic,"—the expectation that women should get and stay married—and codified the sexual double standard, making state aid contingent on the continued celibacy of unwed mothers rather than unwed fathers.[16] Because these programs remained relatively inexpensive and racially exclusive, opposition to them remained limited.[17]

The New Deal period provided maternalist reformers with an unprecedented opportunity to expand and improve mothers' pensions. As unemployment and poverty spread during the Great Depression, the labor movement, elderly pensioners, and unemployed workers mobilized and liberal Democrats gained electoral power.[18] In response to public pressure, President Roosevelt established the Committee on Economic Security to design federal welfare programs and appointed top officials in the federal Children's Bureau—Grace Abbott, Katherine Lenroot, and Martha Eliot—to develop Aid to Dependent Children (ADC).[19] Congress followed the bureau's recommendations by letting states administer ADC, requiring counties to establish a program and adopting a broad definition of "needy children." Other bureau recommendations, intended to make welfare coverage more equitable—national standards for benefits, a merit system for welfare employees, and oversight by the U.S. Children's Bureau—were defeated by congressional committees, however. These committees were dominated by southern politicians, who were concerned about protecting farmers' labor supply and the racial status quo. They gave authority over the program to the more conservative Social Security Board and defended "states' rights" to keep their welfare programs stingy and inaccessible to blacks. Meanwhile, Congress excluded agricultural, domestic, and casual workers, and therefore most blacks, from the core programs of the 1935 Social Security Act. Believing that ADC, like mothers' pensions, would mainly serve white widows, Congress considered it to be one of the least controversial welfare programs adopted in 1935.[20]

As expected, ADC was very selective in its early years, almost exclusively serving white widows.[21] Most states continued to use "suitable home" criteria to discriminate against divorced, separated, and unwed mothers, while discrimination against racial and ethnic minorities was rampant.[22] To reformers' dismay, welfare offices continued to push poor mothers, especially blacks, into low-wage jobs by steering them into employment offices, providing them insufficient aid, or denying them aid.[23] A 1942 federal survey of eighteen states found that, overall, 23 percent of welfare mothers were employed or seeking jobs and this proportion was twice as high in southern states. During World War II, federal welfare officials observed that caseworkers were "taking advantage of the war situation to pressure mothers to work."[24] In 1943 Louisiana adopted the first formal work requirement for ADC, which was used to deny aid to black women and children when they were needed in the cotton fields.[25] Despite increases in the federal share of payments in 1939, 1946, and 1948, aid for poor mothers remained grossly inadequate and uneven in these early years.[26]

In short, employers' demands for labor, fiscal constraints, and discrimination against unwed mothers and racial minorities limited welfare coverage in these early years, which helped minimize opposition to it. Only after most poor widows gained access to the Old Age Survivors' Insurance program in 1939 and ADC began to serve rising numbers of unwed mothers and racial minorities after World War II did strong opposition to the program develop. Since then, efforts to restrict A(F)DC have waxed and waned over time. Under what conditions do these welfare backlashes emerge and gain influence?

THE POLITICS OF WELFARE CUTBACKS

Scholars are currently divided in terms of the relative importance of class, race, and gender politics to efforts to roll back poor mothers' welfare rights in the United States. Some authors highlight the role of business interests, while others point to the importance of patriarchal, classist, and/or racist ideologies. A third perspective focuses almost exclusively on the role of conservative politicians and interest groups in welfare reform. Combining insights from these perspectives, I explore how class, race, and gender politics have historically interacted during conservative political periods to generate strong cross-class support for welfare cutbacks. As Gosta Esping-Andersen notes, "patterns of class-alliance building" shape welfare politics in important ways.[27] This is no less true for the retrenchment of welfare programs than it is for their development.[28]

In the United States, cross-class support for welfare cutbacks has historically been based on political alliances between conservative and low-wage employers and white working and middle classes, alliances rooted in racist sentiments, belief in the Protestant work ethic, and patriarchal family values. To a considerable extent, conservative business leaders and low wage employers, interested in minimizing their tax burdens and protecting their labor supply, provided much of the initiative, resources, and political muscle behind campaigns to roll back poor mothers' welfare rights. Their participation in these campaigns has not always been readily apparent, however, because they often promote cutbacks from behind the scenes or through the mouths of politicians and ideologues—lobbyists, writers, and researchers. Conservative business leaders and their ideologues have been remarkably successful, especially during conservative periods, at courting political allies and manufacturing public consent for welfare cutbacks. They have spewed forth antiwelfare dogma through news stories, editorials, political speeches, and books, effectively appealing to racial resentment, negative stereotypes of the poor, and concern about the rise of single motherhood. My analysis combines insights from three theoretical perspectives on welfare retrenchment, usually kept separate, which highlight (1) political and institutional factors, (2) class, race, and gender ideologies, and (3) business interests.

Political and Institutional Perspectives

A number of recent analyses of contemporary welfare cutbacks emphasize the role of political and institutional factors. The most notable are Paul Pierson's (1994) *Dismantling the Welfare State? Reagan, Thatcher, and the Politics of Retrenchment,* Steven Teles's (1996) *Whose Welfare? AFDC and Elite Politics,* and Kent Weaver's (2000) *Ending Welfare as We Know It.* All three books argue that welfare cutbacks occurred because conservative politicians came to power, public animosity toward welfare grew, and federalism enabled politicians to avoid blame for welfare cutbacks.

Both Pierson and Teles suggest that the 1980s welfare backlash was mainly the work of conservative politicians. Pierson claims that it occurred mainly because conservative politicians came to power and ruled in a climate of budget austerity, which made cutbacks seem imperative. Teles suggests that the main proponents of welfare cutbacks were conservative elites engaged in broader moral debates about "family decomposition, the decline in the work ethic, and the erosion of personal responsibility."[29] Both authors argue that AFDC was particularly vulnerable to welfare cutbacks, because public support for it had declined and its clients were not well organized. Pierson also claims that federal responsibility for AFDC made it easier for public officials to avoid blame for cutbacks. Federal officials blamed local politicians for dragging their feet, while local politicians blamed federal ones for constraining their efforts to reform welfare. Politicians also adopted policies, such as work requirements, that appealed to the work ethic and only affected able-bodied recipients, who tend to be seen as the "undeserving poor." In these ways, politicians were able to minimize reprisals from voters or interest groups.[30]

Weaver provides a very similar account of PRWORA's passage in 1996, although conservative interest groups play a larger role in his analysis. Weaver argues that growing public hostility to welfare opened the door for politicians to restrict benefits. Public opposition to welfare rose in response to widely publicized conservative interpretations of rising welfare caseloads and rates of out-of-wedlock and teen childbirth that blamed them on the welfare system. Researchers, journalists, and policy makers argued that stringent rules for receiving welfare were needed to better regulate the behavior of poor adults. The rise of this view "was fueled in part by increased funding from conservative foundations, the growth of conservative think tanks, and conservative journals."[31] The inability of liberal researchers to find clear-cut solutions to poverty-related social problems also increased support for conservative perspectives. In this context, politicians sought credit for reforming welfare. Republicans, who controlled Congress, had the upper hand in shaping PRWORA, while Clinton and congressional Democrats compromised with them to avoid blame for obstructing welfare reform.

As these authors persuasively argue, conservative politicians and organizations have been major forces behind welfare cutbacks, which were facilitated by rising public antipathy toward welfare and lax federal control over the program. This is no less true of past episodes of welfare retrenchment. Nevertheless, these accounts fail to adequately explain why conservative politicians and organizations became more powerful and hostile to welfare at the end of the century, or how these trends were related to broader social, economic, and political shifts. The role of corporate leaders in the welfare backlash is noticeably absent from these accounts. In contrast to Teles, who claims that "AFDC is almost a pure case of cultural and intellectual politics,"[32] I argue that business interests shaped the retrenchment of AFDC in fundamental ways.

Ideologies of Race, Class, and Gender

Other scholars highlight how public opposition to welfare was linked to racist, classist, and patriarchal ideologies.[33] The classist belief that one's economic status is largely due to individual merit and effort denigrates the poor in American society. This belief, along with the strong Protestant work ethic, fosters the view that people are poor because they are lazy, inept, lack traditional family values, and cannot delay immediate gratification. Such individualistic analyses of poverty direct attention away from structural factors that contribute to poverty, such as the shortage of living wage jobs or racial discrimination.[34] Opposition to welfare also reflects a classist and racist double standard regarding maternal obligations. While white middle-class married women are encouraged to limit work outside the home to take care of their children, the caretaking work of poor mothers, especially non-white ones, is devalued.[35]

As race-centered and feminist scholars point out, opposition to welfare rose after World War II, when it increasingly served women of color and single mothers. Single mothers confront strong moral disapproval because they fail to conform to the "marriage ethic" of getting and staying married.[36] Social disapproval of unwed mothers, long viewed as "fallen women," is especially strong.[37] Moreover, "the faces summoned by welfare discourse are Black—welfare 'queens.'"[38] This stereotype portrays welfare mothers "as dishonest and irresponsible individuals who purchase bottles of vodka with food stamps intended to help feed their children, or as immoral and promiscuous individuals who are said to breed children to rip off the welfare system for more benefits."[39] This stereotype was created and spread in the 1950s by white supremacists who used "old-fashioned," blatant forms of racism to criticize welfare. Since then, it has become so pervasive that the phrase "welfare mother" is now racially coded.[40] Today's welfare mothers are commonly assumed to be "young, inner-city black mother[s]" who stay on welfare for many years and pass on their "bad values" to their children, who become "future welfare mothers, unemployed males, and criminals."[41] Black mothers are thus blamed for the cycle of poverty.[42] Likewise, non-custodial fathers who fail to provide sufficient financial support for their families, disproportionately low-income and nonwhite, are frequently portrayed as lazy and irresponsible "deadbeat dads" who set bad examples for their children.[43] Welfare critics, now as well as in the past, have also employed racist stereotypes of poor immigrants of color to justify cutbacks, claiming that our country has become a "welfare magnet," luring immigrants who abuse welfare at the expense of native-born taxpayers.[44]

The persistence of these stereotypes of welfare recipients is striking, especially since they bear little relationship to reality. While blacks disproportionately receive welfare, they made up only about 39 percent of all cases in 2000, while 31 percent were white and 25 percent were Latino.[45] Teenagers made up only 6 to 7 percent of all adult recipients.[46] Even before PRWORA was implemented, most able-bodied welfare mothers were not avoiding work but rather combining work and welfare, actively seeking work, or cycling between welfare and low-wage jobs. Between 80 and 92 percent of adult recipients had worked at some point before receiving welfare.[47] The vast majority of adult recipients left welfare within two years, with most leaving it within one year.[48] Most of their daughters did not receive welfare later in life. Immigrants actually have similar or lower rates of welfare use compared to their native-born counterparts, and contribute far more in federal taxes than they cost.[49] Despite such facts, antiwelfare myths pervade Americans' consciousness, undermining support for welfare.

While such myths, and the racist, classist, and patriarchal ideologies they stem from, undoubtedly undermine support for poor mothers' welfare rights in important ways, political opposition to welfare has not been constant throughout American history. Negative stereotypes of welfare mothers were mobilized with greater force during some historical periods than others, producing waves of welfare cutbacks that are connected to broader social and political shifts. As Neubeck and Cazenave argue, efforts to roll back welfare in the United States are often part of a broader racist backlash against social or political threats to white power, such as civil rights gains and the in-migration of racial minorities.[50] Purging people of color from the welfare rolls and creating degrading and stigmatizing conditions for welfare receipt provided politically convenient ways to vent racial resentments and reinforce racial inequalities.[51]

The politics of race also interacted with the politics of gender in the development of America's welfare backlashes. AFDC was originally designed to prop up the family wage system, enabling poor mothers to stay at home with their children when fathers, the traditional breadwinners, were absent. As single motherhood and female employment increased and the family wage system declined, so did support for AFDC. This was particularly true as more women of color, traditionally expected to work, gained access to welfare. At first, work requirements were controversial and disproportionately applied to blacks. Yet, as maternal labor force participation rose, it broadened political support for welfare-to-work policies. Welfare critics, past and present, have also readily employed patriarchal family ideologies to demonize unwed mothers, disproportionately women of color, and "deadbeat dads" in order to justify welfare restrictions and reduce support for welfare programs.[52] Patriarchal ideologies shape the content of many welfare regulations that aim to regulate family life. Such rules reinforce the sexual double standard, the institution of marriage, and women's economic dependence on men.[53]

Racist, classist, and patriarchal family ideologies, as well as rising expectations that poor mothers should work, undoubtedly contributed political support for welfare cutbacks. Yet, much of the initiative, resources, and political muscle behind antiwelfare campaigns come from the business community, which dominates American politics.

Class-Based Perspectives

Corporate interests regarding welfare are complex and ambiguous. On the one hand, business leaders generally have an interest in limiting welfare programs to minimize their taxes, ensure a ready supply of cheap labor, and minimize the public sector, all of which help them accumulate more profit. On the other hand, they have a collective interest in maintaining some level of welfare benefits and coverage because it maintains the legitimacy of the state and ensures workers' survival.[54] To understand why, at certain times in history, particular business leaders engaged in antiwelfare campaigns, we must consider the factors shaping their perceived interests.

According to Piven and Cloward's (1993) classic book, *Regulating the Poor*, state and business interests regarding welfare depend greatly on political conditions. Employers and politicians, as a whole, are willing to expand welfare to maintain legitimacy when poor people protest and elect reform-oriented politicians into office. On the other hand, in more quiescent and conservative periods of history, politicians restrict welfare programs in order to discipline workers and regulate employers' supply of cheap labor.[55]

As Piven and Cloward suggest, welfare retrenchment mainly occurs during politically conservative periods and, except for the late 1960s, those marked by relatively little popular mobilization. Yet, Piven and Cloward's analysis oversimplifies business interests regarding welfare, failing to capture significant variations in the views of business leaders. Nor do Piven and

Cloward provide a clear analysis of the mechanisms through which business interests become expressed in welfare policies and interact with racial and gender politics. American welfare policies, after all, regulate not only the labor market, but also gender and race relations.

I argue that ideologically conservative[56] and low-wage employers tend to be the most opposed to welfare. As the literature on "corporate liberals" suggests, there are important ideological splits within the business community, with ideologically conservative employers being the least supportive of welfare spending.[57] Research also shows that small employers and those in labor-intensive and competitive industries have historically been more opposed to welfare spending than is "monopoly" capital. Facing greater pressure to minimize their labor and tax costs, they have been particularly reluctant to support welfare programs that provide a wage floor for workers and increase their tax burdens.[58]

These insights help to explain why business opposition to welfare has become more widespread and why it has been stronger among certain kinds of employers than others. For example, large farmers—racial conservatives and heavily reliant on low-wage, casual labor—were the most active employers in the antiwelfare campaigns of the 1950s. Since then, business support for welfare cutbacks broadened and deepened as corporate politics shifted rightward in response to the rise of neoliberalism and as the demand for low-wage, casual labor increased as a result of economic globalization and economic restructuring. As Jamie Peck's (2001) *Workfare States* suggests, newly expanded workfare programs and stringent welfare rules promised to provide employers with a ready supply of low-wage, flexible labor for the new economy.[59] After the 1970s, business leaders became increasingly concerned with reducing social expenditures and minimizing their taxes.[60] Corporate tax cuts, high military spending, and economic stagflation produced rising deficits and a climate of austerity that increased support for "balanced budget conservativism."[61] For all of these reasons, business support for welfare cutbacks intensified. Conservative corporate leaders' political capacity also increased after the 1950s through the development of broad-based national lobbying groups and an extensive network of right-wing think tanks, making it easier for them to launch national attacks on the welfare system.[62]

Low-wage and conservative employers have not attacked the welfare system single-handedly, however. They worked in alliance with and appealed to socially conservative whites wary of the rise in single motherhood and immigration and resentful of government aid to racial minorities. The contemporary attack on welfare, like previous welfare backlashes, is a "class war," but also a socially conservative war to preserve patriarchal "family values" and the racial status quo.

Cross-class alliances significantly shaped both the development and the dismantlement of welfare programs. In the United States, most of the opposition to welfare historically came from low-wage and ideologically conservative employers and white voters. Their opposition to welfare was rooted in a combination of business interests in minimizing wages and taxes, racial resentments, patriarchal family values, and the Protestant work ethic. In this broad sense, the underlying politics behind welfare cutbacks is not so different at the end of the century than it was at mid-century. On the other hand, as I explore in the rest of this book, the backlash against welfare mothers has grown in scope and severity over the years.

In Part 2, I trace the development of the first major welfare backlash, which first emerged at the state level in the late 1940s and reached the national level in the late 1960s. Chapter 3 provides an overview of the 1950s welfare backlash and examines how federal officials' lax control over ADC encouraged states to develop tough new welfare policies. Chapter 4 examines the role of large farmers and white racists in this welfare backlash and how their opposition to welfare was shaped by perceived threats to their interests and values. Using quantitative evidence, I argue that states were more likely to restrict welfare eligibility in the 1950s, when large farmers played a more important role in the economy, racial conflicts were more salient, and fiscal constraints were greater. Chapters 5 and 6 provide comparative case studies, based on archival data, of these state-level revolts against welfare in four states: California, Georgia, New York, and Kentucky. These states differed in terms of their political economy and race relations, a difference that significantly shaped the contours and outcomes of their antiwelfare campaigns. Nevertheless, all these campaigns were marked by racism and efforts to regulate family life. In the 1960s, as welfare caseloads rose, attacks on welfare mothers spread across the country. At the same time, an emergent welfare rights movement and their liberal supporters were demanding improvements in the welfare system. Chapter 7 explores the political struggles over welfare in this period, leading to several failed attempts to replace AFDC with a guaranteed income program in the 1960s and 1970s.

Failures to replace AFDC with a more popular program paved the way for the rise of the contemporary welfare backlash, the focus of Part 3. Chapter 8 explores the rise of the Republican Right and New Democrats in the 1980s and 1990s. I argue that many corporate leaders became mobilized around a highly conservative domestic agenda in response to international competition, declining profits, and a wave of regulatory reforms, and increased pressure on politicians to move rightward on social policies. At the same time, Republican politicians constructed an emotionally powerful, racially coded conservative discourse and agenda that effectively appealed to white voters' reactionary sentiments. As Republicans' popularity increased, especially among Southern whites and white working-class men, Democrats moved rightward on social issues in an effort to recapture their support. Chapter 9 examines the role of corporate-sponsored, right-wing think tanks in promoting antiwelfare propaganda and why opposition to welfare increased among broad sectors of the corporate community. Chapter 10 analyzes the forces shaping the contemporary welfare backlash that led to the passage of PRWORA and continues to shape Congressional debates about its reauthorization. I argue that attacks on welfare mothers resonated strongly with the public, especially white voters, because they appealed to antitax sentiments, racial resentments, traditional "family values," and rising expectations that poor mothers work. On the other hand, Republican control of Congress after 1994 increased the influence of conservative groups, especially the Christian Right and right-wing think tanks. As a result, despite popular opposition to AFDC, Congress overreached public opinion in a number of respects when they crafted PRWORA. Chapter 11 considers the future prospects for improving poor mothers' welfare rights. I argue that to counter the current backlash against welfare mothers, politicians and activists need to offer a bold alternative to the current welfare system that will help build solidarity rather than divisions among working-class families.

PART II

The First Welfare Backlash

(1945–1979)

3. The 1950s Welfare Backlash and Federal Complicity

In the 1950s, states purged their welfare rolls through all sorts of new rules and regulations. In 1949, for example, Georgia's welfare department required poor mothers to seek court orders of support from fathers and prohibited their supplementation, despite the fact that, as social workers noted, the father's "contribution is often irregular and inadequate." The rule also led to violent reprisals from fathers, as Mrs. Jones's story, recounted by a local welfare official, illustrates:

> Mrs. Jones came to our department . . . seeking assistance, telling of the hardships, physical abuse, deprivation, and worry she had experienced until she finally left her husband in another county. She had one sixteen-year-old son who was trying desperately to be the breadwinner for the forlorn group. This son, mother, and other children were living in a remote area . . . and working in the field, but were unable to earn enough to buy all of their necessities. . . . Mrs. Jones signed the [welfare] application, but seemed to have doubts about pressing charges against her husband for support. . . . [Later] Mrs. Jones returned to the welfare office and reapplied. She took court action against her husband. The sheriff . . . apprehended Mr. Jones and he was tried. . . . The judge ordered him to contribute toward his children's support. This man was [later] released from jail. He lived in a distant county, but he came to his wife's home at 2 A.M., forced his way in with a shotgun. Mrs. Jones and the younger children escaped, but as the sixteen-year old son was trying to leave, his father shot him in the back, killing him instantly, and then committed suicide.[1]

When Georgia adopted even tougher welfare rules in 1952, it aroused many complaints among social workers and welfare recipients, who viewed them as inhumane. As one county official described:

Under our new regulations, employed mothers cannot receive ADC....
Mrs. C., with two children, rents a farm.... Her children are small. She
does her own plowing. She will have no income until the fall, and then
perhaps not enough to pay her debts.... Another ADC recipient has
six children. She has received assistance for four who in years past were
abandoned by their fathers. The father of the last two is a substitute
father living in the home. She has never asked for assistance for his
two children, but he is now responsible for all six, when he stated that
he would not be.[2]

These women were denied welfare by rules that prohibited aid to mothers
who worked fulltime, regardless of their wages, and to families with a "man
in the house," regardless of his willingness or capacity to provide sufficient
financial support. A federal administrator reviewing complaints and eligibility hearings in Georgia the year after these policies were implemented
noted, "The hardships worked on dependent children by the application of
non-supplementation of low wages ... was ... vividly demonstrated. ...
Most of the hearing officers recognized the urgent need of these cases and
efforts were made by some of the hearing officers to seek other sources of
help for them, but according to information revealed in the hearing records
the limited resources of the communities [were] discouraging."[3] Similarly,
another welfare employee claimed that this rule caused "an unfair and terrible hardship."[4]

The deprivations created by these welfare rules continued to be felt many
years later, as revealed by records from a 1967 court case challenging the
state's "seasonal employment" rule. One of the witnesses for that case was
a black widow with eleven children. She reported that at the beginning of
each harvest season, she received notice from the county that she would no
longer receive her check because seasonal employment had become available. The widow had back problems and could not stoop, which made it
impossible for her to work a full day or perform many jobs in the fields.
Worried about how she could possibly provide for her eleven children, she
went back to the welfare department. The social worker told her that "the
children would have to go out and work." The law exempted welfare mothers from working if suitable childcare was not available, but this rule was
often ignored. Forced to work and unable to afford childcare, they took their
children with them so they could watch them as they worked or left their
children with aging parents too old to adequately care for them.[5]

Many other states besides Georgia restricted welfare in the 1950s. This
chapter provides a broad overview of this state-level revolt against ADC and
examines the role played by federal welfare officials in fostering it. After

New Deal officials were replaced with more conservative ones, they became more tolerant of states' efforts to restrict ADC, encouraging the spread of new rules and regulations.

THE POSTWAR EXPANSION OF WELFARE

Attacks on ADC escalated in the postwar period after the program expanded. After wartime employment declined, the number of recipients in the nation more than doubled, from under a million to over two million between 1945 and 1950. After a brief decline between 1950 and 1953, national welfare caseloads increased, so that from 1945 to 1960, the number of ADC recipients more than tripled.[6] ADC also became more inclusive of unwed mothers and racial minorities. The share of national welfare cases made up of black families rose from 31 percent in 1950 to 48 percent in 1961, with the largest concentrations in the North and South. Meanwhile, the percentage of welfare families headed by widows declined from 43 percent in 1937 to less than 8 percent in 1961.[7]

ADC's postwar expansion and its greater inclusion of unwed and non-white mothers were partly due to rising fertility rates, which increased the number of families and their average size. The national rate of out-of-wedlock childbearing, highest among black women, also tripled between 1940 and 1958.[8] At the same time, workplace accidents and deaths declined, lowering the need for welfare because of male disability or death.[9] Federal welfare policies also contributed to changes in the ADC caseload and its size. The 1939 Social Security Act Amendments made benefits available to Old Age and Survivors Insurance (OASI) recipient survivors and dependents, who displaced middle-class white widows from ADC.[10] In 1947 and 1949, federal welfare officials required states to implement new application procedures, making it more difficult for social workers to discriminate against unwed or minority welfare applicants or put them on a "waiting list."[11]

The dramatic postwar rise in welfare caseloads jars with the common image of the 1950s as an age of prosperity, an image not without basis. As Table 1 shows, total unemployment rates remained below 6 percent for most of the decade, while mean incomes rose for all income brackets.[12] The family poverty rate also declined from 32 percent in 1947 to 21 percent in 1960, but it remained high by today's standards.[13] Poverty was most concentrated among nonwhite families, especially those headed by women.[14] Median incomes for all nonwhite workers remained at less than 60 percent of median incomes for whites throughout this period,[15] while women workers generally received less than two-thirds of what their male counterparts were paid. Wages were especially low among women of color.[16] For example, black women, concentrated in low-wage agricultural and service work, "took home yearly paychecks amounting to less than half of white women's."[17] Because most black and Latino households were larger than white households, their incomes, already low, were also spread thin. Black families were also significantly more likely to be headed by women than white households, further reducing their family incomes. As a result, per capita income for black families with children was about 43 percent of the per capita income for their native-born white counterparts in 1950. Among Hispanics, this ratio was 53 percent.[18] National unemployment rates were between 1.5 and 2 times greater among nonwhites than whites, and even greater racial disparities in unemployment were found in major cities (see Table 1).[19]

As the ADC program expanded to include more racial and ethnic minorities, it was subject to greater controversy.[20] As early as 1944, the Bureau of Public Assistance chief noted that regional welfare officials were complaining about community prejudice toward ADC.[21] Journalists, politicians, welfare officials, and business groups helped arouse such prejudices. They attacked the program, claiming that it was wasting taxpayers' money and undermining family responsibilities, sexual morality, and the work ethic.[22] By 1960, researchers studying the program proclaimed, "Aid to Dependent Children has become one of the most controversial and misunderstood programs in the United States. . . . The ADC families are considerably different than in the early years of the program . . . and attitudes of the general public toward them are usually confused, accusing, and hostile."[23]

Along with ADC, Old Age Assistance (OAA) also came under attack in the 1950s. Politicians sought to lower benefits and tighten eligibility for the program through rules requiring relatives to support aging parents and restrictions on property ownership.[24] Attacks on OAA were less severe than attacks on ADC, however, and OAA payments rose more rapidly than ADC payments between 1944 and 1959. OAA was less controversial than ADC, partly because its recipients were more likely to be white and did not include unwed mothers.[25] Unlike ADC recipients, old age pensioners were also organized. In the 1930s, they united behind Upton Sinclair's "End Poverty in California" campaign, the "Ham and Eggs" movement, and the Townsend movement. While these groups later declined, in 1953 there were still more than 550 Townsend clubs in the country, claiming more than 22,000 members.[26] As a result, old age pensioners were better prepared to defend their rights than welfare mothers, who remained unorganized until the 1960s.[27]

Advocates for poor women were also weak or absent. Most social work-

TABLE 1. *National Family Poverty Rate and Average Annual Unemployment Rate, 1947–1960*

Year	Family Poverty Rate*	Total Unemployment Rate**	Nonwhite Unemployment Rate***	Ratio of Nonwhite to White Median Family Income***
1947	32	3.9	—	—
1948	—	—	5.9	0.53
1950	32	5.3	9.0	0.54
1951	29	3.3	5.3	0.53
1952	28	3.0	5.4	0.57
1953	26	2.9	4.5	0.56
1954	28	5.5	9.9	0.55
1955	25	4.4	8.7	0.56
1956	23	4.1	8.3	0.53
1957	23	4.3	7.9	0.54
1958	23	6.8	12.6	0.51
1959	22	5.5	10.7	0.52
1960	21	5.5	10.2	0.55

* Poverty rate is measured as the percent of families with money income less than $3,000, 1947–1960 (expressed in 1962 dollars). SOURCE: *Economic Report of the President*, 1964, p. 57, cited in Miller (1965: 89).
** Annual average unemployment rates are for the civilian labor force sixteen years and over. SOURCE: U.S. Bureau of Labor Statistics (2001).
*** SOURCE: U.S. Bureau of the Census (1975) Part I, Series G 189–204, p. 297, cited in McAdam 1999: 119.

ers emphasized the importance of rehabilitative casework rather than social reform in the 1950s.[28] "Social feminist" groups, such as the National Women's Trade Union League and the National Consumers' League, which had earlier lobbied on behalf of poor women and children, disbanded or became inactive in the 1940s, while wartime coalitions for child care fell apart after the war's end. Although the National Women's Party and the National Business and Professional Women's Clubs remained active in the 1950s, they were small and mainly focused on gaining support for an Equal Rights Amendment.[29] The labor movement, dominated by white men, focused little attention on poor mothers' welfare rights. While black leaders and journalists criticized welfare cutbacks that targeted blacks, the civil rights movement mainly focused on desegregating public facilities in the 1950s.[30] Unorganized and with few active supporters, welfare mothers swiftly came under attack.

A WELFARE BACKLASH SPREADS

Welfare opposition was spurred at the local level in the late 1940s by a series of newspaper exposés and public and private investigations of large cities' welfare programs that focused on fraud, "wasteful" expenditures, and government inefficiency. For example, Baltimore's Commission on Government Economy and Efficiency, dominated by real estate interests concerned with lowering taxes, publicly criticized the welfare department for its "sloppy" eligibility and benefit policies.[31] In cities and states across the country, ADC was coming under attack as a "free love racket" that served "unfit" mothers. Welfare mothers were also accused of cashing their checks at bars and liquor stores and using them to buy luxury items.[32]

By the 1950s, campaigns to tighten welfare eligibility and purge ADC of "undeserving" recipients reached the state level. The most common policies adopted were "employable mother" rules and stricter "suitable home" policies. Between 1949 and 1960, almost half of continental U.S. states, mainly in the South and Southwest, restricted ADC through one or both of these policies through law or administrative fiat (see Appendix 1 and Figure 1).[33] Eighteen states adopted "employable mother" rules that, contrary to the original intent of ADC, made it mandatory that poor women accept available employment if suitable care could be found for their children. These policies formalized what were previously only informal practices. In many states, these "employable mother" rules served only the symbolic function of reaffirming the work ethic. Overall, employment rates for welfare mothers did not vary significantly among states with or without these rules. Southern states enforced their work requirements the most strictly, with thirty-five percent of southern ADC mothers employed in 1958. In other regions, their employment rates were far lower, ranging from 5 to 16 percent.[34] Although "employable mother" rules were only supposed to be enforced if welfare mothers had access to child care, this was seldom enforced. A survey by the federal Children's Bureau, published in 1960, found, "Of the ADC children under twelve whose mothers worked full-time, one in nine had no daytime care arrangements."[35] The scarcity of child care for welfare mothers was even greater in certain areas.[36]

Nine states (eight of them southern) adopted new or tougher "suitable home" policies. Welfare offices routinely used these policies to deny aid to

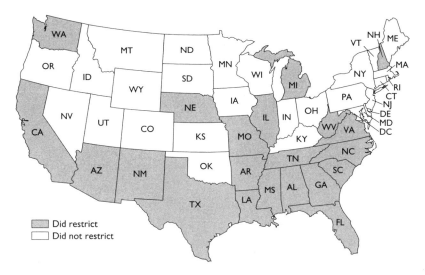

Figure 1. States that did and did not restrict ADC eligibility, 1949–1960. Note: Rhode Island's employment requirement disappears from official records in 1956. Sources: Social Security Administration 1949–60; Bell 1965; and state legislative records.

unwed mothers, who were disproportionately black, and other women considered promiscuous, on the grounds that their homes were "unsuitable" for children. In some states, mothers applying for welfare were forced to pledge "not to have any male callers coming to my home nor meeting me elsewhere under improper conditions . . . and to not knowingly contribute or be a contributing factor to [my children] being shamed for my conduct. I understand that should I violate this agreement, the children will be taken from me."[37] As part of strengthening their "suitable home" policies, four state legislatures (Georgia, Mississippi, Louisiana, and Tennessee) passed laws to exclude children born out of wedlock.[38]

States also adopted various "family responsibility" or "child support" policies to enforce fathers' traditional role as the family breadwinner. Welfare critics chastised recipients' boyfriends, former lovers, and second husbands for not supporting their children and forcing poor mothers to rely on welfare at taxpayers' expense. In response to such sentiments, Congress adopted the "Notice to Law Enforcement Officials" (NOLEO) requirement in 1950. NOLEO required welfare applicants to notify local law enforcement agencies of cases of desertion so they could prosecute "deadbeat dads" and require them to pay child support.[39] Nineteen states implemented this requirement by requiring ADC applicants to take legal action against the father, and fourteen states required those already receiving aid to do so.[40] By 1962, twenty-four states, many of them southern, had adopted "substitute father" or "man in the house" rules that denied aid to mothers if there was an able-bodied stepfather or "substitute father" in the house. In some states, a mother who had a casual affair with a man was considered to have a "substitute father." Such policies both expressed patriarchal disapproval of such relationships and the expectation that men be the family breadwinners. Like "suitable home" policies, "substitute father" rules were commonly used to purge blacks from the welfare rolls.[41]

States adopted other kinds of welfare regulations as well. For example, Iowa established maximum family grants, which forced large families to receive smaller grants per child.[42] Other states adopted property limits, rules denying aid to pregnant women, and requirements that parents accept medical rehabilitation for disabilities. After Congress passed a 1951 law authorizing public disclosure of welfare records, about half of U.S. states passed laws opening the rolls for public inspection.[43] By 1962, eight states and eighteen large cities had established special investigating units to examine potential cases of welfare fraud, while other cities made grand jury investigations of the problem.[44]

FEDERAL COMPLICITY WITH THE WELFARE BACKLASH

This wildfire spread of restrictive welfare rules was facilitated by federal officials' lax control over ADC. According to the 1935 Social Security Act, states were free to develop welfare policies as they saw fit as long as these policies did not conflict with federal law. Every three months, states were required to submit for federal approval a description of their public assistance plans. If federal welfare officials determined that state laws were out of conformity with federal laws, they could withhold, or threaten to withhold, welfare funds from states. Federal officials also persuaded states to change controversial policies by warning them that auditors would find exception to the individual cases affected by them.[45] Given this authority, federal welfare officials could have declared many of the strict new eligibility rules created in the 1950s to be illegal, but they did not.[46] Instead, they allowed welfare critics to pursue their antiwelfare campaigns with few restraints.

Federal officials were not always so permissive. Before 1951, under Arthur Altmeyer's leadership, the Social Security Administration "was calling non-conformity hearings with regard to [states' ADC programs] at the rate of one or two a year."[47] Federal officials also reduced racial discrimination in the distribution of public assistance by requiring states to adopt federal application procedures in 1947 and 1949.[48] Meanwhile, under the leadership of Jane Hoey, a staunch New Deal liberal,[49] the Bureau of Public Assistance (BPA) encouraged states to broaden eligibility for ADC.[50] It repeatedly urged them to eliminate various eligibility rules, including suitable home policies, residency requirements, age limits under eighteen, requirements that adults support needy siblings, and school attendance and work requirements.[51]

As the country became more conservative in the 1950s, so did federal welfare officials. In 1952, Democrats lost both the presidential election and control of Congress. With the reelection of Eisenhower in 1956, the White House was put firmly under Republican control until 1960. Although Democrats recaptured control of Congress in 1954 and 1956, they did not recapture an overwhelming majority in Congress until 1958. Even then, conservative Democrats often allied with Republicans on social issues, so that liberal Democrats experienced "years of exile" during which they were pushed to the right through red-baiting and were unable to achieve desired reforms.[52]

In this context, New Deal liberals did not last long in the federal welfare administration. Top welfare officials appointed under Roosevelt lost their posts as the new Republican administration reorganized the federal welfare department and made its bureau chiefs into presidential appointments. Despite a public campaign to keep her job, Jane Hoey was forcibly replaced. Wilbur Cohen, Altmeyer's principal assistant since 1939, was demoted. He quit his job in 1955, frustrated by the conservative climate in which he had to work. Altmeyer, welfare commissioner since 1936, also quit in 1953, when he reached retirement age. Eisenhower appointed conservative officials to replace these New Deal liberals to lead his newly created Department of Health, Education, and Welfare. Eisenhower, like many business groups at the time, supported a loosening of federal control over welfare, and his appointments reflected those views.[53]

Congress also pressured federal welfare officials to reduce their control over welfare administration. In 1951, these officials overturned an Illinois law authorizing the public inspection of welfare records because it contradicted safeguards protecting recipients' confidentiality. Advocates of the law claimed that it would root out welfare fraud by publicly shaming unworthy recipients. Although the U.S. Court of the District of Columbia upheld the decision, it remained highly contested, and Congress overturned it through the Jenner Amendment to the 1951 Revenue Act. The Jenner Amendment authorized states to allow "public access to public assistance financial records so long as such legislation prohibits any use of any list of names for commercial or political purposes."[54] Afterward, "public inspection" laws spread across the United States, despite the BPA's warning that they would needlessly deter poor people from applying for welfare.[55] The Jenner Amendment discouraged federal welfare officials from calling nonconformity hearings for ADC during the 1950s. As a welfare rights lawyer noted, "After the 1951 [Indiana] hearing a change of view took place within [the federal agency]. No hearings were held whatsoever until 1960."[56] During this period, the federal agency claimed that cutting off funds does "more harm than good."[57]

As a result, federal welfare officials tolerated all sorts of new eligibility restrictions for welfare in the 1950s, including employment requirements, which it had previously overturned in 1945.[58] They also condoned the use of "suitable home" policies as eligibility rules, believing they would prevent states from providing welfare to homes that were harmful to children in order to avoid expenses for foster or institutional care.[59] Federal officials hoped that such policies would not be discriminatory if skilled social workers used "objective standards of health and care" and provided assistance to homes "unfit" for financial reasons.[60] Federal reviews found, however, that states were using these policies to purge welfare rolls of women believed to be sexually immoral.[61] In response, in 1945 federal officials clarified their disapproval of using "suitable home" policies to deny aid to "unfit" mothers, warning states that such practices "will not . . . protect children. It simply precludes them from receiving ADC."[62] Hesitant to interfere with "states' rights," however, the federal agency did not ban or regulate the use of "suitable home" policies.[63] While fifteen states followed federal advice and repealed their "suitable home" policies before 1961, five states (Connecticut, Illinois, Iowa, Mississippi, and South Dakota) adopted new or more stringent "suitable home" policies after 1945.[64] Federal administrative reviews in the 1950s found that parental morality was the "almost exclusive concern of agency staffs in their assessment of homes."[65] Opposing these practices, Social Security Commissioner John Tramburg claimed that "there is nothing in the Federal law that points to the question of morals of the mother or caretaker," and suggested that the court rather than social workers should determine a mother's fitness.[66]

Even so, federal welfare officials permitted the use of "suitable home" policies, overturning only the most blatant forms of discrimination against unwed mothers. For example, the federal agency warned state officials in Georgia that there were serious questions regarding the legality of a 1951 law that denied additional aid to mothers who had more than one child out of wedlock. Similar laws were proposed in nineteen other states in the 1950s, and federal officials warned states that these policies violated equal protection laws.[67] Nevertheless, they tolerated Georgia's policy, adopted in 1952, declaring that " 'repeated births of children born out-of-wedlock" were a sign that a home was "unsuitable" and grounds to deny welfare.[68] Federal officials even authorized a 1958 Mississippi policy that denied aid to children whose parents were not legally married. While federal officials disapproved of the policy, they were hesitant to act because state legislators threatened to withhold state welfare funds if they overturned the policy. Federal officials also reluctantly permitted "substitute father" policies that denied aid to families if a mother had an affair or lived with a man.[69] It was not until 1961, when a new, Democratic administration came into power and Louisiana's "suitable home" law provoked widespread public criticism, that federal officials finally banned the use of "suitable home" policies in eligibility rules for welfare.

THE "LOUISIANA CRISIS" OF 1960

In 1960, Louisiana adopted a thirty-bill "segregation package" that included restrictions on voting and other antiblack measures. Two of these bills revised the state's "suitable home" policy to deny welfare to mothers who gave birth to a child out of wedlock while receiving welfare, cohabited with someone of the opposite sex, or were believed to be promiscuous.[70] William Rainach, founder of Louisiana's segregationist White Citizen's Council, paved the way for the bill's passage with his 1958 gubernatorial campaign, in which he advocated cutting off aid to unwed mothers to reduce "wasteful" expenditures.[71] The bill was clearly aimed at blacks. Ninety-five percent of the 22,501 children affected by the new policies were black, even though black children made up only 66 percent of recipients.[72]

Louisiana's "suitable home" policy provoked considerable criticism. At first, criticism was almost entirely confined to black churches and community groups who gave aid to the affected families. The New Orleans Urban League requested additional assistance from the federal government and the Red Cross, launching a publicity campaign called "Operation: Feed the Babies" with the help of a former president of the National Council of Jewish Women. At first, the only newspaper to give the issue significant press was the *Chicago Defender,* a black newspaper. Black journalists denounced the new welfare laws as racist.[73] Only after outraged British councilwomen from Newcastle-upon-Tyne "airlifted food, money, and clothing to the 'starving babies' of New Orleans did non-southern whites join the Urban League, social welfare activists, and black church groups in pressuring Louisiana's legislature to reinstate the 'innocent children' to the welfare rolls."[74] Welfare advocates, including Elizabeth Wickenden, as well as religious, welfare, social reform, and labor organizations, pressured federal welfare officials to take action against the state.[75]

In early 1961, the Social Security commissioner reluctantly approved Louisiana's policy because "in the face of the many precedents and analogies established during the twenty-five years of experience in the administration of the Social Security Act, no practical alternative was left to me." Nevertheless, the commissioner expressed strong opposition to the policy, claiming it "brought immeasurable and unnecessary privation and suffering upon thousands of children who were completely innocent of any wrong-doing."[76]

The next day, the secretary of Health Education and Welfare, Arthur F. Flemming, issued a new policy, making it illegal for welfare departments "to declare a home unsuitable for a child to receive assistance and at the same time to permit him to remain in the same home exposed to the same environment."[77] Flemming's decision was encouraged both by the public outcry over the "Louisiana crisis" and the fact that Kennedy's Democratic administration would take power in a few days. Congress endorsed Flemming's ruling later that year.[78] A federal review found that eight states had to revise their policies to conform to the new ruling: Arkansas, Florida, Georgia, Louisiana, Michigan, Mississippi, Texas, and Virginia.[79] The federal agency's response to the "Louisiana crisis" was significant because it signaled a decline in federal tolerance for states' restrictive welfare policies. Nevertheless, it was not until the late 1960s that many of the policies created in the 1950s were overturned, mainly through a series of Supreme Court rulings.[80]

As ADC expanded and served more unwed and minority mothers in the late 1940s and 1950s, controversy about the program spread. Critics charged that it had become too lax and was undermining traditional family values and the work ethic. In response, many states adopted work requirements, "suitable home" policies, and other tough rules designed to purge the "undeserving poor" from the welfare rolls. Federal welfare officials encouraged the wildfire spread of these welfare regulations by its lax control over ADC. In part, this was because New Deal liberals had been replaced with more conservative officials under the Eisenhower administration. In 1951, Congress overturned welfare officials' ruling that public inspection of welfare rolls was illegal, putting increased pressure on federal officials to respect "states' rights" in setting welfare policies. Not until 1960, when a new Democratic administration came to power and a broad public campaign was waged against Louisiana's draconian "suitable home" policies, did federal officials begin to exercise tighter control over state welfare policies. In the next chapter, I examine the forces behind these early antiwelfare campaigns and why they were more influential in some states than others.

4. Explaining the Postwar Rise of Welfare Opposition

> Many of these [welfare] children merely have been abandoned by
> one or more parents, simply because the parent or parents know that
> the welfare department will provide funds for rearing these children,
> leaving the parents free to earn, spend, and beget other children
> to become wards of the government. . . . To me, this type of thing
> is weakening the moral fiber of which strong families are built.
> Children from homes supported by the government funds arrived
> at the conclusion that support comes easy and without work.
>
> GEORGIA COUNTY WELFARE OFFICIAL, 1952

THE 1950S WELFARE BACKLASH AND COLD WAR LIBERALISM

The notion that poor people were using welfare to avoid work and their familial obligations was encouraged by the rise of conservative ideas in the 1950s. Structuralist views of poverty and the belief that the state had a responsibility to help the poor declined as a "cold war liberal" ideology took hold. This ideology viewed the free enterprise system and economic growth as the key to economic prosperity, democracy, and equality.[1] Such beliefs flourished amid the relative affluence of the period, as average family income rose for all income brackets. Not only were the poor less numerous, but they were also less visible as white working- and middle-class people moved to suburbs and increasingly relied on cars for transportation.[2] Cold War anti-communist hysteria—stirred up by the House Un-American Activities Committee's investigation of communism in the Hollywood Motion Picture Industry in the late 1940s and Senate hearings led by Joseph McCarthy on communist subversion of the U.S. government in the early 1950s—also undermined support for welfare.[3] Conservative politicians viciously attacked New Deal programs, claiming they were infiltrated by communists, contrary to the free enterprise system, and un-American.[4]

On the other hand, while the decade's prosperity reduced the sense of urgency for social reforms, it also undercut the notion that welfare would ruin the economy.[5] Most Republicans, especially the cosmopolitan "eastern establishment," and conservative Democrats treated the New Deal as a per-

48

manent feature of politics. Reflective of this, President Eisenhower was a moderate Republican, whose administration brought "some retrenchment and much consolidation" to New Deal programs.[6] As Eisenhower explained to his brother in 1954, "Should any political party attempt to abolish Social Security, unemployment insurance, and eliminate labor laws and farm programs, you would not hear again of that party in our political history."[7]

Congress even improved federal welfare programs in the 1950s. It expanded housing assistance, improved vocational and rehabilitation services, created permanent veterans' readjustment benefits, and improved unemployment benefits. In 1952 and 1954, Old Age and Survivors Insurance was extended to cover more farmworkers, and disability insurance was created in 1956.[8] Congress even improved ADC, establishing caretaker grants in 1950 that gave adults an allowance in addition to their children's grant. It also increased the federal government's share of public assistance payments in 1946, 1948, 1950, 1952, and 1956.[9]

Even at the state level, campaigns to restrict ADC were only partially successful. Nearly half of all states refused to restrict poor mothers' access to welfare through employment requirements or "suitable home" policies. There were three reasons for this. First, opposition to welfare remained concentrated among conservative business leaders and low-wage employers, especially farmers, in the 1950s. Second, racialized opposition to welfare was only just emerging in the 1950s, since the color barrier for welfare receipt had only recently been lowered. There was also a fairly low level of immigration, which limited opposition to immigrants' use of welfare. Third, maternal employment was still uncommon, which limited support for work requirements for welfare mothers.

The most active support for the welfare backlash during this decade came from two partly overlapping social groups: large farmers and conservative whites. Large farmers, occasionally joined by other business leaders, were interested in limiting poor mothers' welfare rights in order to minimize their taxes and ensure a supply of cheap labor. Conservative whites, concerned with maintaining the racial status quo, also pressured the state to restrict welfare. In this chapter, I examine in greater detail the role of these two groups in the antiwelfare campaigns of the 1950s and the conditions under which these campaigns succeeded. Using quantitative evidence, I argue that welfare critics were more successful in restricting welfare eligibility where agribusiness was more important to the state's economy, racial conflicts were more salient, and states were more fiscally constrained.

My account of the 1950s welfare backlash differs from previous research in several ways. Bell (1965) and Solinger (1992) argue that desire to purge black families from the welfare rolls was the most important driving force behind these antiwelfare campaigns. Soule and Zylan (1997) claim this welfare backlash was more complex, reflecting state managers' "racial, fiscal, and . . . patriarchal motivations." They claim that work requirements were designed to reduce expenditures and decrease the "representation of black, unmarried, divorced, and deserted women among the recipient population."[10] Consistent with this, they found that enactment of work requirements was more rapid in states with high per capita caseloads and relatively large black populations.[11] While otherwise insightful, these accounts underplay the importance of business interests in this welfare backlash. Other scholars do acknowledge this, noting that "employable mother" rules were primarily used during the harvest season in rural areas to coerce poor mothers and children to do farm work.[12] Yet, these analyses fail to explain how large farmers carried out their antiwelfare campaigns and why they were influential in some states but not others. In addition, previous accounts of the 1950s welfare backlash focus almost exclusively on the South and overlook the role played by racism against Mexicans and Puerto Ricans in antiwelfare campaigns in the North and West.[13]

THE ROLE OF LARGE FARMERS

Historical records provide ample evidence of farmers' participation in antiwelfare campaigns. For example, minutes of the North Carolina State Board of Public Welfare noted that its newly adopted "employable mother" policy "is expected to be of particular value in counties where there is a considerable amount of seasonal work in agriculture."[14] Minutes of the last quarterly meeting of this board reveal that this policy's author had been in contact with "farm leaders" about the state's welfare policies before making his motion, suggesting that farmers were not simply passive beneficiaries of the new policy. Documents also reveal that farm bureaus lobbied for work requirements in other states, such as California and Illinois.[15] Once adopted, rural county welfare departments in many states, including Arkansas, Georgia, Illinois, and California, used seasonal employment requirements to coerce poor families to work in the fields during harvest times.[16] Restricting access to welfare during the harvest season provided farmers with an ample supply of people desperate for work, while allowing benefits in the off-season prevented out-migration of workers and reduced farmers' responsibilities to their workers.[17]

Work requirements and rules prohibiting supplementation of low wages were the most obvious ways that farmers regulated their labor supply, but farmers also benefited from, and lobbied for, other kinds of restrictive rules. For example, legislative records and minutes of the California Farm Bureau Federation annual meeting show that they actively lobbied for a whole host of new welfare regulations in the early 1950s.[18] Newsletters from the Illinois Farm Bureau Federation show that in 1956 the federation urged the state to deny aid to mothers who had more than one child out of wedlock.[19] New York's State Conference Board of Farm Organizations, representing eight major farm groups, urged their state to open up the welfare rolls to public inspection in an effort to reduce welfare fraud.[20]

The political influence of agribusiness should not be underestimated. They were, by the postwar period, a highly organized political group. The biggest and most powerful farm organization was the American Farm Bureau Federation, or AFBF.[21] Farm bureaus, dominated by large farmers, had a strongly conservative, pro-business and anti-union political agenda, which they actively promoted.[22] Farm leaders also belonged to a variety of political associations organized around the interests of particular commodity groups, which amplified their political voice.[23] Agribusiness also benefited from unequal state legislative apportionment. By 1955, "inequality of legislative representation was solidly entrenched in all but a handful of the forty-eight states." Rural areas were overrepresented in at least one house in most states, and both houses in many. As a result, "organized agricultural interests [were] usually in a favorable position to influence state legislation."[24]

Why were corporate farmers so concerned about purging the welfare rolls in the 1950s? Planters generally have a great need for low-wage, casual labor since agricultural production is labor intensive, seasonal, and involves perishable goods, and they have little control over the price of their goods.[25] Minimizing poor mothers' access to welfare, especially during the harvest season, ensured a ready supply of cheap female and child labor. As the secretary of New York's Conference Board of Farm Organizations noted, "Farmers felt particularly 'touchy' about rising welfare costs because of continued difficulties in recruiting farm manpower among rural residents who, they said, are on relief and content to remain there."[26] Restricting welfare also promised to reduce their tax burdens.

Large farmers' interest in restricting welfare was further enhanced by a number of historical events and trends that increased the instability of their labor supply in the 1940s and 1950s. First, farmers increasingly relied on wage workers. The number of southern sharecroppers was cut nearly in half between 1930 and 1950, and the number had declined again by more than half by 1959.[27] Wage workers were more mobile than sharecroppers, who risked forfeiting their share of the crop if they left a farm during the harvest season. By contrast, wage workers often left farms in search of better employment opportunities before the harvest season was finished.[28]

Blacks' postwar migration out of the rural South and their civil rights gains posed other problems for farm labor recruitment. Between 1940 and 1950, nearly a third of blacks left the rural South for urban areas and northern and western states, while another third left in the next decade. Whereas 51 percent of blacks lived in rural areas in 1940, 65 percent of them lived in urban areas by 1960.[29] In part, blacks were pushed out of the rural South because of declining employment opportunities as a result of the mechanization of agriculture, the reduction of cotton acreage, and the planting of less labor-intensive crops.[30] Yet, blacks also left the South voluntarily in search of better jobs, as wartime labor shortages and civil rights agitation improved blacks' employment opportunities in the 1940s. In the 1950s, blacks continued to move out of the rural South because of the promise of better public services and better wages in urban white-collar, public sector and industrial jobs.[31]

A third threat to planters' labor supply was the expansion and consolidation of welfare programs. Before the 1950s, large farmers relied on all sorts of informal practices to deny welfare to poor families, especially poor black families. For example, welfare departments routinely put applicants on waiting lists, freezing the number of recipients. Social workers also discouraged women from filling out welfare applications and urged them to seek employment instead. Through such means, rural officials expanded and contracted welfare programs in response to farmers' shifting labor demands.[32] In the late 1940s, however, federal welfare officials pressured states to follow federal application procedures, making it more difficult for them to deny welfare to poor families.[33] In response, AFBF called for a reduction of federal control over welfare programs and "urged Farm Bureau members to take a 'more active interest' in the selection of state and county committees responsible for the administration of federal programs."[34]

Old Age and Survivors' Insurance (OASI) was expanded to include temporary, part-time, and self-employed farmworkers in 1952 and 1954, posing another threat to farmers' labor supply. Before this time, elderly farm laborers did not have access to retirement benefits, putting pressure on their families to work. AFBF strongly opposed the expansion of OASI to these workers, ranking this issue "near the top of the list" in terms of "long-run importance to the American farmer."[35] In response, in 1955 Congressional politicians authored at least five bills to limit OASI coverage of farmworkers. Farm leaders claimed they opposed coverage of temporary workers because it would require costly bookkeeping and increase their tax burdens.[36] More likely, they wanted to protect their supply of casual labor. Indeed, even before OASI was expanded, rural welfare officials noted that "some of the Old Age Assistance recipients are taking care of young relatives, thus creating a problem for farmers to secure labor."[37]

Mechanization of agriculture and the increased use of foreign labor decreased large farmers' demand for cheap domestic labor, but only partially. Mechanization was gradual and uneven. It had only just begun in the early 1950s for many crops, including cotton.[38] Vegetables and fruits were only mechanized in the 1960s and 1970s.[39] Even after mechanization, farmers desired an ample supply of casual labor to keep wages low, maintain labor discipline, and ensure the availability of labor throughout the harvest season.[40]

Although farmers became more reliant on foreign workers in the 1950s, they never made up the bulk of the farm labor supply.[41] Even in California, where the use of foreign contract labor was by far the heaviest,[42] they made up only 34 percent of all seasonal workers in 1957, the peak year of their use.[43] The future of the bracero program, which allowed farmers to hire contract workers from Mexico during World War II, was uncertain. After the war's end, the program had to be reauthorized every year or two.[44] Labor unions, humanitarian groups, and independent farmers lobbied Congress to either end or improve the program, claiming that it lowered wages and work opportunities for domestic workers, put small farmers out of business, and encouraged the abuse of Mexican workers.[45] In response, liberal politicians and the U.S. Department of Labor regularly tried to better regulate the program.[46] The Mexican government also sought improvements, which temporarily delayed the program's continuation in 1954.[47] The supply of undocumented workers was insecure because they could be suddenly deported. Through Operation Wetback, immigration officials raided factories, restaurants, bars, and homes between 1953 and 1956, resulting in the deportation of about four million Mexicans.[48]

In short, the decline of southern sharecropping, an increase in black migration, and the expansion of Social Security to part-time and temporary farmworkers threatened farmers' ready supply of casual labor, while mechanization and the use of foreign labor only partially reduced farmers' demand for cheap domestic workers. Both southern and national farm wage rates rose in the post–World War II period and the early 1950s, indicating a shortage of cheap farm labor.[49] As the ADC program expanded, large farmers acted to protect their labor supply and reduce their taxes by pressuring states to restrict welfare coverage. At the same time, they lobbied for all sorts of reductions in public spending, continuation of the bracero program, restrictions on labor organizing, and reductions in wage and hour regulations, especially for agricultural workers.[50] Efforts to purge blacks from the welfare rolls were also part of the pro-segregationist movement, which many planters actively supported.[51]

RACIST POLITICIANS AND ORGANIZATIONS

Racist organizations and politicians were the other major group pushing for welfare cutbacks. In response to civil rights gains and the influx of blacks, Puerto Ricans, and Mexicans in the North and West, whites mobilized to maintain the racial status quo. As more nonwhite women gained access to welfare, this racial backlash lent support to the 1950s welfare backlash. Attacks on black, Puerto Rican, and Mexican welfare mothers' rights provided an outlet for racial anger, reinforced the racial status quo among poor mothers, and maintained a ready supply of cheap labor for employers.[52]

In the South, pro-segregationists mobilized mainly against blacks' civil rights gains. Blacks achieved a number of important political victories in the 1940s and 1950s. For example, in 1945, in response to protests and a growing black electorate, President Truman endorsed a bill to establish a permanent Fair Employment Practices Commission. He later appointed a civil rights commission by executive order and issued two executive orders prohibiting racial discrimination in the military and the federal civil service. The Supreme Court gave blacks two more important victories when it declared unconstitutional the segregation of public schools in 1954 and the segregation of public transportation in 1955.[53] "Massive resistance" rose in response to these legal gains, especially in the South, where the legacy of slavery left its mark, and where most blacks continued to live.[54]

Southern politicians mobilized white racist sentiments into a powerful pro-segregationist movement. Opposing Democrats' endorsement of civil rights in the 1940s, the governor of Mississippi organized a "states' rights" meeting attended by four thousand people. Through the 1948 "Dixiecrat Revolt," J. Strom Thurmond ran as a white supremacist presidential candidate for the States' Rights Democratic Party and won the nomination in four southern states (Alabama, Louisiana, Mississippi, and South Carolina) and thirty-nine electoral votes.[55] During the 1950s, southern politicians passed bills to obstruct the desegregation of public schools in four states and to outlaw the NAACP in three states. State registrars also barred many blacks from registering to vote, claiming they were unqualified.[56]

White anger over civil rights gains also took the form of racial violence, which rose significantly in the postwar period and in the wake of the 1954 Supreme Court decision.[57] Between 1955 and 1959, there were 210 recorded incidents of racial intimidation and 225 incidents of racial violence in the eleven former Confederate states. Mob violence erupted when blacks tried to enter formerly all-white public schools in four southern cities, and other schools were bombed. The desegregation of public transportation, housing, and voter registration initiated by blacks also sparked violent responses from whites.[58] Thousands of southern whites joined pro-segregationist organizations. By the end of 1955, Citizens' Councils spread across the South. With over 200,000 members in 568 groups, they engaged in racist lobbying campaigns and harassed civil rights supporters.[59] The racist Ku Klux Klan experienced a revival after the Brown decision, with membership ranging from 25,000 to 50,000 nationwide in the late 1950s.[60]

As more black women gained access to welfare in the period following World War II, opposition to welfare merged with this racist backlash. The southern "Dixiecrat Revolt" opposed not only blacks' civil rights gains, but also liberal economic and social policies.[61] White supremacist organizations were strongly opposed to the postwar expansion of welfare. As William J. Simmons, a Citizens' Council leader, explained to a newspaper reporter in 1955, "I consider the Citizens' Council movement the beginnings of a fundamental conservative revolt throughout the country. Much more is involved than the school segregation issue. Many of our membership is [sic] concerned also about the trend toward the welfare state."[62] Pro-segregationist politicians and Ku Klux Klan leaders also criticized the "communistic welfare state" in the postwar period, adding support to farmers' antiwelfare campaigns.[63]

In northern and western states, opposition to welfare was linked to white resentment toward the influx of Puerto Ricans and Mexicans, as well as blacks. Between 1950 and 1960, more than one million blacks moved to the North, and nearly 400,000 moved to the West.[64] As a result, 40 percent of blacks lived outside the South in 1960, compared to 23 percent in 1940. Eighty-nine percent of black migrants between 1940 and 1950, and 86 percent between 1950 and 1960, went to seven states: New York, New Jersey, Pennsylvania, Ohio, California, Illinois, and Michigan.[65] The in-migration of blacks met with white hostility, especially when blacks tried to enter formerly white neighborhoods, public parks, or beaches. In Chicago, 485 racial incidents were reported between 1945 and 1950, 357 of them in response to housing.[66] In Philadelphia, the supposed "City of Brotherly Love," there were more than 200 racial incidents related to housing reported within a six-month period in 1955.[67]

The continental Puerto Rican population increased from about 70,000 in 1940 to over 300,000 in 1950 and 893,000 in 1960.[68] The vast majority came to New York City, although many also moved to other northeastern cities or

Chicago as the decade wore on.[69] Many Puerto Ricans left because of rising unemployment brought about by the dramatic decline in the sugar and garment industries.[70] Puerto Rican immigration was also encouraged by cheaper air transport after World War II, U.S. employers' aggressive labor recruitment, the promise of higher wages, and U.S. military service.[71] Like the in-migration of blacks, the postwar migration of Puerto Ricans was often portrayed negatively. For example, one daily newspaper's 1946 headline claimed that a "tidal wave of Puerto Ricans" was "swamping" New York City, while a well-known anthropologist claimed that they had "invaded" the city.[72] Like northern blacks, Puerto Ricans experienced intense employment and housing discrimination, forcing many to live in poor, segregated neighborhoods, such as "Spanish" Harlem.[73] Prejudice against them was so widespread in the 1950s that the Puerto Rican government began to issue a pamphlet called "What is Prejudice?" to prepare migrants for the racism they would experience in the United States.[74]

Meanwhile, the Southwest experienced a wave of Mexican immigration. Mexican braceros, mainly concentrated in California, Arizona, and Texas, increased from 32,000 in 1946 to 448,000 in 1959.[75] The bracero program also stimulated undocumented immigration, as braceros "skipped" their contracts and returning braceros spread news of economic opportunities abroad. In the 1950s, the number of undocumented immigrants may have even exceeded the number of braceros.[76] Most Mexican migrants in this period were male sojourners, but women also migrated to the United States, often following their husbands. These Mexican immigrants joined other Mexican Americans living in the United States, contributing to the growth of rural and urban barrios.[77] According to the census, the Spanish surname population increased by more than 50 percent in the Southwest and by nearly 90 percent in California between 1950 and 1960.[78]

While not as widespread as black-white conflicts, Chicano-white conflicts did flare up in this period. In 1943, violent skirmishes between Mexican gang members and American sailors led to large-scale attacks by thousands of white servicemen and civilians on Mexicans, blacks, and Filipinos in Los Angeles's "zoot suit" riots. Similar disturbances broke out that summer in San Diego, Chicago, Detroit, Philadelphia, and Harlem, as well as Beaumont, Texas and Evansville, Indiana.[79] Like blacks, Chicanos were frequently refused service at stores, barred from moving into white neighborhoods,[80] and prohibited from swimming in public pools.[81] Organized groups of white parents, who claimed that they "didn't want their children in the same schools with dirty ignorant foreigners," actively defended racial segregation in public schools.[82] In response, Mexican-

Americans organized throughout the West and Southwest, forming Defense Committees, Unity Leagues, the Community Service Organization, and local chapters of the G.I. Forum. These groups registered voters and organized protests and lawsuits to combat racial discrimination and segregation of public facilities.[83] They won several court cases in 1945 and 1946 related to the segregation of Mexican Americans in public schools.[84]

In this racially charged climate, black, Puerto Rican, and Mexican welfare recipients came under attack in northern and western states. As I discuss in Chapter 6, welfare critics appealed to racial resentment toward these groups, claiming that they had become overly reliant on welfare in order to avoid work. They also claimed that some states had become "welfare magnets," attracting newcomers with their generous welfare payments, even though little social scientific research supports this view.[85] Such views legitimized residency requirements, which kept black, Puerto Rican, Mexican-American and other migrants from receiving public assistance, usually for one or two years. By 1966, thirty-nine states had adopted some sort of residency requirement for welfare.[86] While many of these rules were adopted in earlier years, support for them rose in the 1950s.

Racialized opposition was most commonly directed at blacks, however. Welfare critics in the 1950s constructed a new association between welfare and blacks in the public mind, an association that continues to this day.[87] One of the most enduring legacies of this backlash was the stereotype of the black welfare queen. In the context of justifying new restrictive welfare policies, welfare critics often portrayed black welfare mothers as purposefully having children so that they could avoid work and receive welfare. While new, this image drew on old stereotypes, constructed during slavery, of blacks as lazy and hypersexed, reckless breeders.[88] Black unwed mothers were commonly viewed as the product of "an 'accepted way of life' in an inferior culture."[89] The black welfare queen stereotype also drew on the long-standing view of unwed mothers as "fallen women" who deserved punishment for their sins.[90]

PROMOTING MARRIAGE AND WORK: PATRIARCHAL CONTRADICTIONS

The welfare backlash both drew strength from and challenged the patriarchal family ideology that flourished in the late 1940s and 1950s and glorified the fulltime housewife. At the time, most psychologists, social workers, and early childhood and family experts argued that proper childhood development was predicated on an ideal family composed of a male breadwinner and a subservient fulltime mother.[91] Citing Bowlby's infamous study, published in 1951, which concluded that deprivation of maternal care in young children produced psychiatric disturbances, family experts claimed that maternal employment contributed to a variety of psychological and social problems, including juvenile delinquency.[92]

The effects of this postwar patriarchal propaganda, spread through advertisements, television shows, movies, and women's magazines, convinced many couples to marry and have children.[93] So did the economic prosperity of the period and the creation of federal home loans for veterans, which made it easier for a male breadwinner to support several children.[94] Marriage rates rose dramatically. Couples were also staying married and having more children. The divorce rate declined in the 1950s, while the fertility rate rose between 1940 and 1955.[95] Women increasingly conformed to the housewife ideal. After rising precipitously during World War II, the rate of women's labor force participation declined sharply in the mid- to late 1940s, and increased only very gradually in the 1950s.[96] By 1960, only 31 percent of married women and 19 percent of married mothers with children under six were in the labor force.[97] Female labor force participation remained below wartime levels until the mid-1960s and was concentrated in part-time employment.[98] Postwar propaganda that discouraged women from working was mainly directed at white, middle-class women, however. Poor women, especially poor women of color, were expected to work, even when they had children.[99] In 1950, black women's labor force participation rate (37 percent) remained significantly higher than the rate for white women (25 percent).[100]

There were also significant racial differences in family patterns. While the marriage rate for young white women (age twenty to twenty-four) increased in the 1950s, it decreased for young black women, partly because of the higher incidence of poverty and unemployment among black males, which discouraged many from marrying.[101] More black men than black women also migrated in the 1950s, contributing to a shortage of eligible bachelors in the South. Black women were also more likely than white women to be separated, divorced, or widowed and to have children out of wedlock. While women of all races were having more children out of wedlock in the 1950s, this increase was sharper among blacks.[102] Between 1950 and 1960, the rate of out-of-wedlock childbearing rose from 6 to 8 per one thousand for whites and from 71 to 90 per thousand for nonwhites.[103] As a result of these combined trends, black women were twice as likely as white women to raise their children on their own. In 1950, female-headed households made up nearly 18 percent of black households, compared to 9 percent for white households.[104]

Because out-of-wedlock childbearing was more prevalent among black women than white women, efforts to restrict unwed mothers' access to welfare served as a proxy for a race-based exclusion. While about one-quarter of nonwhite welfare mothers were unwed in 1950, only about 6 percent of white welfare mothers were. This was because black mothers were more likely to be unwed, not because they were more likely to rely on welfare. Indeed, only 16 percent of nonwhite unwed mothers received ADC, compared to 30 percent for white women in 1959.[105] The race gap in the percentage of welfare mothers who were unwed remained substantial in the 1950s although it declined somewhat. By 1960, 19 percent of nonwhite welfare mothers were unwed, compared to 6 percent for white welfare mothers.[106] Commenting in the late 1950s, a government official noted that because black welfare mothers were more likely to be unwed, "much of the venom in the current attacks on ADC" was focused on them.[107] Once adopted, "suitable home" and "substitute father" rules, especially popular in the South, were used to purge blacks from the welfare rolls. As a 1961 study showed, blacks were about twice as likely as whites to be denied welfare on the grounds that their homes were "unsuitable."[108]

The "black welfare queen" stereotype figured prominently in politicians' and welfare officials' justifications for "suitable home" policies. For example, the Florida Department of Public Welfare justified its new "suitable home" policy on the grounds that many recipients, especially blacks, misunderstood the purpose of ADC:

> There is an almost universal belief by this group of [black] families that the State unquestionably has the responsibility to support children when they do not have a father. In some few cases, clients even believe that the State pays them for the illegitimate child. As one fourteen year old unmarried mother explained, "I was always told when you got to be fourteen or fifteen, you had a baby and the State started sending you a check of your own." It is believed by many clients that the State is subsidizing deserted and illegitimate children, since the check is given only for those children where the mother can prove there is no father in the home.[109]

Given the racist attitudes of the state's welfare officials, it is not surprising that about 90 percent of the cases denied under Florida's new "suitable home" policy were black.[110]

Antiwelfare rhetoric also appealed to racist stereotypes in implicit ways. Describing Governor Faubus's address to a convention in Hot Springs, Arkansas in 1959, a newspaper reporter wrote:

> Governor Faubus mounted the well-worn hobby horse of criticizing welfare payments to mothers of illegitimate children: "By taxing the good people to pay for these programs, we are putting a premium on illegitimacy never before known in the world." To anyone who has ever heard this line before, which includes all of us in Arkansas, there was little doubt that Mr. Faubus was referring primarily to Negro unwed mothers and not to any "good, honest, hard-working" white folks who have been remiss in getting down to the licensing bureau. . . . It is a fairly safe theme. Nobody, of course, wants to be put in the light of defending both bastardy and Negroes in the same breath, and the few who might point to lack of educational opportunity and generally depressed economic and social conditions as a factor in illegitimacy are soon shushed into silence.[111]

As this account suggests, politicians appealed to racist images of black welfare mothers to justify cutbacks and generally received a favorable public response when they did so.

The stereotype of the black welfare queen was even used to justify sterilization of unwed mothers. For example, a Mississippi state politician explained why he authored a bill to sterilize unwed mothers: "During the calendar year 1957, there was born out of wedlock in Mississippi, more than seven thousand Negro children. . . . The Negro woman because of child welfare assistance [is] making it a business, in some cases, of giving birth to illegitimate children . . . The purpose of my bill was to try to stop, or slow down, such traffic at its source."[112]

To justify "suitable home" policies, welfare critics appealed to racist sentiments as well as patriarchal norms of family life. They attacked unwed mothers who failed to conform to expectations that women marry and have children only in wedlock. In this case, welfare critics' patriarchal, racist, and business-oriented goals converged. Limiting unwed mothers' access to welfare simultaneously upheld traditional gender roles, purged blacks from the welfare rolls, reduced welfare expenditures, and maintained a ready supply of cheap labor. By contrast, campaigns for "employable mother" rules challenged the patriarchal expectation that mothers should stay at home with their children.

Supporters of work requirements argued that welfare interfered with the work ethic and the principle of self-sufficiency. For example, the California Farm Bureau defended the idea of work requirements for welfare recipients on the grounds that it would "encourage a return of the philosophy that each should diligently try to support himself."[113] Critics claimed that such rules were needed because welfare was breeding a culture of dependency. For example, as a Georgia county welfare board member put it, "I fear the outcome of such a program is that these children will grow into citizens who feel the government should support them."[114] An attorney in Tulsa County, Oklahoma, was even more critical, claiming, "[Welfare] raises new generations of twisted, subnormal people bred in the foulest environments, who are candidates for our swelling ranks of unemployables, criminals, and insane."[115]

Welfare critics also justified work requirements in economic terms. For example, when Georgia state officials first introduced a work requirement for welfare mothers in 1949, they claimed they were forced to adopt it because they did not have enough money in the state welfare budget.[116] They claimed that they "especially regretted" it because " 'a mother's place is in the home with these children,' but the rule seemed necessary."[117] Critics also appealed to taxpayers' interests. For example, the California Farm Bureau Federation warned that "the California taxpayer is bearing a needlessly heavy and ruinous tax burden."[118] Similarly, an exposé about "welfare cheats" in the *Saturday Evening Post* suggested that taxpayers were "paying the bills for lazy, apathetic, ne'er-do-wells satisfied to eat the bread of idleness."[119]

To justify work requirements, welfare critics appealed to the racist view that black women were more employable than white women. As a social worker employed in the 1950s explained, black welfare mothers were attacked because "the Negro mother has always worked in the past."[120] While white middle-class women were encouraged to stay at home with their children, poor black mothers were chastised for doing so.[121] Large farmers were not the only ones concerned that the postwar expansion of welfare would drain the supply of black labor. For example, a 1952 county grand jury report on ADC claimed, "It was apparent in a number of cases, *largely among colored people*, that unwarranted welfare aids were provided with the result that many such recipients of aid were unwilling to work at jobs for which they were physically and mentally suited."[122] Similarly, a member of a 1945 grand jury in Louisiana observed, "What the people who make these criticisms [about welfare] are chiefly interested in is cheaper servants. It makes no difference to them one way or the other what happens to Negro children. They are not interested in whether the mother has someone to leave the children with or not. What they want is to get a cook at $5 a week as they used to."[123]

Ten years later, a top federal welfare official also linked public hostility to welfare to white women's demand for black household help.[124] After World War II, many black women were forced to leave their factory jobs and return to white women's homes, but they were often not employed in the same kitchens because they had migrated out of the rural South.[125] White southerners blamed rural labor shortages on urban welfare programs. For example, a juror serving on a grand jury in Shreveport, Louisiana questioned a local welfare director: "I should like to know why you have so many Negro women on your payrolls. Why can't they go back to the country and work instead of staying in the city and living on public welfare?"[126] In response to such pressures, southern social workers routinely used employment requirements to deny aid only to black women when domestic service jobs became available. They justified such practices by claiming that domestic service was more suitable to black women than white women.[127]

Perhaps because they were disproportionately applied to blacks, restrictive welfare rules adopted in the 1950s enjoyed considerable public support. In a 1961 Gallup poll, 90 percent of respondents said that the amount of aid to unwed welfare mothers should not be increased each time they had an illegitimate child. While most felt that relief for unwed mothers should be stopped, others suggested that they should be forced to accept employment, institutionalized, or even sterilized. Seventy-three percent of respondents agreed that it was "a good idea . . . to get a court order to require the mother of an illegitimate child to name the father and then require him to pay the extra relief costs for the child." The poll also found that 85 percent of those surveyed supported employment requirements for relief recipients, and 74 percent agreed with a plan to make ADC applicants prove they were looking for a job.[128] Popular acceptance of work requirements for welfare mothers reflected long-standing expectations that poor women, especially poor women of color, work.[129] As maternal employment became more common, the idea that aid was needed to prevent the negative consequences of maternal employment lost more of its political appeal.[130]

While support for work requirements and "suitable home" policies were strong, they were not accepted by everyone, especially those directly affected by it. For example, an administrator reviewing eligibility hearings in Georgia noted, "The ADC policy relating to the employability of the mother was frequently protested. Both the mothers and their witnesses felt that the mothers were needed in the home for the job of homemaker for their children."[131] Individual complaints about the implementation of work rules did not lead to collective protest among welfare mothers, however, as they remained unorganized until the mid-1960s.

The U.S. Children's Bureau was also highly critical of "employable mother" rules in the 1950s. Its chief, Martha Eliot, promoted ADC as a "preventive mental health" policy that ensured that young children could have a close relationship with their mothers, which she believed was crucial to their healthy development.[132] Her replacement, Katherine Oettinger, was more tolerant of maternal employment. Yet, she also defended poor mothers' right to stay at home with their children on the grounds that it would enable mothers to make responsible choices regarding maternal employment. She claimed that public assistance was cheaper than forcing poor mothers to work because "either the community must foot the bill for daytime care or foot the bill for the consequences of inadequate care."[133] Bureau leaders also strongly opposed attacks on unwed welfare mothers, which they attributed to "unenlightened segments of the public."[134] Eliot warned that without assistance, unwed mothers might be forced to exchange their children "through unscrupulous middlemen."[135] While such concerns may have stemmed the welfare backlash in some states, they were disregarded in others. What explains the uneven support for welfare cutbacks across the nation?

UNEVEN SUPPORT FOR WELFARE CUTBACKS

Although most (about 62 percent) of states that restricted ADC eligibility were in the South, there were a number of western and midwestern states that also did so. What socioeconomic or political factors distinguished states that restricted ADC eligibility from those that did not? In general theoretical terms, I believe that states are most likely to experience powerful pressures to restrict welfare coverage when the demand for low-wage contingent labor is high, there are considerable fiscal constraints, or racial conflicts are salient. In the 1950s, the main political forces behind the 1950s welfare backlash were large farmers and white racists. Large farmers had the most political influence where agribusiness made up an important part of the local economy. In states dominated by family farming or industrial enterprises, large farm operators had to contend with other corporate elites for political power and had less control of the state's economy. Though economic dominance does not always lead to political dominance, the two are often related. States were also more likely to respond favorably to antiwelfare campaigns when racism was rampant and when states were fiscally more constrained. Racist opposition to welfare was likely to be more powerful where there was a larger black population and blacks made up a greater share of welfare cases. Welfare cutbacks were also more likely to occur where the tax base was lower.[136] Such states were more financially burdened by the post–World War II expansion of ADC, making cutbacks seem imperative.

Table 2 shows the characteristics of states that did and did not restrict ADC eligibility in the 1950s by adopting either a work requirement or a stricter "suitable home" policy. This table shows that most states that restricted ADC had a significant agribusiness sector, measured in terms of whether the percentage of farms reporting ten or more employees was

TABLE 2. *Characteristics of States That Did and Did Not Restrict ADC Eligibility*

	High Percentage of Large Farms**	Low Per Capita Income***	Large Proportion of ADC Recipients Black****
RESTRICTED ADC ELIGIBILITY*			
South and Border South			
Alabama	Yes	Yes	Yes
Arkansas	Yes	Yes	Yes
Florida	Yes	Yes	Yes
Georgia	Yes	Yes	Yes
Louisiana	Yes	Yes	Yes
Mississippi	Yes	Yes	Yes
Missouri	No	No	Yes
North Carolina	Yes	Yes	Yes
South Carolina	Yes	Yes	Yes
Tennessee	No	Yes	Yes
Texas	Yes	Yes	Yes
Virginia	Yes	Yes	Yes
West Virginia	No	Yes	No
West and Midwest			
Arizona	Yes	Yes	No
California	Yes	No	No
Illinois	No	No	Yes
Michigan	No	No	Yes
Nebraska	No	No	No
New Mexico	Yes	Yes	No
Washington	Yes	No	No
Northeast			
New Hampshire	No	Yes	No
Summary Measure			
Percentage of states with this characteristic	67	71	67

* State adopted an employment requirement or adopted a new or more restrictive suitable home policy between 1949 and 1960. *Source:* Federal Security Agency, Social Security Administration, Bureau of Public Assistance; Bell 1965; state legislative records.

** Percentage of state's farms that reported ten or more hired workers in 1950 was above the median. SOURCE: U.S. Department of Commerce, Bureau of the Census 1956.

*** State per capita income in dollars in 1950 was below the median. SOURCE: U.S. Department of Commerce 1958.

**** Percentage of state's ADC recipients in 1948 that were black was above the median. SOURCE: Alling and Leisy 1950.

TABLE 2. *(continued)*

	High Percentage of Large Farms**	*Low Per Capita Income****	*Large Proportion of ADC Recipients Black*****
DID <u>NOT</u> RESTRICT ADC ELIGIBILITY			
Northeast			
Connecticut	Yes	No	Yes
Delaware	No	No	Yes
Maine	No	Yes	No
Maryland	Yes	No	Yes
Massachusetts	Yes	No	No
New Jersey	Yes	No	Yes
New York	No	No	Yes
Pennsylvania	No	No	Yes
Rhode Island	No	No	No
Vermont	No	Yes	No
West and Midwest			
Colorado	Yes	No	No
Idaho	No	Yes	No
Indiana	No	No	Yes
Iowa	No	No	No
Kansas	No	Yes	Yes
Minnesota	No	No	No
Montana	Yes	No	No
Nevada	Yes	No	No data
North Dakota	No	Yes	No
Ohio	No	No	Yes
Oregon	Yes	No	No
South Dakota	No	Yes	No
Utah	Yes	Yes	No
Wisconsin	No	No	No
Wyoming	Yes	No	No
Border South			
Kentucky	No	Yes	No
Oklahoma	No	Yes	Yes
Summary Measure			
Percentage of states with this characteristic	37	33	37

above the median for all states in 1950.[137] Most of these states also had a per capita income below the median for all states in 1950[138] and an above-median share of welfare cases that were black.[139] By contrast, most states that failed to restrict ADC eligibility did not have these characteristics.

As Table 2 also suggests, the southern political economy was distinct from other regions in having a *combination* of a relatively large black population, an agricultural economy, and a small tax base. This combination of characteristics appears to be strongly associated with the development of restrictive welfare policies. It is likely that these southern states experienced pressures to restrict ADC from multiple, overlapping groups: racist whites, fiscal conservatives, and large farmers. Under this combined pressure, many southern states restricted welfare eligibility. By contrast, most of the midwestern and western states that restricted ADC eligibility (as well as the northern, midwestern, and western states that did not restrict ADC eligibility) only had one or two of these characteristics. Such states probably experienced more isolated *and also less decisive* pressure to restrict welfare.

A logistic regression analysis also indicates a statistically significant, positive relationship between these characteristics and the odds that a state would restrict welfare eligibility (see Table 3).[140] This quantitative analysis indicates that both the size of the black population and caseload and the strength of agribusiness had a statistically significant independent effect on the odds that states would restrict welfare in the 1950s. This suggests that in the absence of a high demand for agricultural labor, states with larger black populations and caseloads were still likely to adopt tougher eligibility policies. The results also indicate that states with large agribusiness sectors were likely to restrict welfare even where racial conflicts were less salient. Indeed, racial animosity toward black welfare mothers was probably not very important to the development of work requirements in Nebraska, where less than two percent of the total population was black (see Appendix 2 for details on measurements and sources).

My quantitative analysis also explored the role of other factors, such as the strength of the labor movement and the presence of a Children's Bureau office, in determining whether or not states restricted ADC eligibility. I did not find that the presence of a Children's Bureau office, the unionization rate, or the strike rate had statistically significant effects on the odds that states would restrict welfare in this period. Most likely, Children's Bureau officials and the labor movement were too weak to effectively defend poor mothers' welfare rights when states experienced strong pressures to restrict them. Besieged with anticommunist red-baiting and dominated by white men, the labor movement was also not very active in defending the ADC

TABLE 3. *Logit Coefficients, Standard Errors, and Odds for the Regression of Adoption of Restrictive ADC Eligibility Rules (in 1960) on Independent Variables*

Variable	Coefficient S.E. Odds				
	Model 1	Model 2	Model 3	Model 4	Model 5
Intercept	1.3413	0.9693	-0.1186	-4.7278	-1.0563
	(4.7773)	(4.5124)	(4.3645)	(5.6821)	(3.8040)
Agricultural labor demand (1 high; 0 low)	5.3879**	—	5.1983**	4.6815*	3.9881**
	(1.9593)		(1.8927)	(1.9679)	(1.6102)
	218.748		180.959	107.928	53.951
Percent of farms that are large	—	0.9442*	—	—	—
		(0.4183)			
		2.571			
Percent of ADC population black	0.0995**	0.0682*	—	—	0.0769*
	(0.0343)	(0.0296)			(0.0319)
	1.105	1.071			1.080
Percent of ADC population nonwhite	—	—	0.0926**	—	—
			(0.0349)		
			1.097		
Percent of population black	—	—	—	0.3540**	—
				(0.1444)	
				1.425	
Per capita income	-0.0080*	-0.0060*	-0.0073*	-0.0040	-0.0041*
	(0.0034)	(0.0029)	(0.0030)	(0.0030)	(0.0020)
	0.992	0.994	0.993	0.996	0.996
Union density	0.1280*	0.0803	0.1208*	0.1039	—
	(0.0666)	(0.0553)	(0.0597)	(0.0643)	
	1.137	1.084	1.128	1.109	
Strike rate	—	—	—	—	0.0318
					(0.1264)
					1.032
Children's Bureau (1 high; 0 low)	-1.5701	-0.6876	-1.3057	-1.1992	-0.7195
	(1.0882)	(1.0263)	(1.0028)	(1.0847)	(1.3205)
	0.208	0.503	0.271	0.301	0.463
Majority of legislature liberal (1 high; 0 low)	-1.3562	-0.7110	-0.8720	-1.5414	-0.7195
	(1.6143)	(1.4107)	(1.4069)	(1.8143)	(1.3205)
	0.258	0.491	0.418	0.214	0.487
Index of rural overrepresentation	0.0571	0.0342	0.0611	0.0726	0.680
	(0.0437)	(0.0377)	(0.0432)	(0.0471)	(0.0406)
	1.059	1.035	1.063	1.075	1.070

* One-tailed T-test is statistically significant at the 0.05 level.
** One-tailed T-test is statistically significant at the 0.01 level.

program, which was increasingly associated with racial minorities and unwed mothers. I found that states with legislatures dominated by conservative politicians (Republicans or southern Democrats) or rural representatives were not significantly more likely to restrict welfare than other states. This may have been due to the fact that state welfare boards, rather than the legislature, were the ones to adopt tough welfare rules in the 1950s. My case studies in chapters 5 and 6 reveal that there were sometimes significant intraparty divisions on welfare issues, with liberal Republicans sometimes defending welfare and conservative or rural Democrats attacking it.[141] Contrary to what one might expect, welfare was not more controversial in the South because poverty was more visible there. Rural poverty was substantial and southern wage rates were lower than the rest of the nation. Unemployment was high in the 1950s in many large northern and midwestern cities, however, especially as rising numbers of blacks moved there from the South. Indeed, southern unemployment rates were equal to or less than national unemployment rates in 1950 and 1960.[142]

The 1950s welfare backlash was shaped by the politics of race, class, and gender. Business leaders, especially large farmers, opposed the expansion of welfare because it threatened to increase their tax burden and interfere with their supply of cheap casual labor. Southern whites were concerned that as more poor black women gained access to welfare, there would be fewer to iron their shirts and clean their houses. The 1950s welfare backlash was also part of a broader racist backlash against postwar civil rights gains and the influx of blacks, Mexicans, and Puerto Ricans in the North and West. Welfare critics targeted nonwhite women for cutbacks and justified this through various racist stereotypes, such as the black welfare queen, or the lazy black, Mexican, or Puerto Rican migrant.

Welfare critics appealed to patriarchal norms of family life, which experienced a resurgence after World War II, but not consistently. While they attacked unwed mothers and "deadbeat dads" for failing to conform to traditional family roles, they also urged poor mothers to work. This contradiction reflected the limits of postwar patriarchal propaganda, which was mainly directed toward white middle-class women. Yet, this contradiction was also indicative of welfare critics' underlying racist and class-based goals. While limiting aid to unwed mothers and enforcing fathers' role as the male breadwinner was consistent with their goals of reducing welfare costs, ensuring a ready supply of low-wage workers, and purging blacks from the welfare rolls, subsidizing poor mothers to take care of their children was not.

Opposition to welfare was not as widespread in the 1950s as it has become today, however. By 1960, more than half of all states still had no formal work requirements for welfare mothers. This welfare backlash was most powerful in southern and southwestern states, where agribusiness flourished, blacks were more numerous, and fiscal constraints were considerable. Even in those states, welfare critics called for restrictions on welfare use rather than abolishing welfare entitlements. Welfare programs still enjoyed considerable public support in this period when maternal employment rates were still low and racialized opposition to welfare was only beginning to emerge. Moreover, large farmers benefited from the provision of welfare in the off-season, which helped prevent the out-migration of their workforce. In the next few chapters, I provide a close-up look at this welfare backlash and how it varied across four states: Georgia, Kentucky, California, and New York.

5. Southern Welfare Backlashes
Georgia and Kentucky

The 1950s welfare backlash was the strongest in the South, where planters dominated the political economy and white racism against blacks was rampant. Yet, it was more powerful in some southern states than others. In this chapter, I compare Georgia's large-scale purge of its welfare rolls with Kentucky's welfare backlash, which was not nearly as powerful. The relative strength of these two welfare backlashes reflected broader differences in these states' political economies and race relations.

Georgia was more typical of the Deep South than was the border state of Kentucky. Like most other states in this region, large farmers dominated Georgia's political economy. In 1950, one out of five workers in the state was employed in agriculture, while the state's main manufacturing industries— textiles, food, apparel, and paper—involved agricultural goods.[1] While there were many small farmers in the state, large farms, many of which were former slave plantations, played a dominant role in the state's economy. The disenfrachisement of blacks and a "one-party" political system dominated by rural counties ensured that planters continued to dominate state politics, even as agriculture declined.[2] Although one-third of Georgia's population lived in its six largest urban counties, representatives from those areas only made up 9 percent of the assembly and 7 percent of the senate in the 1950s.[3] Racism toward blacks, who made up more than one-third of the population but lacked real voting power, was also extensive and shaped state politics considerably.[4] These conditions fostered the development of a powerful welfare backlash and adoption of a host of new welfare regulations in 1952.

By contrast, Kentucky adopted only a few new welfare rules in the 1950s. This is somewhat surprising, since the state had a substantial agricultural sector and considerable racism, conditions conducive to a strong welfare backlash. In 1950, about one-quarter of its labor force was employed in agriculture, and corn and tobacco products were among the state's principal manufactured products.[5] As in other southern states, there was also considerable white resistance to the desegregation of the state's public facilities.[6] On the other hand, labor unions, especially strong in the state's mines, and numerous small farmers provided strong support for New Deal programs and liberal Democrats. Kentucky's political system was also more competitive than the rest of the one-party Deep South, a situation that encouraged politicians to compete for the black vote.[7]

GEORGIA'S WELFARE BACKLASH

The Rise of Welfare Opposition

Georgia's welfare backlash developed in response to a dramatic rise in welfare cases. Four times as many welfare applications were approved in 1950 as in 1945, while the percentage of black families among those served by ADC rose from 32 in 1948 to 43 in 1953.[8] The demand for welfare increased partly because of the demobilization of the wartime economy and the displacement of agricultural workers.[9] Federal welfare officials also put greater pressure on welfare officials to stop discriminating among applicants. Before then, Georgia's welfare department limited its welfare budget by freezing the number of recipients who could receive aid. Counties discouraged people from applying or simply put new applicants on a "waiting list" until another welfare case was closed.[10]

To stem rising caseloads and expenditures, state welfare officials first cut benefits and tightened eligibility rules for ADC in 1949.[11] The new regulations reinforced family self-sufficiency by requiring men to support their stepchildren, welfare mothers to seek support from deserting fathers, and able-bodied mothers with children over eighteen months to work.[12] In 1952, the state welfare board adopted an even more stringent policy package.[13] Like the 1949 policies, the new rules reinforced the male breadwinner role in families. Welfare mothers were required to seek support from their child's father before receiving state assistance. Court orders of support, even if inadequate, could not be supplemented with welfare. The state also denied eligibility if there was an able-bodied stepfather or "substitute" father (i.e., a boyfriend) in the home. Meanwhile, mothers deemed promiscuous were denied welfare on the grounds that their homes were "unsuitable." While those policies reinforced traditional gender roles, the state's new "seasonal work requirement" undermined them. Able-bodied mothers with children over one year of age were expected to find employment if work was available. Another rule prohibited supplementation of full-time wages, even if they were inadequate.[14] The federal Bureau of Public Assistance criticized these policies for conflicting with the purposes of ADC, but only insisted that the state develop more detailed procedures for evaluating the "suitability" of a home. State officials responded by declaring various behaviors to constitute unsuitable parental behavior, including "repeated births of children born out-of-wedlock."[15]

The implementation of Georgia's new "policy package" purged nearly 6,000 families and more than 21,000 children from the rolls, representing more than one-third of all cases in 1952–53.[16] The new rules also halted the trend toward more equitable treatment of African Americans. The percentage of the caseload that was black increased by 6 percent between 1948 and 1953, but increased by only 1 percent over the following five years.[17]

Why did welfare officials restrict welfare eligibility in the postwar period? Budget constraints were the immediate impetus. By June 1947, state funds for public assistance were exhausted, but the caseload continued to rise. Initially, the state welfare department adopted a dual strategy of reducing benefits and tightening eligibility. When the caseload continued to grow, the state welfare department was forced to make more cutbacks.[18] As the director recalled, the state welfare board adopted the 1952 policy package "to keep the Department's budget from being over-spent."[19] Another top welfare official similarly recounts that they "had to do something to live within the money that the legislature had given us."[20]

Nonetheless, the problem was more political than financial. At the time, the "Talmadge faction" still dominated the state's Democratic Party. This faction backed Eugene Talmadge, who won four gubernatorial campaigns before his death in 1946, afterward transferring its allegiance to his son Herman, elected governor in 1948. The Talmadge machine was financed by bankers, industrialists, and large corporations but appealed mainly to farmers, who provided most of its votes. The Talmadge faction was known for its "anti-Negro rantings," its fiscal conservatism, and its strong opposition to welfare.[21] Eugene Talmadge, who viewed most recipients as "chiselers," told the state welfare director that "if she wanted to end the depression, she should 'line [the poor] up against a wall and give them castor oil'" so that they would return to work. Because of his opposition, Georgia received no federal welfare funds until Governor E. D. Rivers replaced him in 1937.[22] Like his father, Herman Talmadge was highly critical of the state's welfare program.

So was the legislature. As the former welfare director recalled, the 1951 legislature had the "general attitude" that "the ADC program [was] getting out of hand moneywise."[23] Some legislators were so dissatisfied with ADC that they "even threatened to introduce a bill to abolish it."[24] They also passed a resolution urging Congress to authorize public inspections of welfare records, claiming that confidentiality made welfare administration "conducive to fraud."[25] Governor Talmadge wholeheartedly supported this resolution, claiming it would reduce the number of ineligibles receiving welfare.[26] Politicians also disapproved of the rising number of unwed mothers receiving welfare, claiming that they put the program in "disrepute."[27]

Because unwed mothers were disproportionately black, limiting their access to welfare served as a proxy for race-based exclusion.[28] Focusing on the racially charged issue of unwed motherhood, politicians appealed to racist sentiments that were strong in postwar Georgia, where blacks' civil rights gains sparked a wave of racist violence.[29] Denying aid to black unwed mothers also appealed to large farmers in the state, since blacks made up 67 percent of agricultural workers.[30] In 1951, legislators considered two bills to limit aid to unwed mothers. The first bill, not enacted, presumed any unwed mother to be "an unfit and unsuitable parent" and authorized county officials to be the children's legal guardian.[31] The second bill, which was enacted, denied additional aid to mothers who had more than one child out of wedlock. To justify this bill, politicians constructed and used the stereotype of the "black welfare queen." For example, Governor Talmadge, who authored it, claimed it was intended to "put an end to 'illegitimate baby-having as a business in Georgia.'"[32] Similarly, a legislator claimed it was designed to stop the practice of "putting a premium on illegitimacy" and then reported that 95 percent of out-of-wedlock children receiving aid were black.[33] Meanwhile, the state welfare director claimed that the new law would arrest a "'growing tendency' to regard producing illegitimate children as 'good business.'" He went on to report that this "growing tendency" was particularly prevalent among blacks, who made up 70 percent of cases of multiple illegitimacy.[34] A state welfare official recalls that Talmadge's bill "passed so fast it would make your head swim."[35] Representative Wood urged the house "not to punish children for the wrongs of their mothers." Sensing the strength of his adversaries, he simply suggested that the bill be limited to those giving birth to a second illegitimate child after the bill's enactment. This amendment was "shouted down."[36] However, the new law was never put into effect. Because the Social Security Administration viewed the law as unconstitutional, it threatened to withhold federal funds if the state put it into practice.[37] The following year, Georgia's legislature replaced the law with one that required unwed mothers to seek child support from their child's father.[38] While more mild than the original law, it was still highly punitive toward unwed mothers who were unable to name the father or feared the consequences of doing so.[39]

Legislators also investigated the state welfare department in 1951, showing particular concern with its racial politics.[40] Legislators accused the chief of the Children's Welfare Division of being a communist because she supported equal rights regardless of race, and they asked several other welfare officials if they had signed a petition supporting the establishment of a Fair Employment Practices Commission.[41] Appealing to both anticommunist and racist sentiments, Senator Mims claimed that "the taxpayers have a right to know whether or not state employees are consorting with Reds and whether or not they are for upsetting the present racial patterns."[42]

Meanwhile, county welfare officials were becoming increasingly adamant that welfare needed to be distributed more selectively. As early as 1949, one rural county welfare department noted, "One of the chief criticisms which the general public in our county has expressed is that we are encouraging, first laziness, second illegitimacy, and third abetting in lowering the standard of social behavior. The consensus of the community thinking is that every capable person should work."[43] While such views were attributed to the "general public," many county welfare boards represented the views of the large farmers who staffed them. For example, the director of the Grady County Department of Public Welfare recalled in 1966 that for the past twenty-nine years, "the Board has been made up of farmers or allied fields other than a few instances where it was businessmen. . . . We have had predominantly, at least a majority of the Board's members have been farmers [sic]."[44]

In the early 1950s, county welfare officials protested the liberal administration of welfare through a series of well-publicized resignations. In 1951, two members of the Sumter County Welfare Board resigned from their posts after state officials overrode their decision to deny aid in certain cases.[45] In 1952, the chairman of the Peach County welfare board resigned in protest when state and federal requirements prevented the county from reducing its welfare rolls.[46] About a week later, the chairman of the Clarke County welfare board commended his action. In a letter to the governor, he urged the state to give county welfare officials greater control over welfare administration, claiming that at least one-third of his county's recipients were unworthy.[47]

Later that year, the state welfare director, after examining minutes from recent meetings, reported that most county welfare boards were concerned that welfare administration had become too lax.[48] One county board member claimed, "Children from homes supported by the government funds

[will] arrive at the conclusion that support comes easy and without work."[49] Other county officials argued that welfare "encourages illegitimacy" and urged enactment of "stricter regulations regarding the responsibility of parents."[50] Similarly, another welfare board noted that there had been "increasing public criticism" of ADC for providing aid to unwed mothers, because their "homes are not suitable." Welfare officials in Houston County urged the state to deny welfare to mothers with more than one child out of wedlock.[51] County officials also sought to punish men for failing to support their families. Appealing to the stereotype of black men as reckless breeders, a county welfare official in Georgia provided this account of the postwar rise in his county's welfare rolls:

> Many of these children merely have been abandoned by one or more parents, simply because the parent or parents know that the welfare department will provide funds for rearing these children, leaving the parents free to earn, spend, and beget other children to become wards of the government. There is one case of one irresponsible man who was the father of 10 children by 10 different women in one 12-month period here in this county, and all of these children were potential wards of the welfare department. . . . Many [ADC] cases are the direct results of divorces, wife swapping, drinking, and desertions. There are other families in the same communities who maintain sound homes based on high moral standards, sharing what income they have as families should, doing without things they can't buy, paying their bills, paying taxes, saving some and bearing their share of the burden of supporting families whose purpose is to get something out of the government instead of assuming their own responsibilities. . . . To me, this type of thing is weakening the moral fiber of which strong families are built.[52]

In these ways, county welfare boards, often staffed by large farmers, increased pressure on the state to restrict welfare eligibility. Meanwhile, the state welfare director, appointed by Governor Talmadge, publicized a study finding that at least sixty-nine welfare mothers cashed their checks in liquor stores, claiming it demonstrated the need for tougher welfare rules.[53] Likewise, the chief of the Finance and Statistics Division for the department publicly testified that "we've got too many people on the rolls" and that federal regulations were "too liberal."[54]

Welfare officials' support for tougher welfare rules was strengthened by their experience in 1949, when they attempted to lower expenditures through a combination of benefit reductions and eligibility restrictions for Old Age Assistance and ADC. They claimed that tremendous public outrage arose in response. As the state welfare director described, "There was a hue and cry from one end of Georgia to the other when those grants were reduced." After that, "we felt like we needed to do whatever was possible . . . to curtail the rolls so that we would not be faced again with the proposition of reducing grants percent-wise across-the-board."[55] Top welfare officials believed it would be more acceptable to provide adequate assistance to the "most needy" and "worthy" recipients rather than reducing grants across the board.[56] As another top welfare official explained, the welfare department adopted the 1952 "policy package" in order to "discontinue the payments of those cases that were casting unfavorable criticism upon the program."[57]

In addition to county welfare officials, journalists and judges were critical of ADC and portrayed its recipients as undeserving. For example, editors of the *Atlanta Constitution* claimed, "The *Constitution* has been saying all along there are gross abuses of Georgia's welfare rolls. Persons genuinely in need find it more difficult to get assistance, and in amounts far below subsistence levels, because there are so many chiselers and leeches taking the taxpayers' money." The editors advocated a number of policies aimed at purging the welfare rolls, including making them public and requiring deserting fathers to support their children.[58] Meanwhile, a county judge lashed out in the press about an alleged "racket," in which poor families falsely charged fathers with abandonment in order to receive welfare, "milking the welfare department of funds."[59]

Large Farmers' Influence

One of the main forces pushing for welfare cutbacks in Georgia, and one of the main beneficiaries, was large farmers, who have a long history of controlling the distribution of welfare. In the early 1930s, when welfare was still heavily reliant on private charities, planters "complained that during the picking season, 'people in Red Cross lines won't work.'" Many prohibited their tenants from receiving Red Cross supplies during the harvest. After Georgia's welfare program became federally funded, it was common for large landowners to serve on local rural relief committees controlling the distribution of work relief and welfare.[60] They "tended to disburse it sparingly for fear they would lose their labor."[61] Business leaders, especially farmers, claimed that public work programs drained the labor supply because they provided greater job security and higher wages than employers could offer. In response, county administrators frequently voted to give no work relief to farm laborers during and sometimes before the harvest season.[62]

In the welfare backlash of the 1950s, the state continued to respond to large farmers' labor supply needs. Both the rule prohibiting the supplementation of low wages and the seasonal employment requirement adopted in

1952 protected their supply of cheap labor. According to the seasonal work requirement, welfare was denied during the harvest season to all mothers who were within reasonable proximity of seasonal farm or cannery work, had previous experience with it, and had children older than one year and could make child care arrangements.[63] Child care regulations were loosely enforced. For example, in an administrative review of eligibility hearings, welfare officials noted that one ADC recipient was denied welfare even though "there was no agreement as to whether the claimant, if employed, had adult care for her six small children and testimony was introduced that claimant's mother was unwilling and perhaps unable to provide this care."[64] There were also cases in which mothers of one-year-olds were denied welfare, even though the "seasonal employment" rule only applied to mothers with children at least two years old.[65] Caseworkers also informed mothers that their older children would have to work with them in the fields.[66] Farmers serving on local welfare boards controlled the implementation of this seasonal work requirement by determining when the period of seasonal employment began and ended, often in response to farmers' complaints about labor shortages.[67] During the seasonal employment period, large farmers and cannery operators recruited workers through the welfare department.[68]

Georgia's seasonal employment rules were only applied to women who had previous experience doing farm work, which meant that white women were more likely to be exempt.[69] As a result, court records indicate, "there are twice as many Negro mothers on the welfare rolls as whites, but during the course of the entire year, four times as many Negro mothers are cut off as white mothers under this [employable mother] rule. During seasonal employment, six times as many Negroes are cut off."[70] Exempting women with no previous farm experience thus reinforced racial inequities between white and black women. Most likely, this was the main purpose of these exemptions, since seasonal farm workers could be trained in a few hours.[71]

The implementation of Georgia's "policy package" suggests that employers were its main beneficiaries. In the first year of their use, nearly 60 percent of all the cases terminated due to the 1952 regulations were attributed to the rule prohibiting the supplementation of low wages and the seasonal work requirement (see Table 4). By contrast, less than 1 percent of these terminations were due to the suitable home rule, nor was this rule used more frequently over the next eight years. Cases denied due to the "suitable home" or "substitute parent" policies account for less than 10 percent of discontinued grants between 1952 and 1960. Nevertheless, the assistant director of the welfare department claimed in a Georgia newspaper that "in the main, two 1952 regulations accounted for the dip in the rolls. They involved

TABLE 4. *Number and Percent of Closures Due to Georgia's 1952 Regulations*

By Type of Rule, July 1952–June 1953 in Rank Order

Rule	No. Closed	% of Closures
1. Prohibition of supplementation of low income wages from full-time employment	2,244	44.4
2. No deprivation of parental support because of able-bodied stepfather who is in the home	770	15.2
3. No deprivation of parental support because parent is employable and able to obtain adult care for children without cost beyond financial ability	625	12.4
4. No deprivation of parental support because of able-bodied substitute father who is in the home	447	8.9
5. No deprivation of parental support because of income contributed voluntarily by an absent parent	358	7.1
6. No deprivation of parental support because of support being furnished the children as a result of court action	338	6.7
7. No deprivation of parental support because parents left children voluntarily in home of ADC payee	224	4.4
8. Home unsuitable according to new agency regulations	47	0.9
All 1952 regulations	5,053	100.0

SOURCE: Georgia Department of Public Welfare 1953b.

'suitability of the home' and the presence of a 'substitute father.'" He went on to describe these policies in this way: "An ADC home can be held 'unsuitable' for children if the mother is promiscuous, carries on with a man, or has illegitimate children. . . . Get right, the parents are told, and the grants will be resumed."[72] The state welfare department's emphasis on these rules despite their negligible use by welfare staff was "politically strategic" given the "social, moral, and political atmosphere" in Georgia.[73] By publicizing its attempts to regulate poor mothers' sexual behavior and obscuring its more questionable practice of coercing poor families into low-wage employment, the department ensured support for its welfare policies.

Public Responses to the Cutbacks

When these restrictive policies were first announced, there was "a flurry among civic and professional groups in Georgia, notably the League of Women Voters," who were concerned about their effects, especially on black children.[74] The league claimed that these policies "have resulted in decreases in the number of persons receiving . . . ADC and undoubtedly have deprived some desperately needy persons of aid."[75] They were not the only ones concerned about the new welfare rules.

Following their implementation, a county welfare worker reported, "Communities were aroused. Workers could not stop in small towns after office hours or on a Saturday without explanations of the ADC program being made to interested individuals." Yet she also noted that the public was easily convinced of the need for strict welfare rules. "When the people in the county understood, they seemed to have a better feeling about the department, and to think that it was right for the responsibility to be placed on the parent, for this department had been accused of encouraging illegitimacy and laziness."[76] For the most part, however, Georgia's new welfare restrictions were quietly accepted. One county welfare official even noted that "reaction to the new rules . . . was extremely favorable."[77]

Even those most affected by the policies—welfare recipients and social workers—did not really contest them much. There were individual complaints about the new polices: as one county welfare department noted, the new regulations "caused dissatisfaction among recipients."[78] Another commented, "It hurt to tell mothers that low income wages could not be supplemented. Are welfare workers so cruel that little children will suffer from want of food?"[79] Recipients occasionally challenged the implementation of the new rules through eligibility hearings.[80] Nonetheless, welfare mothers remained unorganized, making it difficult for them to mobilize opposition to the new regulations.

By contrast, efforts to tighten eligibility rules for old-age pensions sparked considerable controversy. In 1951, Georgia's legislators enacted a law that required financially able children to support their parents, as well as a property lien provision for pensioners; the governor, the welfare department, and state legislators were so deluged with complaints about these new policies that they were subsequently revised.[81] Not only were old-age pensioners more likely to be perceived as the "deserving poor" than were welfare mothers, but they were also more organized. Between 1930 and 1950, sixty-one Townsend clubs formed in Georgia.[82] Although only two of these clubs were still considered active by the national organization between 1951 and 1953, the prior history of these organizations probably increased pensioners' sense of entitlement and their ability to mobilize opposition to the cutbacks.[83] Pensioners' adult children may also have opposed the expectation that they support their parents, and were better able than welfare mothers' young children to complain about welfare cutbacks.

KENTUCKY'S WELFARE BACKLASH

Kentucky's welfare backlash was much less extensive, and was more contested, than it was in Georgia. Whereas Georgia adopted a whole slate of restrictive welfare policies in the early 1950s, there were relatively few legislative attempts to restrict welfare in Kentucky. Between 1948 and 1960, the state's politicians introduced only three bills to restrict welfare and seven bills to strengthen parental support laws, and adopted only a few of them.[84] By 1961, Kentucky's eligibility rules for ADC remained relatively lenient compared to most southern states. To receive welfare, a needy child had to live in the state for at least a year and attend school regularly. Mothers were required to take legal measures to gain support from their children's fathers and stepfathers. The state did not adopt an employment requirement for welfare mothers until the early 1960s. Though state officials noted that the rule was "used as a means of keeping assistance payments at a minimum level," it was not rigidly enforced. Less than 7 percent of welfare mothers were employed in the state and less than 2 percent were employed fulltime.[85]

The Rise of Welfare Opposition

Kentucky's welfare caseloads rose sharply, with almost three times as many children receiving welfare in 1949 compared to the end of World War II. As the state welfare commissioner pointed out, this was "probably the largest relative increase made by any state in the country."[86] The welfare department attributed this partly to economic factors, and partly to the state's "less restrictive eligibility requirements" compared with other states.[87] To reduce the state's caseload, politicians adopted three new policies. First, in 1950, the state made stepparents and common-law fathers legally responsible for supporting their families. A total of 1,716 welfare cases (about 9 percent of the caseload) were discontinued in the first six months of this rule's implementation.[88] Unwed fathers were also legally obligated to support their children. If they failed to show up for their "bastardy proceeding," they were liable to pay court fees in addition to child support or be thrown in jail.[89] There is no record of the number of cases affected by this rule, but the welfare department estimated that it "could theoretically affect up to 12 percent of children receiving aid."[90] Apparently, the policy was more effective in punishing poor fathers than in restricting welfare coverage, however. Welfare officials reported, "A large percentage of fathers in such cases plead guilty and elect to serve ten days in jail and take the pauper's oath. Thereafter, prosecution necessarily ceases."[91] Nevertheless, the rule did temporar-

TABLE 5. *Number of ADC Recipients in Kentucky by Year,*
1949–1953

Year	No. of Families	% Change	No. of Children	% Change
1949*	19,363	—	48,697	—
1950**	22,951	+18.5	57,953	+19.0
1951**	23,228	+1.2	59,920	+3.4
1952**	19,827	-14.6	51,883	-13.4
1953**	20,297	+2.4	54,183	+4.4

* Data is from July. SOURCE: Kentucky Department of Economic Security, 1949, *Statistical Journal.*
** Data is from June. SOURCE: Kentucky Department of Economic Security, 1950–53, *Statistical Journal.*

ily deter some women from applying for welfare. According to a county welfare report, "In Floyd County, there are instances of mothers of illegitimate children waiting until the child is older than 3 years before applying for aid. Three years is the limitation for prosecution of the father under the bastardy law."[92] Probably, these mothers either felt mercy for these poor fathers or feared their reprisals. While the number of welfare cases continued to rise in the year after this rule was enacted, caseload growth was substantially slowed from the year before (see Table 5). In 1954, the state became even more punitive toward "deadbeat dads." It authorized punishment of one to five years in jail for failing to comply with court orders of child support.

The third policy making it tougher for poor mothers to get welfare was a one-year residency requirement. This rule, adopted in 1952, may have contributed to the 15 percent decline in the number of cases that year (see Table 5). While residency requirements in northern and western states served as a way of targeting blacks for cutbacks, it was not clear that they did so in Kentucky, which, like other southern states, was experiencing greater out-migration than in-migration of blacks.[93]

Kentucky's other antiwelfare campaigns were thwarted. For example, there was strong opposition to a 1950 bill to open the welfare rolls for public inspection to reduce "fraud and scandal." A similar but even harsher bill was considered and rejected in 1948. That bill would have required all counties to publicize in general-circulation newspapers the names and addresses of all public assistance recipients. Supporters of this policy suggested that many of the state's new recipients were unworthy of aid and that politicians were distributing welfare to gain electoral support at taxpayers' expense. They argued that "secrecy permits political manipulation of the assistance rolls by state administrations."[94] Top welfare officials, who supported recipients' rights to privacy, strongly opposed the public inspection bill and claimed there were enough checks on the use of public assistance. The state auditor, the attorney general, and grand juries were already authorized to inspect public assistance records, while the welfare department had a special unit to investigate fraud.[95] Apparently such arguments were influential, since the senate rejected, by a large margin, a public inspection bill in 1952.[96]

In 1952, the legislature also opposed a measure to deny welfare to children born out of wedlock, who made up about 14 percent of all cases. The Legislative Research Commission, led by the lieutenant governor and the minority and majority leaders, claimed that unwed mothers' access to welfare should not be limited: "The charge that support of this group of illegitimate dependent children may have offered unwed mothers a new career does not appear valid in Kentucky. . . . The average ADC 'family' with illegitimate children has only 1.7 children, and there aren't many such families in Kentucky. Limiting payments to one illegitimate child per family . . . would probably do little more than reduce the already small amount available to each child in a family with more than one illegitimate child."[97] Their recommendation was apparently influential. No bills were proposed to limit aid to children born out of wedlock until 1960, when another welfare backlash erupted.

In 1961, a legislative research commission reported, "Of all the forms of public assistance provided by the state, the ADC program is the most criticized by the general public."[98] Most criticisms were directed at unwed welfare mothers, who made up almost one-quarter of welfare mothers in 1958, and who were disproportionately black. Newspaper editorials, magazine stories, and pamphlets by "interested groups" all focused on that issue.[99] As a legislative report described, "Some have charged that ADC is 'subsidizing immorality' and that unmarried mothers deliberately bear illegitimate children in order to become eligible for assistance. Others believe that illegitimate children raised in a home supported by public assistance funds will tend to follow the behavior patterns of their mothers."[100] Traces of this backlash against unwed welfare mothers are found in county child welfare reports. At least eight of these reports suggested that ADC was encouraging out-of-wedlock childbearing and that unwed mothers' aid should be limited.[101] For example, based on its survey of "responsible people," such as "teachers, housewives, PTA members, public officials, social workers, and businessmen," the Davies County committee claimed that "the general public links the increase in illegitimacy with welfare grants."[102] It also noted that survey respondents were "concerned about public welfare causing families to become more dependent." It recommended limiting aid to the first one or two illegitimate children and requiring "those who are able" to work.[103] The Scott County committee even suggested that unwed mothers be sterilized after the birth of their second child.[104] Legislative researchers noted that similar suggestions were made in other parts of the state.[105]

In 1960 and 1962, legislators introduced several bills to limit aid to mothers who gave birth to more than one child out of wedlock, promoting racist stereotypes to justify them. Their 1961 legislative report, "Illegitimacy in Kentucky," claimed, "Some evidence exists . . . which indicates that the Aid to Dependent Children program may retard the acceptance by certain groups of moral patterns held by the majority of Americans. Particularly among some less sophisticated Negroes in the South, the purpose of the ADC program may be misunderstood."[106] The 1960 bill, which prohibited public assistance for more than one illegitimate child, never even reached the floor, however. Most likely, state politicians were wary of enacting it because of federal disapproval of a similar policy in Louisiana.[107] Instead, legislators adopted a resolution requesting Congress to authorize states to pass such policies.[108]

The 1960 legislature also established an advisory committee to study the issue. That committee, along with top welfare officials, opposed efforts to restrict welfare to unwed mothers, however. During a public hearing, the state welfare director emphasized that "denial of public assistance payments would not solve the illegitimacy problem." He also claimed the shortage of adoptive homes "was a serious barrier to removal of children from their parents."[109] The committee's 1961 report opposed the idea that welfare encouraged illegitimacy and claimed that compulsory sterilization laws were immoral. It also warned that putting children born out of wedlock in orphanages would be expensive, psychologically damaging to the children, and unconstitutional.[110] The commission advised the state to enact a suitable home policy instead. The proposed policy conformed to federal guidelines and would be used to remove children from "unsuitable" homes rather than to deny welfare.[111] In 1962, politicians introduced another bill to "limit aid to dependent children to one illegitimate child per mother," but it was rejected.[112]

Explaining Kentucky's Limited Welfare Backlash

Why was Kentucky's welfare backlash so limited? First, unlike most southern states, liberal Democrats had considerable political support and opposed welfare cutbacks. Liberal Democrats' political strength was related to the state's unusual political economy. Unlike the "one-party" South, Kentucky was a "three-party" state, with conservative Democrats, liberal Democrats, and Republicans. These political divisions were linked to regional differences in the economy. Large farmers and high-income residents in the western and Bluegrass areas were mainly conservative Democrats, as they had been since slavery. Support for liberal Democrats came from coal miners in the east, the state's numerous small farmers in the west, urban voters, union members, and blacks.[113] Republicans also won black votes, but were mostly popular among urban and suburban professionals and business leaders, especially in the southeastern part of the state.[114]

Unlike most southern politicians, "the Kentucky group remained loyal, and some became more fervent supporters of the New Deal as time passed."[115] A national congressman in the 1940s, Governor Clements, who ruled between 1947 and 1950, "ardently defended the New Deal."[116] It is likely that Clements's successor, Governor Lawrence Weatherby, held similar views, since he served as Clements's lieutenant governor and agreed with him on most issues. The state welfare commissioner, V. E. Barnes, who was appointed by Clements and held his post until 1960, frequently defended ADC against attacks in the 1950s. Although Governor Chandler, who ruled between 1955 and 1959, was a strong advocate of limited government and taxes, his efforts to cut back social programs and indigent relief were strongly opposed by younger, more liberal state legislators.[117]

Second, racialized opposition to welfare was more limited in Kentucky than elsewhere in the South. In part, this was because in 1950 only 7 percent of the state's population and only 15 percent of ADC recipients were black.[118] Yet, even efforts to limit unwed mothers' access to welfare—a measure that would disproportionately affect blacks—failed. The state's factionalism encouraged Republicans and liberal Democrats to compete for black votes, which may have increased resistance to such policies. Indeed, Kentucky's politicians were fairly supportive of blacks' civil rights gains. Governor Clements, a longtime supporter of blacks' civil rights, attempted (unsuccessfully) to initiate desegregation in the state's universities and professional schools.[119] His successor, Weatherby, also supported desegregation of public schools, "effectively quieting segregationist critics."[120] Even Governor Chandler defended blacks' civil rights, sending in the National Guard to repress protests directed against the desegregation of public schools at the end of the decade.[121] By the time support for limiting unwed mothers' access to welfare gained ground in the early 1960s, federal opposition to these policies prevented their adoption. In short, Kentucky's welfare backlash was more limited than elsewhere in the South both because large farmers played a less dominant role in the state's political economy and because white racism toward blacks was less influential.

As the campaigns to restrict welfare in Kentucky and Georgia demonstrate, the southern welfare backlash was intimately tied to racial politics. In both states, politicians justified welfare cutbacks by appealing to white racism, which was very strong in the wake of blacks' postwar civil rights gains. They rhetorically constructed black welfare mothers as undeserving "welfare queens" who purposefully had children in order to receive welfare and avoid work. They also proposed or adopted regulations, such as rules limiting unwed mothers' access to welfare, that would disproportionately affect blacks.

On the other hand, the welfare backlash was more extensive and influential in Georgia than in Kentucky. In 1952, Georgia adopted a whole slate of restrictive welfare policies, many of which benefited large farmers. This is not surprising, given that planters dominated the state's political economy. Racism was also rampant in the state, where about one-third of the total population and nearly half of all ADC recipients were black. Some professional groups publicly criticized Georgia's restrictive welfare policies, and social workers and poor mothers privately complained about them. Overall, Georgia's welfare backlash met with very little political resistance, however.

By contrast, there was greater resistance to restricting ADC in Kentucky, which only adopted a few new welfare regulations in the 1950s. There, corporate farmers played a less decisive role in state politics. The state's numerous small farmers and heavily organized coal miners provided support for liberal Democrats and New Deal programs. Moreover, about 85 percent of the state's welfare recipients were white, which limited the spread of racialized opposition to welfare. Some politicians may have been particularly reluctant to target blacks for cutbacks because factionalism within the "three-party state" encouraged Republicans and liberal Democrats to court the black vote.

6. Western and Northern Welfare Backlashes

California and New York

The 1950s welfare backlash was not simply shaped by black-white race relations, nor was it confined to the South. In northern and western states, welfare critics appealed to racist resentment over blacks' civil rights gains and the in-migration of blacks, Puerto Ricans, or Mexicans. This chapter explores how racism interacted with other factors to shape the welfare backlashes in California and New York. Attacks on welfare mothers were more powerful in California than in New York, mainly because large farmers played a politically dominant role there. Although only 7 percent of California's labor force was employed in agriculture in 1950,[1] the sheer size of agribusiness gave it a significant role in the state's economy.[2] Agricultural products—processed foods and lumber—were also among the state's principal manufactured products.[3] More importantly, rural legislators dominated the state senate. California's four largest urban counties made up 59 percent of the state's population but were represented by only 10 percent of senate seats in the 1950s.[4] This gave the "farm lobby" considerable influence as it and its allies lobbied for welfare cutbacks. California's welfare critics appealed to antiblack and anti-Mexican sentiment, as well as anticommunism and taxpayers' interests, to justify welfare cuts.

Welfare opposition also emerged in the northern, highly industrial state of New York, where less than 3 percent of the labor force was employed in agriculture in 1950. There, farmers, business groups, and upstate rural residents pressured legislators to restrict welfare eligibility. Welfare critics appealed to racist resentment toward the blacks and Puerto Ricans entering the state, suggesting that they came to take advantage of the state's generous welfare programs. They mainly lobbied for a residency requirement for welfare so as to deny aid to newcomers. However, organized labor, the state's highly developed network of private social agencies, and liberal Republicans and Democrats mobilized considerable opposition to this proposal.

CALIFORNIA'S WELFARE BACKLASH

The Rise of Welfare Opposition

At first, welfare opposition in California was provoked by a successful campaign to expand old-age assistance by the California Institute for Social Welfare (CISW).[5] CISW was one of a series of old-age pension movements in the state that included Upton Sinclair's unsuccessful bid for governor under his "End Poverty in California" platform, the Townsend movement,[6] and the "Ham and Eggs" movement.[7] George McLain, a former "Ham and Eggs" organizer, founded CISW in 1941.[8] By 1948, the group claimed a hundred thousand members, most of who were old-age pensioners living in lower-middle-class neighborhoods.[9] CISW's biggest policy victory was the passage of Proposition 4 in 1948, an initiative supported by labor unions and liberal politicians.[10] Proposition 4 made the director of aid to the aged and blind programs an elective position and named a CISW leader for this position, increased benefits to old-age and blind pensioners, and broadened eligibility for benefits.[11] Business groups, including the California Chamber of Commerce, were concerned about the proposition's cost and launched a five-million-dollar campaign to repeal Proposition 4 by Proposition 2. To broaden support for their campaign, they allied themselves with women's organizations and social welfare groups that expressed concerns about how the measure might affect welfare administration, especially CISW leaders' authority over it.[12] Opponents of CISW depicted it as a corrupt organization dominated by a power-hungry man.[13] Two senate committees investigated corruption charges against the organization,[14] and several unsuccessful lawsuits were filed against CISW.[15] Following these highly publicized attacks and a five-million-dollar campaign, voters repealed Proposition 4 by a fairly wide margin in 1949.[16]

The campaign against Proposition 4 helped unite business leaders around an antiwelfare agenda. Buoyed by their victory, they quickly turned their attention to ADC, which had been dramatically expanded in 1949 by a new state law that significantly broadened the definition of a "needy child" to conform to federal guidelines.[17] Welfare officials and organizations,[18] Catholic leaders, and urban officials actively supported the bill.[19] County and state supervisors' associations also sent letters and telegrams in favor of the bill, which promised to reduce the number of families receiving county-funded general relief.[20] With so much support, the bill passed the legislature by a fairly wide margin and was signed into law.[21] After the bill's passage, ADC caseloads, already increasing in the 1940s, more than doubled.[22]

Opposition to ADC's expansion surfaced almost immediately. After the bill's passage, county officials urged the state welfare board to restrict eligibility for the program. Minutes from the board's meeting noted that "the Supervisors were very concerned that at no time the program develop into one of supplementation of full-time wages." In response, state welfare officials adopted a narrow definition of parental disability, denied coverage to children whose fathers were absent due to military service, and eliminated a requirement to aid needy families for up to three months after an absent parent returned or a disabled parent recovered. Yet, to county officials' consternation, the state welfare board refused to require documentary proof of eligibility, do more to secure support from absent parents, or prohibit aid to unborn children.[23] Frustrated, county officials and their allies urged state legislators to restrict welfare eligibility.

Large farmers, represented by the California Farm Bureau Federation, with more than 59,000 members, were highly active in this antiwelfare campaign.[24] Restricting welfare eligibility was an important part of the bureau's political agenda in the early 1950s. In 1950, the bureau made a number of policy recommendations. First, it disapproved of the state board's "liberal" welfare administration, claiming that too many ineligible people were receiving aid. The bureau urged the legislature to reduce the state welfare board's administrative power, require applicants to "provide documentary proof" of their need, authorize public inspection of welfare records so that "private citizens" could help to "purg[e] the rolls of unworthy recipients," make welfare fraud a misdemeanor, and deny pregnant women aid. The bureau also recommended policies to increase poor mothers' dependence on men rather than the state, such as penalties for deserting parents and rules making men responsible for their stepchildren.[25]

The farm bureau also sought to increase the poor's work incentive through a number of measures. It urged the state to ensure that

> allowances under public charity . . . be . . . sufficiently lower than the wage rates of unskilled workmen to retain the incentive for such workmen to continue to work and to enable them, as taxpayers, to bear a fair share of the welfare burden;
>
> Require all minor children living at home to share in the costs of the home to the extent of their ability to do so;
>
> Encourage parent or other caretaker to seek employment and become self-supporting;

Require that able-bodied applicants work for relief payments;
Encourage a return of the philosophy that each should diligently try
to support himself.[26]

These policies clearly reflected large farmers' concern that a liberal welfare
program would undercut their labor supply.[27]

Farmers' interest in restricting welfare in California is not surprising
given their labor supply concerns at the time. The state's agricultural production was still largely unmechanized,[28] and braceros made up only about
15 percent of the state's agricultural labor force in the early 1950s.[29] Maintaining an ample supply of domestic agricultural workers helped to keep
wages low and maintain labor discipline, especially since labor unrest and
union organizing were spreading among the state's farm workers.[30] As
landowners, farmers were also interested in minimizing state expenditures.
Although ADC was financed through general state revenues, the farm
bureau urged that welfare revenues "provided by the property tax be kept
as low as possible."[31] It warned that "the California taxpayer is bearing a
needlessly heavy and ruinous tax burden. This tax burden is rapidly increasing by the attraction of persons to welfare rolls, and will cause financial
chaos unless stopped."[32]

Other business associations, concerned about minimizing welfare expenditures, also supported this antiwelfare campaign. In 1950, the California
Chamber of Commerce made the following legislative recommendations:

> That . . . a deserting parent be absent for 6 months before an application
> for assistance can be made . . . [and] . . . a maximum contribution be
> obtained from the parent of his or her children.
>   That the maximum amount of aid be limited generally to the com-
> pensation of unskilled labor in the community and be realistic with
> respect to the normal earnings of recipients.
>   That the program be administered so that families become self-
> supporting. . . .
>   That the cash permitted in qualifying for aid be reduced drastically
> from the present $600 cash now allowed on application.
>   That local administration be given greater jurisdiction in administer-
> ing cases.
>   That the section "liberally construed" be removed from the act.
>   That parents misusing funds given for food, clothing, rent, etc., be
> placed on an "in kind" basis where the county will pay vendors directly
> for such items.[33]

In 1951, the chamber issued a pamphlet urging the state to reduce public
assistance costs by lowering limits on the amount of property recipients

could own, eliminating provisions for 'special needs,' pressuring responsible relatives to support their family members, and reducing benefit levels.[34] The California Real Estate Association and the California County Supervisors' Association, whose director was a banker, also lobbied for more restrictive welfare laws.[35]

The California Taxpayers' Association, which aimed to "promote efficiency and economy in government operations,"[36] also urged welfare cutbacks. This association was not led by ordinary taxpayers. Its board of directors was almost entirely staffed by business leaders representing agriculture and various other industries.[37] Numerous contributors to the association's monthly publication, *The Tax Digest*, criticized the expansion of welfare in the early 1950s. Like the farm bureau, these authors opposed funding and administration of welfare by the state or federal government, claiming that it encouraged liberal policies.[38] One author claimed, "California is the prize sucker State of the Union when it comes to dishing out public assistance." He urged the association to fight the expansion of welfare, which was "growing to beat the band."[39] *The Tax Digest* also promoted the views of three welfare directors who supported tougher welfare regulations and lower grant levels.[40] *The Tax Digest* appealed to taxpayers' interests to justify cutbacks and portrayed the expansion of welfare as a menacing threat to capitalism. For example, one author criticized "the New Deal philosophy which for sixteen years has led this nation toward the abyss of gray communism."[41] Another author warned his readers, "We have launched experiments of such magnitude that they threaten to alter fundamental ways of thought and life to which we have been long accustomed. . . . In the name of security we are steadily socializing the economy."[42] Similarly, the president of the California Chamber of Commerce claimed that "our slide into the welfare state" has led people to be "unwittingly drawn into the whirlpool of socialism."[43]

Business and political groups opposed to welfare were closely interconnected. Urban business leaders dominated the California Chamber of Commerce, but its board of directors included prominent farm leaders, such as the president of the California Prune and Apricot Growers' Association, and the president of the California Farm Bureau Federation.[44] Farm leaders were also active in the California Taxpayers' Association. In the early 1950s, its president was a farmer from Santa Paula and its board of directors included two other farm leaders.[45] County supervisors in Los Angeles and San Diego hired the California Chamber of Commerce staff to lobby for welfare cutbacks.[46]

Welfare critics' most important political allies were rural county officials and rural politicians who dominated the state legislature. Two senate com-

TABLE 6. *Selected Characteristics of Members of California's Senate Interim Committee on Social Welfare, 1949–1951*

Name	Occupation	County	% of County Labor Force Employed in Agriculture, 1950
Weybret, Fred (Chair)	Retired	Monterey/San Benito	23.9
		Monterey	21.4
		San Benito	43.7
Cunningham, Roy	Real estate and insurance	Kings	33.9
Johnson, Ed C.	Retired	Sutter/Yuba	28.6
		Sutter	38.7
		Yuba	16.7
Watson, Clyde A.	Citrus grower	Orange	11.1
Abshire, F. Presley	Farmer	Sonoma	23.8

SOURCES: California State Legislature 1951b; U.S. Department of Commerce, Bureau of the Census 1952.

mittees—the Senate Interim Committee on Social Welfare and the Senate Interim Committee on State and Local Taxation—spearheaded the campaign to restrict ADC eligibility in 1951. Members of the former committee sponsored sixteen bills affecting ADC, while the latter committee sponsored fourteen such bills.[47] As one observer noted, these committees represented the views of "the State Chamber of Commerce, the Supervisors' Association, the State Taxpayers' Association, [and] the California Farm Bureau,"[48] all of which testified at their public welfare hearings in favor of restricting welfare eligibility.[49] As Tables 6 and 7 indicate, with the exception of Senator Harry Parkman, all of the members of these committees were either farmers or represented areas where more than 15 percent of employed workers were engaged in agriculture (almost double the figure for the state as a whole). Dominated by rural senators, these committees were particularly sympathetic to farmers' interests. Business leaders also received tremendous support from Assemblyman Levering, a businessman, who in 1951 sponsored sixteen bills to make ADC more restrictive.[50] Rural county supervisors were also active in efforts to push through welfare cutbacks. Eight of the twelve speakers at the senate's 1950 hearings on ADC were from counties where more than 15 percent of those employed were engaged in agricul-

TABLE 7.   *Selected Characteristics of Members of California's Senate Interim Committee on State and Local Taxation, 1949–1951*

Name	Occupation	County	% of County Labor Force Employed in Agriculture, 1950
Hulse, Ben (Chair)	Rancher	Imperial	36.6
Ward, Clarence	Attorney	Fresno	23.3
Burns, Hugh	Funeral director	Santa Barbara	15.4
Powers, Harold	Rancher	Modoc/Lassen/ Plumas	12.8
		Modoc	30.2
		Lassen	9.8
		Plumas	3.7
Parkman, Harry	Wholesaler and jobber	San Mateo	2.7

SOURCES: California State Legislature 1951b; U.S. Department of Commerce, Bureau of the Census 1952.

ture.[51] The role of rural politicians and officials in California's antiwelfare campaign is not surprising, given that farmers were among their most powerful constituents.

Racism and California's Welfare Backlash

California's welfare backlash also had a racial dimension. Like other southwestern states, California had a long history of denying welfare to Mexican Americans. During the Great Depression, hundreds of thousands of indigent Mexican Americans, including women and children, were persuaded or coerced into leaving the country through government-funded repatriation programs. Southern California's welfare officials carried out some of the earliest and most aggressive repatriation programs in the country, boasting that it saved hundreds of thousands of taxpayers' dollars and exaggerating Mexicans' reliance on welfare.[52]

Given this history, it is not surprising that opponents of welfare quickly resorted to long-standing negative stereotypes of Mexicans as lazy and overly dependent on others.[53] The minutes from the State Welfare Board meeting capture how these racist stereotypes were employed to criticize the liberalization of the ADC program:

Father Markham: A practical question came up in a conversation I had with Mr. Sell. He is afraid that the Negroes and Mexicans and Okies in his area will take advantage of a program like this. He claims that they are very ignorant people and that they make a profession almost of getting as much assistance as possible. Then they will buy cars and fur coats and the children don't get the money, and he is worried about that and so I was wondering how that objection could be answered. When the county finds out that a parent is misusing assistance, what can be done about it? . . .

Mrs. MacLatchie: . . . I think actually—Mr. Sell is thinking from the viewpoint of Mr. Sell's area. Mr. Sell represents a cotton-picking area and he has always been concerned with the present program because the Negro women who come in there in the wintertime were more or less unattached, probably not a marriage, have a rather fluctuating situation. He has wanted to offer—the county has wanted to offer a work program to the man in order to make certain that the man in the house is working even though he is not the father and the woman has said that he is not and wants aid for the children. Now just as soon as they offer a work program they say that some of those men melt off. I think that is probably true. And they are not going to want those people in the program. I think we are going to have trouble. But you have trouble no matter what you do with it, Mr. Koenig. It seems to me wherever we put this line there are going to be some people who take advantage of it but the big bulk who don't.

Father Markham: That is what I wanted to get. He said that was the biggest problem, these kind of people. I didn't think that they did constitute a large number or a large portion of cases, and I told him so, but he said in his county they certainly did.[54]

As this quote shows, racist stereotypes of poor blacks, Mexicans, and southern whites ("Okies") as lazy, dishonest, and self-serving were not unknown in California. The fear expressed in this quote—that welfare recipients were misusing assistance—was commonly directed at nonwhites.[55]

Racist resentment toward blacks and Mexicans migrating to California also contributed support for longer residency requirements for welfare receipt. Between 1940 and 1950, the percentage of the total population that was black doubled, from 2 to 4 percent, mainly in response to wartime employment opportunities.[56] Between 1950 and 1960, the Spanish surname population also nearly doubled, encouraged by the expansion of the bracero program and the rise of Mexican immigration that followed.[57] By 1960, official census counts, which exclude most undocumented immigrants, indicate that Latinos made up almost 14 percent of the state's population.[58] In response to this influx of new residents, welfare critics lobbied the state to lengthen its residency requirement for welfare. In 1950, the state already denied welfare to anyone who had lived in the state for less than one year, while counties imposed local residency requirements. Even so, members of the California Taxpayers' Association and the Farm Bureau complained that California's generous welfare programs were luring people into the state.[59] In response, legislators proposed, but did not adopt, bills to lower welfare grants and lengthen the residency requirement for welfare from one to three years.[60]

Nonetheless, racialized opposition to welfare was less common in California than it was in other states. For example, welfare critics did not appeal to the racially charged issue of unwed welfare mothers, as they did in the South. There are a number of reasons for this. First, although blacks made up almost 16 percent of ADC recipients by 1948, most of the initiative for welfare cutbacks in California came from rural areas where few blacks lived. Farmers relied far more heavily on Mexican than black labor at this time. In 1950, black women made up only about 3 percent of female agricultural workers. By contrast, Mexican contract laborers (braceros) made up about 15 percent of seasonal agricultural workers in California in 1951, and by 1960, this proportion had doubled.[61] Black-white racial struggles were also more politically salient in other regions, where more blacks resided and White Citizens' Councils and the Ku Klux Klan were more organized. They had much less influence in California, where blacks comprised only 4 percent of the state's population in 1950.

Meanwhile, it is likely that Mexican Americans made up only a very small share of ADC cases, because they faced tremendous barriers to receiving aid.[62] As Martha Eliot, chief of the Children's Bureau, noted, despite meager wages, "children of migratory families [are] treated too often as outcasts from social and health services."[63] California's migrant workers were disqualified from receiving welfare because of citizenship or state and county residency requirements. Language, cultural barriers, and discrimination by social workers also prevented Mexican Americans from using welfare.[64] Most unemployed Mexican or Mexican American agricultural workers, if they received any public relief at all, received locally distributed federal food surpluses or "migrant relief" through county-funded work relief projects, which were frequently underfunded and inadequate.[65] To survive, Mexican immigrants usually relied on friends, family, mutual aid societies, and child labor.[66] Thus, there were few Mexican or Mexican American welfare mothers for welfare opponents to target in 1951. Scapegoating Mexican Americans in antiwelfare campaigns could have also backfired for farmers, lending support to efforts to further restrict Mexican immigration and end the bracero program.

Welfare Critics' Impact

In response to the lobbying efforts of business groups and rural officials, ADC came under heavy attack in 1951. As a leading welfare reformer commented, "Never before in the history of the California Legislature had there been such a flood of anti-welfare bills as those that came before the 1951 session."[67] The following policies were adopted in 1951:

1. Parents are required to accept suitable employment when available.

2. Child or parents are required to accept medical treatment or rehabilitation.

3. Mother and father are equally responsible for a child's education and support.

4. Stepfather is required to support a needy child.

5. Uniform Reciprocal Enforcement of Support Law enables state to cooperate with other states in enforcing family support laws.

6. The district attorney is required to investigate cases of desertion.

7. The personal property limit is revised to include a number of specific items in the $600 maximum for personal property.

8. Real property other than a home must be utilized for the needs of a child.

9. Pregnant women may not receive ADC.[68]

Both houses unanimously approved almost all of these tough new welfare laws.[69] These policies reduced welfare dependency by strengthening parental support laws and property ownership restrictions. They also required recipients to work. Together, these policies halted the postwar growth of ADC cases. By 1953, the ADC program was serving 5,380 fewer families than in 1951.[70]

CISW lobbied vigorously against many of the restrictive welfare bills introduced in 1951, occasionally joined by the Welfare Council of Metropolitan Los Angeles.[71] But more often, "No one else spoke up for the needy children . . . no PTA, no women's clubs, no church or welfare group."[72] Perhaps in response to CISW's efforts, politicians revised or killed the following bills, which advocates claimed kept more than 47,000 children eligible for welfare:

1. Restoration of the definition of needy child that existed prior to passage of AB 40.

2. Increase in the state residency requirement from one to three years.

3. Requirement that for cases of desertion to be considered eligible, the period of continued absence be lengthened to one year or more.

4. Requirement for notification by payee of the return of an absent parent within fifteen days of their return.

5. Requirement that stepparent (not just stepfather) support needy child.

6. Requirement that category of "responsible relatives" (i.e., those required to provide financial assistance to a needy child if able) include: (1) adult brother or sister of child living in same house, and (2) emancipated minor brother or sister in same house.

7. A ceiling of $300 on families of eight or more persons.

8. Repeal of the requirement that the welfare code "should be liberally construed."

9. Clarify legislative intent of welfare code to inspire needy children and caretakers to be self-sufficient.[73]

The defeated bills would have introduced new or tougher welfare restrictions and made the program less liberal in intent.[74] The Assembly Committee on Social Welfare rejected most of these.[75] Unlike the rural-dominated senate welfare committee, urban politicians dominated this assembly committee. Five of its eight members represented Los Angeles or San Diego, two of the state's largest cities.[76]

Farmers continued to shape welfare administration in California in ways that suited their labor supply interests. In the 1960s, California adopted an AFDC Unemployed Parents program that enabled two-parent families to receive welfare but required recipients to accept all offers of reasonable employment. In Alameda County, the welfare department made a contract with the local growers, agreeing to transport unemployed fathers from Oakland to the outlying rural areas. Most of these men had no previous experience with farm work and were fired for not working hard enough. The welfare rights organization later figured out what was going on: "A lawyer in our committee got . . . a phone call from a grower who actually confirmed what we had heard from individuals who had gone out on this strawberry picking. This grower informed us that the growers were very happy to get welfare recipients to do strawberry picking because if they were worked hard and quit or if they were all fired for not working hard enough, this would be evidence that American labor would not tolerate these kinds of working conditions and the bracero system was absolutely needed."[77] The welfare commission later confirmed this story. According to them, the growers later stopped their contract with the welfare department because they were dissatisfied with the number of recipients that showed up and the quality of their work. They then used this claim to argue for a continuation of the bracero program.[78]

NEW YORK'S WELFARE BACKLASH

Like elsewhere in the nation, opposition to welfare in New York rose, following a sharp rise in cases after World War II. Between 1945 and 1947, the ADC caseload nearly doubled, from 68,000 to 132,000, and nearly tripled between 1945 and 1950.[79] Critics charged that New York City's welfare department had become too lax because of the influence of communists, unions, and liberals.[80] In response, the State Board of Social Welfare investigated the department in 1947, while the city welfare commissioner tightened eligibility procedures and purged communists from the department. After he resigned under fire, his successor engaged in a "war on relief frauds,"[81] put thousands of Home Relief recipients to work,[82] and purged additional communists from the department.[83]

Meanwhile, employer and taxpayer groups lobbied the state to reduce welfare costs. In 1949, the New York State Conference Board of Farm Organizations, representing eight major farm groups and a hundred thousand farmers, issued a report claiming that "it seems possible . . . that some have adopted the philosophy that the country owes them a living."[84] A few years later, farmers urged Governor Dewey to give counties greater administrative responsibility to reduce local welfare costs. The Conference Board of Farm Organizations' secretary claimed, "Farmers felt particularly 'touchy' about rising welfare costs because of continued difficulties in recruiting farm manpower among rural residents who, they said, are on relief and content to remain there. [He] said that many of the rural counties now spend as much as 40 per cent of their annual budgets for welfare costs. 'We have no sympathy for those who rely on [welfare] as a substitute for working for a living.'"[85] Meanwhile, the State Grange (another association of farmers), the New York Commerce and Industry Association, and a taxpayers' group called the Citizens Public Expenditure Survey urged state legislators to reduce the state's share of public assistance costs.[86] The state supervisors' association also called for local investigations of welfare administration.[87]

In response to growing allegations of welfare abuse, the state adopted two laws: a 1950 law requiring welfare officials to report cases of fraud to the district attorney and a 1951 law to punish taverns and liquor stores that cashed welfare checks.[88] New York's Conference Board of Farm Organizations, the Nassau Taxpayers' League, and the Citizens' Public Expenditures Survey also successfully lobbied in 1953 for a law authorizing public inspection of public assistance records.[89] Compared to other states, however, there were few legislative attacks in New York that specifically targeted welfare mothers. Instead, legislators authorized workfare programs in 1948 for recipients of veterans' assistance and Home Relief, which served indigent adults not eligible for federal public assistance.[90] They also restricted seasonal workers' access to unemployment insurance in 1952, and reduced the state's share of costs for other welfare programs in 1953.[91]

Even this limited welfare backlash confronted strong opposition, however. State and local welfare officials, labor unions, and a highly developed network of Jewish, Protestant, Catholic, and nonsectarian private social service agencies actively defended New Deal programs.[92] They strongly opposed the public inspection law, for example, which was passed only after more stringent bills were defeated two years in a row.[93] Opponents claimed the policy would not reduce fraud, but instead would deter poor people from applying for welfare and "simply humiliate the needy."[94] The *New York Times* editorialized against the bill, claiming that it would cruelly subject recipients to the prying eyes of neighbors.[95] Even the New York State Chamber of Commerce urged deferment of the bill.[96] The bill that eventually passed was a watered-down version of the original that authorized local officials to allow only particular groups, rather than the general public, to inspect welfare records.[97] By 1954, 46 out of 62 counties permitted some public inspection of welfare records. The New York State Federation of Women's Clubs urged the other sixteen counties to follow suit, claiming that "the end of secrecy . . . deters ineligibles from applying for or continuing to claim assistance."[98]

Since welfare critics faced so much opposition at the state level, they often limited welfare at the local level. The Federal Security Administration threatened to withhold federal welfare funds from New York in 1951, charging that some counties' welfare budgets were too low and decisions regarding eligibility were being made according to the "whims of a local welfare administrator."[99] State politicians and welfare officials vocally defended state and local autonomy.[100] They begrudgingly agreed to create a statewide budget standard for welfare benefits, but one that could be modified according to local conditions. Even this flexible standard was strongly opposed by many local officials and upstate politicians.[101]

Efforts to cut welfare faced the greatest opposition in New York City, a long-time Democratic stronghold with several active left-wing parties,[102] well-organized unions, and an extensive network of private social agencies. In 1950, encouraged by state officials and the New York Commerce and Industry Association, the city welfare commissioner reduced public assistance benefits 5 percent on the grounds that food prices had decreased.[103] The cuts met with strong criticism from the city council and groups such as "the Liberal and American Labor parties, the New York Tenant Council, the United Public Workers, Congress of Industrial Organizations, the United War Veterans Board of New York, the United Neighborhood Houses."[104] After their implementation, state and city officials continued to confront a "storm of protest" from AFL-CIO labor leaders, the American Labor Party, private social welfare agencies, and welfare organizations.[105] The left-wing American Labor Party even organized a 350-person protest of the cutbacks.[106] At first, state and city officials defended the cuts.[107] The chair of the state welfare board claimed they would deter the use of welfare as a "way of life," while the city welfare commissioner tried to prove the adequacy of the new food budget by imposing it on his own family.[108] Nevertheless, they continued to be confronted with "tremendous agitation."[109] Liberal Party leaders circulated petitions, others testified at public hearings, the *New York Times* editorialized against the cuts, and East Harlem church groups organized food drives to help those affected.[110] Fifty-five people, including recipients, even held a sit-in protest against the cuts.[111] Several months later, the city welfare commissioner relented and sought permission from state officials to increase relief allowances, using unexpected savings from caseload declines to do so.[112]

State-level opposition to welfare re-emerged in 1954 after the caseload rose for the first time in three years, continuing to rise through the end of the decade.[113] Each year between 1954 and 1961, upstate legislators campaigned for a one- or two-year residency requirement for welfare receipt. Senator Cooke, one of the leading advocates of the policy, claimed that aid to nonresidents "made the state 'a dumping ground for ne-er-do-wells.'"[114] Similarly, Senator Mahoney claimed that "it would put an end to the mass migration of the impoverished, lured by the dangerously deceptive magnet of quick relief."[115] The United Taxpayers' Association and business groups, such as the Buffalo Chamber of Commerce and the New York Commerce and Industry Association, supported the residency bill. They viewed the bill as a cost-cutting measure, even though nonresident relief recipients made up less than two percent of the state's overall caseload.[116] Conservative white upstate residents, resentful of southern black and Puerto Rican migrants, supported the measure. As the head of the State Association of Councils and Chests explained, "Residence is being used as a symbol to hide the real issue—an objection to the entrance of new cultural and ethnic groups."[117] According to a 1957 report, 52 percent of nonresident relief recipients in New York City were Puerto Rican, while 24 percent were from the South. In the upstate area, where only 4 percent of migrants were from Puerto Rico, the proposed policy would mainly affect black migrants.[118]

Along with racist stereotypes of black welfare recipients, myths about Puerto Rican welfare use were used to justify the residency requirement.[119] Although only 11 percent of Puerto Ricans and 10 percent of blacks received aid in New York City, "unsympathetic and bigoted social workers" and politicians spread negative stories about their welfare use.[120] For example, one politician claimed that Puerto Ricans were "almost impossible to assimilate. . . . [T]he lure was relief."[121] Another told the press that "many persons, particularly Puerto Ricans, came to this city simply to get on relief."[122] In fact, most blacks and Puerto Ricans came to New York in search of work, not welfare, but employment discrimination and a lack of good job opportunities forced many to seek welfare.[123] Unemployment levels among Puerto Rican men in New York City were more than double the figures for whites and even exceeded the figures for blacks.[124] Puerto Ricans were concentrated in low-wage jobs, such as garment manufacturing, semiskilled factory work, hotel and restaurant services, and agricultural work, forcing many to seek welfare even while they were employed.[125]

The campaign for residency requirements, like previous attacks on welfare, confronted tremendous opposition, especially from New York City public officials. For example, the city's mayor claimed the policy would cause "widespread human suffering," and would impose "an arbitrary, discriminatory, and unfair barrier against ambitious newcomers."[126] City welfare officials countered the racist stereotypes used to justify the policy, pointing out that most Puerto Ricans were self-supporting[127] and disagreeing with "the rumor that a major cause of the swelling relief rolls was the influx of Puerto Ricans."[128] To support their claims, the city welfare department released reports showing that employment was more common among black and Puerto Rican welfare recipients than other recipients and that Puerto Ricans and southern migrants were slower to apply for welfare compared to other new residents.[129]

Puerto Rican groups, becoming more organized and politically active in the late 1940s and 1950s, also countered the negative publicity surrounding Puerto Rican welfare use.[130] For example, when a magistrate testified that residency requirements were needed because Puerto Rican immigrants were contributing to the growth of slums and juvenile delinquency in the city, a Puerto Rican "self-help" group pointed out their positive economic contributions. The Puerto Rican bar association also dismissed the judge's testimony, claiming that he "tends to subject the Puerto Rican and Negro people to the contempt of the rest of the community."[131]

State and local officials, such as the state welfare department, the Interdepartmental Committee on Low Incomes, and Westchester's Board of Supervisors also criticized the residency bills. So did private social welfare professionals and welfare groups and charities, including Catholic, Protestant, and Jewish organizations.[132] Airing their concerns, the Community Council of Greater New York claimed that the proposed policy was "reactionary, inhumane, and objectionable" and would "saddl[e] private charities and philanthropic givers" with new financial burdens.[133] The Consumers' League of New York opposed it for similar reasons.[134] Labor leaders, including the head of the AFL-CIO, also opposed the residency bill,[135] as did the editorial board of the *New York Times*.[136]

With so much opposition, the campaign for residency requirements was soundly defeated several years in a row, with both liberal Republicans and Democrats opposing it.[137] Although Republicans dominated both houses of the state legislature in the 1950s, liberal Republicans were fairly supportive of welfare and played an active role in defeating a number of the residency bills. For example, journalists credit the Republican speaker of the house with the defeat of the 1958 residency bill. After his speech, fifteen Republicans switched their votes to oppose the measure, just enough to defeat it.[138] Conservative Republicans, however, strongest in upstate rural counties, remained highly supportive of the measure.[139]

Finally, in 1960, legislators passed a residency bill for Home Relief, which served indigent adults not eligible for federal public assistance. As one journalist described, a "punitive, repressive attitude toward welfare recipients . . . increasingly dominated the Legislature."[140] Senator Cooke claimed that the measure was necessary to "close our borders to the chiseling free-loader."[141] Other upstate Republicans promised it would help cut "skyrocketing welfare costs."[142] The senate quickly approved the measure. After a "stormy three-hour debate," the assembly also passed it, with just one vote more than the required majority.[143] Most of the bill's opponents were Democrats. The only black state senator claimed that the bill was "designed 'to stop in-migration from the South and Puerto Rico.'" Similarly, a Manhattan Democrat called the bill an "exclusion bill" and criticized its proponents, claiming, "You're not concerned about poor whites. You're concerned about Negroes and Puerto Ricans coming into the state. They are all American citizens and you're trying to keep them out."[144]

Governor Nelson Rockefeller, representing the liberal wing of the state's Republican Party, later vetoed the bill. Opposition to the bill was central to his gubernatorial campaign. Upholding New York's role as a gateway to immigrants, he told the press, "It is a great tradition and I don't think we want to close that opportunity to them."[145] Rockefeller's veto message claimed that the policy contradicted the state's tradition of "stand[ing] behind the individual to prevent suffering and economic want." Nevertheless, Rockefeller conceded that some "idlers" were abusing welfare and promised to back measures to discourage this "slothfulness."[146]

Despite Rockefeller's veto, support for a residency requirement remained strong. Some supported it for fiscal reasons, others because they opposed welfare or "object[ed] to migrants."[147] Racism was thinly disguised among the bill's supporters. For example, defending the measure, a Newburgh city councilman argued, "This is not a racial issue. . . . But there's hardly an incentive to a naturally lazy people to work if they can exist without working."[148] Although Senator Mahoney introduced weakened versions of the bill, Governor Rockefeller initially rejected them as "unsound."[149] However, after Mahoney threatened to drop one of the governor's pet projects—a $15 million Lincoln Center theater—from the state budget, Rockefeller finally relented and approved a new compromise bill. The new law required all welfare applicants who had lived in the state for less than six months to obtain documentation from the state employment office showing that they had looked for work and that none was available to them. Rockefeller claimed that the bill would "eliminate chiseling and other abuses of relief" but would "not prevent anyone legitimately in need from obtaining public assistance."[150] Although the measure gained support from the State Charities Aid Association and the New York State Council of Churches, it was strongly opposed by other welfare advocacy and religious groups and the *New York Times*.[151] Democrats also attacked the bill, claiming that it "violated the state's traditional policy of aiding the needy and was aimed at keeping Negroes and Puerto Ricans from coming into the state."

Despite this opposition, the bill passed both houses and was signed into law. Senator Cooke of Erie County applauded its passage, claiming it would "stop these chiselers from coming into the state for easy relief," while Senator Mahoney claimed it would stop "the migration into this state of unfortunates attracted solely by the magnet of our easy welfare reputation." [152] After the new law was approved, between 42 and 103 relief applicants per month in 1961 were approved for repatriation to Puerto Rico from New York City. Reportedly, they had not attempted to find work and had volunteered to leave.[153] The law remained in effect until 1969, when the Supreme Court ruled, in *Shapiro v. Thompson*, that such laws were illegal because they violated the Fourteenth Amendment's equal protection clause and individuals' right to travel.[154]

As the campaign for residency requirements gained steam, so did other attacks on welfare. The master of New York's Grange, speaking at the group's annual meeting in 1958, claimed that "public welfare is 'a small-time political racket'" and urged the state to reduce welfare expenditures.[155] Similarly, the state's Chamber of Commerce issued a report calling for more "scrupulous" welfare administration.[156] The United Taxpayers' Association suggested that the state "substitute a special scrip" for welfare checks because they "were often cashed in liquor stores."[157] Even the state's Catholic Welfare Committee, usually a strong advocate of welfare, urged the state to tighten welfare administration and prosecute welfare fraud.[158]

After several years of campaigning by upstate Republicans, who claimed that too many "loafers" and "chiselers" were on the state's welfare rolls, the legislature authorized a broad investigation of the state's welfare programs.[159] The New York State Society of Newspaper Editors successfully pushed for passage of a bill to permit journalists access to welfare records. The group criticized the "miasma of secrecy" surrounding welfare and accused the Rockefeller administration of "becoming a government-by-handout." The proposed bill, passed by a Republican-controlled legislature, allowed newspapers to publish names of recipients that had been charged with fraud.[160] State legislators also passed a bill to deny welfare to married women unless they brought criminal abandonment charges against their husbands. Although Governor Rockefeller vetoed the bill, fearing that it would "divide a broken family," he approved a similar bill giving "welfare officials the power to subpoena those responsible for the support of relief recipients."[161] Despite the growing controversy surrounding welfare, there were no strong efforts to force welfare mothers to go to work. As late as 1963, the state welfare department considered welfare mothers to be "potentially employable" only if they expressed interest in employment.[162]

As the welfare caseload grew in the late 1950s and early 1960s, local welfare backlashes surfaced. In New York City—where 83 percent of ADC recipients and 70 percent of all public assistance recipients were black or Puerto Rican—the welfare department came under heavy fire.[163] In 1959 alone, it had to answer to inquiries "from the borough District Attorney's offices, the Brooklyn Grand Jury, the New York State Legislature, and the

City Department of Investigation."[164] Of these, the Kings County (Brooklyn) grand jury investigation, begun in 1958, was the most widely publicized.[165] The judge and jury involved in this investigation promised to crack down on welfare "leeches" and "parasites."[166] To help in this effort, city officials authorized funds for eight new special assistants for the district attorney's office,[167] which visited recipients' homes at odd hours to search for missing and unreported husbands.[168]

Unwed welfare mothers, disproportionately black, became the target of considerable criticism. During its investigation, the Kings County jury reported, "We are deeply concerned with the chronic breeder *[sic]* of illegitimate children who go on their merry sinful way and who well know that the Department of Welfare will not only continue her on the rolls but will increase her budget allowance with every additional out-of-wedlock child she produces."[169] It recommended "that when more than one illegitimate child was found in a family on relief, the children be placed in foster homes or children's centers."[170] Meanwhile, a welfare investigator, in fifty public speeches, testimony before state legislators, and statements to the press, claimed that he "frequently found children living in the same rooms in which their mothers entertained men." Before being dismissed for his irresponsible statements, he beseeched his audiences, "Are we paying to have these children raised like animals? Are we paying to keep them in homes where immorality is constantly practiced?"[171]

City welfare officials opposed proposals to deny additional aid to unwed mothers who had more than one child out of wedlock. They claimed that the policy would wrongly separate children from their mothers and would cost too much.[172] The State Social Welfare Department backed their position, claiming that "the care of the child is paramount, not the morality of the mother."[173] Nevertheless, the city welfare commissioner conceded, "[Unwed motherhood] is a most deplorable condition and reflects current morality. All of our community resources should be mobilized to reduce the rising rates of out of wedlock births."[174] A year later, the commissioner called a conference on "illegitimacy" and urged the department to locate more fathers and relatives who deserted their children.[175]

A year and a half later, when the Kings County grand jury finally completed its investigation, the county claimed responsibility for 167 indictments of welfare fraud. The *New York Times* added to the antiwelfare hysteria by running a "story a day" and "big headlines" about the fraud convictions, prompting some mothers to give up custody of their children out of fear of getting into similar legal trouble.[176] The grand jury's final report claimed that the welfare department was too lax in administering welfare and recommended that it improve its verification of applicants' documents and identity.[177] In response, the city welfare commissioner introduced new application procedures to make it more difficult for ineligibles to obtain welfare and authorized unannounced visits to recipients' homes to verify their eligibility.[178] Yet, city welfare officials also defended their program, boasting that it had initiated most of the fraud cases brought to court and pointing out that fraud occurred in less than 3 percent of all cases.[179] The city welfare commissioner warned that sending so many welfare recipients to prison might cost the city more than it was saving, since it would have to "care for their dependent children at a cost of at least $12 a day each."[180] Meanwhile, the mayor increased the welfare department's budget to meet rising costs and an expanding caseload,[181] claiming that "we should take pride in the assistance we give our less fortunate citizens."[182]

The backlash against welfare spread to other parts of the state. For example, in 1960, Poughkeepsie's city manager "ordered all relief fund recipients cut off city rolls . . . but directed that any who wished to do so might ask reconsideration of their cases."[183] Newburgh's thirteen-point welfare reform plan, adopted by its city manager, Joseph Mitchell, was even more controversial. This plan was largely directed at black migrants accused of moving to the city to get on welfare. The plan included a "suitable home" requirement, a rule restricting aid to unwed women who had additional children while receiving welfare, and strict work requirements. The welfare plan also required that "all applicants for relief who are new to the city must show evidence that their plans in coming to the city involved a concrete offer of employment, similar to that required of foreign immigrants" and prohibited aid past two weeks for such newcomers. As black journalists pointed out, Mitchell's crackdown on welfare closely followed a highly successful black voter registration drive and campaign against the city's urban renewal plans. Despite such criticisms, Mitchell's plan won support from conservative politicians and journalists around the nation as well as the wider public. A 1961 Gallup poll found that more than 80 percent of those surveyed approved of his plan. Nevertheless, state and federal officials and attorneys challenged the legality of the plan and forced the city to revoke it before it was ever fully implemented.[184]

Just as they did in the South, large farmers, concerned with reducing their taxes and ensuring a ready supply of cheap labor, lobbied for welfare cutbacks in California and New York in the 1950s. Yet, they carried out their welfare backlash in very different political and demographic contexts. In the South, where there was "massive resistance" to blacks' civil rights gains, large farmers allied themselves with white racists. Politicians and other welfare critics justified cutbacks by spreading new racist stereotypes of black welfare mothers. In California, large farmers mainly allied themselves with other business groups and rural county officials. While welfare critics sometimes appealed to racist stereotypes of lazy blacks and Mexicans, racist rhetoric was less commonly employed in California than in other states. With so few black and Chicana welfare mothers in the state, such racist rhetoric did not have wide appeal. In New York, where black and Puerto Rican welfare use was widely publicized, politicians appealed to racial hostility toward Black and Puerto Rican migrants and targeted newcomers for cutbacks.

In both these states, strong resistance to these welfare backlashes developed, especially from urban interest groups. Welfare advocacy groups and urban officials in both states, and unions in New York, lobbied against proposed cutbacks. The groups were most powerful in New York. There, Republicans as well as Democratic leaders rejected a number of restrictive welfare bills. In California, the vast overrepresentation of rural districts in the legislature favored welfare critics. Even so, urban politicians, who dominated the assembly's social welfare committee, killed a number of restrictive bills opposed by welfare advocates.

These case studies help illustrate the limits of this early welfare backlash. In the 1950s, the welfare backlash occurred mainly at the state level, and more than half of all states still had no work requirements for welfare mothers. In states such as Kentucky and New York, some Republicans joined Democrats in defending poor mothers' welfare rights, staving off various restrictive welfare rules. In the 1960s, the backlash against welfare mothers continued to spread, however, reaching the national level by the end of the decade. Growing conservative opposition to welfare, along with the rise of a new welfare rights movement and liberal Democrats' renewed efforts to reduce poverty, produced several failed attempts to replace AFDC with a guaranteed income program in the 1960s and 1970s. The reasons for these attempts, and their failure, are explored in the next chapter.

7. Setting the Stage
The Failures of Liberal Innovation

The blunt truth is that liberals have achieved virtually
no fundamental change in our society since the end of
the New Deal.

SENATOR EDMUND S. MUSKIE,
addressing the Liberal Party in New York in 1971

The 1960s and 1970s were particularly tumultuous decades in welfare history, bringing forth both expansions and contractions in poor mothers' welfare rights. On the one hand, increased electoral power of liberals, the rise of
the civil rights movement and its demands for employment opportunities,
and urban riots in the early 1960s provided new impetus to expand the
rights of poor families. Under Presidents Kennedy and Johnson, Congress
undertook a "service and rehabilitation" strategy for alleviating poverty,
expanding services and job training for low-income people and creating
financial incentives for employment. The rise of a new grassroots welfare
rights movement and a series of legal victories for poverty rights lawyers
undercut many of the restrictive policies and practices that had earlier prevented poor mothers from receiving welfare. Partly as a result of these
developments, the AFDC program experienced its most rapid growth, as the
number of families it served almost tripled between 1960 and 1970, increasing from 787,000 to 2,208,000.[1] This dramatic caseload growth brought
renewed attention to the welfare system, sparking considerable debate.

These policy changes proved to be too limited and too narrowly targeted,
however, to either eradicate poverty or gain broad-based support. Because
AFDC and War on Poverty programs disproportionately served racial
minorities—who were disproportionately unemployed, concentrated in
low-wage jobs, and excluded from other welfare programs—racialized
opposition to their expansion quickly emerged. AFDC also came under
attack from conservative business leaders and low-wage employers. In the
late 1960s, the backlash against welfare reached the national level, culmi-
nating in the creation and strengthening of federal work requirements for
welfare mothers in 1967 and 1971. Along with a broader white backlash

against the civil rights movement, this welfare backlash contributed to Republican Richard Nixon's election.

President Nixon represented the moderate wing of the Republican Party and ruled over a largely Democratic Congress, however, which encouraged the development of innovative policy proposals. Nixon tried, unsuccessfully, to replace the welfare system with a guaranteed income program for the working and nonworking poor. In the late 1970s, Carter revived presidential efforts to revamp the welfare system, and urged Congress to adopt the Program for Better Jobs and Income, which combined a guaranteed income program with job creation. Congress's failure to improve on AFDC, despised by both the Left and the Right, was a crucial turning point in American welfare history, paving the way for more forceful attacks on welfare mothers.[2]

THE SERVICE STRATEGY AND ITS LIMITS

Under the Kennedy and Johnson administrations, the federal government expanded its efforts to combat poverty. Their initiatives provided new job training opportunities, monetary incentives to work, and social services to low-income people, in an effort to rehabilitate the poor and integrate them into mainstream society. Both presidents focused on expanding opportunity, but not on reducing inequality or seriously redistributing the wealth. They emphasized training and services rather than job creation or a guaranteed income because it was a less expensive approach and because they were optimistic that the booming economy would create more jobs in the private sector.[3]

In response to rising concerns about structural unemployment and poverty, popularized through Michael Harrington's (1962) book, *The Other America,* Congress created a number of new job training initiatives through the 1961 Area Redevelopment Act, the 1962 Manpower Development and Training Act (MDTA), and the 1963 Vocational Educational Act.[4] Congress also expanded ADC in 1961, authorizing states to provide aid to two-parent families through the ADC Unemployed Parents program, and thus reinforcing the family wage system for low-income families.[5] Through the 1962 Social Security Act amendments, which renamed the program Aid to Families with Dependent Children, Congress expanded the program's casework services and created a new Community Work and Training (CWT) program to "rehabilitate" current, former, and potential recipients. Like the Area Redevelopment Act and MDTA training programs, CWT authorized federal funds for job training and work expenses, such as child care, for welfare recipients. Reflecting the persistent influence of the family wage model on policy makers, CWT mainly targeted unemployed fathers and was largely voluntary. Most states used the funds to create "work for relief" programs, in which recipients received "on-the-job training." Like other training and service programs begun under the Kennedy administration, CWT was small and meagerly funded.[6]

Before his assassination, Kennedy made a commitment to undertake a major effort to reduce poverty. His successor, Lyndon B. Johnson, followed his direction, declaring an "unconditional war on poverty," and made the development of his "Great Society" programs one of his first priorities.[7] Dominated by Democrats, Congress passed the Economic Opportunity Act in the summer of 1964 in response to the spread of urban riots and the civil rights movement's growing demands for job opportunities, made clear by the 1963 March for Jobs and Freedom and local protests for jobs. By expanding blacks' economic opportunities, Congress hoped to prevent further radicalization and dissent.[8]

Although the secretary of the Department of Labor, Willard Wirtz, and union leaders in the AFL-CIO urged Congress to create more jobs, the Economic Opportunity Act sought to alleviate poverty mainly by expanding services, training, and education for low-income people.[9] Among other programs, the act created job training programs, such as the Neighborhood Youth Corps and Job Corps, and Operation Head Start, a preschool program for low-income children.[10] The War on Poverty represented a major increase in federal expenditure for job training, which increased from $200 million to $1.4 billion between 1964 and 1970.[11] A second prong of the act provided federal money to mobilize poor people through Community Action Agencies, run with "maximum feasible participation" of the poor, which meant that at least one-third of their board members were low-income. These agencies engaged in a variety of campaigns, protesting slum housing, employment discrimination, inadequate welfare, and police brutality.[12]

As part of its effort to expand job training for low-income people, the Economic Opportunity Act provided states with full federal funding for work and training programs through the Work Experience and Training (WET) program, prompting all states except Alabama to take advantage of the program. Like subsequent welfare-to-work programs, the program used a combination of "sticks" (requirements and sanctions) and "carrots" (positive incentives) to increase participation of poor people in the labor force. Conservatives emphasized the importance of work requirements for discouraging welfare receipt, while liberals viewed the carrots—training and support services—as crucial to the "rehabilitation" of the poor. Because WET was so poorly funded, participation was largely voluntary, and only about 150,000 people participated. Most participants, about one-third of whom were African American, were put into "work for relief" programs and assigned to low-wage jobs, such as heavy cleaning, dishwashing, yard work, and domestic service, which provided few opportunities for recipients to learn new job skills.[13] As urban riots spread across the country, policy makers sought to quell dissent by expanding training opportunities for blacks. In 1966, Congress amended MDTA, which mainly served white men, to focus more attention on the "hard core unemployed," commonly understood to mean young inner-city blacks.[14] They also created the Concentrated Employment Program, which provided job training and support services to disadvantaged adults, most of whom were black.[15]

The expansion of federal job training and employment services was intended to not only prevent riots, but also to strengthen the family wage system and reduce the number of black female-headed households. The circulation of Daniel Patrick Moynihan's infamous 1965 report, "The Negro Family: A Case for National Action," helped to raise concerns about black family structure. Reviving old behavioralist explanations of black poverty, Moynihan attributed the growth of welfare caseloads and social problems in the black community to the rise in female-headed and matriarchal households. According to Moynihan, the shortage of good jobs for black men discouraged them from forming and maintaining families and playing the dominant role within these families. Moynihan urged policy makers to make black male employment a national priority in order to "strengthen the Negro family."[16]

Consistent with this view, job training and employment services were directed mainly toward unemployed men. Like CWT, WET targeted unemployed fathers. As the labor market improved, however, male participation in the program declined from 61 percent in 1965 to 48 percent in 1966. Concerned about the growing number of female participants in the program, federal administrators instructed project directors to fill at least half of their positions with men.[17] MDTA and Job Corps programs likewise targeted young men rather than women.[18]

To further reduce poverty, policy makers also attempted to reduce the rates of out-of-wedlock childbearing by expanding low-income women's access to contraceptive services, but this was not a major priority. The Office of Economic Opportunity (OEO) spent only $16.5 million (less than 1 percent of its budget) on family planning services between 1964 and 1968.[19] Although rates of unwed motherhood were rising among whites and declining among blacks in the 1960s, policy makers' concerns were usually directed at black women, who had rates of out-of-wedlock childbirth more than eight times greater than that of white women in 1965.[20]

In 1965, OEO urged Congress to adopt more far-reaching reforms, which included "growth, structural and payment programs that fit together in an integrated War on Poverty."[21] While the decline in unemployment reduced OEO's support for public jobs the following year, it continued to favor income maintenance programs, which promised to provide greater benefits and serve more people than the existing welfare system.[22] OEO experts favored negative income tax (NIT) plans, which provided money to low-income families through the tax system, considering them to be less expensive and more efficient than family allowances, which provided grants to all families with children.[23] In 1967, to build support for this policy, OEO implemented a NIT program in New Jersey, hoping to show that it would increase or fail to affect participants' work activity.[24]

OEO's position was heavily influenced by economists' growing support for NIT proposals. In the late 1940s, Milton Friedman and George Stigler began to advocate NIT plans, but academic support for these policies did not really grow until after the publication of Robert Theobald's (1965) *The Guaranteed Income* and Milton Friedman's (1962) *Capitalism and Freedom*. Whereas Theobald and other radicals emphasized the right to an income, Friedman and other conservatives viewed NIT plans as a more efficient way to provide income to the poor than the bureaucratically unwieldy welfare system. Liberal and conservative scholars emphasized that the NIT created incentives to work and form families by subsidizing low-wage employment.[25]

NIT proposals captured the interest of the Johnson administration. Johnson's 1966 economic report to Congress urged it to seriously consider a NIT program. Weeks later, his Presidential Commission on Technology, Automation, and Progress advocated a GAI (guaranteed annual income) program to deal with problems of structural unemployment, claiming that it would encourage work and family formation among low-income workers.[26] In 1968, in response to the previous year's riots, Johnson established a Commission on Income Maintenance to consider NIT and other welfare proposals.[27]

Yet, support for NIT plans from Johnson and the Democratic Party was weak. Like Kennedy, Johnson remained optimistic about the potential for tax cuts and economic growth to provide more jobs and higher wages, and so was fiscally conservative. Fearing the erosion of business confidence and following the advice of his economic advisors, Kennedy advocated a $10.2

billion-dollar tax cut in 1964. To pass it, Kennedy agreed to reduce expenditures to avoid deficit spending. Congress required greater expenditure reductions in 1965 when President Johnson pursued another tax cut. To maintain business confidence and their commitments to Congress, both presidents kept social spending low. Growing military expenditures during the Vietnam War also created fiscal constraints.[28] President Johnson expanded services for the poor largely by taking money away from other programs, a strategy that increased Congressional opposition to the War on Poverty.[29] However, funding for OEO never cost even 1 percent of the federal budget. As one historian points out, "Until Nixon abolished [OEO] in 1974, its spending never accounted for more than 3 percent of all federal social welfare expenses or 6 percent of all federal funds for the poor."[30]

A fiscal conservative, Johnson was reluctant to give full-fledged support to expansive programs, such as job creation, family allowances, and GAI proposals that threatened to increase expenditures.[31] Whereas OEO officials endorsed GAI proposals, top officials in the Department of Health, Education, and Welfare (HEW) under Johnson favored more incremental reforms, such as expanding services.[32] The Democratic Party was also cautious, endorsing only further assessment of family income support proposals in its 1968 party platform. Even Robert F. Kennedy, one of the most liberal Democratic candidates for the presidency that year, did not favor a GAI policy. Instead, he advocated poverty reduction through financial incentives to stimulate inner-city investment.[33]

Kennedy and Johnson's antipoverty policies undoubtedly helped the poor, but their impact was limited. As Michael B. Katz suggests, the expansion of federal social programs "reduced poverty, hunger, malnutrition, and disease; increased the access of the poor to important social services; and lowered barriers to political participation, employment, housing, and education for black Americans."[34] Meanwhile, Community Action Agencies helped develop black political leadership, contributing to the rapid rise in black elected officials in the 1960s.[35] MDTA and Job Corps programs modestly increased employment among participants, but they served only a fraction of low-income people. More importantly, the service approach did very little to raise wages or ensure the availability of good jobs. Indeed, despite new job training programs for unemployed youth, unemployment among black teens rose in the 1960s.[36]

Although Johnson passed laws to create Medicare and Medicaid in 1965, he did little to expand the reach of AFDC or Food Stamps. Food Stamps, created in 1964, served fewer people than the surplus commodity program it replaced. Johnson refused to expand the program, however, disappointing advocates both within and outside his administration.[37] Average AFDC payments rose 35 percent between 1960 and 1968[38] but remained grossly uneven and insufficient, creating deplorable living conditions for recipients. As Congresswoman Martha Griffiths described welfare mothers, they were often confined to "a room with falling plaster, inadequately heated in the winter and sweltering in the summer, without enough beds for the family, and with no sheets, the furniture falling apart, a bare bulb in the center of the room as the only light, with no hot water most of the time, plumbing that often does not work, with only the companionship of small children who are often hungry and always inadequately clothed—and, of course, the ever-present rats."[39]

Johnson's advisors considered national benefit standards, but the president never introduced the idea to Congress and chastised his advisors when they tried to include a measure in the 1968 budget requiring states to provide aid to two-parent families.[40] The War on Poverty also did little to directly challenge state and local policies that prevented tens of thousands of poor families from obtaining welfare. Instead, it funded legal aid services and Community Action Agencies to do this work.[41] Their work was greatly aided by the rise of a grassroots welfare rights movement.

A WELFARE MOVEMENT ARISES

The National Welfare Rights Organization (NWRO), formed in 1966, represented the first major attempt to build a national grassroots movement among welfare mothers. NWRO was a national federation of welfare organizations, which had been forming locally since the early 1960s under the leadership of recipient leaders, such as Johnnie Tillmon, Community Action Agency staff, student and civil rights activists, and social workers.[42] NWRO was the brainchild of two academics, Frances Fox Piven and Richard A. Cloward, who circulated a "strategy to end poverty" in 1966. Piven and Cloward urged welfare advocates to "end poverty" by flooding the welfare rolls and increasing benefit levels. Not only would this immediately alleviate poverty, it would produce a fiscal crisis, especially in large cities, that would increase political support for replacing the welfare system with a guaranteed annual income. NWRO's "break the bank" strategy informed their decision to focus on urban welfare mothers, who were more numerous than other public assistance recipients and densely concentrated in large cities.[43]

After recruiting George Wiley, a civil rights activist, to direct the organization, welfare rights activists held their first national meeting in 1966.

Participants declared the primary goal of their new movement to be "enough money from either jobs or welfare grants for recipients to live dignified lives as American citizens, above the level of poverty."[44] In this formative period, its slogan was "Jobs or income now!"[45] National leaders publicly criticized the government's failure to alleviate job shortages and advocated the creation of "jobs with adequate income."[46] Some local WROs even organized protest marches for jobs. For example, Johnnie Tillmon, who served as the first chairperson of NWRO, described one such protest: "We wanted jobs—in the state, in the county, in the city. . . . But if they couldn't come up with the jobs, then they should leave us alone and put some more money in the checks."[47] NWRO also worked to secure funds to establish child care centers run by welfare mothers.[48] Nonetheless, jobs were a secondary concern to NWRO leaders, who focused instead on "bread and justice." As Wiley told one reporter, NWRO's "chief concern . . . has been money."[49]

The decision to focus on recipients' consumption rather than employment rights was consistent with NWRO's "break the bank" strategy. Organizers also believed that to be effective they had to address their members' immediate needs[50] and were skeptical about the availability of decent jobs for poor mothers, especially poor black ones, given existing labor market inequalities.[51] NWRO's strategy was a product of its time. In 1970, only about 30 percent of married women with children under six were in the labor force.[52] Like others, the NWRO embraced the family wage system, demanding poor mothers' right to stay at home with their children and "'federal funds for immediate creation of at least 3 million jobs for men' in order 'to permit them to assume normal roles as breadwinners and heads of families.'"[53]

Although most welfare mothers at the time were white, the organization was mostly composed of African American women. Organizers targeted large northern cities because blacks were concentrated there and the civil rights movement had politicized poor blacks, making it easier to organize them. Many welfare rights organizers, like George Wiley, came out of the civil rights movement, and they quickly allied themselves with black leaders and churches.[54] Allies in the women's movement, churches, and middle-class "Friends of the NWRO" also supported NWRO's campaigns.[55]

NWRO lobbied for better welfare laws and used direct action to improve welfare administration.[56] NWRO chapters and Community Action Agencies distributed "welfare rights" handbooks and encouraged poor people to demand the benefits they were entitled to receive.[57] Because of the stigma of welfare receipt, lack of information, and restrictive policies, only about a third of eligible families were receiving AFDC in the early 1960s.[58] Through harassment and protests, NWRO members pressured local welfare departments to end discriminatory practices that prevented applicants from receiving welfare. Legal service lawyers, often affiliated with Community Action Agencies, challenged restrictive welfare policies in administrative hearings and class action suits.[59] Partly through such efforts, the application and acceptance rates for AFDC rose dramatically. By 1971, more than 90 percent of eligible families were participating in AFDC.[60] Fear of rioting and national rhetoric denouncing poverty encouraged social workers to become more lenient.[61] Quantitative research shows that caseload growth and welfare expenditures were positively associated with both urban riots and Community Action Agency activity.[62]

Among NWRO's most successful campaigns were those for "special needs" grants for school clothing and furniture, carried out mainly in Massachusetts and New York.[63] Demonstrations at local welfare offices involved groups of twenty-five to five hundred people, while demonstrations at central offices drew between five hundred and two thousand participants. These campaigns succeeded in obtaining millions of dollars worth of benefits for recipients. The high level of solidarity among poor mothers, social workers' fear of riots, and the influence of liberal welfare administrators contributed to the success of these campaigns.[64] NWRO also demanded, and sometimes received, access to federally subsidized meal programs, medical services for children, and consumer credit at department stores.[65]

Welfare recipients, with the help of federally funded antipoverty lawyers, won important legal victories in the late 1960s. Judges declared residency requirements, "man in the house" policies, and "substitute father" rules to be illegal. These court victories significantly expanded AFDC eligibility and reduced racial inequities in AFDC coverage. For example, the ruling against the "substitute father" regulation affected some five hundred thousand children in nineteen states.[66]

NWRO faced an increasingly hostile political environment as the decade wore on, however. The group's short-term goal of improving welfare for poor, mostly black urban mothers failed to capture broad-based support or galvanize a large-scale movement for a guaranteed income. Although civil rights leaders and organizations, such as the Urban Coalition and the Southern Christian Leadership Conference, women's organizations, such as the League of Women Voters, and "labor, civic, religious, and social welfare organizations" also promoted a guaranteed income, it was mainly through education and lobbying rather than mass action.[67]

Had the organization targeted a broader sector of the working class and coupled its demands for income with demands for jobs, it might have built a more powerful welfare rights movement and countered the racist stereo-type of lazy recipients, which was increasingly used to undermine support for welfare.[68] NWRO's narrow membership base and short-term demands left welfare mothers vulnerable to racial scapegoating, especially given the intense backlash against minority movements at this time. Although mounting welfare caseloads provoked a fiscal crisis in northern cities and states and created political support for restructuring the welfare system among some politicians, it also unleashed greater opposition to welfare among whites and conservative business and political leaders. In reaction to NWRO's "special needs" campaigns, states adopted flat grants, making it more difficult for local chapters to win benefits and attract new members. Meanwhile, conservative forces increasingly dominated national welfare debates.[69]

THE 1960S WELFARE BACKLASH

State and local campaigns against welfare, begun after World War II, con-tinued in the early 1960s. Three of these campaigns received considerable press coverage, bringing racist attacks on welfare mothers into the national spotlight. These included Louisiana's 1960 purge of black unwed mothers from its rolls, Newburgh, New York's "thirteen-point welfare plan" of 1961 directed against black migrants, and the 1962 U.S. Senate hearings on wel-fare fraud in Washington, D.C., where 93 percent of the caseload was non-white.[70] Politicians frequently resorted to racist stereotypes of poor blacks to justify these campaigns, taking attention away from the enduring problems of racial discrimination and inner-city job shortages. For example, during the 1962 Senate hearings on Washington, D.C.'s welfare program, Senator Robert Byrd of West Virginia (a former Klansman) proclaimed: "It is about time . . . that we stop encouraging indolence and shiftlessness, and that we quit furnishing money, food, and rent for indecent mothers and paramours who contribute nothing but illegitimate children to the society of this fed-eral city, most of whom end up roaming the streets and getting arrested for various crimes."[71] Conservative politicians, such as Barry Goldwater, the 1964 Republican candidate for president, endorsed these early antiwelfare campaigns, paving the way for the national welfare backlash at the end of the decade.[72]

As in the 1950s, the popular appeal of these campaigns among whites was linked to the broader backlash against blacks' demands for social justice and their continued migration into northern cities. Although black migration slowed after the 1950s, it remained substantial. On average, 102,000 blacks left the South per year between 1960 and 1966.[73] The civil rights movement also spread northward, and blacks became increasingly radical and militant. In response, white support for black activism diminished.[74] As James L. Sundquist suggested, "The image of the Negro in 1966 [was] no longer that of the praying, long-suffering nonviolent victim of southern sheriffs, it was a defiant young hoodlum shouting 'black power' and hurling 'Molotov cocktails' in an urban slum."[75] Northern as well as southern whites felt threatened by blacks' demands for fair housing policies, school busing programs to integrate schools, and federal enforcement of equal opportunity employment laws. The white racial backlash was evident even in California, where voters overwhelmingly rejected a fair housing law in 1964.[76] Whereas 68 percent of northern whites polled in 1964 supported federal efforts to integrate the South, by 1966, 52 percent said that the government was pushing integration too quickly.[77]

As the decade wore on, many whites became increasingly resentful of expanding welfare rolls and federal social programs, which they viewed as benefiting racial minorities at their expense as taxpayers.[78] The most dramatic decline in public support for greater welfare spending occurred between 1961 and 1973. Whereas more than 60 percent of Americans surveyed in 1961 supported more welfare spending, only about 20 percent did in 1973. Negative media publicity about rising caseloads and the perception that Democrats were doing little to reduce public spending did much to increase opposition to welfare.[79] Popular magazines were also more likely to depict welfare as creating dependency in this period compared to previous ones.[80]

Opposition to welfare was racialized, as most people mistakenly believed that welfare mainly benefited blacks.[81] In fact, blacks' share of the nation's AFDC caseload continued to grow in the 1960s, but remained less than half of all recipients.[82] Blacks' biggest gains from the expansion of welfare in the 1960s were mainly concentrated in the South, where they made up a rising share of the caseload. Elsewhere, the liberalization of welfare rules mainly benefited whites.[83] Racialized images of welfare were encouraged by conservative politicians' rhetoric and distorted media coverage of poverty. While blacks' share of the poor increased marginally, from 27 to 30 percent during the 1960s, the percentage of African Americans pictured in news stories about poverty jumped dramatically, from 27 percent in 1964 to 72 percent in 1967.[84] Overrepresentation of blacks in these stories was related to media coverage of urban riots and civil rights protests, as well as increasingly critical coverage of the War on Poverty.[85] Growing associations between poverty, welfare, and blacks were linked to increasing skepticism about the worthiness of welfare recipients, especially as AFDC served rising numbers of black female-headed households.[86] Popular magazines increasingly portrayed welfare mothers as "black, unmarried women out to cheat the state" in the 1960s and 1970s.[87] Whereas only 37 percent of Americans polled in 1964 blamed poverty on lack of effort, forty-four percent did so in 1967.[88]

There was also considerable white resistance to the War on Poverty, whose job training programs targeted blacks, and to efforts to desegregate employment.[89] Some skilled trade unions helped run federally funded job-training programs, but most fiercely resisted federal interference with their control over job training and employment. Union control over apprenticeships allowed white workers to keep wages high by limiting the supply of skilled labor, protected family members' access to skilled jobs, and kept blacks out of the skilled trades.[90] Meanwhile, campaigns by Community Action Agencies to expand blacks' opportunities and access to services helped erode politicians' support for antipoverty programs, increasingly perceived as tax expenditures used to weaken white political power.[91]

In the 1960s, AFDC was increasingly associated with black mothers, who made up about 40 percent of the caseload. Widespread stereotypes of blacks as lazy, and the racial expectation that they work outside the home, contributed to support for mandatory employment requirements, as did rising levels of maternal employment.[92] "Employable mother" rules continued to spread across the nation in the 1960s, providing an outlet for white resentment toward welfare, black in-migration, and the civil rights movement.[93] These rules also provided a cheap labor source for employers. Congressional testimony from the late 1960s reported that in the South, "During cotton-picking season no one is accepted on welfare because plantations need cheap labor."[94] Whereas these rules spread mainly across the South and Southwest in the 1950s, in the 1960s they were spreading in the North and Midwest. Between 1960 and 1967, eight more states adopted work requirements for AFDC, including Pennsylvania, Massachusetts, New York, Vermont, Kansas, and North Dakota.[95]

Support for federal work requirements was also growing among businesses, increasingly reliant on female labor and concerned about rising welfare expenditures. The U.S. Chamber of Commerce and the National Association of Manufacturers (NAM) urged Congress to enact work requirements for AFDC.[96] The Council for State Chambers of Commerce also supported them, claiming, "We believe this proposal is a refreshing change. We see it as a negation of the attempt to establish an absolute or constitutional right to welfare payments or to a guaranteed income."[97] A representative of the Winter Park, Florida Chamber of Commerce likewise commended conservative politicians for "publicly challenging the concept of welfare as a way of life."[98]

The 1967 Social Security Amendments reflected a compromise between liberals who sought to stimulate employment among poor mothers through work supports and financial incentives and conservatives who demanded "get tough" welfare measures. On the one hand, the law expanded recipients' rights, providing child care funds and employment placement services, allowing recipients to keep the first thirty dollars they earned plus one-third of the remaining income, and paying recipients a thirty-dollar stipend for participating in training programs. On the other hand, the law was extremely punitive toward single mothers, freezing welfare spending for unwed mothers and children deserted by their fathers. It also required, when "appropriate," adults and children over sixteen to register for job training or employment and authorized grant reductions for noncompliance.[99] Support for these measures was rooted in racist images of lazy, irresponsible, and promiscuous blacks taking advantage of the welfare system and in the perceived need to force them into the labor force and cut off support for their children. Senator Russell Long of Louisiana, for example, complained that he could no longer hire anyone to iron his shirts because the welfare system had become too lenient,[100] and dismissed welfare rights activists as "brood mares."[101]

These punitive measures were highly contested. NWRO testified against them and organized a sit-in demonstration after most members of the Senate Finance Committee walked out of the room during their testimony.[102] Fifty-one people testified against the compulsory work features of Work Incentive programs (WIN) during congressional hearings in 1967, claiming they were punitive and would interfere with poor mothers' ability to care for their children. Opposition mainly came from welfare officials, social welfare associations, churches, and women's organizations.[103] The spending freeze directed against deserted and unwed mothers was also highly controversial. Three secretaries of HEW, the majority of state governors (who viewed it as a fiscal burden), NWRO, and welfare advocates opposed the measure. Both Johnson and Nixon delayed its implementation until it was formally repealed in 1969.[104]

In 1968, federal judges upheld the legality of work requirements for recipients, paving the way for WIN's implementation. The case, *Anderson et al. v. Shaefer et al.*, concerned the implementation of Georgia's 1952 "employable mother" rule. The judges claimed that the state could not prohibit the supplementation of full-time employment because it unfairly discriminated against applicants based on their employment status. It also ruled that the state could not deny assistance to all experienced agricultural workers during the county-designated seasonal employment period unless the mother was actually employed or received an actual employment offer.[105] Nevertheless, the court found Georgia's "employable mother" rule to be constitutionally sound because there was "no federally protected right of a mother to refuse employment while receiving assistance and remaining at her home with her children."[106]

Like previous work programs, WIN targeted unemployed fathers and frequently exempted mothers. Sanctions were applied sparingly to welfare mothers, sometimes out of fear that they would spark riots. The program was grossly underfunded, making it difficult for most referrals to be placed in jobs. As a result, only 10 percent of 1.6 million referrals were found suitable for employment. Even so, 81,000 people participated in the program in 1969, and this number rose to 112,000 in 1971.[107] According to Congressional testimony, WIN participants in the South were "made to serve as maids or to do yard work in white homes to keep their checks."[108]

The backlash against welfare and civil rights gains reshaped electoral politics. Liberal Democrats' support for the War on Poverty, the 1964 Civil Rights Act, and the Voting Rights Act of 1965 cemented black support for the party but alienated white racial conservatives. Republicans actively courted this group, moving toward the right on racial issues after 1965.[109] The strategy paid off in the 1966 elections, when Republicans picked up thirteen seats in Congress and eight governorships.[110] As liberal Democrats lent support not only to black civil rights but to a broader "rights revolution" for women, gays and lesbians, the disabled, prisoners, and the mentally ill, it became increasingly perceived by white voters as serving "special interests." Alongside this, the spread of urban riots between 1964 and 1968, the rise of crime, urban decay, sexual liberalism, unwed motherhood, and new left movements gave momentum to Republican calls for "law and order."[111]

George C. Wallace's 1968 presidential campaign paved the way for the electoral realignment of traditional white voters. Appealing to racial conservatives, Wallace portrayed civil rights "as the imposition on working men and women of intrusive 'social' policies by an insulated elitist cabal of lawyers, judges, editorial writers, academics, bureaucrats, and planners."[112] After barely winning the three-way race against Wallace and Hubert H. Humphrey, Richard Nixon carefully courted white racial conservatives while publicly expressing a commitment to racial equality.[113] In its first few years in office, the Nixon administration filed a legal motion to slow down racial desegregation, urged Congress to weaken the 1965 Voting Rights Act and end school busing programs, and nominated racial conservatives to the Supreme Court. Although Nixon introduced affirmative action policies for federal contractors, these were viewed then as a moderate, business-centered approach to achieving racial equality.[114] Reflecting the backlash against blacks' civil rights gains and federal social programs, most Americans polled in 1968 identified "big government" as the greatest threat to their future.[115] Republicans, including Nixon, appealed to such voters, attacking both the "welfare mess" and the War on Poverty.[116]

By the late 1960s, the view was widely held that the current welfare system was not working. Conservatives criticized AFDC, claiming that it encouraged welfare dependency by reducing the incentives to work and marry, especially among blacks. They also portrayed the federal welfare bureaucracy and service strategy as inefficient. Liberal and left observers, on the other hand, viewed the welfare system as too stingy and punitive. Meanwhile, state and urban officials, especially in the Northeast, sought fiscal relief from expanding welfare caseloads and claimed that inequities in coverage encouraged the poor to migrate to more generous states.[117] These criticisms, coming from both the Left and the Right, lent support to replacing the current welfare system with some sort of GAI policy.

NIXON'S FAMILY ASSISTANCE PLAN

While Nixon attacked and gutted the War on Poverty and welfare services, which he believed gave excessive power and resources to federal agencies, he urged Congress to replace the current welfare system with the Family Assistance Plan (FAP), a NIT program.[118] Nixon sought to distance FAP from proposals for a GAI, but it would have guaranteed a minimum income for low-income households, equalizing benefits across states. The plan provided $500 for the first two family members and $300 for each additional member. To encourage work, FAP allowed a low-wage family to earn up to $720 annually and still receive full benefits. It also provided funds for job training and child care.[119] The plan contained work requirements but exempted women with children under six.[120] Nixon made the passage of FAP his top domestic priority in 1970. It came close to passing, winning the approval of the House in 1969 and 1971, but was rejected both times by the Senate Finance Committee.[121]

Nixon's advisors, along with the Ripon Society, a Republican research and policy organization, urged him to back a NIT proposal to gain greater popular electoral support among white workers, the "forgotten Americans." The largest beneficiaries of the program would be the working poor in the

South, most of whom were white.[122] Other Republican leaders, such as Congressman Melvin R. Laird, also promoted the policy.[123] Whether or not FAP would increase Republicans' popular support remained a point of controversy among Nixon's advisors, however, especially after it became clear that neither labor leaders nor southerners were particularly supportive of the policy.[124]

Nixon actively courted white workers and taxpayers in his speeches for the policy by portraying it as a "workfare" policy that would simultaneously reduce welfare dependency and help low-income workers.[125] FAP's supporters also claimed that it would help to prevent urban riots, which had quickly spread across the country, with sixty-four disorders occurring in 1967 alone.[126] Daniel Patrick Moynihan, then an advisor to Nixon, linked the riots to the broader social disintegration of the black community, which he believed was related to black male unemployment and the rise in female-headed households. By providing extra income to low-wage workers, FAP's supporters claimed it would encourage family formation among poor blacks and so reduce their propensity to riot.[127] This argument helped gain the support of big city mayors and the National Association of Counties. State and local officials also embraced FAP, believing it would provide fiscal relief and reduce interstate migration by equalizing benefits across states.[128]

Nixon's FAP had active support from larger corporations, some of which had been pushing for an income maintenance program for several years. Participants in Nelson Rockefeller's 1967 Arden House Conference—which included representatives of Xerox, Metropolitan Life Insurance, the New York Stock Exchange, Inland Steel, Mobile Oil, and the Ford Motor Company—favored replacing the welfare system with a NIT or family allowance program. They publicized these recommendations through a full-page ad in the *New York Times*. Business leaders participating in President Johnson's Commission on Income Maintenance, headed by Ben W. Heineman, head of Northwest Industries, recommended that Nixon adopt a NIT plan that would provide at least $2,400 to low-income families. For these business leaders, NIT plans promised to subsidize low-wage employment, increase work incentives, and prevent riots.[129]

Once introduced, FAP received favorable responses from business organizations, especially those representing larger corporations such as the National Association of Manufacturers and the Committee for Economic Development (CED, an elite organization of two hundred corporate elites). NAM supported FAP "as a mechanism for calming urban ghettos and encouraging work, particularly among black males."[130] CED's recommendations were even more liberal than Nixon's plan. The National Federation of

Independent Businesses also supported FAP, believing that it would increase the incentive to work among the poor. Major corporations, including those participating in the Arden House conference, such as Ford, Xerox, Lehman Brothers, and Eastman Kodak, were enthusiastic about FAP and sent telegrams and letters in support of it. The Urban Coalition, formed in 1967 in response to the riots, mobilized support for FAP within the business community, gathering over one hundred signatures in favor of it.[131] Support for a NIT plan was also growing among economists. By 1968, 1,200 economists signed a statement endorsing a "national system of income guarantees and supplements."[132]

Union leaders provided more reluctant support for FAP, preferring job creation to GAI plans. They feared that FAP would subsidize low wages and undermine the bargaining power of their members, most of whom were skilled white workers. After the House passed FAP, union leaders sought to amend it. The executive committee of the AFL-CIO endorsed FAP only after Congress eliminated the requirement forcing people to accept work not covered by the minimum wage. To reduce labor market competition, the committee persuaded Congress to create a separate public sector tier for training programs. Labor leaders did not mobilize strong grassroots support for FAP. Despite publicly endorsing the plan, George Meany, head of the AFL-CIO, privately opposed it and believed that most of his members would also oppose it because it would provide aid to those who did not work.[133] Michael Brown argues, "Calls for new and more inclusive social policies—guaranteed incomes, public employment, family allowances—were irrelevant to . . . white union members already securely protected from the ills of industrial capitalism."[134]

Nixon's FAP received largely positive responses in the press and public. About 90 percent of news editorials favored the plan, and the White House received ten times as many letters in support of FAP as opposed to it. Public opinion polls by the Gallup and Harris organizations showed support for Nixon's plan as high as 65 percent. Support for FAP was weak in the South, however, a region traditionally hostile to welfare, especially if it would aid blacks.[135]

As Jill Quadagno argues, southern Congressmen opposed FAP because it threatened to disrupt the southern political economy by raising its wage base, tripling the income of the typical southern farmworker. Southerners were expected to make up 52 percent of FAP recipients, and two-thirds of southern blacks would be covered by it. By making blacks less dependent on whites for their income, FAP would empower workers and encourage them to vote.[136] Whereas liberals feared that FAP's work requirements were too punitive, southern conservatives feared that they were too weak. Georgia representative Phillip Landrum, reacting to FAP, claimed, "There's not going to be anybody left to roll these wheelbarrows and press these shirts."[137] Because of the exemptions, it was estimated that in one Mississippi town, only two out of eighteen maids would have to register for work to receive full FAP benefits. Concerned about its effects on their labor supply and wages, southern business organizations, such as the Restaurant Association, opposed FAP.[138]

Southern businesses were not the only ones concerned about FAP. Although 80 percent of business leaders affiliated with the U.S. Chamber of Commerce supported it, its leaders strongly opposed FAP. Chamber leaders claimed that FAP would increase the size of the federal bureaucracy, the welfare caseload, and expenditures. Unlike NAM, the chamber believed that FAP would reduce work incentives by reducing low-income workers' need to seek a second job or promotion. They also opposed making the government the employer of last resort. For these reasons, the chamber made defeat of the bill one of their top legislative priorities.[139]

Whereas conservative critics opposed FAP because it was too generous, liberal groups opposed it because it was too stingy. Although NWRO had lobbied for a GAI, they denounced FAP as "anti-poor and anti-black . . . a flagrant example of institutional racism."[140] Although FAP promised to raise the incomes of southerners, it would lower the incomes of AFDC recipients in northern states, such as New York. Along with NWRO, the Urban League criticized FAP for being grossly underfunded.[141] As NWRO and feminist and civil rights groups also pointed out, FAP would have done little to reduce racial and gender inequities. FAP was intended to enable poor men to support a family, which would reinforce poor mothers' economic dependence on men and their traditional role as caregiver. FAP's training and employment programs would mainly be directed at fathers, and the plan provided insufficient child care assistance to encourage women's participation. Far from promoting blacks' upward mobility, the measure would simply subsidize low-wage employment.[142] These groups also considered FAP's work requirements overly punitive and racist. NWRO's concerns about FAP were publicized through demonstrations and an unofficial hearing scheduled by Senator Eugene McCarthy of Minnesota, a liberal Democrat. At the hearing, NWRO members criticized FAP and urged politicians to provide a guaranteed annual income of at least $5,500, equal to the average benefits for AFDC recipients in New York.[143] Such criticisms of FAP increased opposition among blacks, the black press, and other liberal groups. Initially, the League of Women Voters, Americans for Democratic Action, and the

National Council of Churches supported FAP, but they later withdrew their support as it became more controversial.[144]

Federal officials tried their best to overcome opposition to the plan. OEO officials released preliminary findings from its NIT experiments, which suggested that concerns that FAP would undermine the poor's incentive to work were unfounded. Nixon's secretary of HEW, Robert Finch, defended FAP, claiming it would reverse the misguided incentives in the welfare system that discouraged work and encouraged family breakup and out-of-wedlock childbearing.[145] Nevertheless, fears that FAP might actually increase family desertion, reduce incentives to work, and raise wages remained strong in Congress.[146]

Southern Congressmen, concerned that it would disrupt their political economy, were the most strongly opposed to the plan. Although the House passed FAP, 79 of the 155 votes against FAP came from representatives from the Deep South. Only seventeen southern Congressmen favored the bill. The South's opposition was central to FAP's demise, since southern politicians dominated the Senate Finance Committee. Nevertheless, three of the six votes against FAP in the committee came from nonsouthern liberal Democrats, probably concerned about FAP's low payments.[147] Although liberal Democrats attempted to pass a more generous NIT plan, the proposal died on the Senate floor.[148]

Shortly afterward, Congress passed, by a large majority, the Talmadge Amendment (WIN II), which strengthened the work requirements for AFDC recipients. The measure was popular not only among southern politicians but among business organizations, such as NAM, that pushed for its passage.[149] WIN II required mothers with children age six and older to register for work or training, emphasized job placement over education and training, and strengthened sanctions.[150] In practice, many welfare mothers were excused for "good cause," especially because WTW programs were not adequately funded. Only about half of the 40 percent of welfare mothers required to register for work activities were selected to participate.[151]

The following year, the Nixon administration urged Congress to pass a revised FAP bill in order to put "a floor under the income of every family with children in America." FAP II was designed to undercut objections from both conservatives and liberals. The plan would replace Food Stamps with cash benefits and strengthen FAP's work requirements. The bill required recipients to work fulltime and register for job training, exempting only mothers with children under three (rather than six) years of age, and it included stricter guidelines for the kinds of jobs that could be refused without losing benefits. FAP II divided the caseload into three categories: (1) the aged, blind, and disabled, (2) families with no employable members, and (3) families with employable members, who would be administered by the Department of Labor. Nevertheless, like FAP I, it put all these groups into the same program and allowed them similar benefits. FAP II also provided greater fiscal relief to states by replacing public assistance programs, funded partly with state money, with a completely federal program that provided higher payments than FAP I. These measures raised the price of the program by $6 billion over the old plan.[152]

Support for the plan remained weakest in the South, where only three governors and three major newspapers supported it. The administration tried to overcome this opposition by emphasizing that the plan would provide fiscal relief to the region and stimulate market demand by raising incomes. Southern politicians were determined to restrict welfare rather than expand it, however.[153] Despite their opposition, the bill, HR 1, passed the House, and a motion to strike FAP II from it was rejected. The Senate Finance Committee, however, voted to replace FAP II with a tougher workfare program that would require all welfare mothers, except those with children under six, to work. Senator Russell Long from Louisiana, who had sought to rid AFDC of "welfare chiselers," introduced the workfare measure. The program, which would subsidize private-sector employers and create public-sector work assignments, would have cost an estimated three to nine billion dollars more than FAP II, suggesting that cost was not the main issue. Along with southern Democrats, Republicans on the committee voted for the measure in place of Nixon's FAP II.[154] Scholars suggest that Nixon's failure to gain support for FAP in the Senate Finance Committee was due to his failure to broker a compromise with Democratic senator Abraham Ribicoff of Connecticut (former secretary of Health, Education, and Welfare under Kennedy) for fear of alienating conservative voters during an election year, and his failure to press for greater support from Republican members whose support he needed for the Vietnam War.[155]

Meanwhile, liberal groups and politicians continued to call for a more liberal GAI program. NWRO, who vigorously opposed the "Family Annihilation Plan," had the most radical vision. Their bill would guarantee a family of four $6,500 per year with no work requirements and provide benefits to half the U.S. population. Senator George McGovern, in his presidential campaign, called for a variety of proposals, including a national income insurance system predicated on work and public service jobs. Senator Ribicoff, who had denounced Long's plan as "slavefare," also proposed a liberal GAI bill. His plan, estimated to cost $3.4 billion more than FAP II, covered all low-income people, including single and childless adults. Ribicoff's plan would ensure a

family of four at least $2,800 per year, phase in annual increases until bene-
fits reached the poverty level, and adjust benefits according to regional differences in the cost of living. It also provided more money than FAP II for
child care and job training. The bill, cosponsored by eighteen senators and
supported by civic, labor, and religious groups, was introduced as an amendment to HR 1 but was rejected 52 to 34.[156]

The final welfare legislation enacted in 1971 contained some of Long's
work-oriented provisions, and created the supplemental security income for
the aged, blind, and disabled but no guaranteed income for the working
poor.[157] After the failure of FAP, Nixon signed into law a major expansion of
the Food Stamp program that made it more accessible to the working poor,
a policy that Johnson had rejected. In 1975, Congress passed the Earned
Income Tax Credit (EITC). The EITC only supplemented the income of the
working poor, however, ensuring that the nonworking poor continued to be
served through separate and stigmatized public assistance programs. The
EITC, unlike FAP, thus subsidized low paychecks without threatening the
labor supply.[158]

THE PROGRAM FOR BETTER JOBS AND INCOME

The next major presidential initiative to replace the welfare system with a
GAI plan was Jimmy Carter's 1977 Program for Better Jobs and Income
(PBJI). The PBJI would create over a million new training positions and
public sector jobs for the unemployed, a consolidated cash assistance program to replace AFDC, SSI, and Food Stamps for those not expected to
work, and an earned income supplement for low-wage workers. Like other
Democrats, Carter was fiscally conservative. He kept welfare expenditures
constant in his initial proposal for PBJI. The cash assistance program would
provide a guaranteed income of $4,200 per year for a family of four, which
would mean benefit reductions for recipients in more generous states.
Carter's proposal also exempted single parents with children under fourteen
years from work requirements.[159] The National Urban League's director,
Vernon Brown, criticized the measure for failing to provide enough jobs,
claiming, "Black people and poor people resent the stress on balanced budgets instead of balanced lives. We resent the unfulfilled promises of jobs . . .
and the continued acceptance of high unemployment."[160]

Initial public support for PBJI was high. A public opinion poll showed 70
percent of respondents supported the measure. According to HEW, 140 out
of 150 newspapers that it surveyed supported the PBJI.[161] Nonetheless, there
was little active grassroots support for the proposal. Civil rights organiza-

tions, though supportive of the measure, criticized it for failing to create full employment, while labor unions claimed that benefits were too low and the jobs program, which paid at or near the minimum wage, would put downward pressure on wages.[162] A more liberal version of Carter's proposal, costing an additional $20 billion, was passed by a House Welfare Reform subcommittee and included "greater flexibility to deviate from the minimum wage, an open-ended appropriation for job creation . . . , and indexing benefits to inflation." The measure died in the House Ways and Means Committee, however, largely because of opposition from southern Democrats and Republicans to guaranteed income proposals.[163]

Carter tried, after consulting with key Congressional leaders, to gain support for a watered down version of PBJI in 1979. Given the difficulties of passing a comprehensive welfare plan, which would have to gain support of multiple Congressional committees, Carter put forward two separate bills, one for job creation and the other for welfare reform. The new welfare plan, which cost about one-third of that allotted by the old plan, set federal benefit standards at 65 percent of the poverty line and increased the federal share of AFDC costs.[164] It also required states to provide AFDC–Unemployed Parents to two-parent households, increased the EITC, and provided fewer jobs.[165] The House passed the measure by 222 to 184, with opposition mainly coming from Republicans and southern Democrats.[166] Once again, however, the bill died in the Senate Finance Committee. Its chair, Senator Long, who represented the views of southern Democrats, was strongly opposed to guaranteed income proposals and viewed the bill as a move in this direction. He was unwilling to support the bill unless the administration capped federal expenditures on welfare, which the administration was unwilling to do.[167] However, Congress was more favorable to the unemployed and working poor than to AFDC recipients, expanding the EITC in 1978.[168]

The antipoverty measures developed under the Kennedy, Johnson, and Nixon administrations represented a major step forward in welfare spending. As Michael Katz points out, between 1965 and 1972, "they fueled a massive increase—from $75 billion to $185 billion—in federal spending for social welfare," which represented a significant growth in the percentage of gross national product spent on welfare.[169] Even so, Liberal Democrats' policy innovations in the 1960s were too little too late. The service strategy pursued by Johnson and Kennedy was fiscally conservative and targeted the underemployed, especially unemployed black men. While it provided needed job training, it did little to ensure the availability of good jobs or help the working poor. The white working class, already resentful of the expansion of civil rights, increasingly viewed liberal politicians as helping the poor and racial minorities at their expense. Courting their vote, Nixon, not Johnson or Kennedy, pushed for the expansion of Food Stamps and a guaranteed income program. By the time liberal Democrats were ready to embrace GAI proposals, they had lost ground to the Republicans, whose own GAI proposals they considered too stingy to pass.

The 1970s also witnessed the decline of NWRO, which had given welfare mothers an organized voice for the first time in history. As other social movements declined and Nixon gutted Community Action Agencies, energy and support drained from the NWRO, just as rising welfare opposition was making it increasingly difficult for NWRO to win benefits and gain new members. NWRO also suffered from internal divisions, as members sought to increase their power within the organization. In the 1970s, staff leaders proposed reviving the organization by broadening its base to include the working poor and other types of welfare recipients around a broad agenda for economic rights. Arguably, this could have strengthened the organization and forged stronger ties to the labor movement. Welfare mothers who led the organization rejected these proposals, however, fearing a loss of control over the only organization representing their interests. They remained firmly committed to "mother power," not class power. In the context of rising hostility toward welfare mothers and minority movements, this strategy proved to be shortsighted. By 1975, the NWRO had dissolved and declared bankruptcy.[170]

Declining support for New Deal policies, the failure of politicians to create a popular alternative, and the absence of a vibrant welfare rights movement created a political vacuum that was quickly filled by the Republican Right, whose rise to power unleashed even greater attacks on welfare mothers. Had politicians replaced AFDC with a guaranteed income program, poor mothers would not have been as vulnerable to welfare cutbacks in the 1980s and 1990s as they became. A guaranteed income program would have put poor mothers, many of whom were already working or cycling in and out of the welfare system, in the same program as the rest of the working poor, who garnered greater sympathy from the public. Instead, AFDC mothers, already highly stigmatized, remained both politically and programmatically isolated and so bore much of the brunt of the attacks on welfare that escalated in the ensuing decades.

PART III

The Contemporary Welfare Backlash

(1980–2004)

8. The Rise of the Republican Right and the New Democrats

The rightward turn in party politics, under way since the 1970s, was deeply shaped by race, class, and gender politics. Under pressure from corporate leaders, politicians of both parties, but especially Republicans, embraced a neoliberal economic agenda that called for minimal governmental interference with labor markets and economic transactions. At the same time, declining participation of working-class voters and the absence of a strong progressive movement reduced political pressure to protect workers' rights. The result was a dramatic rollback in corporate taxes, social services, and environmental and workplace regulations. Meanwhile, Republicans gained popularity among traditional whites—especially southern, evangelical, male, and working-class whites—by constructing an emotionally powerful, racially coded conservative discourse and championing policies that appealed to nativism, racial resentment, and patriarchal "family values." To try to recapture support among traditional white voters, New Democrats moved rightward on social issues. Like Republicans, they championed tough immigration, criminal justice, and welfare policies. Their strategy has not been wholly successful, however. Lacking a bold vision and rhetoric of their own, and unable to effectively address the economic concerns of white working-class voters, Democrats have been unable to recapture the popularity they once had.

CONSERVATIVE CORPORATE POLITICS

During the 1970s, corporate elites became more mobilized politically. One manifestation of this was the growth of coordinated corporate campaign contributions.[1] As Jerome Himmelstein points out, "In 1974 labor Political Action Committees [PACs] still outnumbered corporate PACs by 201 to

89. Within two years corporate PACs outnumbered labor PACs by almost two to one (433 to 224), and by 1984 by more than four to one (1,682 to 394)."[2] By the late 1990s, corporate PACs spent eleven times as much as labor PACs on political campaigns.[3] As Manza and Brooks observe, "the largess available from corporate PAC sources . . . has been important in transforming both parties, but especially the Democratic party, into more corporate-oriented parties increasingly incapable of mobilizing voters from below."[4] American business leaders also hired additional lawyers and government relations staff, funded broad-based lobbying organizations, and opened Washington offices. They invested more money in think tanks that could shape public opinion and policy debates through advertising campaigns, editorials, and research.[5] While business leaders continued to be politically divided, they formed more broad-based coalitions, rather than acting as narrow interest groups representing particular industries or companies.[6]

Conservative corporate heads were especially mobilized. Beginning in the 1970s, business investments in "ultra-conservative" think tanks outpaced those in "moderate-conservative" ones.[7] Right-wing think tanks paved the way for conservative policy reforms by promoting supply-side economics and neoliberalism. Along with corporate lobbyists, they pushed for an agenda that included tax cuts for corporations and the wealthy, decreased social spending, and fewer government regulations on business activity.[8] Conservative business leaders urged the corporate community to favor Republicans rather than incumbents, as they usually did. In the 1980 election, "88 percent of the largest corporate PACs engaged in an ideological strategy by directing more than 30 percent of their giving to Republican challengers, six times the figure for the next closest year, 1984, when 14 corporations did so."[9] This rightward shift in corporate campaign contributions, along with Reagan's 1980 victory, put Democrats on the defensive. In an effort to recapture support from both corporate donors and white voters, moderate Democrats—known as the "new Democrats"—formed the Democratic Leadership Council and moved their party rightward on economic and social issues.[10] Afterward, corporate PACs returned to their pragmatic strategy of giving more money to incumbents.[11]

Increased corporate political activity, and its more conservative bent after 1970, constituted a response to a perceived economic and political crisis. In part, corporate elites were reacting to increasing international economic competition and declining rates of economic growth and profit. Economic restructuring also meant that business leaders were more invested in labor-intensive service industries, which increased pressure on them to reduce labor costs. Many American businesses, especially low-wage employers and small businesses, responded to these economic pressures by pursuing the "low road" to economic growth. They sought to increase profits and out-maneuver their rivals by minimizing taxes and labor costs.[12] At the same time, corporate heads were reacting to the erosion of their political power. From the mid-1960s to the mid-1970s, mass-based movements and public interest groups made considerable gains in terms of consumer and environmental regulations.[13] Along with low-wage employers, industries most affected by government regulation—such as oil, chemical, lumber, paper, pharmaceutical, fabricated metals, rubber, and machinery—donated heavily to Republicans in 1978 and 1980.[14] Conservative corporations were politically powerful because they had tremendous resources to promote ideas and candidates and because they controlled the economy and could disinvest, or threaten to do so, if governmental policies were not perceived as "business-friendly."[15]

Increased political activity by conservative corporate elites led to noticeable shifts in national domestic policies. Under the Reagan, Bush I, and Bush II administrations, Congress cut taxes for corporations and the wealthy.[16] All three Republican administrations oversaw declines in regulatory programs and generally favored business over labor interests. President Reagan began his administration by firing and permanently replacing striking federal air traffic controllers, and then appointed "business-friendly" members to the National Labor Relations Board. Likewise, George W. Bush, at the behest of employer groups, intervened in a contract dispute between the International Longshore and Warehouse Union and the Pacific Maritime Association, ending the employers' eleven-day lockout and reducing the union's bargaining power. He later championed regulations to strip overtime pay from white-collar workers.[17]

Republicans, increasingly followed by new Democrats, championed "balanced-budget conservativism," which made deficit reduction through social spending cuts a major priority in the 1980s and 1990s. However, between 1981 and 1983, under Reagan, deficits doubled as a percentage of federal spending, as military spending rose to new heights, unemployment rose, and huge corporate tax cuts were implemented. Deficits reached unprecedented levels—$200 billion—in the mid-1980s. The sheer magnitude of the deficit—and the threat it posed in terms of raising taxes, inflating interest rates, and reducing the value of government bonds—increased political support among the corporate elite for reducing the deficit. Given the benefits they accrued from a strong military and tax cuts, corporations and wealthy families sought to balance the budget mainly through cutbacks on federal aid to the poor.[18] The spread of such ideas among financiers in the 1980s and 1990s was especially significant, since they could refuse to buy government bonds and raise interest rates, which would hurt the economy and make it difficult to finance federal deficits. President Clinton was warned of this, which encouraged him to make deficit reduction a priority, despite his earlier promises to raise corporate taxes and create jobs.[19] Indeed, although President Clinton pushed for a national health insurance plan, tougher environmental and workplace regulations, and the Family and Medical Leave Act, he favored free trade, deficit reduction, and welfare reform.[20] George W. Bush, who has championed both corporate tax cuts and bloated military budgets, belies fiscal logic. Yet, like his predecessors, he continues to oppose efforts to increase welfare expenditure, while Congressional support for proposals to link spending cuts to tax cuts remains strong.[21]

THE RIGHTWARD TURN IN ELECTORAL POLITICS

Conservative business elites would not have been as influential as they were, however, had Republicans not been able to build a politically effective "top-down" coalition, gaining mass support from white voters.[22] Whereas black support for Democratic presidential candidates has been remarkably stable, white support declined 13 percent between 1960–64 and 1992–96. Almost the entire decline occurred among less educated whites. Whereas support for Democratic candidates declined by only 1 percent among college-educated whites, it declined by 14 percent among those without four-year college degrees.[23] As Manza and Brooks observe, "Non-skilled workers moved from being the most Democratic class in all earlier elections to only the fourth most Democratic class in 1996."[24] Meanwhile, professionals were becoming more supportive of Democrats because of their liberal positions on social issues. By 2000, middle-class whites were more likely to vote Democratic than their working-class counterparts, only 40 percent of whom supported the Democratic presidential nominee, Al Gore.[25]

Republicans' growing appeal among whites was especially strong in the South. Electoral realignment among southern whites, underway since the 1940s, when Democrats stepped up concessions to the civil rights movement, became more marked after 1964, and even more pronounced after 1980.[26] Figure 2 shows the rising share of Congressional seats held by Republicans in the former Confederate states and border states. Between 1980 and 2000, Republicans' share of southern House seats grew from 35 to 58 percent, while their share of southern senators grew from 28 to 59 percent.[27]

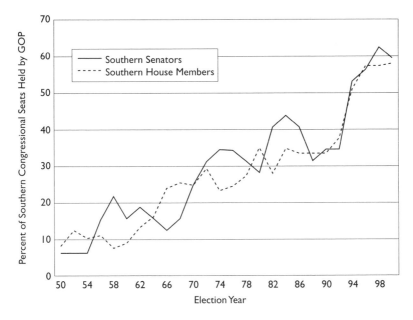

Figure 2. Republican strength in southern congressional seats, 1950–2000. (Southern states include Alabama, Arkansas, Florida, Georgia, Kentucky, Louisiana, Maryland, Mississippi, Missouri, North Carolina, Oklahoma, South Carolina, Tennessee, Texas, Virginia, and West Virginia.) Source: John L. Moore, Jon P. Preimesberger, and David R. Tarr, eds., *Congressional Quarterly's Guide to U.S. Elections,* 4th ed., vol. 2 (Washington, DC: CQ Press, 2001), pp. 1236–66, 1569–77.

Republican gains in the 1980s and 1990s were partly related to their ability to mobilize resources. Unlike the Democratic National Committee, the Republican National Committee controlled the party's campaign fund, making it better able to strategically channel its funds to close races.[28] Because their policies were more favorable to the rich, Republican Party committees were better fundraisers than their Democratic counterparts. For example, they raised more than three times as much as their Democratic counterparts between 1977 and 1984, enabling them to gather more information about the electorate and its attitudes.[29] Yet, resources alone do not sway voters. The decline of progressive social movements, including the civil rights, feminist, and labor movements, and Democrats' lack of an alternative vision provided an ideological vacuum, a vacuum filled by conservative voices that constructed an emotionally powerful, coherent political discourse.[30]

As George Lakoff suggests, conservatives skillfully drew conceptual links between public policy and a culturally resonant metaphor for morality: the strict father. The "strict father" model of morality emphasizes paternal authority and strict rules in order to encourage "self-discipline, self-reliance, and respect for legitimate authority."[31] Drawing on the popular metaphor of the nation as a family, this moral model presents people as naturally weak and in need of paternal protection from external threats and of strict punishment to reinforce self-discipline and self-reliance. This model for morality underlies support for a variety of disparate policies, including opposition to gun control and affirmative action and support for military spending, welfare reform, and restrictive immigration laws. Lakoff argues that conservatives "have learned that politics is about family and morality and myth and metaphor and emotional identification. They have, over the past twenty-five years, managed to forge conceptual links in the voters' minds between morality and public policy. They have done this by carefully working out their values, comprehending their myths, and designing a language to fit those values and myths so that they can evoke them with powerful slogans, repeated over and over again, that reinforce those family-morality-policy links, until the connections have come to seem natural to many Americans, including the media."[32] Meanwhile, liberals have been unable to construct a bold alternative agenda or a coherent and emotionally powerful discourse of their own. Instead, they have engaged in issue-by-issue debates and appealed to rationality and group interest.[33]

Conservative rhetoric was powerful partly because it drew on widely held racist, sexist, and classist beliefs. Invoking the myth of equal opportunity, conservatives bestow moral authority on dominant groups, viewing their success as the result of moral strength, while blaming the misfortunes of disadvantaged groups on personal deficiencies.[34] The appeal of this paternalistic rhetoric grew among white workers, concerned about the rise of single motherhood and increasingly resentful of government programs for racial minorities and the poor. Such resentments were racially motivated but also fueled by the economic losses that workers experienced at the end of the century.

ECONOMIC LOSSES AND PRAGMATIC CONSERVATIVISM

Poor economic conditions during the Carter years undermined Democrats' image among these voters as the party of prosperity.[35] The 1970s witnessed a period of "stagflation," as economic growth and productivity slowed after 1973. Accompanying this was a shift in the economy from manufacturing to services, which helped keep unemployment levels high. For those at the bottom of the labor market, real wages stagnated or even declined after

1973. Meanwhile, inflation rose, increasing the perceived burden of taxes and social expenditures. Worsening this situation, Democrats approved regressive taxation policies, including a rise in Social Security taxes, which hit workers with below-median incomes the hardest.[36]

As Ruy Texeira and Joel Rogers suggest, white working-class voters became pragmatically conservative in this context. Resentful of Democratic politicians, who did little to alleviate their economic woes, they were attracted to Republicans' antitax message because it promised to save them money. White workers did not, however, become more ideologically conservative. As numerous polls show, they still support federal intervention in many policy areas, including economic management, health care, aid for the elderly, and conservation of natural resources.[37] Nevertheless, Republican appeals to "taxpayers' interests" and attacks on federal programs that disproportionately serve minorities, such as AFDC, public housing, and grants-in-aid to cities, struck a chord with white suburban working- and middle-class voters. Republicans' antitax and antistatist messages strategically pitted white middle-class and working-class "taxpayers" against poor, minority "tax eaters." This united them with ideologically conservative corporations around an antiwelfare agenda, despite differences in their interests regarding regressive taxes, government regulation, and social spending.[38]

Promises that Republicans' tax cuts would stimulate economic recovery and benefit workers were unfulfilled, however. Conditions worsened for most white workers in the 1980s and 1990s. The combined effects of downsizing, deindustrialization, and offshore production significantly raised unemployment rates, which peaked at 9.7 percent in 1982 and remained above 5 percent through 1995.[39] Even during the employment boom of the late 1990s, workers experienced economic insecurity. Because employers relied more heavily on contingent workers, it became more difficult for workers to find long-term fulltime jobs. By 1997, about 30 percent of the labor force was temporary, part-time, or contract workers.[40] Real wages for those at the bottom of the labor market stagnated or declined.[41]

Working-class voters became increasingly disaffected and volatile, as neither party seemed capable of improving their lives. In the Clinton-Dole presidential race in 1996, voter participation was the lowest it had been since 1924. That year, less than half (49 percent) of the voting-age population actually voted, compared to 53 percent in 1980 and 62 percent in 1960. Despite "get out the vote" campaigns by both parties, voting participation levels rose only slightly (2 percent) in the 2000 election.[42] Electoral apathy was especially concentrated among low-income and working-class voters, who were traditionally Democratic. The turnout rate was less than 35 percent for the poorest one-fifth of the population in 1996, compared to 75 percent for the richest one-fifth of Americans, a far larger class gap than in most industrialized countries. Likewise, middle-class voters were 15 percent more likely than working-class voters to vote in 2000.[43] Such trends benefited Republicans and pushed Democrats rightward on welfare issues.

Nevertheless, many white workers renewed their support for the Democrats in 1992, helping to elect Bill Clinton. Clinton's southern roots and his promises to expand social programs to "make work pay" increased his popular appeal. Support for Democrats remained weak, however, and the conservative realignment among nonskilled workers became even sharper after 1992, as wages continued to stagnate or decline and Clinton appeared incapable of fulfilling his electoral promises to working families. Stymied by Congressional opposition, he failed to enact his touted public health insurance program. At the same time, under pressure from Wall Street and the Federal Reserve, Clinton made deficit reduction a major priority. He increased taxes, including the gas tax, and toned down his requests for social programs. Such backtracking was encouraged by Democrats' greater reliance on middle-class and affluent voters. Whereas Kennedy received about three times as many votes from working-class voters as from professional and managerial voters in 1960, in 1992 Clinton received about equal numbers of votes from these classes. Only about one-fifth of Clinton's votes came from working-class voters that year, about the same share as his Republican rival received.[44]

Disappointment with the Democrats gave congressional Republicans record gains in 1994. That year, the GOP gained 55 seats in the House, taking control of it for the first time in forty years. They also ruled the Senate, winning eight additional senate seats. For the first time, they won a majority of southern congressional seats and governorships. As Republicans gained critical mass, a number of southern conservatives in Congress and state legislatures switched parties in the mid-1990s, further accelerating the region's realignment.[45] In the 1990s, Democrats lost seats, mainly in the South and in districts that were predominantly white, working-class, and suburban or rural.[46]

Support for congressional Democrats and President Clinton increased as the economy improved, and as congressional Republicans overstepped their reach and attacked popular social policies, such as environmental regulations, education, and Medicare.[47] These gains were modest, though, and Republicans retained control of Congress after 1996.[48] And, despite high approval ratings for the Clinton administration, class differences in presidential voting continued to decline among whites. Although support for

Republicans continued to be greatest among more affluent voters, a majority of working-class whites supported George W. Bush in 2000.[49]

APPEALS TO RACIAL CONSERVATIVISM

White workers' growing support for Republicans did not reflect only their economic concerns but also their racial conservativism. Since 1964, when congressional Democrats stepped up their support for blacks' demands and Republicans became more conservative on racial issues, race has become the largest cleavage among American voters. While white support for Democrats declined, black support for the party remained remarkably stable, with 90 percent of blacks or more supporting Democratic presidential candidates since then.[50]

Republicans courted the white vote by becoming more conservative on racial issues and employing racially charged rhetoric. This strategy was especially important in the South. As Hastings Wyman Jr., a South Carolinian Republican activist, recalls, "Racism, often purposefully inflamed by many southern Republicans, either because we believed it or because we thought it would win votes, was a major tool in the building of a new Republican Party in the south."[51] This strategy apparently paid off, especially among southern white men, who flocked to the GOP more quickly than their female counterparts. Voter surveys show that Republican identification among southern white men became increasingly associated with opposition to busing programs to integrate schools and aid to blacks over time.[52]

In the 1980s and 1990s, Republicans engaged in a series of attacks on affirmative action policies. As Edsall and Edsall recall: "The Reagan administration consistently established not only its opposition to quotas, goals, and timetables, but also demonstrated that it would challenge these practices whenever possible—in the courts, in the enforcement policies adopted by regulatory agencies, and in the negotiation of consent decrees and other agreements with private and public-sector employers."[53] President George H. W. Bush followed in Reagan's footsteps when he vetoed the Civil Rights Act of 1990, calling it a "quota bill."[54] His son, George W. Bush, similarly opposed affirmative action policies.[55] Conservative attacks on affirmative action were also waged at the state level. In California, for example, a majority of voters (80 percent white), passed Proposition 209 in 1996 to abolish affirmative action in college admissions.[56]

This rollback of civil rights gains was justified through a populist discourse of conservative egalitarianism that portrayed Republicans as advocates of equal opportunity and individual initiative and demonized Democrats as creating unfair special preferences for racial minorities and women. This "race-free political language" helped to legitimize racially conservative policies and increase support for Republicans, especially among white Democrats.[57] A 1981 Washington Post/ABC survey, for example, found that Democrats who supported Reagan in 1980 were more conservative on racial issues than were Reagan's Republican supporters or Democratic loyalists.[58]

Republicans' appeal to white racism was effective in gaining white working-class support, and put pressure on Democrats to follow their path. Democrats continued to defend affirmative action, since doing otherwise would have seriously jeopardized their electoral support among blacks. Nonetheless, they joined Republicans in appealing to racism in more subtle and symbolic ways. Along with Republicans, Democrats called for cutbacks in social programs, such as AFDC, that would disproportionately affect blacks and Latinos.[59] Bipartisan campaigns to "get tough on crime" and wage a "war on drugs"[60] likewise targeted poor people of color and preyed on white anxieties about the growing urban minority "underclass."[61] By 2001, nearly 40 percent of federal prisoners were black, and 32 percent were Latino. Most had been convicted of drug offenses.[62] "Apartheid sentencing" for drug offenses, which penalized users of crack cocaine more heavily than users of heroin or powder cocaine, contributed to such racial disparities.[63] Similarly, prosecutions of pregnant drug-users disproportionately targeted blacks, despite studies showing comparable rates of drug abuse among black and white women.[64]

Republicans also appealed to race-based nativism. Between 1980 and 2000, the number of immigrants doubled (from 14 to 28 million), and their share of the U.S. population grew from 6 to 10 percent. With the end of national origin quotas in 1965, immigrants were more likely to be nonwhite, with most immigrants coming from Latin America and Asia.[65] In response, public support for restrictions on immigration grew. In 1965, 33 percent of national survey respondents favored such restrictions, compared to 66 percent in 1995. The share of Americans falsely believing that most immigrants were illegal also rose, from 49 percent in 1986 to 68 percent in 1993.[66] Much of this nativism is racialized. Polls show significantly greater opposition to Asian, Latin American, and African immigrants than to European immigrants.[67]

Nativism did not emerge spontaneously from below. Anti-immigrant politicians, intellectuals, and organizations encouraged a "moral panic" about the negative effects of immigration. In the 1980s, male immigrants, especially Latinos, were accused of taking jobs away from native-born workers and depressing wages. In the 1990s, as the immigrant population became more feminized, attacks on Latino immigrants focused more heavily on women's and children's use of social services. Despite research to the contrary, immigrants were accused of being overly reliant on welfare and creating a fiscal burden for white taxpayers.[68] Nativist groups, such as the Federation of American Immigration Reform (FAIR), blamed immigrants for "overwhelming schools and welfare rolls."[69]

The backlash against immigrants was also a "reactionary impulse to reconstitute the nation as an ethno-culturally homogeneous . . . collectivity."[70] Symptomatic of this, U.S. English and its allies campaigned for state laws declaring English to be the official language. Such campaigns proved to be highly popular, drawing support not only from conservative white racists, but also liberals concerned about barriers to immigrants' upward mobility. By 1996, twenty-three states had adopted "Official English" measures.[71] Anti-immigrant pundits also emphasized the cultural effects of immigration. A good example is Jean Raspail's (1983) *The Camp of Saints*, whose distribution was financed by FAIR and other anti-immigrant groups. *The Camp of Saints* describes how third world immigrants invaded Europe and destroyed its civilization. Similarly, Peter Brimelow's (1995) *Alien Nation: Common Sense about America's Immigration Disaster* claims that non-Anglo immigrants' cultural diversity is the real threat to the nation,[72] although he also confesses his fear of "the fateful day when American whites actually cease to be a majority."[73] To promote anti-immigrant policies, Cordelia Scaife May gave $2.5 million dollars to FAIR, U.S. English, and the Center for Immigration Studies. FAIR received nearly $300,000 between 1985 and 1989 from the Pioneer Fund, a conservative foundation that previously sponsored eugenics research.[74]

Republican politicians mobilized nativist sentiments, especially during the 1992 and 1996 presidential election campaigns. Republican candidates Pat Buchanan, Pete Wilson, and Bob Dole urged their party to adopt tougher immigration policies and made immigrant-bashing central to their campaigns.[75] For example, Buchanan blamed immigrants for "declining living standards, the widening income gap . . . high crime, declining property values and a general sense that . . . communities are veering out of control." As one commentator put it, immigration was the "Willie Horton issue" of the 1996 primary.[76] Nevertheless, the Republican Party remained divided over immigrant issues, as its moderate wing sought to bring more ethnic and racial minorities into their fold.[77]

Restrictive immigration laws also gained bipartisan support, enabling Congress to pass a series of them in the 1980s and 1990s.[78] The Illegal Immigration Reform and Immigrant Responsibility Act of 1996, passed shortly after Congress denied legal immigrants access to public assistance through PRWORA, was especially punitive. It strengthened border enforcement, increased penalties for misusing or forging identification papers, and expanded the crimes for which immigrants could be deported.[79] In 1996, moderate Democrats, such as Clinton, joined Republicans in calling for greater limits on legal immigration.[80]

After 1996, a number of leading Republicans softened their stance, fearing their anti-immigrant positions had hurt their electoral support among Latinos, a growing segment of Catholic voters who might otherwise join the Republican Party because of its emphasis on traditional "family values." For example, Newt Gingrich and other congressional Republicans supported an amnesty program for thousands of Nicaraguans and Cubans in 1997. In 2001, George W. Bush announced support for a bilateral immigration deal with Mexico that combined a guest worker program with limited amnesty for illegal immigrants. The plan was put on hold, however, after anti-immigrant hysteria mounted following the September 11 attacks on the World Trade Center. The revised plan, announced in 2004, excluded the amnesty provision.[81]

"FAMILY VALUES" AND THE RISE OF THE CHRISTIAN RIGHT

Republicans also courted the vote of white traditionalists, especially evangelicals concentrated in the South, by promoting conservative Christian and "family" values. Conservatives upheld the patriarchal, two-parent, heterosexual nuclear family as the ideal, attacking the rights of women, sexual minorities, and nontraditional families. In his 1980 presidential campaign, for example, Reagan attacked the Equal Rights Amendment, endorsed the female housewife, and opposed women's right to abortion.[82] During the 1992 election, Bush's running mate, Dan Quayle, demonized Murphy Brown, a popular television character, for having a child out of wedlock.[83] Despite Bush's initial objections, the Republican National Committee that year endorsed a constitutional amendment to ban abortion and opposed civil rights for gays and lesbians.[84] Likewise, George W. Bush opposed abortion, except in cases of rape, incest, or to save a woman's life, and opposed Democrats' proposal to allow homosexuals to openly serve in the military.[85] While Democrats were more supportive of feminism and civil rights for gays and lesbians, many expressed concerns about the social consequences of single motherhood and supported the 1996 Defense of Marriage Act, which banned same-sex marriage.[86]

TABLE 8. *National Rates of Divorce, Out-of-Wedlock Births,
and Teenage Births, 1960–2000*

Year	Divorce Rate*	Out-of-Wedlock Birth Rate**	Teenage Birth Rate***
1960	2.2	21.6	—
1980	5.2	29.4	53.0
1990	4.7	43.8	59.9
1996	4.3	44.8	54.4
2000	4.1	45.2	48.7

* Per 1,000 people. SOURCES: U.S. Bureau of the Census 2001b, table 68. U.S. Department of Health and Human Services, National Center for Health Statistics 2001c, table 12.
** Per 1,000 unwed women, aged 15–44. SOURCES: Ventura and Bachrach 2000, table 3; Martin, Park, and Sutton 2002, table 5.
*** Per 1,000 women aged 15–19. SOURCES: U.S. Department of Health and Human Services, National Center for Health Statistics 2001a, table 4; U.S. Department of Health and Human Services, National Center for Health Statistics, 2001b, table B.

In promoting conservative family policies, Republicans appealed to, and mobilized, broad social concerns about the decline of the heterosexual, two-parent, patriarchal household. Public outcry over shifting family patterns did not simply correspond to actual trends in family relations. While rates of unwed motherhood increased in the 1980s and 1990s, rates of divorce and teen motherhood fell in the 1990s but nonetheless remained sources of considerable public alarm (see Table 8). Attacks on unwed and teen mothers, often racially coded, resonated with the public because they gave expression to broader concerns about inner-city poverty, welfare dependency, and long-term shifts in family structures and sexual mores.[87]

Politicians' emphasis on traditional "family values" was linked to the rise of the Christian Right, which revitalized the Republican Party and shifted it rightward on social issues. The politicization and conservative realignment of evangelical Christians, underway since the 1970s, escalated after 1983.[88] Before the 1960s and the spread of dominion theology, most evangelicals separated the church from the purportedly corrupt world of secular politics. Dominion theology encouraged Christians to become more active politically and to utilize secular institutions to return America to its biblical principles, including the traditional family and unfettered capitalism.[89] Republican activists, seeking to revitalize their party, also mobilized evangelical and fundamentalist Christian voters.[90] As part of this effort, New Right leaders lent resources to create and expand Christian Right groups.[91] Most notably, Paul Weyrich, Richard Viguerie, and Ed McAteer (of the Conservative Caucus) convinced Reverend Jerry Falwell in 1979 to use his large Baptist church, weekly television broadcasts, and clergy contacts to build the Moral Majority. Within the first year, 400,000 members joined the Moral Majority, contributing $1.5 million. Meanwhile, Pat Robertson mobilized 200,000 charismatic and fundamentalist Christians for a "Washington for Jesus" demonstration in 1980, while 40,000 Christian right activists attended a series of public affairs briefings.[92] Much of the activism of evangelical and fundamentalist Christians in the 1980s and 1990s focused on countering the demands of the feminist and gay rights movements. They also opposed the spread of secular humanism and sexual liberalism, calling for school prayers and an end to pornography and sex education in public schools.[93]

In 1980, the Moral Majority, Christian Voice, and secular conservative groups, such as the Conservative Caucus and Free Congress Foundation, mobilized voters. Appealing to conservative "family values" and "long-standing evangelical and fundamentalist discontents with a secularized, hedonistic, and permissive society," they drew southern whites into the Republican Party. Christian Voice alone raised some $500,000 for voter mobilization for the 1980 election.[94] Altogether, these groups reportedly registered between two and three million new evangelical voters for this election. Evangelical voters supported Ronald Reagan, who endorsed a constitutional amendment for prayer in public schools and several anti-abortion measures. Reportedly, evangelicals made up two-thirds of Reagan's ten-point margin over Jimmy Carter.[95]

After 1980, conservative and Christian organizations, including Pat Robertson's newly formed Freedom Council, continued to mobilize voters. The effectiveness of such mobilization drives is not clear, however. Data from the National Election Studies show no evidence of a mobilization or realign-ment among denominationally conservative Protestants or southern Baptists between 1960 and 1982.[96] Likewise, national surveys show that a relatively constant 11 to 15 percent of whites supported the Christian Right between 1980 and 1988.[97] Nevertheless, by the mid-1980s, the Christian Right had become a significant pressure group within the Republican Party and pushed it to become more supportive of conservative social policies.[98] Jeff Manza and Clem Brooks claim that the rising influence of the Christian Right on the Republican Party was "due not so much to a rapid increase in votes from con-servative Protestants, but instead from the loss of the moderating influence of liberal (and moderate) Protestant voters." Liberal Protestants both shrank in number and became more Democratic after the 1960s.[99]

The Christian Right lost some support in the late 1980s, when its most prominent televangelists became mired in personal scandal.[100] Nevertheless, the Christian Right remained active, raising about $27 million and winning about one million votes (about 9 percent of the total) for Pat Robertson's 1988 bid for the Republican presidential nomination. Robertson was mainly popular among charismatic Christians and evangelicals; surveys indicate that Robertson's supporters tended to be less affluent, less educated, more female, younger, more likely to be from the South and rural areas, and more new to politics than other Republican supporters. After Robertson lost the nomination, 80 percent of evangelical voters supported George H. W. Bush.[101] Although Bush's top advisors consulted with a hundred Christian Right leaders shortly after his election, the Bush administration disappointed them by providing only lackluster support for their causes.[102]

Robertson's defeat and the preacher scandals were only temporary setbacks for the Christian Right. By the early 1990s, the religious broadcasting industry put forward new preachers, who quickly gained large audiences. Meanwhile, conservative Christian leaders focused more heavily on state and local politics, where they made significant gains. They revitalized their movement by reaching out to racial minorities, running "stealth candidates,"[103] and forming alliances with secular conservatives.[104] They also formed new interfaith organizations to replace Jerry Falwell's Moral Majority, which disbanded in 1989. The most important of these was Pat Robertson's Christian Coalition, claiming more than one million members and 1,700 chapters in 1995.[105] Meanwhile, Dr. James Dobson merged his Focus on the Family radio broadcast ministry, heard on 1,300 stations in 1989, with the Family Research Council and used both groups to lobby for conservative family policies. Concerned Women of America (CWA), a conservative, mass-based lobbying organization formed in 1979, also grew, claiming more than 600,000 members by 1992.[106]

In the 1990s, the Christian Right increased their activism within the Republican Party. A 1994 study found that it played a dominant or substantial role in the state Republican Party in thirty-one states, including ten of the eleven former Confederate states.[107] The Christian Right was also active within the national Republican Party. In the 1992 Republican primaries, Pat Buchanan won between 20 and 30 percent of the votes (more than twice the portion garnered by Robertson in 1988).[108] That year, more than 40 percent of the delegates to the Republican National Convention were evangelical Christians, while an estimated 15 to 20 percent were Christian Coalition members. Their members also made up almost 20 percent of the Republican platform drafting committee.[109] Over George H. W. Bush's objections, this committee endorsed home schooling, school prayer, and bans on abortions and pornography, and opposed civil rights for gays and lesbians, public funding of "obscene" art, and the distribution of contraceptives in public schools.[110] The platform helped maintain the religious Right's support for Bush, who won a majority among only two demographic groups: people making more than $100,000 a year and white evangelical Christians.[111]

Clinton's victory in 1992 mobilized the Christian Right and reunited Republicans. The Christian Right, now drawing support from a wider range of faiths, was both a beneficiary of and a political force behind Republicans' unprecedented victories in the 1994 midterm Congressional elections.[112] The Christian Coalition distributed 30 million voter guides in 1994 and 45 million in 1996. According to one survey, about 20 percent of Americans claimed to have relied on this literature.[113] By 1996, religious conservatives who attended church at least once a week and claimed that religion guided their life a "great deal" made up 9 percent of all voters but 23 percent of all GOP voters.[114] In the 2000 election, more than half of George W. Bush's supporters were white Christians who regularly attended church, while two-fifths were evangelicals.[115]

While Republican support for conservative social policies may have helped to garner support from the Christian Right and white men, 60 percent of whom voted for George W. Bush in 2000,[116] it alienated women, especially working women, from the party. Accompanying the rise in women's labor force participation, the gender gap in the vote has increased gradually since the 1950s. The conservative realignment of the white electorate, even in the South, has been most pronounced among men. Based on analyses of data from the National Election Study, Manza and Brooks found that working women's support for social spending and feminism, significantly higher than that of men and nonworking women, accounts for much of this gender gap.[117]

The rise of the Republican Right and the New Democrats at the end of the century reflected shifts in both elite and electoral politics. First, in response to globalization, economic restructuring, and a wave of regulatory reforms in the 1960s and 1970s, many corporate heads embraced neoliberalism and became more politically mobilized. In response, politicians of both parties, but especially the Republicans, championed rollbacks in corporate taxes, economic regulations, and social programs.

Second, both Republicans and Democrats moved rightward on social issues, as they competed for the support of white traditional voters. Republicans revitalized their party by gaining support from white southerners, evangelical Christians, and white working-class males. They did so by constructing an emotionally powerful, coherent conservative discourse that drew support from the widely held "strict father" model of morality, which emphasizes paternal authority and strict rules to encourage self-reliance. This same moral model was used to justify welfare cutbacks, rollbacks in affirmative action, and strict immigration policies, an agenda that appealed to the antitax and racial sentiments of white workers, especially in the South. Republicans also drew support from the Christian Right. Encouraged by the spread of dominion theology and funding from Republican strategists, the Christian Right became a powerful political force by the 1980s, especially in the South. While moderate Protestants generally shifted their allegiance to the Democrats, evangelical and fundamentalist Christians remained loyal, and increasingly active, members of the Republican Party, pushing it to the right on social issues.

As Democrats lost electoral support among traditional white voters, they also moved rightward on social issues, championing tough new criminal justice and immigration policies, expressing alarm about the social consequences of "father absence," and signing into law the 1996 Defense of Marriage Act. This defensive strategy was only partially successful. While it reduced Republicans' lead somewhat, working-class voters were becoming increasingly volatile and disinterested in electoral politics. Without a bold new agenda and rhetoric of their own, Democrats were unable to regain the popularity they once had with working-class white voters.

The growing coalition of Republican voters brought new power to the Republican Party but also increased divisions within it. Serious disputes emerged between social and economic conservatives, between its religious and secular wings, and between racial and gender conservatives and those seeking votes from minority and women voters. Nevertheless, by appealing to the reactionary racist and patriarchal sentiments of white working-class voters, the Republican Party gained considerable electoral ground and broke the back of an already weakened New Deal coalition. Attacks on welfare mothers provided Republicans with fertile ground for attacking liberals and uniting its disparate constituents: racial conservatives, nativists, the Christian Right, and neoliberal corporate elites. Meanwhile, Democrats, seeking to retain their support among white voters and business donors, retreated in their support for AFDC. The welfare backlash that followed is the subject of the next two chapters.

9. Business Interests, Conservative Think Tanks, and the Assault on Welfare

> We know why the welfare bill passed
> Why the Congress puts the moms last
> The bosses want more cash
> Off families they can trash.
>
> "STOP TANF IN 2002,"
> a song by Pat Gowens

> It certainly seems to me, in my most cynical moments, that there
> is a conscious effort to retain a serving class and that there is no real
> intention of thinking through how you effectively pull people out
> of poverty. Somebody's got to serve McDonald's [food], somebody's
> got to do your dry cleaning. Somebody's got to be there to meet the
> needs of the owning class.
>
> 9TO5 WELFARE RIGHTS ACTIVIST

By 1997, the year after PRWORA was enacted, outgoing secretary of Labor Robert Reich noted, "Almost eighteen years ago, inequality of earnings, wealth, and opportunity began to increase, and the gap today is greater than at any time in living memory."[1] Business leaders' dogged pursuit of deregulation and the "low-wage" road to economic growth was apparently paying off. Since the late 1970s, corporations aggressively attacked any possible countervailing power that might get in their way, including organized labor, labor laws, environmental regulations, and welfare.[2]

By 1996, the U.S. Chamber of Commerce, the country's largest business federation, made welfare reform one of its highest priorities. As it testified to Congress, a 1995 survey of their members found that "welfare reform was second (behind unfunded mandates) on a list of 64 issues ranked by importance." An earlier survey of six hundred of their members had found that "99 percent advocated an overhaul of the current welfare system. While 76 percent said that welfare recipients should be eligible for federally funded education and training services, 98 percent believed that those who receive such services should be required to work. An overwhelming percentage—

94 percent—supported placing a limit on the amount of time that one can receive welfare benefits."[3] The chamber was primarily interested in strengthening work requirements and promoting time limits, the focus of its 1995 congressional testimony, but it supported all of the main components of PRWORA.[4] The chamber's testimony was the tip of the iceberg in terms of business efforts to promote welfare cutbacks. Of the nearly six hundred witnesses testifying in welfare reform hearings before the 104th Congress, about one hundred were business representatives.[5] Corporate-sponsored think tanks also shaped wider public debates about welfare, producing a barrage of antiwelfare books, editorials, and research reports, whose findings were picked up and spread through the mass media.

In this chapter, I argue that the rise of a tightly integrated network of right-wing, or "ultra-conservative," corporate-sponsored think tanks, starting in the late 1970s, played a crucial role in shifting political debate about welfare rightward and undermining public support for welfare in the 1980s and 1990s. These right-wing think tanks developed an emotionally powerful antiwelfare rhetoric that drew strength from widely held social values, such as the work ethic and individualism, and from public hostility toward poor minorities, unwed mothers, and immigrants. I then argue that business support for restrictive welfare policies, most concentrated among low-wage and ideologically conservative business elites, is linked to the rise of neoliberalism, economic restructuring, and economic globalization.

THE RISE OF RIGHT-WING THINK TANKS

In response to rising international competition, falling profits, and the wave of environmental and labor regulations of the 1960s and 1970s, the corporate rich increasingly invested in right-wing think tanks.[6] While the budgets of "moderate-conservative" think tanks, such as the Brookings Institution, also rose, they did not keep pace with the rising budgets of "ultra-conservative" think tanks, such as the American Enterprise Institute (AEI), the Hoover Institution, and the Heritage Foundation.[7] Between 1970 and 1983, the budgets for AEI and Heritage grew tenfold, Hoover's budget quadrupled, but Brookings's budget only doubled. Funds for conservative think tanks came from bankers, oil barons, and a range of other large corporations, as well as an influential network of conservative foundations financed through family fortunes and corporate donations.[8] The twelve leading conservative foundations donated more than $1 billion, awarded $300 million in grants, and used $210 million to support particular conservative policy goals between 1985 and 2000.[9] As a result, the budgets of the leading conservative think tanks were about four times the size of the budget for the typical liberal think tank.[10] As right-wing think tanks grew between 1973 and 1990, their directors also became better integrated and prominent in policy planning networks.[11] The appointment of fellows from conservative think tanks to high-ranking government positions under Republican administrations in the 1980s and 1990s also increased their influence.[12]

Right-wing think tanks promoted a highly conservative agenda based on free market principles, which included labor market deregulation, tax cuts for the wealthy, privatization of public social services, and reduced federal spending on and authority over welfare.[13] Their ideologues tirelessly promoted welfare reform, publishing a barrage of books, papers, magazine articles, and editorials by "social scientific" experts, whose "data" and technical jargon legitimated the views of their wealthy donors and leaders.[14] They also organized conferences, sometimes broadcast over C-SPAN, to build consensus on welfare issues among politicians, business leaders, philanthropists, and conservative experts.[15] As one scholar put it, "Conservative think tanks wield great influence simply by being the source of a large portion of available information and analysis on any given public policy issue."[16] Think tank fellows, freed from university teaching and service and endowed with ample travel budgets, spend much of their time talking with journalists, participating in television and radio shows, testifying to Congress, and delivering public lectures. These think tanks also provide politicians and journalists with free copies of streamlined policy briefs and maintain elaborate web sites, giving congressional staffers and journalists instant access to their research reports and recommendations.[17] Too busy themselves to keep abreast of current policy research and ideas, politicians, businessmen, and journalists often rely on these resources to familiarize themselves with the issues and formulate their own positions.[18]

Right-wing think tanks maximize their influence by cultivating ties to policy makers. Their government relations specialists maintain close contact with politicians, organizing special briefings for them, hand delivering publications, and even responding to specific research requests. Along with specialized reports, they provide politicians with broad political agendas, such as the Heritage Foundation's *Mandate for Leadership* and Cato Institute's *Handbook for Congress*.[19] Conservative think tanks also organize special conferences for politicians to promote their policy ideas.[20] For example, in 1995, Governor Pete Wilson urged his fellow governors to support "fundamental changes" in the welfare system at a Heritage-sponsored forum.[21] That same year, Heritage cohosted a conference highlighting welfare issues for incoming congressional conservatives.[22]

In addition, right-wing think tanks sell their ideas to the wider public by hosting their own television and radio shows and building ties to the mass media.[23] Such efforts have apparently paid off. In 1996, the year that PRWORA passed, conservative think tanks were cited seven times more than progressive think tanks by the mainstream media. Heritage's "welfare expert," Robert Rector, was cited by the mainstream news media an average of more than fifteen times a month that year.[24] Journalists often use think tank fellows' "findings," even when they are misleading. For example, Rector charged that the United States had spent $5.4 trillion (later, $8 trillion) on welfare since the onset of the War on Poverty, with little influence over the poverty rate, a claim reported by leading national newspapers and PBS. However, only 30 percent of this figure went to households receiving AFDC, which is what most Americans understand by "welfare."[25] Similarly, a widely publicized Cato Institute study, which claimed that AFDC paid more than low-wage jobs in every state, falsely assumed that most recipients receive additional benefits, such as housing assistance.[26]

Not only did right-wing think tanks monopolize public debates, but they crafted a coherent welfare agenda and an emotionally powerful and culturally resonant rhetoric to justify it. To promote cutbacks, fellows revived "culture of poverty" arguments that blamed poverty on the lack of a strong work ethic and traditional "family values," and on an inability to delay immediate gratification. They thus deflected attention from larger structural problems, such as inner-city job shortages and employer discrimination.[27] They blamed the welfare system for being overly permissive and encouraging laziness and out-of-wedlock childbearing among the poor. In doing so, they forged links between welfare opposition and racist stereotypes of poor blacks and Latinos, white taxpayers' resentment of government spending, and social anxieties about the rise of single motherhood. In addition, right-wing think tanks appealed to the broadly held "strict father" model of morality,[28] the work ethic, and patriarchal family values by advocating paternalistic "get tough" welfare rules to promote self-sufficiency through marriage and work. While they differed in the details of their policy proposals, they agreed that welfare eligibility should be restricted and welfare-to-work (WTW) programs expanded. The similarity in their views on welfare is not surprising. Donors rewarded them for having a shared "free market" political vision, and they often shared major funding sources.[29] Shared policy prescriptions were also encouraged by interlocking boards, close collaboration, and interaction through seminars, conferences, and policy forums on welfare issues.[30] For example, in 2001, Cato Institute hosted a policy forum on President Bush's "charitable choice" provisions, publicized through C-SPAN. Participants included representatives from Heritage Foundation and religious organizations, many of who favored Bush's proposals. The debate was narrowly focused on how charitable services should be financed, and conveyed a consensus that faith-based charities should replace public welfare agencies.[31]

Nevertheless, there were, and continue to be, important differences in the welfare agendas of right-wing think tanks. Socially conservative think tanks promoted tough federal mandates, such as family caps and tough work requirements in the 1990s, and urged Congress to fund marriage and abstinence promotion programs. On the other hand, Cato Institute, a libertarian organization, favored loose federal control over welfare and claimed that workfare programs and marriage and abstinence education were ineffective and expensive.[32] Whereas socially conservative think tanks urged Congress to expand the opportunities for faith-based organizations to compete for government service contracts, Cato argued that these services should be financed solely through charitable contributions.[33] Nevertheless, such differences pale in comparison to the larger similarities in right-wing think tanks' welfare agenda.

By funding multiple experts to reiterate similar principles in slightly different forms, conservative donors have narrowed the political debate on welfare. As one researcher astutely predicted in 1981, "By multiplying the authorities to whom the media are prepared to give a friendly hearing, [conservative donations] have helped to create an illusion of diversity where none exists. The result could be an increasing number of one-sided debates in which the challengers are far out-numbered, if indeed they are heard from at all."[34]

RIGHT-WING THINK TANKS: A SNAPSHOT

Most "ultra-conservative" think tanks promoting welfare cutbacks in the 1980s and 1990s represented a socially conservative perspective that combined free market principles with conservative Christian and patriarchal "family values." The largest and most powerful of these were the American Enterprise Institute and the Heritage Foundation. Founded in 1943, AEI's budget grew remarkably in the 1970s, from $800,000 in 1970 to $11.7 million in 1982. Most of its funding came from corporate contributors and about half from conservative foundations. Dependent on the wealthy, AEI is at their beck and call. In 1986, Olin and Smith Richardson Foundations deemed AEI's agenda too centrist and withdrew their support. When AEI moved its politics farther to the right, it was heavily rewarded. AEI's budget nearly doubled, from $12.6 million in 1994 to $23.7 million in 2000, enabling it to employ more than fifty scholars. Corporate executives not only fund AEI, but also dominate its board of trustees, making up a large majority of its trustees.[35] In the mid-1990s, AEI's president, Christopher Demuth, who served as Nixon's staff assistant and as administrator of the Office of Information and Regulatory Affairs under Reagan, bragged, "We are delighted to be members of good standing of the Washington Establishment, called upon many times each day for Congressional testimony, media commentary, and advice on all manner of current policy issues."[36]

Among those issues was welfare reform. In 1995, House Speaker and antiwelfare champion Newt Gingrich asked Robert L. Woodson Sr., AEI research fellow from 1977 to 1995, to form a national welfare task force to make policy recommendations to Congress. The task force, whose meeting was sponsored by the conservative Bradley and Bader Foundations, advocated tightly regulating the poor, abolishing prevailing wage laws, contracting out welfare services to private agencies, and minimizing government regulations on social services.[37]

The Heritage Foundation, promoting both "free enterprise" and "traditional American values,"[38] experienced even more rapid growth than AEI, becoming one of America's leading conservative think tanks. Heritage was the brain-child of New Right activists Paul Weyrich and Edwin Feulner, who believed that AEI was not aggressive enough in the 1960s and decided to establish a conservative rival to the Brookings Institution. With backing from key Republican leaders, Heritage was launched in 1973 with a $250,000 grant from Joseph Coors (the beer baron).[39] It quickly gained the support of two other conservative business leaders: Roy Rogers (the fast food entrepreneur), and Richard Scaife (heir to the Mellon banking fortune).[40] Ten years later, Heritage's $10.6 million budget almost rivaled AEI's, and then nearly tripled, reaching $28.7 million in 1996.[41] Heritage currently employs more than two hundred staff, including twenty-six research fellows, and is in the process of doubling the size of its Washington-based office.[42] In 1995, the vice president of Heritage boasted that it had "become Congress' unofficial research arm," while another top official claimed it was "involved in crafting almost every piece of major legislation to move through Congress," including welfare reform.[43]

Other right-wing think tanks that pushed for welfare cutbacks in the 1980s and 1990s were the Hudson Institute, Empower America, and the Manhattan Institute. Hudson, founded in 1961 and well endowed by conservative foundations, had a $7 million budget in 1995.[44] Hudson's interest in welfare reform grew in the 1980s, when the federal Department of

Health and Human Services channeled big research projects on "dependency" to it.[45] Formed by Republican leaders shortly after Bush's defeat in 1992, Empower America aimed to revitalize the Republican Party and promote conservative policies.[46] The Manhattan Institute for Policy Research, a New York-based think tank founded in 1978, was conceived by Anthony Fisher, a British economist who greatly influenced Prime Minister Margaret Thatcher's policy agenda. William J. Casey, CIA chief under Reagan, served as Manhattan's first chair, and early trustees included Edwin J. Feulner, head of the Heritage Foundation. Initially begun with $500,000, Manhattan's budget tripled in the 1990s, from $2 million in 1991 to $6.3 million in 1998. In 2002, Manhattan employed nearly thirty senior fellows representing a range of conservative thought. Its welfare specialists tended to be socially conservative, however, promoting traditional family and religious values. About half of Manhattan's budget came from private, mostly conservative foundations, while one-quarter was from corporate donations. Manhattan shaped national policy debates mainly by influencing the agenda of New York's opinion leaders and policy makers through its quarterly magazine, *City Journal*, and lavish luncheons.[47]

Working alongside these large, multi-issue conservative think tanks to promote welfare reform were specialized think tanks affiliated with the Christian Right, such as the Acton Institute for the Study of Religion and Liberty, the Family Research Council (FRC), and Institute for American Values (IAV). Acton, founded in 1990 and led by conservative Christian leaders, heads of corporations, and representatives from AEI, Heritage, and Cato Institute, seeks to unite religious scholars, ministers, and business leaders around free market and Christian principles.[48] In 2002, Acton claimed twenty-seven staff members and seven affiliated scholars.[49] FRC was co-founded in 1983 by James C. Dobson, a leader of the conservative "pro-family" movement who served as a consultant on family policies under Reagan. Until recently, it was led by former Reagan administration officials.[50] Like other conservative Christian groups, FRC views the two-parent, patriarchal, heterosexual family as superior to other family forms, and designs policies to strengthen it.[51] In the mid-1990s, it had a $10 million operating budget to promote its policy agenda.[52] IAV, founded in 1987 and heavily funded by the Bradley, Scaife, and Olin foundations, also provides research for the conservative "pro-family" movement. Scholars and policy advocates make up most of its board of directors, but nearly half are corporate executives. Although it has only one-tenth FRC's operating budget, its leaders are some of the most prominent advocates of conservative family policies.[53]

Like these socially conservative think tanks, the libertarian Cato Institute, founded in 1977, also promoted welfare cutbacks. In 2002, Cato had a $13 million budget, employed ninety full time employees, sixty adjunct scholars, and sixteen research fellows. Currently, eleven of thirteen members of its board of directors are corporate heads.[54] Since 1998, Cato has been the second most cited think tank in the mainstream press after the Brookings Institution.[55]

These right-wing think tanks frequently collaborate with each other, Republican policy makers, and Christian Right groups. Experts, leaders, and activists affiliated with the Christian Right frequently participate in seminars and policy forums on welfare issues put on by conservative think tanks. For example, religious leaders and representatives of grassroots Christian Right organizations, such as the Traditional Values Coalition, participated in a series of welfare reform conferences between 1999 and 2001 on the role of the faith-based community that were sponsored by the Brookings Institution, Manhattan Institute, and Heritage Foundation.[56]

Together, these socially conservative think tanks promoted a fairly consistent set of welfare policies at the end of the century. Through tough new welfare rules, marriage and abstinence promotion, and faith-based services, they aimed to promote the three W's among the poor: work, wedlock, and worship. They also called for reducing federal authority over welfare and for replacing AFDC with a system of fixed block grants.

THE RIGHT-WING WELFARE AGENDA

Promoting Wedlock

In attacking the existing welfare system, right-wing think tanks claimed, despite evidence to the contrary, that it encouraged unwed and teen motherhood. Such criticisms demonized unwed welfare mothers, disproportionately black and Latina, portraying them as modern-day "welfare queens" who would pass on their bad values to their children and were incapable of competently raising children on their own. For example, the president of the Institute for American Values, David Blankenhorn, who wrote *Fatherless America* (1995) and served on the National Commission on America's Urban Families under the George H. W. Bush administration, claimed that "father absence," encouraged by welfare, is "the leading cause of declining child well-being in our society [and] the engine driving our most urgent social problems."[57] Likewise, William Bennett, cofounder of Empower America, warned that "illegitimacy is the surest road to poverty and social decay."[58] To support such arguments, conservative experts point to the high rates of delinquency, school dropouts, and other problems among the children of female-headed households, ignoring evidence that such connections are due primarily to poverty rather than "father absence" per se.[59]

The argument that welfare should be abolished because it encourages unwed motherhood was made most forcefully by Charles Murray in his book, *Losing Ground: American Social Policy, 1950–1980* (1984). According to Murray, a former fellow at the Heritage Foundation, contemporary poverty is mainly due to the twin evils of "dependency" and "illegitimacy" that were encouraged by the expansion of welfare. Playing the race card, Murray blamed white liberals for the "welfare mess": "Race is central to the problem of reforming social policy . . . because the debate has been perverted by the underlying consciousness among whites that 'they'—the people to be helped by social policy—are predominantly black and black people are owed a debt. . . . Whites began to tolerate and make excuses for behavior among blacks that whites would disdain in themselves or their children. . . . The system had to be blamed, and any deficiencies demonstrated by blacks had to be overlooked or covered up—by whites."[60] Murray thus claimed that poor blacks' behavior, encouraged by white liberals' permissive policies, was the real cause of their poverty, reviving long-standing stereotypes of poor blacks as lazy, promiscuous, and irresponsible. Manhattan Institute paid Murray $35,000 to write *Losing Ground*, and then promoted it through a $125,000 advertising campaign, funded mainly by grants from the Scaife and Olin Foundations.[61] With funding from the Pioneer Fund, Murray later wrote *The Bell Curve* (1994) with Richard Hernstein,[62] which argued that whites are naturally more intelligent than blacks and Latinos, and advocated "ending welfare to discourage births among low-IQ women."[63]

Murray later became AEI's leading spokesman on welfare. Realizing that Congress would not end welfare, he advocated a "realistic" plan in 1994, which included family caps and rules banning welfare payments to teen mothers. He hoped such draconian measures would scare young women into using contraceptives, abstaining from sex, or marrying their partners.[64] Murray did not stay "pragmatic" for long, however. In 1998, he was once again arguing that the only real way to significantly reduce the "under-class" was to eliminate welfare.[65]

Along with Murray, Heritage fellow Robert Rector urged Congress to eliminate welfare for unwed teen mothers, adopt federal family caps, and expand adoption services.[66] Doug Besharov from AEI likewise argued that unwed motherhood was encouraged by "the idea that welfare is an alternative lifestyle."[67] He attributed the rising rate of black unwed motherhood to behavioral problems, such as the spread of crack cocaine, rather than inner-city job shortages and high male unemployment rates, which discouraged family formation. Appealing to the "strict father" model of morality, Besharov advocated restrictions on teen mothers' welfare benefits, claiming that this policy was how most parents would handle the problem, "which is say: stay at home, finish school, take care of your kids, get a job, and we are not going to finance you in a separate apartment."[68]

William Bennett, a former research fellow at Hudson and Heritage and cofounder of Empower America, was another leading champion of welfare reform. After serving as Reagan's secretary of education and George H. W. Bush's former drug czar, Bennett became a leading expert on public morality, authoring numerous books, including his best-selling collection of morality tales, *The Book of Virtues*. Despite his well-known habit of high-stakes casino gambling, Bennett urged the public to confront their personal vices and blamed liberal social programs for the nation's moral laxity.[69] Through numerous editorials, talk show appearances, and public speeches, Bennett promoted the idea that welfare encouraged women to bear children out of wedlock and urged Congress to adopt punitive policies to discipline poor young women.[70] Bennett confidently proclaimed: "Here's 'tough love' on a large scale: end welfare, and young girls considering having a baby out-of-wedlock would face more deterrents, greater social stigma, and more economic penalties arrayed against them if they have their babies. There would, therefore, be far fewer births to unwed mothers." Realizing that Congress would not "end welfare," Bennett urged Congress, through testimonies, advertisements, and radio appearances, to devolve responsibility for welfare onto the states, enabling them to experiment with restrictive regulations and to cut off welfare to unwed teens.[71]

Hudson fellow Michael Horowitz testified to Congress in 1995 that welfare was encouraging dependency and "illegitimacy," and urged them to make major cutbacks.[72] Horowitz, who served as general counsel for the Office of Management and Budget under President Reagan and as chairman of Reagan's Domestic Policy Council on Federalism, urged Congress to stop providing welfare to unwed teens living alone, claiming that "taxpayers have suffered, but the children of those mothers have suffered most of all from this arrangement."[73] The Family Research Council (FRC) worked hand in hand with conservative think tanks and the Christian Right to promote family caps and bans on benefits for teens.[74]

In addition to these punitive policies, some socially conservative think tanks promoted state-sponsored programs to promote abstinence, marriage, and "responsible fatherhood" among low-income families. Heritage and a coalition of conservative "pro-family" groups were the main advocates for using welfare money in 1996 to promote abstinence and marriage.[75]

Meanwhile, the Institute of American Values and the National Fatherhood Initiative, cofounded by IAV's president in 1994, promoted the spread of federally funded "responsible fatherhood" programs across the nation. These programs, often administered through child support enforcement offices, put unemployed fathers to work and encouraged them to be more involved in their children's lives.[76]

Since 1996, socially conservative think tanks, such as Heritage Foundation, pushed for expansions in abstinence, marriage, and "responsible fatherhood" programs, policies that were quickly embraced by the George W. Bush administration.[77] Heritage's Robert Rector, complaining that states did not make serious efforts to reduce out-of-wedlock childbearing, claimed that Congress's "first priority" for welfare reform reauthorization should be to "strengthen marriage and reduce illegitimacy."[78] Heritage proposed that states should lose welfare money if they failed to reduce their nonmarital birth rate. Defending such proposals, Rector claimed that "the collapse of marriage is the principal cause of child poverty and a host of other social ills."[79] Another Heritage fellow, Patrick Fagan, pushed for even broader policy reforms to reinforce the traditional two-parent family, such as covenant marriages to make divorce more difficult, adoption reform, and church-based outreach programs to encourage unwed teen mothers, especially black ones, to give up their children for adoption.[80] Meanwhile, William Bennett, of Empower America, published a revised edition of *The Index of Leading Cultural Indicators* (1999), which proclaimed that "the break-up of the American family is the most profound, consequential, and negative social trend of our time."[81]

Hudson also pushed for expansion of marriage promotion and "responsible fatherhood" programs. Teaming up with IAV, it published Wade Horn and Andrew Bush's *Fathers, Marriage, and Welfare Reform* (2002). Horn and Bush, cofounders of the National Fatherhood Initiative, urge politicians to use the "bully pulpit" to restigmatize single motherhood, give married couples priority for certain social benefits, such as Head Start and public housing, and pass adoption reforms to make it easier for unwed mothers to put their children up for adoption.[82] Horn, serving as George W. Bush's assistant secretary of Children and Family Services, and Andrew Bush, serving as director of the Office of Family Assistance, wield considerable influence over welfare policies.[83]

Promoting Work

Along with Charles Murray, Lawrence Mead, whose research was sponsored by a variety of conservative foundations and think tanks and who served as an advisor to the Reagan and George W. Bush administrations,[84] was another leading thinker who promoted the idea that welfare was overly permissive and encouraged indolence. Whereas Murray called for welfare's abolition, Mead advocated strict rules to enforce social obligations among recipients in two widely circulated books, *Beyond Entitlement: The Social Obligations of Citizenship* (1984) and *The New Politics of Poverty: The Nonworking Poor in America* (1992).[85] Appealing to long-standing racial stereotypes, Mead argued that strict work requirements were needed because "the worldview of blacks makes them uniquely prone to attitudes contrary to work, and thus vulnerable to poverty and dependency."[86] He claims that, like blacks, the Irish, Southeast Asians, Native Americans, Mexicans, and Puerto Ricans were prone to poverty because they were not diligent workers.[87]

Consistent with Murray and Mead's views, right-wing think tanks urged Congress to adopt hard time limits and strict work requirements, claiming that it was necessary to instill work discipline among welfare recipients in the mid-1990s. For example, Acton Institute's Reverend Robert A. Sirico, a Catholic priest, urged Congress to make deep cuts in public assistance, claiming, "When welfare no longer offers an easy way out, millions more will be persuaded to become more independent."[88] Likewise, AEI's Doug Besharov lobbied Congress to adopt strict time limits and work requirements to discourage welfare "dependency" by increasing the "inconvenience level of being on welfare."[89] Similarly, Heritage's Robert Rector urged Congress in 1995 to adopt stricter work requirements to reduce recipients' "addiction" to welfare.[90] Such testimonies reinforced the racist image of welfare recipients as lazy and drew attention away from the structural bases of unemployment and poverty.

After PRWORA's passage, right-wing think tanks, including AEI and Heritage, urged Congress to strengthen and expand WTW programs.[91] Rector claimed that "work first" policies were necessary for instilling "responsible behavior" and "self-discipline" among the poor.[92] Hudson designed and promoted a draconian new welfare program for Wisconsin, called Wisconsin Works, infamous for its rigid work requirements.[93] Manhattan promoted Wisconsin's policies in a conference highlighting welfare reform's "success stories" and featuring Wisconsin's governor Tommy Thompson, who later became secretary of the Department of Health and Human Services under President George W. Bush.[94]

Block Grants, Devolution, and Privatization

Ultimately, right-wing think tanks sought the abolition of federal welfare programs, claiming they encouraged indolence, out-of-wedlock childbearing, and intergenerational dependency.[95] These groups were optimistic that free of government regulations, the labor market would provide the jobs necessary to employ the poor. As the editor of Manhattan's *City Journal* explained, "We believe the best way to help the poor is to promote economic growth . . . and that the welfare state has been a horrible, terrible mistake that ended up making miserable the people we all hoped it would help."[96] Likewise, Cato urged Congress to deregulate the economy in order to stimulate entrepreneurship among the poor and argued that private charities and adoption services, rather than federal welfare, should serve any remaining needy families.[97]

Right-wing think tanks promoted greater reliance on private agencies to provide welfare services. AEI spread these ideas through a series of books. First, it published Peter Berger and Reverend John Neuhaus' *To Empower People: The Role of Mediating Structures in Public Policy* (1977), which argued that churches and voluntary associations should be revitalized to promote good citizenship. It then produced *Meeting Human Needs: Toward a New Public Philosophy* (1983), which argued that the private sector should play a larger role in the delivery of social services, and hand delivered a copy to President Reagan.[98] In the 1990s, it published *To Empower People: From State to Civil Society* (1996), which it promoted through a conference involving welfare "experts" and congressional politicians. The conference, like the book, explored how poverty and other social problems could be confronted through private charities and churches rather than federal bureaucracies, with all of their "pathologies."[99]

Other right-wing think tanks promoted the privatization of social services and the adoption of "charitable choice" policies.[100] For example, Heritage funded Marvin Olasky's research for *The Tragedy of American Compassion* (1992), which claimed that "successful anti-poverty programs emphasize . . . some level of spiritual involvement."[101] The Acton Institute's publications similarly called for "replacing a failed welfare system with one that lifts its eyes to God."[102] Its president, the aforementioned Reverend Sirico, urged Congress in 1995 to replace the "faceless" federal welfare bureaucracy with faith-based charities that could impress upon unwed mothers the magnitude of their sins.[103] The Cato Institute also urged Congress to replace federal welfare with private charities,[104] promoting these ideas through Michael Tanner's *The End of Welfare: Fighting Poverty in Civil Society* (1996).[105]

Since 1996, conservative think tanks have continued to promote "charitable choice" policies. For example, Heritage's fellow James Payne published *Overcoming Welfare: Expecting More from the Poor and from Ourselves*

(1998), which argued that public services should be replaced with private charities modeled after nineteenth-century "smart samaritans," who expected work in exchange for help.[106] Another Heritage fellow, William E. Simon, who served as the secretary of the treasury in the Nixon and Ford administrations, backed President Bush's proposal to expand "charitable choice" policies, dismissing government assistance as "impersonal, bureaucratic, and empty of any moral or spiritual perspective on life."[107] The Hudson Institute and Manhattan Institute are leading champions of state-church welfare partnerships. Since 1996, they have carefully documented purportedly successful models of these partnerships.[108] John Dilulio, who briefly headed the Bush administration's Faith-Based Initiative, oversaw Manhattan's "faith-based" research project, which produced three books, seven articles, and two conferences.[109]

Right-wing think tanks urged Congress to end federal welfare entitlements, give states greater control over welfare administration, and replace AFDC with a block grant system.[110] These policies represented a backlash against the expansion of federal grants-in-aid programs and the reduction of local discretion over welfare distribution in the 1960s. Reducing federal control over welfare allowed states to adopt more restrictive welfare policies, while the block grant system put a cap on federal welfare expenditures.[111] Defending the block grant proposal, Heritage's Rector argued: "By slowing the outpouring from the federal welfare spigot, such a welfare spending limit would gradually reduce the subsidization of dysfunctional behavior: dependency, non-work, and illegitimacy. . . . With a cap on the growth of future federal funds, state governments would, for the first time, be forced to adopt innovative and aggressive policies that would reduce the welfare rolls."[112] As Rector predicted, following PRWORA's passage, "get tough" welfare policies and schemes for diverting recipients and applicants from the welfare rolls spread across the nation. State governments have a strong fiscal incentive to adopt these policies, because caseload reductions enable them to allocate welfare funds for other purposes.[113]

NARROWING THE DEBATE: THE BROOKINGS INSTITUTION

A shift in the Brooking Institution's welfare agenda exemplifies how public debates on welfare narrowed after PRWORA's passage. Founded in 1916, Brookings remains one of the largest and most reputable think tanks in Washington circles. After a conservative period in the 1930s and 1940s, Brookings became more moderate in the 1950s. In the 1960s, it was well connected to the Democratic Party establishment. Keynesian economists from Brookings counseled the Kennedy and Johnson administrations and supported President Johnson's War on Poverty. Beginning in the 1970s, however, Brookings became more conservative. By the 1980s, Brookings' scholars were criticizing Keynesian economics, governmental regulations, and welfare spending and claiming that the budget deficit and unions were the main obstacles to economic growth. Robert Roosa, Brookings's chair from the mid-1970s until the mid-1980s, commented, "We do some things on the conservative side—and more so now." Indicative of this, Michael Armacost, Brookings president between 1995 and 2001, was Reagan's former undersecretary of state.[114]

In the mid-1990s, when welfare reform was being debated, Brookings employed about two hundred people, including fifty fulltime scholars, and since then its operating budget has grown considerably, from $21 million in 1997 to $33 million in 2001. Among its many corporate supporters are a number of top national and multinational companies.[115] Wealthy individuals, such as Washington Post owner Kathryn Graham, have also contributed generously to Brookings.[116] Its board of trustees includes executives from major corporations, including Chiquita, CBS/Westinghouse, Fannie Mae, Goldman Sachs, U.S. Airways, and State Farm Mutual Automobile Insurance.[117]

Although Brookings's welfare agenda shifted rightward, it remained more moderate than that of Heritage, AEI, Hudson, Manhattan, or Cato in the mid-1990s. During congressional welfare debates, Brookings criticized many of the more preposterous claims made by right-wing think tanks. For example, they disputed the claim that welfare was the main cause of rising rates of unwed motherhood, pointing out that women on welfare tend to have fewer children than other women and that higher benefits were not correlated with higher rates of unwed motherhood. In contrast to "ultraconservative" think tanks, they defended welfare entitlements and opposed block grant proposals, federal bans on benefits to teen mothers, and strict time limits. They also urged Congress to provide more job training and day care for poor mothers. Nevertheless, like other conservatives, they supported the expansion of WTW programs and greater state control over welfare.[118]

After the passage of PRWORA, Brookings fellows ceded considerable ground to their right-wing counterparts, providing only mild criticism of PRWORA. Fellow Ron Haskins, who was a Republican staff member for the House Ways and Means Committee when it considered PRWORA and a senior advisor on welfare policy for the George W. Bush administration, claimed that "none of the disasters predicted when Congress debated [this] legislation has occurred."[119] In fact, Haskins argued that the law was "the most successful large scale social reform since the New Deal" because it helped to increase work and marriage among poor single mothers.[120] He also recommended that Congress retain many of the policies that Brookings fellows had criticized five years previously, including the block grant system, the five-year lifetime limit, and the elimination of welfare entitlements.[121]

Brookings advocated only minor modifications to right-wing policy proposals. For example, Brookings fellows urged the retention, rather than reduction, of current spending levels. Rather than opposing full-family sanctions, Brookings fellows argued that studies on the "the relative effectiveness of full-family and partial sanctions" were inconclusive, and urged Congress to allow states to use either kind and study the matter.[122] Brookings also called for only "modest" rather than full benefit restorations for legal immigrants.[123] While social conservatives called for more funds for abstinence and marriage promotion, Brookings fellows urged state flexibility in the content of sex education and provided contradictory testimonies regarding marriage promotion.[124] Unlike other right-wing think tanks, Brookings called for more job training and better outreach about Medicaid and Food Stamps to "make work pay."

BUSINESS INTERESTS IN WELFARE REFORM

Views on welfare reform were not uniform within the business community. Support for cutbacks was strongest among the ideologically conservative wing of the business community and low-wage employers, represented by groups such as AEI, Heritage, and the Chamber of Commerce. While each of these groups actively promoted welfare reform, the Conference Board, the Committee for Economic Development, and the Business Roundtable, which represented "the largest, most capital-intensive multinational corporations" did not.[125]

There were also divisions in the 1990s among the business groups promoting welfare reform. For example, mainstream business organizations, such as the Chamber of Commerce, were more supportive of job training for recipients than "ultra-conservative" think tanks, and less enthusiastic about the "pro-church" and "pro-family" welfare policies promoted by socially conservative think tanks.[126] While "ultra-conservative" think tanks called for federal full-family sanctions and abstinence-only sex education, "moderate-conservative" think tanks, such as the Brookings Institution, urged greater state flexibility in setting such policies. Domhoff suggests that these policy differences between "moderate" and "ultra-conservative" think tanks are mainly ideological: "There is a tendency for the moderate organizations to be directed by the most internationally oriented of corporations, but there are numerous exceptions to that generalization. Moreover, there are corporations that support policy organizations within both policy subgroups. Then, too, there are instances in which some top officers from a corporation will be in the moderate camp, and others will be in the ultraconservative camp."[127] The policy differences among these organizations pale in comparison to their larger similarities, however. By 2000, all of these organizations supported time limits, strict work requirements, and the elimination of welfare entitlements.

Why did such large sectors of the politically active business community support welfare reform at the end of the century? First, welfare cutbacks were part of a broader antistatist agenda known as "balanced budget conservativism," which sought to reduce governmental deficits mainly through cuts in social programs. This agenda, increasingly powerful in the 1980s and 1990s, reflected corporate interests in minimizing their taxes and government responsibility for social needs.[128] Although AFDC made up less than one percent of the national budget, dismantling it paved the way for larger cutbacks in Social Security, Medicaid, and education.

For similar reasons, big business also supported the privatization of welfare services. Corporations claimed that the private sector could provide social services more efficiently and cheaply than the public sector, despite the many instances in which private contractors have overcharged the government.[129] Some corporations also sought to enter the multi-billion-dollar welfare business. After the passage of PRWORA, large for-profit companies aggressively pursued and won multi-million-dollar state and local welfare contracts, mainly for WTW case management, job training, and placement services. Maximus and Lockheed Martin (one of the country's largest weapons manufacturers) became two of the nation's leading welfare contractors. By 1998, Lockheed Martin Information Management Systems had landed fifteen welfare contracts in four states, and Maximus had won contracts for welfare services in almost every state by 1999.[130]

Perhaps the biggest reason why corporations support welfare cutbacks, however, is to maintain a supply of cheap labor. Rather than taking the "high-road" strategy for economic growth by investing in technological innovations and skilled labor, American business leaders have pursued the "low-road" strategy of deregulating the labor market, cheapening labor, and making labor contracts more "flexible."[131] Without a safety net and forced to comply with time limits and stringent WTW requirements, poor people are forced to accept—even desperate for—jobs, no matter how menial, temporary, or low-wage. For similar reasons, the business community supported the expansion of the Earned Income Tax Credit, even as they clamored for cutbacks in AFDC. Because eligibility is dependent upon employment, the EITC helps to maintain a ready supply of contingent, low-wage labor for employers.[132] Both TANF and EITC require employment and subsidize the low-wage labor force, ensuring its continued reproduction and survival while minimizing employers' labor costs.

As Peck and Theodore argue, "work-first" models of WTW, on the rise since 1996, nicely complement the need for a flexible, low-wage labor market.[133] The "work-first" model emphasizes initial employment rather than long-term career success and requires participants to accept the first job offered to them. It also concentrates on developing participants' "soft skills," such as resume writing, interview preparation, and wardrobe selection, rather than education or skill development. These programs are attractive because they ensure "a continuously job-ready, pre-processed, 'forced' labor supply for the lower end of the labor market," where turnover rates are high.[134] Acknowledging this, one businessman claimed that PRWORA "created an unprecedented chance for employers to fill their payrolls with new workers, just as a booming economy was making that job more difficult than ever."[135] Across the nation, county welfare departments are administering free drug and skills tests to potential employees, subsidizing customized job training, and funding job fairs. Employers also benefit from free labor and lucrative tax breaks offered to WTW participants who hire welfare recipients in unsubsidized jobs.

WTW programs are especially popular among low-wage employers. According to Welfare to Work Partnership, "Businesses like Burger King franchises . . . swear by it." CVS Pharmacies was another major employer of WTW participants, hiring twelve thousand participants between 1999 and 2001, mostly in entry-level positions.[136] In Missouri, the main beneficiaries of WTW programs were meat processing plants, temporary agencies, and nursing homes.[137] In Milwaukee, Wisconsin, hundreds of WTW participants were placed in temporary jobs, mainly in light industrial, assembly, or warehouse positions.[138] Maximus, one of the city's five welfare contractors, even funneled its own clients into jobs through its for-profit temporary agency, profiting twice from the arrangement.[139] In areas of high unemployment, local governments lowered their municipal labor costs by employing recipients themselves. In New York City, for example, almost seven thousand WTW participants were assigned to work for the Parks Department in 1998.[140]

On the other hand, many employers are reluctant to hire recipients, and WTW programs may not provide the best means of recruiting new workers.

Welfare to Work Partnership, a business-led organization, claims that between 1997 and 2001, it helped a total of 22,000 companies to hire 1.1 million welfare recipients (mostly in minimum-wage jobs), but this was during an employment boom.[141] In fact, WTW programs implemented after 1996 were not as strongly work-oriented as their creators had hoped. Because states received credits toward meeting federal WTW participation requirements for caseload reduction and because of exemptions, only about 34 percent, rather than 50 percent, of adult recipients were actually working by 2002.[142] Even so, welfare reform protects low-wage employers' labor supply interests by symbolically reaffirming the work ethic at a time when workers are experiencing greater employment insecurity and stagnant and declining wages.[143] Time limits and other eligibility rules also increase competition at the bottom of the labor market, putting downward pressure on wages.[144]

Strong evidence supports the idea that corporate support for welfare reform is linked to their need for cheap labor. First, corporate-sponsored think tanks publicly acknowledge that the purpose of welfare reform is to increase the supply of low-wage workers. For example, Robert Lerman, an AEI economist who served as special assistant for youth and welfare policy at the Department of Labor under Carter, claimed: "We have had tremendous job growth in this country. Every quarter 10 to 15 million new hires takes place, even when employment is not growing at all, because of high job turnover. Single mothers should be able to compete with teenagers and immigrants for these jobs; if adequate child care is made available, they will be able to do so."[145] The president of the Chamber of Commerce also claimed that welfare reform would force recipients to compete for low-wage jobs that they might otherwise have avoided: "There are lots of jobs. Anytime there's high unemployment, there's also the long list of jobs that go a-begging. The fact of the matter is everyone wants to start at the middle or upper middle, and now you're going to be driven to start at the bottom and begin to work your way up. And that's the beginning of the end of dependency."[146] As these quotes suggest, business leaders and their experts see welfare reform as a way to increase the low-wage applicant pool.

Second, business groups tried to cut labor costs even further by seeking exemptions from minimum wage and other labor laws for WTW participants. The well-publicized attempt of New York City employers to do this was not an isolated occurrence.[147] The Chamber of Commerce sought to waive the regulation of minimum wages, maximum hours, and overtime payments during a "reasonable probationary period" after welfare recipients were hired by employers. They also sought exemptions from other laws, such as "prevailing wage" policies for government contract employees, medical and family leave laws, and antidiscrimination policies.[148] Business groups continued to press for the exclusion of WTW participants from protective labor legislation, even after the Department of Labor ruled that the Fair Labor Standards Act should apply to WTW participants. In response, Congress included a provision in its budget act stating that WTW participants were not regular employees, but the Clinton administration refused to approve it. Since then, corporate-sponsored think tanks, such as Heritage, have continued to oppose the application of federal labor laws to WTW participants, claiming such laws would increase expenditures.[149] In 1999, Heritage even advocated state flexibility in minimum wages for all workers, so that employers would hire more welfare recipients.[150]

Is corporate support for welfare reform a rational response to economic restructuring and the pressures of the global economy? As international business competition rose and corporations increasingly moved production abroad, employers experienced increased pressure to lower labor costs.[151] At the same time, employment in the labor-intensive service sector rose while employment in the capital-intensive industrial sector fell, further increasing business incentives to cut labor costs.[152] Yet, labor costs are only one factor determining success, and not always the most important one. Many companies remain competitive through technological and organizational innovations or new product designs, a strategy that depends on hiring highly skilled workers.[153] As Esping-Andersen has noted, "It would, indeed, be a sad irony if the West engaged in welfare state dismantling in its drive to remain competitive if, at the same time, the main competition were to raise its labor costs."[154] Lowering labor costs also threatens to decrease product markets.[155] The claim that welfare expenses add to government deficits, which drive up interest rates and taxes and discourage investment, contradicts research showing that investment rates are not very responsive to tax and interest rate variables. For example, in the 1980s, when business investments fell and government deficits rose, interest and taxation rates actually declined.[156] Business's antiwelfare agenda may be more the product of the ascendancy of neoliberalism, racism, and socially conservative ideas than a rational response to new economic realities.[157] It is how corporations perceive and act on their economic interests that ultimately matters in politics.[158]

By the 1990s, the argument that welfare cutbacks were essential to American businesses' ability to compete in the global economy had "become a political force, helping in the creation of the institutional realities it purportedly merely describes."[159] Some claim that business owners needed welfare cutbacks to reduce labor costs and taxes in order to produce cheaper goods and compete with foreign imports. However, the growth in trade openness in the 1980s and 1990s was marginal among highly industrialized countries, and some of the most generous welfare states were in Scandinavian countries with high levels of trade openness.[160] Nevertheless, "the issue lent itself to powerful rhetoric from business and the right and thus may very well have contributed to legitimizing cuts."[161] Cross-national research shows greater support for the argument that capital mobility, which has risen significantly over the past few decades, increased political pressure on governments to reduce welfare spending.[162] Capital mobility puts employers and investors in a good position to pressure policy makers, through either disinvestment or the threat of it, to adopt "business-friendly" policies.[163] Yet, this may be just as much a political as an economic constraint on policy makers. While the availability of cheap labor and low tax rates are particularly important in the decisions about production location of low-wage employers, factors such as access to markets, skilled workers, or infrastructure also shape these decisions. Indeed, the bulk of foreign direct investment flows to other affluent democracies, not third world countries. Nevertheless, economic globalization made "the threat of exit more credible and thereby has enabled business to extract concessions by arguing that a given country's business climate was noncompetitive."[164] Such pressures are especially influential in the United States, given the weakness of third parties capable of countering the power of big business.[165]

In response to the rise of neoliberalism, economic restructuring, and global competition, ideologically conservative and low-wage companies aggressively promoted welfare reform to reduce expenditures and protect their supply of low-wage, casual labor. In addition to lobbying through well-established business organizations, such as the U.S. Chamber of Commerce, they sponsored a powerful, highly integrated network of right-wing think tanks that spewed forth antiwelfare propaganda in books, news editorials, and television and radio programs. This propaganda demonized poor black and brown mothers and blamed teen and single motherhood on "permissive" welfare policies. Right-wing think tanks did not simply promote a neoliberal agenda calling for welfare cutbacks. Most promoted a socially conservative agenda that included rules denying benefits to teens and unwed mothers, public funding for the promotion of marriage, sexual abstinence, and "responsible fatherhood," and government partnerships with faith-based organizations to deliver welfare services. Meanwhile, business groups such as the Chamber of Commerce, representing the interests of low-wage employers, pushed for tougher work requirements, a block grant system, and time limits for welfare mothers. Before the enactment of PRWORA, moderate think tanks, such as the Brookings Institution, defended welfare entitlements and opposed block grants and strict time limits for welfare receipt. After PRWORA's passage, however, they ceded ground on these issues, further narrowing public debates about welfare.

10. Congressional Attacks on Welfare, 1980–2004

> Washington has promoted welfare programs which encourage
> illegitimacy, discourage work, mock marriage, and require
> dependence, consigning generations to hopelessness and despair.
>
> SENATOR JOHN ASHCROFT

The contemporary welfare backlash, on the rise since 1980, was broader in scope and intensity than previous ones, as Democrats as well as Republicans stepped up their attacks on welfare. This chapter provides an overview of this welfare backlash and analyzes the political forces that shaped it. I argue that antiwelfare propaganda and bipartisan attacks on welfare mothers, spread through the mainstream media, increased public opposition to AFDC. Antiwelfare rhetoric resonated with the broader public, especially more affluent and traditionally minded whites,[1] because it tapped into broadly held values, resentments, stereotypes, and concerns. Attacks on welfare mothers exploited racist stereotypes of poor blacks and Latinos and appealed to white resentment toward taxes, civil rights gains, and the recent wave of immigration. The rise in women's labor force participation also increased expectations that poor mothers work. Finally, traditional "family values" and concerns about the rise in single motherhood, especially among blacks and Latinos, created support for punitive policies toward "deadbeat dads," unwed mothers, and teenage mothers. Rising public opposition to welfare in turn put increased pressure on politicians to champion tough welfare policies.

In the 1990s, President Clinton and other new Democrats sought to revive electoral support for their party, especially in the South, by "ending welfare as we know it." However, they lost the upper hand in welfare debates after Republicans gained control of Congress in 1994. Republican control of Congress and of key congressional committees gave conservative groups, especially right-wing think tanks and the Christian Right, considerable influence over the design of the 1996 Personal Responsibility and Work Opportunity Reconciliation Act (PRWORA). Although there was broad public support for strengthening work requirements and adopting time limits for welfare, Congress overreached public opinion in the details of the legislation, adopting more punitive policies and fewer work supports than most people supported. After 2000, with Republicans in control of the White House and Congress, Democrats moved even farther to the right on welfare issues.

THE RISE OF A NEW WELFARE BACKLASH

In the 1980s, as politicians responded to the rise of neoliberalism and competed for the white southern vote, attacks on welfare mothers, under way since the late 1960s, hit new heights. Although Reagan was frequently stymied by Democrats' control of the House, he pushed through a number of tough welfare measures. He did so with the support of moderate Democrats, led by the Democratic Leadership Council, who sought to recapture support among traditional white voters by championing more conservative social policies.[2] In 1981, Reagan gained congressional support for the Omnibus Budget Reconciliation Act (OBRA), which tightened welfare eligibility, cut payments, and encouraged states to develop work demonstration programs, removing an estimated five hundred thousand recipients from the program. In 1982, Congress cut AFDC expenditures again, mostly through penalties to states.[3] However, Reagan did not gain congressional support for his most radical proposal: transferring administrative responsibility for Food Stamps and AFDC to state governments. His workfare proposals were somewhat appeased by the Family Support Act of 1988. The act, which created the Job Opportunities and Basic Skills (JOBS) program, represented a compromise between conservatives and moderates who called for more workfare, and liberal Democrats who called for more education and training for recipients. Administered by the states, the implementation of JOBS varied widely. To conservatives' consternation, most states expanded education and training for recipients rather than workfare.[4]

Politicians and the media frequently appealed to racial stereotypes in their attacks on welfare, although racist antiwelfare rhetoric was more subtle and coded than in the past. For example, as early as 1976, Reagan criticized the welfare system by evoking the image of a Chicago "welfare queen" who lived high on the hog with her fraudulently claimed AFDC check. In a later political campaign, he described a similar welfare cheat, a "woman in Chicago" who "has eighty names, thirty addresses, twelve Social Security cards, and is collecting veterans' benefits on four nonexistent deceased husbands. . . . She's collecting Social Security on her cards. She's got Medicaid, getting food stamps, and she is collecting welfare under each of her names. Her tax-free cash alone is over $150,000."[5] Racialized images of poor people were also promoted by popular magazines and television news stories, which disproportionately portrayed the poor as black, especially when coverage was negative or focused on the "underclass."[6] Magazine articles criticizing welfare as a cause of dependency were significantly more likely to feature unwed mothers and African Americans than articles portraying welfare in a more positive light.[7]

In addition to championing national welfare cutbacks, Reagan stimulated state-level retrenchment through revisions in the federal waiver system. This system, created in 1962, authorized experimental welfare projects that bypassed federal regulations. To conservatives' frustration, the Department of Health and Human Services granted these waivers sparingly, with fewer than twelve significant exemptions approved by 1977. In 1987, Reagan created a new federal commission, the Low-Income Opportunity Advisory Board, to oversee state waiver requests. This board, continued under the George H. W. Bush administration, actively solicited and approved waiver requests to stimulate welfare reform. Most of these waivers sought to increase the employment, training, and education of recipients.[8]

In the early 1990s, both Republicans and Democrats stepped up their attacks on welfare, courting traditional white working- and middle-class voters, especially southern voters and those adhering strongly to traditional social values. Championing the ideas of the Democratic Leadership Council, presidential candidate Bill Clinton promised to "end welfare as we know it" in 1992 through tougher work requirements and two-year consecutive time limits.[9] Clinton's support for tougher welfare rules dates back to the late 1980s, when he urged passage of the Family Support Act as the chair of the National Governors' Association.[10]

As in previous periods, rising attacks on welfare mounted in response to rising caseloads. After fluctuating between ten and eleven million the decade before, the number of AFDC recipients rose from 10.9 million to more than 14 million between 1988 and 1994. After 1994, when economic conditions improved, national caseloads declined. By then, however, politicians were already committed to "end welfare."[11] All this fury over welfare was not a response to the growing expense of AFDC. Since the 1980s, combined state and federal AFDC expenditures actually declined, mainly because politicians did not increase the value of benefits to keep up with the rising cost of living.[12] Welfare was vulnerable to attack, however, because its adult recipients, mainly able-bodied single mothers, were increasingly seen as undeserving. In 1995, 57 percent of cases involved an unwed mother, while another 25 percent involved a divorced or separated mother. While most welfare mothers received welfare for less than two years, about one-fifth received it for more than five years, which contributed to concerns about long-term dependency.[13] Most, or 58 percent, of adult recipients were black or Latino, racial groups more likely to be perceived by the public as lazy.[14]

Along with right-wing think tanks, politicians and the media promoted racist stereotypes of the poor through subtle, and not so subtle, means. Politicians readily engaged in racially coded attacks on "welfare queens," and chided black men for being hypersexed and irresponsible. For example, Ross Perot, presidential candidate for the Reform Party in 1996, appealed to racist stereotypes of black men to explain to his television audience why there were such high levels of welfare dependency among blacks: "I'm just kind of a dumb dude who never finished the fourth grade. I'm wandering around the streets with my baseball hat on backward and $150 tennis shoes I knocked another kid out to get. I'm looking for real trouble to prove that I am a man. Well, how do I define what a man is? I define what a man is from the rap music I hear. . . . A man is defined in that culture as a breeder who gets the woman pregnant and then she gets welfare."[15] Similarly, New Jersey governor Christine Todd Whitman told a London reporter that young African American men often played a "jewels in the crown" game, in which the object was to impregnate the most women.[16] In the late 1980s and early 1990s, blacks were overrepresented in news stories about poverty on television and in national news magazines, especially when these stories were negative in tone, contributing to the false impression that most poor people were black, and feeding racist stereotypes of the black poor.[17]

Politicians also appealed to negative stereotypes of Mexican immigrants as lazy and overly dependent on welfare to justify rules denying public assistance to most legal immigrants. For example, Republican senator Phil Gramm of Texas declared in 1996, "Immigrants should come to the U.S. with their sleeves rolled up, ready to work, not with their hands out, ready to go on welfare,"[18] despite census data showing that most immigrants were working.[19] Like other anti-immigrant pundits, politicians claimed that immigrants were more reliant on welfare compared to their native-born counterparts, despite research contradicting this claim.[20]

The Clinton administration and other moderate Democrats agreed with many of the key features of PRWORA, including time limits for welfare receipt, stricter employment requirements, and looser federal control over welfare administration. Initially, Clinton supported new training and job creation programs and improvements in healthcare and child care to facilitate employment, but the cost of these measures contradicted his top advisors' deficit reduction agenda. By the time his welfare proposals were considered (and rejected) by Congress, Clinton's job creation program had been cut in half and the budget for his job training program represented a 2–3 percent decrease from the job training budget of the George H. W. Bush administration. The president's interagency Welfare Reform Working Group's proposals were highly similar to the bills proposed by Republicans.[21]

Frustrated by congressional opposition to his welfare proposals, Clinton eased restrictions on the approval of welfare waivers to show his commitment to reform. Although he returned authority over these waivers to the Department of Health and Human Services, in 1995 he eliminated the rule that programs be cost neutral, encouraged states to apply for waivers, and adopted a fast-track review process. By the end of 1996, states had registered some four hundred waiver requests.[22] State-level reforms increased political support for federal reforms, especially with the National Governors' Association. As one commentator put it, "What the waiver programs provided was a perception that the central ideas of welfare reform, particularly time limits, had been tested and worked."[23] States received waivers to regulate the reproductive lives of poor mothers through "family caps" (which denied additional aid to mothers who had children while on welfare), incentives for recipients to use Norplant (a birth control drug), and requirements that teen mothers live with their parents. Waivers for tough new welfare-to-work rules, immunization requirements, rules to reduce aid to recent migrants, and across-the-board grant cuts were also approved.[24]

An analysis of state waiver adoptions between 1992 and 1996 suggests that they were shaped by states' racial, economic, and political context. Consistent with the idea that these tough new measures were mainly directed at blacks, states were more likely to adopt these waivers when a higher proportion of AFDC recipients were black. States were more likely to adopt time limits and stringent work requirements when they had a larger low-wage sector, suggesting that these measures were responsive to employers' demand for low-wage labor. States ruled by Republican governors were more likely to adopt welfare waivers, but only when the Christian Right was powerful. States were also more likely to adopt waivers when party competition was more intense or fiscal constraints were greater, suggesting that politicians viewed them as vote-getting and cost-cutting measures.[25]

As new welfare regulations spread across states, the activist Republican Congress that came to power after the 1994 elections, led by southern politicians such as Newt Gingrich, pushed aggressively for welfare reform as part of its "Contract with America." Conservatives were not wholly united on the issue, however. While some were willing to increase funds for WTW programs and work supports, others sought to minimize expenditures.[26]

Some Republicans supported tough federal mandates, while others supported greater state control over welfare regulations.[27]

Because Republicans had a majority in Congress, Democrats were forced to move rightward in order to pass a welfare reform bill. Clinton and many congressional Democrats wanted to avoid blame for obstructing welfare reform and viewed the issue as key to regaining the support of white voters, especially in the South. Already, Clinton had failed to enact a healthcare plan because of Republican opposition, and he did not want to appear to be unable to keep his campaign promises.[28] Clinton was not, however, entirely compromising. Early on, he made it clear that he would not support a bill that included a federal family cap or a ban on benefits for teen mothers, which some Republicans supported. Such policies had little public support and were strongly opposed by organized women's groups, whose support Clinton courted. He also vetoed several bills, one that included cuts to politically popular Medicare and Medicaid programs and another that contained cuts to Food Stamps, federally subsidized school lunches, and deep cuts to legal immigrants' benefits.[29] Eventually, Clinton signed PRWORA into law in 1996, despite reservations, anxious to fulfill his promise to "end welfare as we know it." The bill included a number of policies he did not support, including hard time limits, an end to entitlements, authorization for states to adopt family caps, and deep cuts to legal immigrants' rights to public assistance.[30] Nevertheless, a year later, Clinton was quick to claim credit for declining welfare rolls, claiming that "the debate is over. We now know that welfare reform works."[31]

After PRWORA's passage, many states adopted welfare measures even tougher than those adopted by Congress. Quantitative research shows that states were more likely to adopt shorter consecutive time limits when their unemployment rate was lower, suggesting that politicians were responsive to the demand for labor. States were also more likely to adopt more stringent welfare regulations when a larger proportion of their caseload was black or Latino[32] and when their rate of unmarried births was higher, suggesting that policy makers were more punitive toward unwed mothers and racial minorities. States with more conservative politicians and those that had previously requested a welfare waiver were also more likely to adopt tougher regulations.[33]

PUBLIC OPPOSITION TO WELFARE

Although the U.S. Chamber of Commerce, corporate-sponsored think tanks, and politicians aggressively promoted cutbacks, the welfare backlash also had considerable public support. While opposition to welfare spending decreased somewhat during the recession of the 1980s and in response to Reagan's cutbacks, it remained substantially higher than it had been in the 1960s.[34] Public hostility to welfare reached new heights after Democratic presidential nominee Bill Clinton and other New Democrats called for "an end to welfare as we know it" in 1992, giving legitimacy to Republicans' long-standing criticisms of the welfare state.[35]

The antiwelfare rhetoric of politicians and conservative groups, spread through the media, appealed to many Americans, especially white Americans with higher incomes. Popular media discourse about AFDC was not, however, entirely negative in the 1980s and 1990s. In fact, about twice as many articles in popular magazines contested as supported the idea that welfare creates dependency. Greater numbers of articles emphasized the importance of helping the needy, compared to literature of the previous two decades.[36] Nevertheless, criticisms of AFDC, increasingly promoted by national political leaders from both parties, resonated with much of the public and increased public alarm about the welfare system.

Antiwelfare rhetoric was effective because it spoke to the sentiments and concerns of the white working and middle classes. First, attacks on AFDC provided an appealing target for white working and middle classes' resentment toward taxes, which ran high in the face of stagnant and declining wages, regressive tax policies, and the rising national deficit.[37] Significantly, most Americans did not oppose aid for poor people, especially poor children. However, they were hostile toward "welfare," or AFDC, which was increasingly associated with women of color and single mothers.[38] Attacking welfare mothers and "deadbeat dads," conservatives blamed dependency on the lack of a strong work ethic and traditional family values among the poor. In doing so, their attacks appealed simultaneously to these values, concerns about the rise of single motherhood, and negative stereotypes of poor blacks and Latinos. Conservatives also appealed to the widely held "strict father" model of morality by emphasizing the importance of strict rules and punishments for disciplining the poor.[39]

Rising opposition to welfare was, however, only partly rooted in reactionary sentiments; it also reflected rising expectations that mothers work. Maternal labor force participation, increasingly common even among white middle-class women, undercut support for subsidizing poor mothers to stay at home with their children.[40] Labor force participation rates for married mothers with children under six more than doubled between 1960 and 1980, from 19 to 45 percent, and continued to rise after 1980. By 1996, nearly 63 percent of married mothers with children under six were employed, al-

though not always fulltime.[41] Demands for expanding welfare-to-work programs came in multiple forms: conservative attacks on welfare mothers for
shirking work, working-class resentment of welfare mothers who were able
to stay at home with their children, and liberal concerns about poor mothers' lack of training and work experience. Demands for putting poor mothers to work also reflected long-standing expectations that women of color,
now the majority of adult welfare recipients, should work.[42]

Rising public hostility to welfare was captured in many national public
opinion polls. For example, in 1994, 60 percent of those surveyed said that
the government was spending "too much" on welfare, compared to 40 percent in 1984.[43] Concerns about the efficacy of the welfare system also
increased. In 1995, 72 percent of those surveyed said that public assistance
was not working well, compared to 55 percent of those surveyed in 1985.
Approximately 73 percent of respondents said that welfare discouraged
work, up from 55 percent in 1985. Similarly, about 69 percent of respondents agreed that the "welfare system does more harm than good, because
it encourages the breakup of the family and discourages the work ethic."[44]
A 1995 survey found that 79 percent of respondents thought that most
recipients were "so dependent on welfare that they will never get off of it,"
despite the fact that most received it for less than two years.[45] In 1994, most
Americans claimed that "families getting more welfare benefits than they
need" was a more serious problem than "families not getting enough welfare to get by."[46]

By 1996, welfare had come to be seen as one of the most important problems facing the nation. In this context, politicians viewed welfare reform as
a way to gain political credit rather than incur blame.[47] Surveys taken
between 1993 and 1995 found that between 45 and 64 percent of respondents supported work requirements for mothers of "young children," and
most favored them for mothers of children under three. Polls taken between
1994 and 1996 found that between 67 and 78 percent of respondents favored
a two-year consecutive time limit on welfare use, and most favored a five-
year lifetime limit.[48] Other measures also enjoyed strong public support.
Most Americans favored greater state control over welfare and rules requiring unwed teen welfare mothers to live with their parents. Following conservative campaigns for family caps, most Americans also supported these
by 1993.[49]

National surveys show that opposition to welfare spending was greatest
among politically conservative whites and those with middle or high
incomes. Democrats were more likely than Republicans to support welfare
spending and to believe that poor people wanted to work. There were also

significant class differences in support for welfare spending, with affluent Americans the most opposed to it, followed by middle-income Americans, and then low-income people. Most likely, this is because more affluent Americans are less likely to have personal experience with welfare or know people receiving it, experiences that might counter the negative stereotypes about welfare recipients. Indeed, affluent Americans are generally more likely than lower-income Americans to view poverty as a result of a lack of effort rather than social circumstances. High-income people with personal or familial experiences with being on welfare are less likely than other high-income people to approve of cuts in welfare spending.[50]

Racism against blacks also undermines support for welfare. According to Martin Gilens's analysis of General Social Survey data, the common association that Americans make between blacks and welfare and the racist stereotype that blacks are lazy are important sources of opposition to welfare spending. Indeed, only 35 percent of those who viewed blacks as hardworking wanted to lower welfare spending, while 63 percent of those who viewed blacks as lazy did. Since whites are more likely than blacks to hold negative stereotypes of poor blacks, it is not surprising that 53 percent of white Americans wanted to reduce welfare spending, compared to only 33 percent of blacks.[51] Similarly, another survey of middle-class Americans found that "young black women were more likely to be held responsible for their plight and much less worthy of government support than single white welfare mothers."[52] Other research shows that public support for increased welfare spending is significantly lower in states where higher proportions of recipients are black.[53]

Support for "get tough" welfare policies is highest among whites and is linked to negative views of minorities and the poor. For example, an analysis of 1990 General Social Survey data found that support for benefit reductions was linked to beliefs that blacks and Latinos were lazy. This study also found that support for work requirements and benefit reductions was significantly related to the belief that personal income should be solely tied to one's work and that poverty is mainly due to lack of effort.[54] Other studies show that while a majority of blacks and whites support family caps and time limits, support is significantly higher among whites and is linked to antiblack and anti-Latino prejudice.[55] Long-standing perceptions of black mothers as "employable" and the devaluation of their caretaking work also undermined white support for welfare.[56]

Congress did not simply adopt the policies that the public supported, however. While public support for welfare reform was strong, it was also shallow. A 1996 CBS/New York Times poll about welfare reform found that

44 percent of survey respondents said they did not know enough to give an opinion.[57] Public polls suggest that the public also supported more liberal welfare measures. Whereas 82 percent of respondents favored PRWORA, 91 percent had favored Clinton's initial welfare proposal.[58] There was also strong public opposition to some of PRWORA's provisions. For example, at the time of its enactment, only 27 percent of the public supported the bill's anti-immigrant provisions and, after its passage, a strong majority favored repealing them.[59] Polls also indicated that about 70 percent of Americans opposed the use of federal funds for abstinence-only sex education.[60]

Most of the public supported softer time limits and work requirements than those adopted in 1996.[61] In contrast to the "work first" philosophy embraced by welfare reform advocates, polls taken in the 1990s show very high levels of public support for job training for welfare recipients, with most respondents indicating a willingness to pay more in taxes to provide it.[62] Congress provided very limited funds for work supports, such as child care, health insurance, and transportation services for WTW participants and the working poor in 1996 despite strong public support for such expenditures.[63] Underlying this support, most Americans believe that most of the jobs available to welfare recipients do not pay enough to support a family.[64]

In short, by the mid-1990s, public opposition to welfare spending was strong, especially among Republicans and middle-class and upper-middle-class whites, paving the way for PRWORA's passage. Many of the reforms enacted by Congress in 1996, such as family caps, work requirements, and time limits, enjoyed broad public support. However, Congress enacted more stringent work requirements and time limits, adopted deeper cuts to legal immigrants' benefits, and spent more on abstinence-only education and less on job training and work supports than most Americans wanted.

These discrepancies between PRWORA and public opinion reflected the disproportionate influence of conservative groups on the 104th Congress, which was under Republican control. Republicans and southern Democrats, who tend to agree with Republicans on welfare issues, dominated the two major committees reviewing welfare reform bills, the Senate Finance Committee and the House Ways and Means Committee, making up 75 percent of the former and nearly 70 percent of the latter.[65] Not surprisingly, these committees chose to hear eleven times as many representatives from right-wing and moderate-conservative think tanks as from liberal ones. Nearly one-quarter of the advocacy groups testifying to these committees were from socially conservative groups, such as Christian Right organizations.[66] Because the views of these groups resonated with those of conservative politicians, these testimonies carried considerable weight. The high level of public opposition to welfare also gave politicians room to maneuver, since any reform would be considered better than the status quo.[67] On the other hand, conservative groups were not all-powerful, and they faced considerable opposition to some of their proposals. They were most successful when their demands had broad public support and dovetailed with other powerful demands on Congress, such as reducing social expenditures.

To examine more carefully how conservative groups lobbied for their policy proposals, and the extent of their influence, I will examine their campaigns for three types of policies: those denying public assistance to legal immigrants, those that aimed to discourage out-of-wedlock childbearing, and "charitable choice" policies. These case studies help to illustrate how conservative groups drew on conservative ideologies to justify cutbacks and how elite-sponsored and grassroots conservative organizations worked together to promote similar proposals.

PRWORA'S ANTI-IMMIGRANT PROVISIONS

As rising numbers of Latina and Asian women immigrated to the United States in the 1980s and 1990s, often through family reunification policies, and Mexican immigrants increasingly settled down permanently in the United States, the use of social services by immigrant women and children came under attack. Such attacks were most powerful in California, home of the nation's largest immigrant population.[68] In 1991, a Californian congressman proposed a constitutional amendment to deny citizenship to the children of undocumented parents who were born in the United States, promising to "save taxpayers millions of dollars in welfare payments." The following year, another Congressional representative from California proposed a bill to end federal health and welfare benefits for illegal immigrants, arguing, "Unless you take away the incentives, there's no way to keep them out."[69]

Opposition to immigrants' welfare rights gained even greater prominence through the widely publicized campaign for Proposition 187 in 1994. This initiative, authored by two former Immigration and Naturalization Service (INS) commissioners, sought to deny undocumented immigrants access to public social services.[70] Supporters claimed it would solve the state's fiscal problems by discouraging immigrants' overuse of government social services (despite research showing that they used them at rates similar to or lower than their native-born counterparts).[71] The ad-hoc group Save Our State (SOS), the Federation of American Immigration Reform (FAIR), the Christian Right, and other conservative groups promoted the proposition, and the Republican Party contributed over $100,000 to the campaign.[72] An impressive media campaign preyed upon anti-Mexican sentiment and the economic anxieties of white workers and taxpayers. One television commercial, for example, warned viewers, "Those illegal aliens streaming across the border are taking your jobs and abusing your social services."[73] Courting white voters, Governor Pete Wilson made support for Proposition 187 central to his reelection campaign.[74]

Critics portrayed Proposition 187 as an inhumane, racist, and divisive measure that threatened public health and forced teachers and doctors to become arms of the police state. Others pointed out that it would jeopardize millions of dollars in federal funds and increase emergency healthcare costs.[75] Despite such criticism, polls showed strong public support for the proposition in California,[76] where about 40 percent of the nation's immigrants resided.[77]

In 1994, the measure passed with 60 percent of the vote.[78] Whites, comprising about 80 percent of actual voters, along with Republicans, were the most supportive.[79] The proposition's passage was a call to arms for immigrants and their advocates. In 1994, a hundred thousand people, mostly Latino, marched against the measure in Los Angeles.[80] Civil rights groups and their allies filed at least nine court cases against the law. They won a significant victory when a federal judge declared Proposition 187 illegal on the grounds that immigration was a federal rather than a state matter.

Meanwhile, national politicians used the issue to build support for immigration restrictions. Although some national Republican leaders, such as Jack Kemp and William Bennett, opposed Proposition 187 as divisive, others applauded its passage.[81] Pat Buchanan asserted that the new law would discourage further immigration and stabilize the national culture. As he put it, "We need to call a time out on immigration, to assimilate the tens of millions who have already arrived."[82] Similarly, Dana Rohrabacher, a Republican congressman from California, warned that if the law did not pass, "the flood of illegal immigrants will turn into a tidal wave, and a huge neon sign will be lit up above the state of California that reads, 'Come and get it.'"[83]

Such political rhetoric lent support to proposals to restrict public assistance to legal (noncitizen) immigrants. Although undocumented immigrants were disqualified from receiving federal public assistance, legal immigrants and children of undocumented immigrants born in the United States were eligible. As immigration increased, the share of adult AFDC recipients who were noncitizens rose from 5.5 percent in 1983 to 9 percent in 1993.[84] Through the 1986 Illegal Immigration Reform and Control Act, Congress created a limited amnesty program for undocumented immigrants who had been in the country since 1982 and barred public assistance to them for the first five years after they applied for temporary residency.[85] By 1996, anti-welfare forces were pushing for broader restrictions on welfare for legal immigrants.

Drawing on long-standing stereotypes of Mexican immigrants as lazy, conservative politicians claimed that the United States had become a "welfare magnet" that lured poor immigrants into the country through the promise of easy welfare money, creating a fiscal burden for taxpayers. Anti-immigrant organizations, scholars, and newspaper editorials promoted these stereotypes. For example, a mailing from the American Immigration Control Foundation claimed that immigrants were wasting taxpayers' money through their use of social services, while the Federation of American Immigration Reform's literature highlighted "immigrant-related welfare rip-offs." FAIR also described Mexican women crossing the U.S. border "with the sole intention of having a child who is automatically an American citizen" and eligible for social services.[86]

Conservative scholars added professional legitimacy to such negative stereotypes. Dr. Donald Huddle produced a study showing that immigrants cost the United States $44 billion more than they contributed in 1993.[87] Dr. Lawrence Mead argued that "many of the newer immigrants feel, and display, fatalistic attitudes about getting ahead" that are "alien to the dominant culture," because they have a "passive, Third World temperament."[88] Most of the coverage in newspaper editorials of elderly immigrants' use of Supplemental Security Income (SSI) prior to PRWORA's passage was negative, frequently portraying recipients, especially Asian immigrants, as purposefully immigrating to the United States to obtain it and refusing support from their middle-class and affluent relatives.[89] One scholar, testifying to Congress, claimed that this practice was especially common among Chinese immigrants.[90] Southeast Asians, who have high poverty rates and many of whom are refugees, were also "demonized as culturally unassimilable and over-dependent on welfare."[91]

Based on such propaganda, immigrants became increasingly associated with welfare. While most Americans viewed recent immigrants as hard-working, national surveys taken between 1985 and 1993 showed that a majority, or close to a majority, of respondents believed that most would end up on welfare. Most, or nearly half, also believed that immigrants were using up more tax resources through welfare than they were contributing,[92] despite the National Academy of Science's finding that "the average immigrant pays nearly $1,800 more in taxes than he or she costs in benefits."[93] In line with such views, only 27 percent of those polled in 1994 supported government aid for immigrants who come here with very little, compared to 43 percent in 1986.[94] Such nativist sentiments were primarily directed at undocumented immigrants, however; polls showed that more than two-thirds of respondents opposed proposals to deny welfare to legal immigrants.[95]

Nevertheless, conservative think tanks, such as the Heritage Foundation, and anti-immigrant groups urged politicians to restrict the benefits of legal immigrants, hoping to capitalize on anti-immigrant hysteria and propaganda blitzes mounted during congressional debates over immigration reform. The Heritage Foundation was especially concerned with reducing legal immigrants' use of Supplemental Security Income (SSI) for disabled and retired immigrants, since it was the most expensive outlay of benefits to legal immigrants. During congressional hearings on welfare reform, Heritage fellows Robert Rector and William Lauber argued, "The United States welfare system is rapidly becoming a deluxe retirement home for the elderly of other countries. This is because many individuals are now immigrating to the United States in order to obtain generous welfare that far exceeds programs available in their country of origin." Rector and Lauber also argued that most noncitizens receiving SSI "have relatives capable of supporting them," and their support obligations should be permanent, not time-limited.[96] After PRWORA passed, Robert Rector, dismissing proposals to restore SSI for legal immigrants, commented, "Washington is excellent at finding stupid things to do with taxpayer dollars."[97]

FAIR also lobbied Congress to deny public assistance to noncitizen legal immigrants, arguing, "Immigrants should pay their own way. No federal or state taxpayer should have to pay a dime for immigration. . . . Welfare programs are an incentive to attract immigrants without education, skills, or literacy to move to the United States." They supported revisions in "public charge" policies so that immigrants could be deported for "using means-tested public assistance for at least 180 days within five years of the date of entry." In addition, they urged Congress to create "enforceable sponsorship pledges" through which sponsors of immigrants could be held financially responsible for their use of welfare.[98]

Republicans championed many of these proposals. In 1994, as part of their "Contract with America," House Republicans promised to cut off virtually all federal benefits for legal immigrants under seventy-five years of age, affecting their access to at least sixty-one programs.[99] Defending the proposal, Republican representative Clay Shaw of Florida argued, "Our welfare benefits are an attraction to people to come to this country, and they should be cut off. We should take care of our own with the resources we have."[100] Republican senator Phil Gramm of Texas even proposed in a television interview that immigrants not be eligible for public welfare during their lifetime, but later retracted it under fire.[101]

Moderate and conservative Democrats known as the "Mainstream Forum" supported immigrant cutoffs as a way to finance welfare reform without raising taxes. The cutbacks were expected to generate $21 billion over five years. A spokesman for Representative Dave McCurdy, a Democrat from Oklahoma, said in support of this policy, "We believe that American citizens are the priority. The welfare system is not designed to [help] immigrants adjust to their new country."[102] The Clinton administration was not much kinder. Its plan would have limited some legal immigrants' access to Food Stamps, SSI, and AFDC for the first five years after their arrival, leaving their eligibility for Medicaid unchanged.[103]

These cuts were highly controversial, especially since many politicians were wary of alienating the growing Latino electorate. For example, 1994 Republican gubernatorial candidate Ron Unz of California, who led the "English Only" movement, wrote an editorial claiming that immigrants were not a fiscal drain on taxpayers and that welfare, not immigration, was the real problem. Unz emphasized that targeting immigrants for welfare cuts would alienate Latino voters, "classic blue-collar Reagan Democrats," from the Republican Party.[104] Immigrant, ethnic, and welfare rights groups also campaigned heavily against the cuts.[105]

Nonetheless, with PRWORA Congress denied federal public assistance to most legal immigrants for their first five years in the country. The 1996 Illegal Immigration Reform and Immigrant Responsibility Act, passed shortly after PRWORA, required sponsors to sign a legally enforceable "affidavit of support." Sponsors had to promise to maintain immigrants' income above 125 percent of the poverty level until they became citizens or until they, or their family, had worked in the country for ten years.[106] Targeting immigrants for cutbacks promised to be a politically strategic way to minimize welfare expenditures while expanding costly welfare-to-work programs. The Budget Enforcement Act of 1990 required that "any legislated changes that increased spending in a program needed to be offset by cuts in that program or in other entitlements or by raising additional revenues."[107] Republicans and New Democrats, however, sought not only to keep welfare costs constant, but to decrease them to meet deficit reduction goals without raising taxes.[108] Nearly half (44 percent) of the projected savings from PRWORA, $25 billion over five years, was expected to come from restrictions on immigrants' access to welfare.[109] As immigrant rights activists pointed out, "It's welfare elimination for a group of people who are currently out of favor and don't vote."[110] Immigrants were also geographically concentrated, with about 75 percent of them living in seven states in 1996, which further reduced the political risk of supporting these restrictions.[111]

Nevertheless, after PRWORA's passage, opposition to its anti-immigrant provisions mounted. Clinton vowed to restore aid to legal immigrants, while ethnic, immigrant, and welfare rights organizations mobilized grassroots support for benefit restoration. Even Republican governors, fearing the fiscal impact of immigrant cutoffs, urged Congress to ease these restrictions.[112] In response, Congress partially restored Food Stamps and SSI to legal immigrants in the late 1990s. Most states also restored legal immigrants' right to at least one public assistance program.[113]

In short, proposals to deny benefits to legal immigrants passed, despite the fact that most Americans opposed them. Appealing to nativist sentiments, anti-immigrant groups and right-wing think tanks urged Congress to adopt these policies. They spread racist myths about Latino and Asian immigrants, claiming they were entering the United States to take advantage of its social services. Like conservative politicians, who viewed these policies as a way to deter immigration to the United States, many moderate Republicans and Democrats supported these cutoffs as a politically expedient means of minimizing the cost of welfare reform. But after 1996, state officials, concerned about the fiscal impact of these measures, as well as immigrant rights activists and their allies, pressured Congress to restore these benefits. Although they won partial restorations, they were not wholly successful.

PROMOTING WEDLOCK AND WORSHIP: "PRO-FAMILY" AND CHARITABLE CHOICE POLICIES

In many respects, socially conservative think tanks—such as the Heritage Foundation, the American Enterprise Institute, the Hudson Institute, and Empower America—and grassroots Christian Right groups presented a united front on welfare issues. These socially conservative groups were antimodernists who wanted to return to a romanticized nineteenth-century past in which women sought protection, sustenance, and moral guidance from male household heads and church leaders, and Victorian values—civic virtue, self-reliance, chastity, and familial obligations—prevailed.[114] According to their view, the decline of both religious and family values was caused by the rise of a hedonistic, sinful, secular culture embodied in and encouraged by an overly permissive welfare state. Welfare benefits reduced the economic risks and responsibilities associated with single motherhood, which purportedly encouraged women to be promiscuous, men to neglect their familial duties, and the poor to be lazy. These groups claimed that civic virtue and religiosity would flourish in the absence of federal welfare programs, when private charities and churches were the main distributors of welfare.[115] They thus overlooked the gross inadequacies of such assistance before 1935.[116] As part of their "pro-family" political agenda, these groups pushed for policies that would deny benefits to unwed and teen mothers, increase child support enforcement, and promote sexual abstinence, marriage, and "responsible fatherhood."[117] In the short term, the Christian Right supported greater state and local control over welfare policies in order to increase its influence over them and to strengthen its ties to secular conservatives. Ultimately, however, it sought to replace public welfare with religious charity.[118]

Perhaps the most influential Christian Right group to promote welfare cutbacks was the Christian Coalition, claiming 1.7 million members. The group's founder, Pat Robertson, framed his hostility to welfare in populist terms, claiming, "It doesn't take a rocket scientist to deduce that this [welfare] system promotes illegitimacy, discourages stable families, and promotes dependency."[119] Beginning in 1993, executive director Ralph Reed called for a "devolutionary approach" to welfare so that states could experiment with "pro-family" policies, the most effective of which would serve as a model for federal reforms.[120] In 1994, the Christian Coalition pledged to spend more than one million dollars lobbying for welfare cuts, as well as other proposals in Republicans' "Contract with America" agenda. In 1995 and 1996, it actively lobbied for "pro-family" welfare policies, and some commentators claimed welfare reform was even given priority over anti-abortion policies during those years. Along with other groups, coalition members "visited and telephoned senators and their staffs" and even "stake[d] out hallways outside the Senate Chamber during the floor debate" on welfare reform.[121]

The Concerned Women of America (CWA), claiming 600,000 members, was also highly critical of welfare, claiming it was "encouraging out-of-wedlock childbirth and subsidizing irresponsible choices."[122] Working in conjunction with these groups was the Traditional Values Coalition (TVC), representing pastors and church members in 31,000 Protestant churches,[123]and Focus on Family, popularized through the radio show and widely circulated magazine of its founder, Dr. James Dobson.[124] Eagle Forum, founded in 1972 by Phyllis Schlafly, the Christian Right activist who spearheaded opposition to the ERA in the 1980s, also joined the antiwelfare bandwagon. Eagle Forum, claiming about 800,000 members, enjoys wide influence through

TABLE 9. *National Rates of Out-of-Wedlock and Teenage Motherhood by Race, 1996*

Race	Out-of-Wedlock Birth Rate*	Teenage Birth Rate**
White	37.6	48.1
Black	74.4	91.4
Latino	93.2	101.8

* Per 1,000 unwed women, ages 15–44. SOURCE: United States Department of Health and Human Services, National Center for Health Statistics 2001a, table 18.
** Per 1,000 women aged 15–19. SOURCE: United States Department of Health and Human Services, National Center for Health Statistics 2001a, tables 4 and 9.

Schlafly's syndicated column, which appears in a hundred newspapers, and daily radio commentaries on more than 450 radio stations.[125] Schlafly blamed the "liberal" welfare state for "destroying the work ethic and subsidizing illegitimacy,"[126] as well as a whole host of other social problems: "It's bad enough that the war on poverty took so much spendable income out of the pockets of hard-working Americans. . . . But the worst of it is that the liberal welfare system has . . . broken up millions of families, prevented more millions of families from forming, produced seven million illegitimate children, created a pathetic underclass that will never achieve what we like to call the American Dream, virtually destroyed our great cities, and spawned the social problems that flow from illegitimacy such as drugs, delinquency, and dropouts."[127] Eagle Forum backed the punitive welfare proposals contained in Republicans' 1994 "Contract with America."

Highlighting the theme that welfare subsidized "immorality" and "illegitimacy," the Christian Right echoed the concerns of right-wing think tanks. Both groups viciously attacked the right of unwed and teen mothers to receive welfare. Such attacks were racialized, given that the out-of-wedlock and teen birth rates were far higher among blacks and Latinos than among whites (see Table 9). Social conservatives readily appealed to racist stereotypes of black and Latina women as "unfit parents," irresponsible "breeders," or "welfare queens" to justify cutbacks.[128] In congressional testimony, conservative groups frequently portrayed welfare mothers as "unmotivated shirkers, drug addicts, and irresponsible parents" and accused them of neglecting their children and "refusing" to get married.[129] In these ways, black, Latina, and single welfare mothers were portrayed as needing discipline from a paternalistic and punitive welfare state.[130]

Right-wing think tanks and the Christian Right were pleased with the opening paragraph of PRWORA, which proclaimed the promotion of heterosexual, two-parent households to be a major goal of the law, based on the following "findings": "(1) Marriage is the foundation of a successful society. (2) Marriage is an essential institution of a successful society, which promotes the interests of children. (3) Promotion of responsible fatherhood and motherhood is integral to successful child-rearing and the well-being of children."[131] To discourage out-of-wedlock childbearing, Congress allocated $100 million annually for "the illegitimacy bonus," used to reward states for reducing out-of-wedlock births,[132] and $50 million annually for abstinence-only education and marriage promotion.[133] Such programs teach that non-marital sex and out-of-wedlock childbearing are morally wrong and likely to be psychologically and physically damaging.[134] After 1996, in response to demands by social conservatives, Congress provided additional funds for community-based abstinence-only sex education and federal welfare officials authorized $10 million annually to reward the ten states with the highest percentage increase in the number of children residing in married, two-parent families.[135] Federal efforts to promote marriage were supplemented by state-level initiatives. In 2001, five states (Arizona, Oklahoma, Michigan, Wisconsin, and Utah) allocated welfare funds for marriage skills and anger management classes, premarital counseling, "healthy marriage" handbooks, and clergy-developed community marriage standards. West Virginia put financial pressure to marry on poor women by adding $100 to a family's monthly benefits if there was a legal marriage in the household.[136]

The Christian Right and right-wing think tanks, such as the Acton Institute and the Heritage Foundation, were the main advocates for PRWORA's "charitable choice" provisions, which allowed faith-based organizations to compete for government service contracts and incorporate religious beliefs and symbols in their services.[137] After passage of PRWORA, faith-based welfare initiatives spread. By 2002, churches in at least thirty-three cities sponsored WTW participants and provided them with child care and biblical education.[138]

The Christian Right and most of the major right-wing think tanks faced opposition, however, to their proposals for federal family caps and bans on benefits to unwed teen mothers.[139] Urging Congress to adopt such policies, a lobbyist for Concerned Women of America claimed they would "break the cycle of dependency" and encourage greater reliance on churches, which would demand "moral accountability" from the poor.[140] Welfare advocacy, feminist, and liberal organizations argued strongly against these policies.[141] Mainstream religious organizations, such as Catholic Charities and the Evangelical Lutheran Church of America, also opposed them, claiming such policies were ineffective and harmful to families.[142] Even the National Right to Life Committee, otherwise allied with social conservatives' "pro-family" agenda, opposed these policies on the grounds that they would encourage poor women to have abortions.[143] This widespread opposition, along with Clinton's strong objections, led politicians to reject these policies. Instead, Congress gave states the option of establishing a "family cap" and adopted a federal requirement that unwed teen mothers must attend school and live with their parents to receive welfare.[144] Nevertheless, social conservatives have shown a striking ability to gain Congressional support for other "pro-family" welfare policies, "charitable choice" policies, and state-level family caps.

Why were the Christian Right and other social conservatives so influential? Certainly, it was not because of the veracity of their claims, which contradicted studies showing that rates of out-of-wedlock childbearing bear no strong or consistent relationship to welfare generosity across U.S. states or internationally.[145] Mothers who never marry are more likely to live in poverty and less likely to work compared to other mothers, as social conservatives are quick to point out,[146] but liberals use these same statistics to argue for job creation, living wages, child care, and other work supports, so as to reduce poverty among single mothers and make family formation more feasible.

Social conservatives gained congressional support for "pro-family" and "pro-church" policies partly because of the growing power of the Christian Right within the Republican Party. Having distributed millions of voter guides in the 1990s, the Christian Coalition held considerable sway over congressional Republicans.[147] Right-wing think tanks and the Christian Right also engaged in effective coalition work. During the 1995–96 welfare reform debates, "pro-family" organizations and Heritage Foundation's Robert Rector met informally to agree on common positions and strategies, coordinating phone calls and letters to Congress.[148] They also organized joint actions and meetings. In 1995, when the Senate Finance Committee excluded family caps and bans on welfare for teen mothers from its bill, the Heritage Foundation, the Traditional Values Coalition, and their allies organized a meeting with the chief of staff for Bob Dole, the majority leader.[149] The unity among social conservatives around welfare issues made it difficult for politicians, especially Republicans, to ignore their demands.

In addition, social conservatives' policy proposals were influential because they dovetailed with other powerful demands on Congress. The family cap was consistent with the desire to reduce welfare expenditures, while calls for

"charitable choice" were consistent with corporate demands to privatize welfare. Social conservatives' emphasis on "responsible fatherhood" and paternity establishment echoed liberals' and feminists' calls for better enforcement of child support policies. Liberals actively promoted aggressive child
support enforcement to save money and improve child welfare. Seeking to
turn the blame for poverty away from single mothers and toward "deadbeat
dads," feminist politicians and women's organizations, such as the National
Women's Law Center and the Women's Legal Defense Fund, pushed for
tougher child support enforcement measures in the 1990s.[150] This chorus of
concern about paternal responsibility increased congressional support for
tougher child support provisions[151] and "responsible fatherhood" programs.
"Responsible fatherhood" programs urge fathers, especially fathers of children on welfare, through parent training, education, and counseling programs, to financially support their children and become more involved in
their lives. Many of these are part of job training programs run by child support enforcement offices for unemployed fathers. While such programs can
be psychologically empowering, they do little to address social structural
barriers, such as racial discrimination and job shortages, which reduce men's
earning power. Like child support requirements, they can also make it difficult for welfare mothers to avoid contact with abusive men.[152]

In sum, a coalition of Christian Right groups and right-wing think tanks
championed "pro-family" and "pro-church" welfare policies in the 1990s.
They wielded considerable influence over the contents of PRWORA
because of Republican control of Congress and the growing power of the
Christian Right within the Republican Party. In addition, their demands for
"family caps," "responsible fatherhood," paternity establishment, and welfare privatization dovetailed with other powerful demands on Congress.
Social conservatives' arguments for these policies drew support from, and
reinforced, racist stereotypes of the poor and negative images of the welfare
state as inefficient and overly indulgent.

WELFARE REFORM REAUTHORIZATION

After the passage of PRWORA and the dramatic decline in welfare caseloads
that followed, public views of recipients became less negative, and opposition to welfare spending declined. In 2000, only 37 percent of respondents
stated that the government was spending too much on welfare.[153] PRWORA
remained very popular, however, with most Americans crediting the law,
rather than the booming economy, for caseload declines, paving the way for
further cutbacks under its reauthorization.[154]

The influence of the Christian Right and socially conservative think tanks on policy debates has clearly increased since President George W. Bush took office. Bush, a born-again Christian, two-fifths of whose support in the 2000 election came from evangelical Christians, was a strong supporter of socially conservative policies.[155] Shortly after coming to office, Bush worked vigorously to expand charitable choice policies. As part of this agenda, he established an Office of Faith-Based and Community Initiatives and appointed Don Eberly, a born-again Christian and cofounder of the National Fatherhood Initiative, to lead it.[156] He also promoted legislation to expand charitable choice policies to most social services.[157] About thirty-five conservative organizations, including right-wing think tanks and Christian Right groups, held a joint press conference to push Bush's proposals.[158] After the bill was killed in the Senate, largely because of concerns that it might increase employment discrimination based on religion, Bush issued executive orders directing federal agencies to issue guidelines for implementing charitable choice policies and ensuring compliance. He also backed provisions in a 2002 appropriations bill to provide $30 million in grants to charitable organizations to create model service programs and to study these projects.[159]

Bush made marriage promotion a central goal of welfare, clearly pleasing Christian Right groups and right-wing think tanks that called for more funding for marriage counseling, "responsible fatherhood" programs, and sexual abstinence education among teens.[160] In 2002, Bush proposed allocating more than $300 million in federal and state funds over five years for community and religious groups to run such "healthy marriage" programs, a proposal given revived media attention in 2004, as controversies over gay marriage heated up and the presidential election neared.[161] Bush made clear his allegiance to the conservative "family values" movement by appointing Wade Horn and Andrew Bush, cofounders of the National Fatherhood Initiative, as assistant secretary for Children and Family Services and director of the Office of Family Assistance, respectively.[162]

Proclaiming welfare reform to be an "unalloyed success," the George W. Bush administration, to the delight of right-wing think tanks, pushed aggressively for stronger work requirements.[163] Bush's welfare plan would expand welfare-to-work (WTW) initiatives by requiring 70 percent of a state's adult recipients to participate in work activities by 2007. It would also increase, from thirty to forty hours, the time recipients were required to spend in WTW activities each week.[164] Bush's proposal defined work activities narrowly and stipulated that twenty-four hours per week had to be spent in actual work, four more than the current requirement.[165] This despite polls showing that most respondents favor WTW policies that enhance recipients' skills over those that simply move people quickly into jobs.[166] According to the Congressional Budget Office, Bush's WTW plan would raise state welfare costs by more than $11 billion, largely because of increased demand for child care.[167] Nevertheless, Bush proposed freezing federal welfare and child care expenditures, denying federal responsibility for these extra expenditures.[168]

Courting the Latino vote, Bush actively supported provisions of the 2002 farm bill that restored the right of most legal immigrants to receive Food Stamps.[169] His welfare reform plan did not, however, include other benefit restorations for immigrants. Most likely, this was mainly to keep welfare expenditures low, but it clearly pleased anti-immigrant groups and conservative politicians, who continue to oppose legal immigrants' welfare rights.[170]

Conservative think tanks, the Republican Governors' Association, and congressional Republicans quickly embraced Bush's welfare plan.[171] The House bill, passed in 2002, closely resembled Bush's proposals but authorized an additional $2 billion for child care.[172] The bill passed, with only fourteen Democrats voting for it and only four Republicans voting against it.[173] Leaders of the National Governors' Association and the National Conference of State Legislatures criticized Bush's plan, however, claiming that its work requirements were "unrealistic" and inflexible, given rising levels of unemployment and a lack of child care. The governors' association called for more education and training opportunities for recipients, greater welfare spending to keep up with inflation, and federal money to help states cover benefit restorations for legal immigrants. It also supported exemptions from welfare time limits for employed recipients.[174]

Democrats, courting the white vote and lacking control of Congress, generally followed Republicans' lead. As one journalist noted, "What is striking about the current debate over welfare . . . is the lack of anger."[175] Another observed that "the current ideological divisions are far less sharp than they were in 1996."[176] Indeed, partisan debates over welfare focused on how much work requirements should be increased and whether to soften time limits, not whether to eliminate time limits or restore entitlements.[177] By 2001, the prevailing consensus in Washington was that liberal Democrats had lost credibility on welfare issues when poverty rates declined and employment levels rose following PRWORA's passage.[178] Even when welfare caseloads and poverty rates later rose as economic conditions worsened, politicians of both parties continued to insist that work requirements and time limits were essential to the success of welfare reform.[179] As Democratic senator Evan Bayh of Indiana explained to the press, "The traditional approach of our party has been not to emphasize work requirements. But those requirements have been important in moving people from dependence to self-sufficiency."[180]

Nevertheless, partisan differences on the details of WTW policies, the levels of funding for child care and marriage promotion, and other issues were sufficient to stall the passage of welfare reform reauthorization legislation in 2002 and over the next two years.[181] Some of Democrats' concerns in 2002 were reflected in the Senate Finance Committee's welfare reform bill. Compared to the Republican House bill, this version included a more modest increase in the proportion of recipients required to participate in WTW activities and their required hours, and gave states more discretion in education and training for recipients. The bill also proposed an additional $5 billion over five years for child care services and allocated only one-third of the amount Bush had sought for marriage promotion.[182] Nearly threatening to veto the bill, Bush claimed it would "hurt the very people we're trying to help" because its work requirements were not tough enough.[183] Stymied by partisan conflicts, the Senate bill never reached the floor for a vote, and PRWORA was temporarily extended through a series of authorization votes.[184]

Just as in 1994–96, Democrats were pressured to move rightward on welfare issues in 2002–2004, because Republicans controlled Congress and key congressional committees. In 2003, Republicans and southern Democrats, who tend to be conservative on welfare issues, made up two-thirds of the Senate Finance Committee and about 70 percent of the House Ways and Means Committee.[185] As a result, Democrats were forced to give up or compromise on welfare reform proposals clearly supported by the public. For example, Democrats gave up the fight to repeal PRWORA's anti-immigrant provisions, despite polls showing that a strong majority favored this.[186] Democrats were also forced to give up or roll back proposals to increase the minimum wage and expand training, child care, and other work supports, despite strong public support for such measures.[187]

As Democrats moved farther to the right in 2003–2004, the House and Senate bills grew more similar. Both required states to increase the portion of recipients engaged in WTW activities to 70 percent by 2008, and contained at least $1.5 billion over five years for marriage promotion schemes. Nevertheless, the Republican House bill included tougher federal mandates. While the House bill required that single parents spend forty hours per week in work activities regardless of the age of the child, the Senate bill required only twenty-four hours for single parents with a child under six and thirty-four hours for other single parents. The House bill gave states less flexibility in counting participation in school or rehabilitation and training programs toward work hours, required states to sanction the entire family for noncompliance, provided $6 billion less in child care funding over five years, and greatly expanded the executive branch's authority to grant waivers of federal welfare laws to states.[188] Despite Democrats' considerable concessions, Republicans were firmly committed to tougher work requirements and less funding for child care than Democrats would support. Such partisan differences stalled the passage of reforms, forcing Congress to temporarily extend the existing law in 2003 and 2004.[189]

As chapter 9 revealed, the corporate rich, especially its ideologically conservative wing and low-wage employers, financed the spread of antiwelfare dogma by conservative think tanks and pressed politicians to restrict welfare beginning in the late 1970s. Politicians were not simply prodded from above to attack welfare mothers at the end of the century, however. Racially coded campaigns for tough new welfare rules formed an important part of politicians' strategy for capturing and retaining the support of white voters, especially traditional white voters in the South. As Republicans stepped up attacks on welfare and made significant electoral gains among this sector of the electorate, Democrats followed their lead, providing bipartisan legitimacy to assaults on welfare. The antiwelfare rhetoric of politicians and right-wing think tanks, spread by the popular media, effectively channeled into welfare opposition broadly held moral values, antitax sentiments, concerns about the rise of single motherhood, and racial resentments and stereotypes. Thus, reactionary sentiments rooted in patriarchal family ideologies and racism and aroused by shifts in gender and race relations, conservative rhetoric, and the rise of conservative movements provided important sources of mass support for business leaders' attacks on welfare. Rising expectations that poor mothers work contributed additional public support for welfare reform. As maternal employment spread, becoming common even among white middle-class women, the public became less tolerant of subsidizing the caregiving work of poor women, especially poor black and brown women. In turn, rising public concerns about AFDC and its recipients' worthiness increased political pressure on politicians to overhaul the welfare system.

Because Republicans controlled both houses of Congress, conservatives had the upper hand in shaping welfare reform legislation in 1996. As a result, Congress overreached public opinion by enacting more stringent time limits and work requirements than what the public supported. Along with right-wing think tanks, grassroots anti-immigrant and Christian Right organizations pushed for punitive policies that targeted for cutbacks unwed mothers, teen mothers, and legal immigrants, in spite of meager public support. Congress rejected bans on benefits for unwed and teen mothers, strongly opposed by Democrats and organized women's groups, but adopted "charitable choice" policies, measures to promote marriage, abstinence, and "responsible fatherhood," and restrictions on welfare for legal immigrants. Legal immigrants, a relatively small constituency concentrated in a handful of states, were politically vulnerable, especially as Congress sought to minimize expenditures and anti-immigrant fervor mounted amid immigration debates.

After 2000, with Republicans in control of both Congress and the White House, right-wing think tanks and Christian Right groups continued to wield considerable influence over Congress and Democrats moved farther to the right on welfare issues. Although Democrats pushed for more work supports in reauthorization bills, they supported Republicans' efforts to strengthen work requirements and marriage promotion programs and offered only weak challenges to other restrictive measures, such as time limits and restrictions on welfare for legal immigrants. Even so, right-wing Republicans sought more far-reaching reforms than other politicians were willing to support, stalling the passage of welfare reform for several years.

11. Rebuilding the Welfare State

Forging a New Deal for Working Families

> Our demands are quite simple: Give us a real chance towards
> self-sufficiency.
>
> A WELFARE MOTHER

> We want caps and gowns, not wedding gowns.
>
> A WELFARE RIGHTS SLOGAN

> We've forgotten good old-fashioned common sense about how to
> spend our money. We have to invest it in our children and in our
> families.
>
> A FAITH-BASED WELFARE RIGHTS ACTIVIST

> This is a very rich country. Why can't we all share in the
> prosperity?
>
> A PROVIDER OF SUBSIDIZED CHILD CARE

Despite the country's vast economic resources, the Census Bureau's latest report shows that 12.9 million children in the United States—about 17.6 percent—are officially poor. This crisis is even greater for young children. One out of every five children under the age of five is poor. For Latinos, this figure is nearly one out of every three, and for blacks it is nearly two out of every five. More than half, or 54 percent, of all female-headed households with a child under five years are below the poverty line.[1] However, the definition of poverty, developed in 1963 according to family consumption patterns in the 1950s, underestimates the extent of the problem, since most families now spend a greater share of their budget on housing, child care, and other necessities.[2] After 1996, when Congress restricted welfare for low-income families, overall poverty rates initially declined from 13.7 percent in 1996 to 11.3 percent in 2000, as economic conditions improved. But with the onset of the recession, they rose from 11.7 percent in 2001 to 12.5 percent in 2003. Meanwhile, the depth of poverty rose sharply throughout this period. By 2002, the average margin by which the poor were below the official poverty line was $2,813, the highest since it was first recorded in 1979.[3] Between 2002 and 2003, even as the number of people in poverty rose by 1.3 million, 149,000 fewer people received welfare. As both welfare and jobs became more scarce, families with children made up a growing share, about 40 percent, of the nation's homeless population and about 59 percent of people who request emergency food.[4] By international measures, the U.S. child poverty rate is the highest among industrialized countries, about 50 percent higher than that of the country with the next highest rate. Other affluent democracies are far more effective at eliminating child poverty than the United States because they have fewer low-wage workers and they provide families, even middle-class families, with far more generous benefits, including universal allowances, national health insurance, subsidized child care, and paid family leave.[5]

The stingy, exclusive, and stigmatizing character of welfare in the United States is partly the result of the arrested development of the American welfare state. It is also the product of successive, and increasingly powerful, waves of welfare cutbacks. In this book, I traced the history of political attacks on poor mothers' right to welfare in the United States from the late 1940s to the present, examining how and why a regional revolt against welfare grew into a powerful, national-level assault on welfare. Following Esping-Anderson, I argued that welfare state development is deeply shaped by the kinds of cross-class alliances that form within a nation.[6] In the United States, cross-class opposition to welfare was shaped by a complex interplay of race, class, and gender politics. Since the late 1940s, ideologically conservative and low-wage employers, concerned with protecting their supply of cheap labor and minimizing their taxes, and politicians representing their interests have been on the forefront of campaigns against poor mothers' welfare rights. During politically conservative periods, when racial conflicts were heightened and patriarchal family ideologies resurgent, antiwelfare campaigns gained popular support, especially among whites. Antiwelfare rhetoric appealed to white voters' reactionary beliefs and sentiments, including the belief that single mothers are immoral or are incapable of rearing children independently, the stereotype that poor blacks and Latinos are lazy, and the desire to discipline the poor through strict rules. Calls for putting poor mothers to work also lent popular support to welfare cutbacks, especially as maternal employment became more common and women of color, traditionally expected to work, gained greater access to welfare. In this sense, there are important continuities in past and present efforts to roll back poor mothers' welfare rights.

On the other hand, opposition to welfare moved through several distinct phases, growing more powerful over time. The first major backlash against AFDC began after World War II, when the program became more accessible to women of color and unwed mothers. This welfare backlash was fueled by the broader backlash against blacks' civil rights gains and white resentment toward the in-migration of blacks, Puerto Ricans, and Mexicans in the North and West. With the help of racist politicians, large farmers, concerned with protecting their supply of cheap labor, led many of the antiwelfare campaigns of this period, which frequently targeted unwed mothers and "deadbeat dads." In the 1950s, this welfare backlash was mainly concentrated in the South and Southwest, where there was a significant agribusiness sector, racial conflicts were salient, and state fiscal constraints were considerable. While other business groups occasionally joined large farmers in these antiwelfare campaigns, most did not actively oppose welfare for poor mothers. Even farm organizations, who were the most strongly opposed to welfare, did not call for the end of welfare entitlements. After all, keeping welfare available in the off-season helped to prevent out-migration of their workforce. Low levels of immigration and maternal employment in this period also helped limit public support for welfare cutbacks.

In the 1960s, the backlash against poor mothers spread to the North, often in reaction to the in-migration of blacks. As AFDC expanded to serve rising numbers of black and unwed mothers and the War on Poverty empowered poor urban blacks, white voters became increasingly resentful of federal social programs. This welfare backlash continued to be fueled by a broader racist backlash against the civil rights movement, especially when that movement spread and became increasingly militant and radical, and as urban riots erupted across the nation. Meanwhile, national business organizations and southern employers, concerned about the expansion of welfare, urged Congress to adopt and strengthen federal work requirements for AFDC recipients, which they did in 1967 and 1971. Seeking to curb the rise in out-of-wedlock childbearing, Congress voted to freeze payments to unwed and deserted mothers, although this policy was not implemented.

Unlike today, rising criticism of AFDC in the 1960s and 1970s led to national proposals to replace it with a guaranteed annual income program that would have served both the working poor and the unemployed. Whereas conservatives embraced the administrative efficiency behind these proposals, liberals viewed them as expanding and improving welfare entitlements. In the late 1960s, a wide variety of social groups, including welfare rights activists, women's groups, civil rights organizations, liberal business leaders, economists, and federal welfare officials, actively supported guaranteed annual income proposals. Both Nixon and Carter championed bills to create a negative income tax program that would have created a guaranteed annual income. However, neither of these bills gained sufficient congressional support to pass. Liberal Democrats viewed Republican proposals as too stingy, while southern Democrats and northern Republicans, reflecting the concerns of conservative and southern business groups, worried that they would undermine the work ethic. Unable to replace AFDC with a more popular alternative, politicians left welfare mothers vulnerable to attack.

With the rise of right-wing Republicans and "new" Democrats, a new backlash against welfare mothers emerged in the 1980s and rose to new heights in the 1990s. In part, rising attacks on welfare reflected the spread of neoliberal ideas among business leaders, particularly ideologically conservative and low-wage employers, who were experiencing increased pressure to cut costs in the new postindustrial and global economy. To promote their ideas among politicians and the public, these business leaders sponsored the development of a highly integrated network of right-wing think tanks. By the 1990s, these think tanks and the U.S. Chamber of Commerce were calling for an end to welfare entitlements, time limits on welfare receipt, and substitution of work for welfare. Right-wing think tanks defended these cutbacks in terms of a socially conservative discourse that drew on the "strict father" model of morality, patriarchal family ideologies, and racist stereotypes of poor blacks and Latinos. Antiwelfare propaganda, picked up by politicians and the media, effectively appealed to white voters' antitax sentiments, concerns about the rise of single motherhood, and resentment toward minorities and immigrants. It thus channeled the anxieties and resentments of voters, especially white voters, into deep-seated hostility toward "welfare" and "welfare mothers." At the same time, the rise in mothers' labor force participation undercut political support for the provision of benefits to stay-at-home mothers. By the 1990s, most adult recipients were also women of color, who were traditionally expected to work.

As public hostility toward welfare grew, the class gap in voter turnout widened, and corporate campaign contributions increasingly outweighed those of organized labor,[7] politicians felt greater pressure to restrict welfare. Republicans and Democrats also formed campaigns for tough new welfare regulations in order to capture the support of traditional white voters, especially southern whites, white men, and evangelical Christians. As Republicans made electoral gains among these groups, Clinton and other New Democrats sought to revive support for their party by "ending welfare as we know it." Republican control of Congress after 1994 gave the upper hand to southern and other conservative politicians in designing welfare reform. As a result, the legislation closely mirrored the agenda of the Christian Right and right-wing think tanks, even when it conflicted with popular opinion. With both Congress and the White House under Republican control, this same dynamic continues to shape congressional proposals for welfare reform reauthorization.

Was this welfare backlash inevitable? Some pundits and scholars argue that the decline of the welfare state is inevitable within a global economy, since nation states must compete for investments from business leaders who demand a minimal safety net and few tax burdens. This argument, far from being a neutral description of inexorable economic pressures, is a powerful rhetorical weapon used by conservative business groups to ensure that policy makers bend to their will.[8] Such arguments might not have become as politically powerful as they did, however, were they not accompanied by an emotionally powerful socially conservative discourse that appealed to widely held racial stereotypes, patriarchal "family values," the work ethic, and a "strict father" model of morality.[9] It is largely this discourse and the rise of mass-based conservative movements, such as the Christian Right, that revitalized the Republican Party and provided popular legitimacy to welfare cutbacks. The triumph of welfare cutbacks thus cannot simply be understood in terms of class politics, the rise of neoliberalism, and shifts in the global economy. It depended heavily on elites' ability to build coalitions with conservative groups and mobilize white voters' moral values and racist and patriarchal sentiments.

Other scholars suggest that the backlash against welfare reflected the political limits of a welfare system designed to "shore up" an increasingly antiquated family wage system.[10] With most mothers of young children in the labor force, the old welfare system, designed to enable poor mothers to stay at home with their children, does seem outdated. On the other hand, recent Republican proposals and state laws requiring mothers of infants to participate in WTW programs and mothers of young children to work more than thirty hours per week do not conform to current patterns of maternal labor force participation. Most mothers of young children temporarily drop out of the labor force or limit their work hours. On average, mothers in two-parent families with children under three years of age only work twenty-four hours per week.[11] Surveys from the 1990s also suggest that 60 percent of voters favor part-time work hours for welfare mothers with preschool children and exemptions from work requirements for mothers of infants.[12] Political support for work requirements thus does not simply reflect shifting expectations regarding maternal employment; rather it reflects the disproportionate influence of conservative groups and the political vulnerability of a highly stigmatized program for poor mothers, most of whom are nonwhite and unwed.

To portray the contemporary welfare backlash as inevitable obscures the role of political choices and alternative historical possibilities. Politicians could have responded to rising maternal employment and rising opposition to AFDC by replacing it with something new and better, rather than simply gutting an unpopular program. Had liberal Democrats embraced guaranteed income proposals earlier, when they controlled a larger share of Congress, they might have been able to do this. Had they done so, welfare mothers would have received aid through the same program as other members of the working poor, making it much more difficult for welfare critics to undermine support for welfare through racially coded attacks and appeals to patriarchal "family values." Politicians might even have competed for the white vote in the 1980s and 1990s by expanding, rather than contracting, welfare.

Today, Democratic leaders, traditionally the champions of welfare programs, continue to fail to mobilize working-class voters around a bold alternative to current New Deal policies. Even though the public is hostile to "welfare," they remain strongly supportive of assistance for poor children and working families.[13] A 2002 survey, for example, showed that 69 percent of Americans are willing to pay more in taxes to provide additional assistance to low-income working families with children.[14] Recent public opinion polls also show that a large majority favors government support for paid family leave, while 63 percent of American parents in working families supported government assistance with child care.[15] Democratic leaders have failed to galvanize this latent public support around a bold program to support working families. Instead, they have tried to counter Republicans' gains by moving rightward on social issues and pushing for incremental, piecemeal gains for low-income families, such as gradual expansions in EITC, subsidized child care, or health coverage. Meanwhile, their electoral support among low-income voters continues to decline. Politicians' lack of political vision and leadership reflects their class, race, and gender biases, which insulate them from the problems faced by single mothers, working-class families, and communities of color. It also reflects the long-standing presumption that care work should mainly be a private, and female, concern.[16]

History suggests that American politicians are only willing to expand and restructure welfare programs when they are confronted with deep electoral shifts and widespread social protest, as occurred in the 1930s and 1960s.[17] Thus, politicians' lack of vision and leadership also reflects the limits of the current welfare rights movement. In the wake of PRWORA's passage, there was a resurgence of welfare rights activity. Antipoverty organizations, immigrants' rights activists, welfare advocates, feminist organizations, service providers, legal advocacy organizations, labor unions, faith-based organizations, and other concerned citizens mobilized to defend poor people's welfare rights. New grassroots welfare rights groups also emerged.[18] These welfare rights activists won some significant victories, restoring some of the welfare and labor rights that had been lost or threatened by welfare reform. For example, in late 1996, feminist organizations pushed through national legislation giving states the option of waiving time limits and work requirements for survivors of domestic violence.[19] Immigrant rights activists and their allies succeeded in restoring some of the welfare benefits taken away from legal immigrants at both the state and federal level.[20] Public employee unions successfully challenged employers' efforts to exempt workfare workers from federal minimum wage and health and safety requirements.[21] While these and other victories were significant, they were also limited, reflecting the political weakness of a movement that remains small and highly fragmented. With good reason, this movement has been largely defensive in character. Without a bold alternative to current welfare policies, however, it fails to capture much interest from the broader public or the labor movement, itself weak and under attack. While coalitions among antipoverty organizations, and between community organizations and labor unions, are growing, they tend to be built around particular campaigns rather than a broad political program.

To move forward, activists and politicians need to promote a second "New Deal," one that will address the needs of, and promote solidarity among, poor single mothers and other working families. Poor single mothers' struggles to find work, make ends meet, and take care of their children are not isolated; rather they are bound up with the larger plight of working-class families in the United States. The economic security of working families has declined considerably over the past few decades, as union density declined, policy makers rolled back social programs and labor rights, and the economy restructured. While real wages for most American workers declined or stagnated, employers became more reliant on temporary and part-time workers, many of whom lack benefits.[22] Many workers, especially blacks, are still recovering from the latest round of job losses. A recent survey of American workers by researchers at Rutgers University found that nearly one-fifth of respondents had experienced a layoff since 2001, when the recent recession began. While more than 70 percent of these workers found new jobs, half reported that their earnings had declined. Such findings are not surprising, given that five of the largest ten employers in the country are now low-wage employers, such as Wal-Mart and McDonald's.[23] Meanwhile, the cost of living, especially housing, transportation, health care, and child care, continues to rise, making it increasingly difficult for families to make ends meet.[24] A rising share of the population, 45 million people or about 15.6 percent of the American population in 2003, lack health insurance. The number nearly doubles, to 81.8 million, when those who lack health coverage for part of the year are considered. Although this problem is most acute among blacks, Latinos, part-time, and less educated workers, about 17.5 percent of all full-time workers lack health coverage.[25]

For financial or other reasons, American workers are working more hours than they used to, making it difficult for them to spend time with their families. The joint weekly hours of dual-earner couples has increased from an average of 77 hours in 1970 to 80 hours in 1997, while the average work year increased for all American workers, from 43 to 47 weeks. Much of this increase is due to women's greater participation in the labor force. Yet, American workers' access to paid vacations, holidays, and sick leave also declined, while their work days grew longer. With few regulations of work hours in place, American employees report the longest annual hours of work and shortest vacations in the industrial world.[26]

During the Great Depression, politicians adopted the first "New Deal" to provide a safety net for the unemployed and those out of the labor force, at a time when few mothers worked. Today, with most mothers working and millions of workers struggling to make ends meet, a second "New Deal" is needed to help working families, both in and out of the labor force, to avoid poverty and balance their work and family obligations. While targeted efforts to reverse employment and wage discrimination, such as Affirmative Action and comparable-worth policies, remain necessary to combat poverty, such policies should be combined with universalistic policies to support working parents. Rather than preaching marriage and abstinence and demonizing unwed mothers, immigrants, and people of color, Congress needs to provide greater economic support and protection for all working families. The "New Deal for Working Families" that I envision would have three major goals: (1) to increase access to jobs, education, and training, (2) to help workers make ends meet, and (3) to help workers balance their obligations to work and family.

First, the New Deal for Working Families would increase access to jobs, education, and training. Many people who want to work lack access to jobs or are underemployed. At the same time, low-income communities are in need of many vital services, such as transportation, preschool, child care, and health care. Job creation programs must address both of these problems. At the same time, public subsidies for education and training should be expanded to improve employment prospects for low-income people and enable them to provide high quality services for their communities.

Second, the government needs to help working families make ends meet. Earnings from low-wage jobs (a rising share of all jobs) are simply insufficient to pay for basic needs, creating hardships for workers across the country and a growing health and housing crisis that can no longer be ignored.[27] The minimum wage, whose real value has declined significantly over the past few decades, should be raised. Income supplements are also necessary, especially if workers are unable to secure sufficient employment. TANF and EITC, which provide inadequate benefits to lift recipients out of poverty and fail to reach many who are eligible,[28] should be replaced with a more generous and expansive negative income tax program. By serving both low-income workers and the unemployed, this program would streamline our welfare state and reduce the stigma associated with "welfare." At the same time, Congress should make it easier for working families to afford basic goods and services, such as transportation, health insurance, and housing, by expanding subsidies or regulating prices.

Finally, Congress should help working parents balance their dual obligations to their employers and dependents by improving work time regulations, providing paid family leave, and expanding subsidized early education and child care programs.[29] In terms of such policies, the United States has much to learn from Western European social policies. Members of the European Union have much stricter regulations regarding work time than the United States, giving European workers more time with their families. For example, European workers are guaranteed at least four weeks of paid vacation each year. Workers have no similar rights in the United States, giving employers tremendous discretion over vacation policies. "In practice, American employees at large and medium-sized enterprises are granted an average of ten days a year during their first five years of service, fourteen days after their first five years of service and about seventeen days after ten years." Workers at smaller companies tend to receive even shorter vacations.[30] Across Europe, the normal weekly hours are less than forty hours, which is the legal norm in the United States. The European Union also requires its members to take measures to discourage employers from requiring more than forty-eight hours of work per week from their employees and to prohibit discriminatory treatment of part-time workers. By contrast, the United States requires employers to pay higher rates for overtime but sets no limits on the number of hours employees can be compelled to work.[31] Many employers avoid overtime regulations by contracting out work or through various loopholes in the law. Employers also commonly pay part-time workers less and provide them with fewer benefits, making it difficult for parents to limit their work hours when taking care of young children.[32]

The New Deal for Working Families would provide paid family leave and expand subsidized child care. The 1993 U.S. Family and Medical Leave Act allows workers to take up to twelve weeks of unpaid leave following the birth or adoption of a child or to care for "seriously ill" family members. It exempts private companies with fewer than fifty employees, however, leaving more than 40 percent of private-sector workers ineligible for benefits. Employees who have worked for their employer for less than a year or 1,250 hours are also exempt. Even if they qualify, many families cannot afford to take advantage of these benefits because they are unpaid. By contrast, most Western European countries provide workers with paid leave after the birth of a child or to take care of sick relatives. Such policies are most generous in the Nordic countries of Denmark, Finland, and Sweden, where workers are guaranteed one to three years of leave after the birth of a child and receive about two-thirds of their usual pay during most or all of this period.[33]

Currently, only very poor families qualify for subsidized child care in the United States, and only 10 to 20 percent of families that qualify for this care actually receive it. Most working parents rely on the private market or informal arrangements with friends or family members for child care. Such policies do "little to ensure that care is accessible, affordable, or of high quality."[34] On average, working families spend about 9 percent of their monthly earnings on child care per month, while working families that are officially poor spend about 18 percent of their monthly earnings on it. Meanwhile, child care workers receive little education and training, earn low wages, and lack benefits, which encourages high employee turnover and reduces the quality of care. By contrast, the Nordic and continental countries of Western Europe provide working parents with far greater access to subsidized child care and early education, which is delivered by better educated and better paid staff. The most generous child care systems are in Nordic countries; these programs integrate care with early education and provide "a nearly universal entitlement for care (with a modest co-payment) during the early years before the start of primary school."[35]

The New Deal for Working Families would be expensive, but it is not out of reach, given the country's enormous wealth and vibrant economy. The policies described above could be easily financed through national general tax revenues. Despite being one of the wealthiest nations in the world, the United States spends far less on family-related benefits compared to most European welfare states. Those countries spend at least three times as much on such benefits per child and as a proportion of their gross domestic product.[36] In good part, this is because potential revenues in the United States are not tapped or are diverted to other purposes, particularly the military. Over the past twenty-five years, Congress has significantly reduced taxes for corporations and the wealthy, robbing the government of billions of dollars in revenue. At the same time, much of our federal budget has been used for military. Military spending, including both current and past military expenditures, such as veterans' benefits and interest on the national debt, uses up nearly half, or about 49 percent, of the federal budget.[37] Military cutbacks and tax hikes for corporations and the wealthy could provide much of the revenue needed to support working families, so that the cost does not overburden ordinary Americans.[38]

Clearly, the United States can afford a second New Deal. The real question is whether this investment is worthy. Many scholars claim that such social policies and labor market regulations hurt the economy and increase unemployment, pointing to the high unemployment rates in European countries in the 1980s and early 1990s. Yet, during the 1990s, when European countries were increasing investments in family-related social programs, their economies improved. As Gornick and Meyer point out, "As of 2002, the average unemployment rate was less than 8 percent across Europe and less than 5 percent in some of the most extensive welfare states, including Denmark, Sweden, and the Netherlands."[39] Thus, programs to help working families are not likely to hurt the economy. Instead, they will provide important social and economic benefits by improving the education, skills, economic security, and well-being of current and future workers. They will also make it easier for parents, especially mothers of young children, to work and avoid poverty. As research shows, paid family leave and subsidized child care significantly reduce maternal poverty and increase maternal labor force participation, especially during the preschool years.[40]

At the moment, policy makers hardly seem ready to adopt such a bold agenda for working families. As I write this, the George W. Bush administration just proposed massive new budget cuts for social programs, reduced funding for subsidized housing, and created new exemptions for overtime laws, while Congress just significantly increased military spending.[41] Democratic presidential hopeful John Kerry promised to expand health insurance coverage, but his emphasis on deficit reduction and his support for military spending would have led to further cuts in social programs had he been elected in 2004.[42] Enacting a New Deal for Working Families would require building a strong movement and reframing debates about values, taxes, welfare, and spending. Such a feat depends on revitalizing the labor and welfare rights movements and creating more solid links between them. Bolder political leaders, with greater initiative and more responsiveness to the needs of ordinary Americans, must also be elected. All of this might require fundamental changes in our electoral system and gender, race, and class relations. This is a very tall order, but certainly the cause is worthy of the fight.

States That Restricted Eligibility for ADC, 1949–1960
By Type of Restriction, Mechanism, and Year Adopted

State	Employment Requirement	Stricter Suitable Home Policy
Alabama	Yes (law, 1951)	No
Arizona	Yes (law, 1949)	No
Arkansas	Yes (policy, 1950–1953) No (policy dropped by 1956) Yes (law, 1957)	Yes (law, 1951)
California	Yes (law, 1951, 1953)	No
Florida	Yes (policy, 1953–1956)	Yes (law, 1959)
Georgia	Yes (policy, 1952)	Yes (policy, 1952)
Illinois	Yes (law, 1949)	No
Louisiana	No	Yes (law, 1957; law, 1960)
Michigan	Yes (policy, 1953–1956)	Yes (unknown, 1955)
Mississippi	Yes (policy, 1950–1953)	Yes (policy, 1954, 1956; law, 1958)
Missouri	Yes (law, 1955)	No
Nebraska	Yes (law, 1949)	No
New Hampshire	Yes (law, 1949)	No
New Mexico	Yes (policy, 1953–1956)	No
North Carolina	Yes (policy, 1952)	No
Rhode Island	Yes (policy, 1950–1953) No (policy dropped by 1956)	No
South Carolina	Yes (policy, 1953–1956)	No
Tennessee	Yes (policy, 1950–1953)	Yes (unknown, 1960)
Texas	Yes (policy, 1953–1956)	Yes (law, 1959)
Virginia	No	Yes (unknown, 1956)
Washington	Yes (law, 1955, 1957)	No
West Virginia	Yes (policy, 1953–1956)	No

Sources: Social Security Administration, 1949–60; Bell 1965; state law records.

Variables and Data Sources Used in Quantitative Analysis

DEPENDENT VARIABLE AND ITS MEASURE

Restrictive Program. Coded 1 if state had an employment requirement in 1959 or adopted a new or more restrictive suitable home policy between 1949 and 1960; coded 0 otherwise.

Sources: Federal Security Agency, Social Security Administration, Bureau of Public Assistance, *Characteristics of State Public Assistant Plans* (Washington, D.C.: Government Printing Office, 1959); Winifred Bell, *Aid to Dependent Children* (New York: Columbia University Press, 1965); State Legislative Records.

INDEPENDENT VARIABLES AND THEIR MEASURES

1. Importance of Agricultural Capitalism to State's Economy

Agricultural Labor Demand. Coded 1 if state was above the top quartile for "percent large farms" and above the bottom quartile for the percentage of the female labor force age fourteen and over employed in agriculture, 1950; coded 0 otherwise. Note: other break points were also tried and similar results, as reported in Table 3, were obtained.

Sources: Department of Commerce, Bureau of the Census, *United States Census of Agriculture: 1954,* vol. 2, *General Report* (Washington, D.C.: Government Printing Office, 1956); Department of Commerce, Bureau of the Census, *1950 Census of the Population,* vol. 2, *Characteristics of the Population* (Washington D.C.: Government Printing Office, 1952), table 79.

Percentage Large Farms. Percentage of farms that reported ten or more hired workers in 1950.

Source: Department of Commerce, Bureau of the Census. 1956. *United States Census of Agriculture: 1954, Volume II: General Report.* Washington, D.C.: Government Printing Office.

2. *Racial Context*

Percentage of ADC Population Black. Percentage of ADC recipients in 1948 who were black.

Percentage of ADC Population Nonwhite. Percentage of ADC recipients in 1948 who were nonwhite.

Source: Elizabeth Alling and Agnes Leisy, *Aid to Dependent Children in a Postwar Year: Characteristics of Families Receiving ADC, June 1948* (Washington, D.C.: Federal Security Agency, Social Security Administration, 1950).

Percentage of Population Black. Percentage of total population in 1950 who were black.

Source: Department of Commerce, Bureau of the Census, *1950 Census of the Population,* vol. 2, *Characteristics of the Population* (Washington D.C.: Government Printing Office, 1952).

3. *State Fiscal Capacity*

Per Capita Income. Per capita income in dollars in 1950.

Source: Department of Commerce, *U.S. Income and Output* (Washington, D.C.: Government Printing Office, 1958).

4. *Working-Class Mobilization*

Percentage of Labor Force Organized. Percentage of labor force that belonged to a labor union in 1953.

Source: Leo Troy and Neil Sheflin, *U.S. Union Sourcebook: Membership, Finances, Structure, Directory,* 1st ed. (West Orange, NJ: Industrial Relations Data Information Services, 1985), table 7.2.

Strike Rate. Percentage of nonagricultural workers who were involved in a work stoppage in 1953.

Sources: Department of Labor, Bureau of Labor Statistics, *Analysis of Work Stoppages, 1953: Major Developments and Annual Statistics,* Bulletin no. 1163 (Washington, D.C.: Government Printing Office, 1954), Table 6:

Work Stoppages by State, 1953; Leo Troy and Neil Sheflin, *U.S. Union Sourcebook: Membership, Finances, Structure, Directory*, 1st ed. (West Orange, NJ: Industrial Relations Data Information Services, 1985), tables 7.1 and 7.2.

5. Institutional Strength of Children's Bureau

Children's Bureau. Coded 1 if the state had a Children's Bureau office in 1949; coded 0 otherwise.

Source: Department of Labor, Bureau of Labor Standards, *Labor Offices in the United States and Canada* (Washington, D.C.: Government Printing Office, 1949).

6. Degree of Rural Overrepresentation in State Legislature

Index of Legislative Representation. This index is computed for the whole legislature; it was "computed by simply adding the minimum population percentage that can elect a majority of each house—a procedure that gives equal weight to each house and produces an index on an approximate scale of 100. This the result of the fact that a figure of 50 percent for either house in the underlying calculations is an indication of near perfection, from a mathematical point of view, in giving representation in that house," p. 6.

Note: the smaller the number, the more urban and suburban areas are underrepresented and rural areas are overrepresented in 1955.

Source: Paul T. David and Ralph Eisenberg, *Devaluation of the Urban and Suburban Vote: A Statistical Investigation of Long-Term Trends in State Legislative Representation* (Charlottesville: University of Virginia, 1961), table 4.

7. Strength of Nonsouthern Democrats in State Legislature

Majority Legislature Liberal. Coded 1 if state legislature had a majority of state legislators that were nonsouthern Democrats in 1948.

Source: National Governors' Association, *The Book of States* (Lexington, KY: Council of State Governments, 1949).

Notes

CHAPTER 1

Epigraphs: Testimony at a protest organized by the Los Angeles Coalition to End Hunger and Homelessness, August 2001. Interview with 9to5 staff (August 2001, Milwaukee, WI). Testimony for the Workers' Rights Board Hearing on W-2, Milwauakee, WI, December 1997.

1. Hays 2003: 11.

2. Mettler 2000; Patriquin 2001: 72.

3. K. Weaver 2000: 345.

4. Sparks 2003.

5. U.S. Department of Health and Human Services 2002: 11–37.

6. Loprest 2003. Other studies report more variable employment rates among former recipients, from 11 percent in Maryland to 67 percent in Washington. This may be due to differences in their labor market and demographic conditions, program rules, or survey designs (Lindhorst, Mancoske, and Kemp 2000: 188; see also Rogers-Dillon 2001: 11).

7. Savner, Strawn, and Greenberg 2002: 3.

8. Albert and King 2001; Hays 2003: 58; Rogers-Dillon 2001: 8–9; Weicher 2001: 19; Loprest and Wissoker 2002. The expansion of the Earned Income Tax Credit, child care services, publicly subsidized health insurance, and minimum wage increases in the 1990s also made it easier for poor mothers to leave welfare for work (Savner, Strawn, and Greenberg 2002: 3–5).

9. U.S. Committee on Ways and Means, House of Representatives. 2000: 64.

10. Loprest 2003; Savner, Strawn, and Greenberg 2002: 3–5; New York Times 2002; An Urban Institute survey found that "32 percent of welfare recipients were in paid jobs in 1999. That number dropped to 28 percent by 2002. Employment also declined among those who had just come off of the welfare rolls, slipping from 50 percent in 1999 to 42 percent in 2002" (Zedlewski and Loprest 2003).

11. Loprest 1999; Rogers-Dillon 2001; Urban Institute 2001; Savner, Strawn, and Greenberg 2002: 3.

12. Schram 2001: 6; Hays 2003: 112.

13. Marks 2003.

14. Sherman, Amey, Duffield, Ebb, and Weinstein 1998; Simon 2002a, 2002b; U.S. Conference of Mayors 2003.

15. Savner, Strawn, and Greenberg 2002; Albelda 2001; Loprest 1999; Urban Institute 2001.

16. Burnham 2001; Loprest 1999; Hays 2003: 226.

17. Annie E. Casey Foundation 2002; Peterson 2001; U.S. Bureau of the Census 2004.

18. The average amount of income by which poor people were below the poverty line rose 23 percent between 1996 and 2002, after adjusting for inflation. This figure was $2,813 in 2002, an amount greater than in any other year since these data were first collected in 1979 (Center on Budget and Policy Priorities 2003).

19. These exemptions vary across states and are not always implemented correctly (Hegar and Scannapieco 2000; Mink 2001: 81; Brzuzy et al. 2000).

20. Burnham 2001: 45; Institute for Women's Policy Research 1994; Loprest and Zedlewski 1999; Duncan 2000: 440; Cancian and Meyer 2000: 79–80.

21. On the other hand, a few studies show it has negative effects on adolescents' behavioral and school-related problems (Morris 2002; see also Rothstein 2002).

22. Sparks 2003: 184.

23. Testimony for the Workers' Rights Board Hearing on W-2, Milwaukee, Wisconsin, December 1997.

24. I borrow the quoted phrase from Acela Ojeda.

25. By comparison, 12.7 percent of adults between eighteen and fifty-four lacked a high school diploma or GED. A study conducted in urban Michigan in 1997 found that only 39 percent of welfare mothers without a high school degree worked at least twenty hours per week, compared to 66 percent of those with high school degrees (Goldberg 2002: 4, 7).

26. Savner, Strawn, and Greenberg 2002: 5.

27. Albelda 2001: 69. This was encouraged by PRWORA's stipulation that states allow education to count as a work activity for not more than 20 percent of their caseload. The policy was later revised so that 30 percent of recipients in each state are allowed to participate in educational activities as part of their mandatory WTW hours (R. Gordon 2001: 13).

28. This welfare reform philosophy, first adopted in Riverside, California, quickly spread across U.S. states and shaped policy debates in Western Europe, Canada, and Australia (Peck 2001).

29. This research was produced by Susan Gooden, cited in Burnham 2001: 44.

30. Testimony at a protest organized by Los Angeles Coalition to End Hunger and Homelessness, August 2001.

31. Interview with a welfare mother and her daughter at the 2001 Mothers' Day Protest in Los Angeles. Ernest Savage, "The Price of Poverty," raw footage, Savage City Productions.

32. Testimony, Los Angeles Coalition to End Hunger and Homelessness Town Hall meeting on welfare reform (June 15, 2002, Los Angeles).

33. Testimony, Los Angeles Coalition to End Hunger and Homelessness Town Hall meeting.

34. Testimonies for Workers' Rights Board Hearing in Milwaukee, Wisconsin, December 1997.

35. Interview with former welfare mother (August 2000, Milwaukee, Wisconsin).

36. Institute for Wisconsin's Future 1998a: 4.

37. R. Gordon, 2001: 13; U.S. Student Association 2002: 5.

38. United States Student Association 2002: 17.

39. Testimony, Los Angeles Coalition to End Hunger and Homelessness Town Hall meeting on welfare reform (June 15, 2002, Los Angeles).

40. Interview, Pat Gowens, Welfare Warriors (July 1999, Milwaukee, Wisconsin).

41. A 1999 California study found that 87 percent of Vietnamese-American and 48 percent of Mexican-American recipients were not proficient in English, while a 1999 Wisconsin study found that this was the case for 90 percent of Hmong-American recipients. In Los Angeles, 41 percent of the total caseload has limited proficiency in English (Burnham 2001: 45; Goldberg 2002: 5).

42. Testimony, Los Angeles Coalition to End Hunger and Homelessness Town Hall meeting on welfare reform (June 15, 2002, Los Angeles).

43. Asian Pacific American Legal Center 2001: 4–5.

44. Testimony of Dennis Kao, director of the Asian Pacific American Legal Center. Los Angeles Coalition to End Hunger and Homelessness Town Hall meeting on welfare reform (June 15, 2002, Los Angeles).

45. Institute for Wisconsin's Future 1998b: 11; interviews with three former welfare mothers (August 2000, Milwaukee, WI); testimony by welfare mother for Workers' Rights Board Hearing, Milwaukee, Wisconsin, December 1997.

46. Heuler-Williams 1998: 22–25. Temp agencies placing W-2 recipients qualify for federal WTW tax credits of up to $8,500 per placement (9to5 2000).

47. Testimony of Milwaukee ACORN's W-2 Workers' Organizing Committee member for the Workers' Rights Board Hearing on W-2, December 1997.

48. Interview, 9to5 staff (August 2001, Milwaukee, WI).

49. Citizens for Workfare Justice 1998; Krinsky and Reese 2000.

50. Interview with welfare mother at Mothers' Day Protest, 2001 by Ernest Savage for his documentary, "The Price of Poverty," Savage City Productions.

51. Testimony for Workers' Rights Board in Milwaukee, Wisconsin, December 1997.

52. J. McBride 1998.

53. Interview, former welfare mother (August 2000, Milwaukee, Wisconsin); Hays (2003: 41) also observed, in her ethnography of two welfare offices, that child care problems were not considered to be "good cause" for quitting a job.

54. By 1999, only 12 percent of potentially eligible low-income families were receiving assistance through the Child Care and Development Fund

(Savner et al. 2002: 6, 9). The Center for Law and Social Policy similarly reported that while 15 million children are eligible for child care subsidies (which aid the working poor as well as welfare recipients), only 2.2 million are receiving it. Poor outreach and lack of services contribute to these problems. By October 2002, waiting lists for child care subsidies emerged in 21 states, and are as high as 280,000 families in California (Peterson 2002d).

55. Testimony, Los Angeles Coalition to End Hunger and Homelessness Town Hall meeting on welfare reform (June 15, 2002, Los Angeles).

56. Albelda 2001.

57. This finding was based on a sample of 989 mothers in the National Longitudinal Survey of Youth who had left welfare before 1987 (Cancian and Meyer 2000: 74).

58. Burnham 2001; Weicher 2001: 17. About half of former welfare recipients find jobs in service industries, and a quarter find them in wholesale or retail trade (Loprest 1999: 10). Often, these jobs are in food preparation, sales, or clerical support (Hays 2003: 55).

59. Cited in Milwaukee Women and Poverty Public Education Initiative 2000: 9.

60. Interview, former Lockheed Martin Information Management Systems employee, Southern California, October 2001 (cited in Reese 2001).

61. Interview of former Maximus employee by Ernest Savage (November 1999, Los Angeles), in "The Price of Poverty," raw footage, Savage City Productions.

62. According to national surveys taken between 1980 and 1987, about 40 percent of those who leave welfare for work return for another welfare spell, and about one quarter of welfare mothers worked while they received welfare (Duncan 2000). The Institute for Women's Policy Research (1994) also found that it was common for welfare mothers to cycle between welfare and work or combine welfare and work.

63. Urban Institute 2001. Similar findings were reported for recipients who left welfare for at least one month between 1995 and 1997 (Rogers-Dillon 2001: 11–12).

64. Albelda 2001; Hays 2003: 55; Weicher 2001: 19. Another review of more than thirty recent state-level "leaver studies" found that median wages ranged from $6.00 to $8.47 an hour, while a national survey by the Urban Institute found that the national median hourly wage for welfare leavers was $6.61 in 1997 and $7.15 in 1999 (Savner et al. 2002: 4; Loprest 1999, chart 7).

65. Cancian and Meyer 2000.

66. Hays 2003: 59.

67. Testimony by ACORN member. Los Angeles Coalition to End Hunger and Homelessness Town Hall meeting on welfare reform (June 15, 2002, Los Angeles).

68. Weicher 2001: 19–20.

69. Burnham 2001: 39; Edin and Lein 1997.

70. Interview, member of Los Angeles Child Care Providers for Action (March 2002, Los Angeles).

71. Loprest and Zedlewski 1999.

72. Difficulties paying utility bills are more common among recipients in northern and midwestern states, which experience colder winters. For example, an Illinois study found that 61 percent of former recipients who didn't work and 48 percent of those who were working had trouble paying their utility bills (Burnham 2001: 40; Shram 2001).

73. Loprest and Zedlewski 1999. While food insecurity declined nationally between 1995 and 1999 because of improved labor market conditions, it rose among households with incomes below 130 percent of the poverty line (U.S. Department of Agriculture 2000, cited in Seavey and Sullivan 2001: 27). Rising food insecurity among these households is partly due to the loss of welfare benefits, which is frequently accompanied by a withdrawal from the Food Stamp program (Burnham 2001; Savner et al. 2002).

74. For example, a 1999 Massachusetts survey of former welfare recipients found that overall levels of hunger were about fifty percent higher after they left welfare than before they did so (Seavey and Sullivan 2001: 48, 50). For example, a 1998 Wisconsin survey found that 37 percent of employed former recipients reported falling behind on a rent or mortgage payment, versus 30 percent before leaving welfare. Thirty-two percent said that they had no way to buy food on at least one occasion after leaving welfare, versus 22 percent beforehand (Institute for Wisconsin's Future 1999; see also Burnham 2001: 41 and Patriquin 2001: 87).

75. Fix and Passell 2002: 2. Restrictions on legal immigrants' access to welfare affected legal immigrants and families of mixed immigration status, who make up 10 percent of American families and one-quarter of families in California (Fix and Zimmerman 1999).

76. Burnham 2001: 46.

77. Fujiwara 1999: 188–93; see also Reese and Ramirez 2002.

78. In her field research on two welfare offices, Hays (2003: 104–5) observed that nearly half of those at diversion workshops she attended left before filling out a welfare application.

79. Sherman et al. 1998; Brockland 2002.

80. Five private agencies—three nonprofit and two for-profit—run Milwaukee's welfare program. The nonprofit agencies are United Migrant Opportunities, Opportunities Industrialization Center, and Employment Solutions. The two for-profit agencies are Maximus and YW Works.

81. Testimony of Debra Silas Green (AFSCME Local 594) for Workers' Rights Board Hearing in Milwaukee, Wisconsin, December 1997.

82. Interviews, Institute for Wisconsin's Future (August 1999, Milwaukee, WI); Milwaukee Hunger Task Force (September 2001, Milwaukee, WI); HOSEA activist (September 2001, Milwaukee, WI); Pat Gowens, Welfare Warriors (July 1999, Milwaukee, WI).

83. Lindhorst, Mancoske, and Kemp 2000: 189; Rehner Iverson 2000; R. Gordon 2001; Brzuzy et al. 2000: 199.

84. Mink 1998a: 87; Hays 2003: 41, 224.

85. Findings are based on a 1998 telephone survey of 347 welfare recipients who had left the welfare rolls in a southern metropolitan region (Lindhorst, Mancoske, and Kemp 2000: 188–98).

86. Patriquin 2001: 90.

87. Albelda 2001: 70; Brandwein and Filiano 2000; Rogers-Dillon 2001: 10. A recent Michigan study found that physical health problems, depression, limited work experience, few job skills, perceived discrimination, and transportation and child health problems significantly lowered employment rates among welfare mothers (Goldberg 2002: 7).

88. Federal law does not fully count recipients' participation in rehabilitation and other programs in work participation rates, which puts pressure on welfare employees to limit their use (Testimony, Mark Duhammil, outreach specialist for Behavioral Services for Los Angeles Department of Public Social Services, Los Angeles Coalition to End Hunger and Homelessness Town Hall meeting on welfare reform (June 15, 2002, Los Angeles); Goldberg 2002; Savner et al. 2002: 2).

89. Brandwein and Filiano 2000: 226.

90. Loprest and Zedlewski 1999; Hays 2003: 82, 164–65.

91. A multi-city survey by the Manpower Demonstration Research Corporation indicates that one-third of recipients with multiple employment barriers were sanctioned, compared to one-fourth of those with no such barriers (Goldberg 2002).

92. Testimony for Workers' Rights Board Hearing in Milwaukee, Wisconsin, December 1997.

93. Interview with welfare mother at 2001 Mothers' Day Protest by Ernest Savage (Los Angeles), in "The Price of Poverty" (raw footage), Savage City Productions.

94. National Low Income Housing Coalition 2002: 3.

95. Findings from the national survey are based on Pamela Loprest's analysis of the National Survey of America's Families, as described by Rogers-Dillon 2001: 11–12; and other studies reported in the press (Wilgoren 2002).

96. National Low Income Housing Coalition 2002; Ernst and Young Kenneth Leventhal Real Estate Group 1998; see also J. Sanchez 2003 and A. Rosenberg 2003. Quantitative research on California reveals that there is a statistically significant greater incidence of homelessness where the poverty rate is higher and the ratio of the fair market rent to per capita income is greater (Quigley et al. 2001).

97. Patriquin 2001: 87. Likewise, a survey conducted in Milwaukee County found that 39 percent of families losing welfare benefits since 1997 were evicted or threatened with an eviction (A Job Is a Right Campaign 1998).

98. Burnham 2001.

99. Marks 2001; Ascribe Newswire 2001; Knox 2002.

100. Burnham 2001: 40–41.

101. Simon 2002a, 2002b.

102. Burnham 2001: 41.

103. Testimony, Los Angeles Coalition to End Hunger and Homelessness Town Hall meeting on welfare reform (June 15, 2002, Los Angeles).

104. Nichols and Gault 1999; Sherman et al. 1998; Patriquin 2001; U.S. Conference of Mayors 2003; Peterson 2002a.

105. U.S. Conference of Mayors 2003; Patriquin 2001: 88.

106. Interview with shelter worker (June 2001, Milwaukee, WI).

107. Cited in Burnham 2001: 41.

108. Berry 2001; Rivera 1998, 2001, 2002.

109. U.S. Conference of Mayors 2003.

110. "Child only" cases rose from 22 percent of AFDC/TANF cases in 1996 to 37 percent in 2001 (U.S. Department of Health and Human Services 2002: I-6).

111. A child can also receive these grants if their parent receives Supplemental Security Income, were sanctioned from welfare, or were denied welfare due to their immigration status (Bernstein 2002).

112. Patriquin 2001: 87; R. Gordon 2001: 4.

113. After PRWORA's passage, many states began to use welfare funds to screen sanctioned recipients to determine if their child was at risk of abuse or neglect (Mink 2001: 87).

114. Interview with shelter worker (August 2000, Milwaukee, WI).

115. Ibid.

116. Interviews with three former welfare mothers (August 2000, Milwaukee, WI).

117. Burnham 2001: 41; interview with shelter worker (August 2000, Milwaukee, WI).

118. For a good review of research on the ineffectiveness of abstinence-only sex education, see Brody 2004.

119. Title IX, Section 912, cited in A. Smith 2001: 313.

120. A. Smith 2001: 313–14.

121. De Lollis 2001.

122. Edin 2000: 113.

123. Hays 2003: 132–36.

CHAPTER 2

Epigraphs: George W. Bush, from a speech at St. Luke's Catholic Church in Washington, D.C., cited in Los Angeles Times 2002. Interview, Pat Gowens, Welfare Warriors (July 1999, Milwaukee, Wisconsin).

1. L. Gordon 1994.

2. The purpose of Aid to Dependent Children (later known as AFDC) was to provide aid to needy children under sixteen years who have " 'been deprived of parental support or care by reason of death, continued absence from the home, or physical or mental incapacity of a parent'" (cited in Bell 1965: 27).

3. For example, see Pierson (1994, 1996, 2001c).

4. Pierson 1994: 17.

5. For example, middle- and upper-class families benefit from tax credits for dependents, special tax breaks for homeowners, and federally-funded retirement benefits.

6. Previous to this, there were campaigns against outdoor relief in the nineteenth century (Katz 1996; Piven and Cloward 1993) as well as opposition to, and curtailment of, state-level mothers' pensions, which predated AFDC (Goodwin 1997).

7. For example, see Abramovitz 1989; Chang 1994; Piven and Cloward 1993; Rose 1995; Rowe 1993; Solinger 1992; Soule and Zylan 1997. The most comprehensive study of it, Winifred Bell's book *Aid to Dependent Children*, published in 1965, was mainly a descriptive account focusing heavily on the South.

8. L. Gordon 1994.

9. Machtinger 1995: 37; Skocpol 1992: 425.

10. Skocpol 1992: 424–478; Sklar 1993.

11. Mink 1990: 94–106; Mink 1995.

12. Gooden 1995; Skocpol 1992: 471–77.

13. Rowe 1993: 144.

14. Skocpol 1992: 471–77.

15. Goodwin 1995: 257–8, see also B. Nelson 1990: 142.

16. Abramovitz 1989; L. Gordon 2001: 16, 19; Mink 1998b.

17. Handler and Hasenfeld 1991; Mink 1990, 1995; B. Nelson 1990; Orloff 1991; Skocpol 1992; Mink 1990: 110; Abramovitz 1989: 201; Gooden 1995; Mink 1995: 49–50; Hondagneu-Sotelo 1995: 174–75.

18. Piven and Cloward 1993: 45–119.

19. Abramovitz 1989: 315; L. Gordon 1991: 35; Zylan 1995: 101.

20. L. Gordon 1994: 266–75; Quadagno 1988; Quadagno 1985: 577; Quadagno 1994: 21.

21. Even so, the number of poor mothers receiving welfare increased significantly following the implementation of ADC. While mothers' pension programs served 300,000 recipients in 1934, the ADC program served over 700,000 by 1939 (Mettler 1994: 318–321).

22. Abramovitz 1989: 329; Mettler 1994: 332–41; Bell 1965: 35; Gooden 1995; Komisar 1977: 84.

23. Rowe 1993: 446–55.

24. Forty percent of welfare mothers in Arkansas were at work, and 47 percent were at work in North Carolina (Rowe 1993: 446–55; Goodwin 1995).

25. Bell 1965: 46. Louisiana's requirement later disappears from official records. This may have been due to pressure from federal welfare officials who advised states against denying ADC in order to pressure mothers to work (Chang 1994: 274).

26. Zylan 1995: 101; Cauthen and Amenta 1996: 436; Mink 1995: 134.

27. Esping-Andersen 1985: 223, see also Esping-Andersen 1990 and Esping-Andersen and Korpi 1984.

28. Pierson 2001a: 6.

29. Teles 1996: 17.

30. Even so, Pierson (1994) claims there was a public backlash against these welfare cutbacks. Following these cuts, public support for welfare spending grew, especially as the recession deepened.

31. Weaver 2000: 104.

32. Teles 1996: 12.

33. For example, see Bashevkin 2000, Gilens 1999; L. Gordon 2001, Mink 1998a; Neubeck and Cazenave 2001.

34. They also undergird the long-standing distinction between the able-bodied poor, viewed as undeserving, and the poor who are not able-bodied (the disabled, the elderly, and children), viewed as deserving (Handler and Hasenfeld 1991; Katz 1996; Block and Somers forthcoming; L. Gordon 2001).

35. Mink 1998a; L. Gordon 2001.

36. The term "marriage ethic" was coined by Abramovitz (1989).

37. L. Gordon 2001: 19.

38. Mink 1998a: 86–87.

39. Neubeck and Cazenave 2001: 3.

40. Collins 1990: 77; Mink 1998a; Roberts 1997; Neubeck and Cazenave 2001.

41. Handler 1995: 3–4.

42. Collins 1990: 77; Roberts 1997.

43. Folse 2001.

44. Neubeck and Cazenave 2001; Chang 2000.

45. While blacks made up the largest share of recipients in 2000, this is a recent development. As late as 1994, 37.4 percent of recipients were white, while 36.4 percent were African American (U.S. Department of Health and Human Services 2002: 110).

46. U.S. Department of Health and Humans Services 2002; U.S. Committee on Ways and Means, House of Representatives 2000: 112.

47. Albelda 2001: 71; Institute for Women's Policy Research 1994; Duncan 2000: 435.

48. Previous research shows that about half of all AFDC recipients exited welfare during the first year, and three-quarters departed within two years. Only about 15 percent of welfare mothers remained on welfare continuously for five years (W. Wilson 1996: 166–67, see also Handler 1995: 48–49).

49. One exception to this is the higher rate of Supplemental Security Income usage among immigrants in 1989, especially Asian refugees (Bean, Van Hook, and Glick 1997: 448). Blau 1984; Chang 2000: 21–32; Jensen 1988; Kposowa 1998: 147–59; Tienda and Jenson 1986. Clark and Passel (1993), cited in Calavita 1996: 290; National Research Council of the National Academy of Sciences, cited in S. Moore 1998, Suárez-Orozco and Suárez-Orozco 1995: 28–35.

50. Neubeck and Cazenave 2001: 118.

51. Piven 2003.

52. Orloff 2002.

53. Abramovitz 1989; Folse 2001.

54. Hicks 1986: 93–94; J. O'Connor 1973; Offe 1985; Piven and Cloward 1993; Rose 1995; Stephens 1979.

55. Hicks and Swank 1983; Isaac and Kelly 1981; Piven and Cloward 1993; Swank and Hicks 1984.

56. According to Clawson, Neustadtl, and Weller (1998: 38–39), corporations that are "pragmatically conservative" act on the basis of short-term interests to support incumbent politicians, while "ideologically conservative" corporations pursue a long-term conservative agenda and seek the election of conservative politicians.

57. Domhoff 2002, 1990: 36; Eakins 1969.

58. Domhoff 1990; Hicks 1986; Noble 1997: 20; Post 1997; Quadagno 1984; Quadagno 1988: 12–13; Quadagno 1990. During the New Deal period, monopoly businessmen or "corporate leaders" were more supportive of broader welfare coverage than southern planters and competitive manufacturing industries (Domhoff 1990: 29–34; Quadagno 1984, 1988). Similarly, the National Association of Manufacturers, representing large monopoly businessmen in capital-intensive firms, supported the establishment of a guaranteed annual income in the late 1960s, whereas the U.S. Chamber of Commerce, dominated by small service-sector firms, opposed it (Quadagno 1990).

59. Peck 2001: 36. This promise was not fully achieved, however. Because most states received credits for caseload reductions and because of various exemptions, only about 34 percent of adult recipients were actually working by 2002 (Pear 2002d).

60. Ferguson and Rogers 1986; Hicks 1999; Huber and Stephens 2001.

61. Plotkin and Scheuerman 1994; see also Pierson 1994: 150–55; Pierson (2001b) suggests that welfare retrenchment in affluent democracies is partly a response to long-term budgetary pressures associated with a postindustrial economy, which lowers economic growth rates and income, making it more difficult to finance welfare programs. Wage rates depend more on the relative power of capital and labor than on economic growth, however (H. Schwartz 2001: 29–30). As Pierson (1994) argues, fiscal constraints were more politically than economically driven. Similarly, Huber and Stephens (2001) suggest that welfare cutbacks in the United States were "ideologically driven," unlike cutbacks in Western European countries, which were "unemployment driven."

62. Himmelstein 1990; Ferguson and Rogers 1986.

CHAPTER 3

1. Calhoun County Welfare Department 1950; I disguised Mrs. Jones's actual name for reasons of confidentiality.

2. Chatham County Department of Public Welfare 1953.

3. Georgia Department of Public Welfare 1953a: 27.

4. Hancock County Department of Public Welfare 1953.

5. This court case challenged the legality of Georgia's "employable mother"

rule (Civil Action Number 10443. Georgia Federal Records Center, East Point, GA. Accession Number 69 A 2139, Box 30–31. Location 86559–60).

6. Brown 1999: 171–72; U.S. Department of Health, Education, and Welfare 1961a.

7. Abramovitz 1989: 321; Brown 1999: 185.

8. Bureau of Public Assistance 1957b; U.S. Department of Health, Education, and Welfare 1960, 1961a, 1961b.

9. Zylan 1995: 102.

10. The 1939 amendments also established a merit system for personnel (Mettler 1994: 337–38).

11. Bell 1965: 53; Conrad 1989: 346–47; Piven and Cloward 1993: 194.

12. Turner and Starnes 1976: 52.

13. The U.S. Census Bureau only provides data on poverty rates beginning in 1959. The figure for that year (20.8 percent) is comparable to the figures shown in Table 1, which come from the 1964 Economic Report of the President, page 57, cited in Miller (1965: 89).

14. By the end of the 1950s, about half of blacks were poor, compared to one-third for the total U.S. population (Coontz 1997: 44).

15. Although black-white income inequality was greater in the South than the North, northern blacks still confronted tremendous employment discrimination and remained at the bottom of the labor market (Kraly and Hirschman 1990: 34).

16. By 1960, 60 percent of all black working women were in institutional and private household service jobs, compared to 16 percent for white women (Jones 1985: 235). On Chicanos' occupational segregation, see Bullock 1972: 96–99; Stevens 1969: 19; Camarillo 1990: 79.

17. Jones 1985: 261.

18. Kraly and Hirschman 1990.

19. For example, in Chicago, Cleveland, Detroit, New York, and Philadelphia, unemployment rates were three to four times as high among black women than foreign-born white women (Jones 1985: 262).

20. Gordon 1994.

21. Hoey 1944a.

22. Bell 1965; Brown 1999; Handler and Hasenfeld 1991; Solinger 1992.

23. Greenleigh Associates 1960: 1–2, cited in Bell 1965: 75.

24. Brown 1999: 198–99.

25. Lansdale 1961: 38.

26. The Townsend movement was the most significant of these old-age pension organizations. At its peak in 1939, the Townsend movement claimed 761,624 dues-paying members, and organized 12,302 clubs between 1934 and 1950 (Pinner, Jacobs, and Selznick 1959: 4–5; Holtzman 1975: 50–51).

27. West 1981; Piven and Cloward 1977.

28. Trattner 1974: 249–253.

29. Daniel 1987: 210–12; Rupp and Taylor 1987.

30. Levenstein 2000.

31. Brown 1999: 173.

32. Howard 1948.

33. I excluded Rhode Island from this count because its employment requirement disappears from official records in 1956.

34. Brown 1999: 172.

35. Herzog 1960: 15.

36. Herzog 1960: 16.

37. Cited in Mink 1998a: 37.

38. Georgia passed its law in 1951, and because of federal disapproval replaced it with an administrative policy (see chapter 5). Mississippi adopted this policy through administrative decision in 1954 and by law in 1958. Louisiana adopted it by law in 1957. Tennessee's state legislature approved their law in 1957, but the governor vetoed it (Bell 1965).

39. Komisar 1977: 89.

40. Brown 1999: 175.

41. Bell 1965: 76–92.

42. The court ruled in *Pearl B. Collins v. State Board of Social Welfare* in 1956 that this rule was illegal because it discriminated against families based on family size. Despite this ruling, other states continued to establish maximum family grants (Bell 1965: 66–67).

43. Komisar 1977: 89.

44. Bell 1965: 87.

45. The Bureau of Public Assistance (BPA) had considerable influence over these decisions, since its regional and central staff initially recommended approval of them (Social Security Administration 1949, 1957). The Social Security Board almost always followed the BPA's recommendations (Cates 1983: 115–27; Lund 1953; Social Security Administration 1949).

46. Originally, federal oversight over ADC, and other federal welfare programs created by the Social Security Act, was given to the Social Security Board when it was created in 1935. This agency was replaced with the Social Security Administration in 1946 and the Department of Health, Education, and Welfare in 1953.

47. Mr. Sparer, cited in Transcript of Proceedings Had Before the Honorable Griffin B. Bell, the Honorable Lewis R. Morgan, and the Honorable Sidney O. Smith, Jr. in Atlanta, Georgia, April 7, 1967, p. 36. Records of Civil Action Number 10443.

48. Bell 1965: 53; Cauthen and Amenta 1996: 433; Conrad 1989: 346–47; Piven and Cloward 1993: 194. Federal welfare officials also provided states with considerable freedom and failed to develop firm guidelines for implementing public assistance programs. In part, this was because they were more concerned with other matters, such as building support for social insurance (Bell 1965; Cates 1983; Mettler 1994: 313–14).

49. Cates 1983: 112. Before becoming the director of the bureau, Hoey was the associate director of the Welfare Council of New York City, and was

appointed to serve on the seven-person Advisory Committee on Child Welfare to Roosevelt's Committee on Economic Security that drafted the Social Security Act in 1935 (L. Gordon 1990: 259).

50. Keam 1954; Mettler 1994: 323.

51. Hoey 1944b, 1944c, 1945b, 1946; Keam 1954; Federal Security Administration 1952: 18–19.

52. Bresler 1995; Congressional Quarterly Service 1965; Lazarowitz 1982: 1–55; Manley 1973.

53. E. Berkowitz 1995: 41–96; Berkowitz and McQuaid 1980: 143–44.

54. The law became effective in October 1951. Despite all the controversy, the Jenner Amendment was not widely used. Altmeyer claims that "few persons other than newspaper reporters inspected the rolls, and these only in the first few months after the Jenner Amendment became law" (Altmeyer 1966: 191).

55. The Revenue Act of 1951 enabled states to pass this type of legislation so long as recipient lists were not used for political purposes.

56. Mr. Sparer, cited in Transcript of Proceedings Had Before the Honorable Griffin B. Bell et al. 1967: 36.

57. Transcript of Proceedings Had Before the Honorable Griffin B. Bell et al. 1967: 37.

58. This decision was made when it reviewed Wisconsin's Chapter 585. That law allowed judges to "require the mother to do such remunerative work as in his judgment she can do without detriment to her health or the neglect of her children." The board approved of this law with the stipulation that it "will not result in a reduction of public assistance payments based on sound determination of need, or that acceptance of assistance will not be conditioned on compliance with such direction of the judge" (Social Security Board 1945).

59. Bell 1965: 31.

60. Bureau Circular No. 9, May 1, 1940, cited in Bell 1965: 35–36.

61. Cited in Bell 1965: 44.

62. Hoey 1945a.

63. Possibly, they believed such actions would have conflicted with the intent of Congress that states be free to use "moral considerations" as eligibility conditions for ADC, which was expressed in congressional debates about and reports on the 1935 Social Security Act (Bell 1965: 52).

64. The fifteen states were Alaska, Arizona, Idaho, Indiana, Kansas, Louisiana, Missouri, Montana, Nebraska, New Mexico, North Carolina, North Dakota, Oklahoma, Texas, and Wyoming (Bell 1965: 51).

65. Bell 1965: 110.

66. Tramburg 1954.

67. Bell 1965: 71–73.

68. Bell 1965: 94.

69. Bell 1965: 98–99.

70. Levenstein 2000.

71. Brown 1999: 197.

72. Bell 1965: 137–38.

73. Bell 1965: 147; Levenstein 2000.
74. Levenstein 2000: 11.
75. Levenstein 2000.
76. Cited in Bell 1965: 146.
77. Cited in Bell 1965: 147; Komisar 1977: 76.
78. Bell 1965: 149.
79. These states subsequently revised their policies, except for Michigan: "In the end Michigan was permitted to continue excluding children in 'unsuitable homes' from ADC by a 1962 amendment to the Social Security Act which, in effect, accepted the principle of maintaining Title IV as the 'elite' program so long as the state provided general assistance to the 'unworthy' families" (Bell 1965: 150).
80. On these rulings, see Davis 1993 and chapter 7 below.

CHAPTER 4

Epigraph: St. John 1952a.
1. Axinn and Levin 1975: 225; Himmelstein 1990: 20–23; Hodgson 1976: 76; Patterson 1986: 96; Schrecker 1989:100.
2. Coltrane and Collins 2001: 140–43; Harrington 1962; Jackson 1985: 238–43; Turner and Starnes 1976: 52; Zieger 1994: 122. "A Bureau of Labor Statistics survey of home building in 1946–1947 in six metropolitan regions determined that the suburbs accounted for at least 62 percent of construction. By 1950 the national suburban growth rate was ten times that of central cities, and in 1954 the editors of *Fortune* estimated that 9 million people had moved to the suburbs in the previous decade." Between 1946 and 1956, about 97 percent of all new single-family dwellings were detached with a yard (Jackson 1985: 238–39).
3. McCarthy's supporters included "conservative politicians and publicists, businessmen, and retired military leaders discontented with the New Deal" who sought to move the Republican Party farther to the right (Hixson 1992: 30).
4. Theoharis 1971: 14. Associations between the New Deal and communism were originally developed by conservatives and the House Committee on Un-American Activities in the 1930s (Goldstone 1973: 20–34).
5. Himmelstein 1990: 57.
6. Himmelstein 1990: 22–23.
7. Cited in Bresler 1995: 14.
8. Lansdale 1961.
9. By 1956, the federal share for ADC had increased to fourteen of the first seventeen dollars, plus half of the balance (Cauthen and Amenta 1996: 436; Mink 1995: 134; U.S. Department of Health, Education, and Welfare 1961a: 18–19).
10. Soule and Zylan 1997: 737.
11. Soule and Zylan (1997) also found that enactment of state-level work requirements for A(F)DC between 1950 and 1967 was more rapid among states that were generally innovative in policy construction and less rapid in states where there were greater institutional protections for public assistance recipi-

ents. They also found that diffusion was more rapid among states that belonged to the same Social Security Administration region.

12. Abramovitz 1989; Chang 1994; Goodwin 1995; Piven and Cloward 1993; Rose 1995; and Rowe 1993.

13. Levenstein (2000) briefly mentions nativist attacks on Puerto Ricans' welfare use in New York. Besides the 1930s, scholars have neglected Mexican Americans' experiences of welfare in the first half of the twentieth century (Weinberg 1998: 55).

14. North Carolina State Board of Public Welfare 1952.

15. California Farm Bureau Federation 1950b; California Senate Interim Committee on State and Local Taxation 1951: 10; Illinois Agricultural Association 1956: 31.

16. Evidence from Georgia comes from court records from the late 1960s, which indicate that this was a long-standing practice (Goodwin 1995: 267). Evidence on Illinois comes from testimony given in a 1966 hearing by the Illinois State Advisory Committee of the U.S. Commission on Civil Rights. Unfortunately, information about such practices is more readily available for the 1960s than the 1950s. Welfare departments came under greater public scrutiny in the 1960s as welfare rights and civil rights advocates and organizations fought many of the eligibility restrictions established in the 1950s (Piven and Cloward 1993: 125). On Arkansas, see Mink 1998a: 37–38.

17. Holmes 1975; Mertz 1978: 54–56; Piven and Cloward 1993; Quadagno 1984, 1988; Southworth 2002.

18. California Farm Bureau Federation 1950b; California Senate Interim Committee on State and Local Taxation 1951: 10.

19. Illinois Agricultural Association 1956: 31.

20. Weaver 1951; New York Times 1951q.

21. Dyson 1986: 14. The AFBF was founded in 1920 by representatives of county and state farm bureaus that formed between 1902 and 1919. County agents of the Department of Agriculture's Extension Service organized many of these to carry out research (McConnell 1953: 46–47).

22. From the start, the AFBF allied itself with business rather than labor (McConnell 1953: 51). Even at the height of the New Deal period, the AFBF expressed little interest in the plight of farmworkers or poor farmers and was hostile to organized labor (Dyson 1986: 14–20). In the late 1940s and 1950s, the AFBF supported passage of the Taft-Hartley Act, opposed raising the minimum wage, and endorsed state "right-to-work" laws that gave employers the right to hire scabs (McConnell 1953: 149–50, 163; McCune 1956: 21–24).

23. McConnell 1953.

24. Baker 1955: 24.

25. Mann 1990: 39; Pfeffer 1986: 259–62; Pfeffer 1983: 541–42.

26. New York Times 1952i.

27. These figures are for the sixteen southern states and Missouri (Mann 1990: 96). Scholars attribute this decline to a number of factors, including federal acreage reduction policies, the mechanization of agriculture (particularly

cotton), and the lure of defense industry jobs during World War II (Goldfield 1982: 140–42; Mann 1990: 95–127).

28. Galarza 1964; 1977; Pfeffer 1983, 1986; Quadagno 1988: 240.

29. Heinicke 1991: 1, 30, 33.

30. Heinicke 1991; Johnson and Campbell 1981: 101–51. Based on his quantitative analysis, Heinicke concludes that "at most, 31 percent of the total black migrants [from the rural South] were displaced by the mechanical cotton picker" (Heinicke 1991: 99).

31. Hawkins 1973: 147–50; Heinicke 1991; Johnson and Campbell 1981: 101–51.

32. Rowe 1993: 446–55; see also Holmes 1975; Mertz 1978, 54–56; Piven and Cloward 1993; Quadagno 1984, 1988; Southworth 2002.

33. Piven and Cloward 1993.

34. American Farm Bureau Federation 1954g.

35. American Farm Bureau Federation 1954e, f.

36. American Farm Bureau Federation 1955a, b, d, e; 1956b, 1957; 1958.

37. Calhoun County Department of Welfare 1950.

38. In 1949, only 6 percent of cotton produced in the United States was mechanically harvested. In 1955, this had increased to only 23 percent (Wright 1986: 245).

39. Bean and Tienda 1987: 18; Pfeffer 1986: 254.

40. Galarza 1964; 1977; Pfeffer 1986: 280. For this very reason, California growers frequently reported labor shortages to the Department of Labor when they did not exist in order to keep up their supply of labor (Galarza 1977: 43–46).

41. The two main programs through which farmworkers were recruited from other countries was the bracero ("farmhand") program, begun in 1942 and terminated in 1964, and the H-2 program (created in 1952). By 1947, Mexican braceros worked in twenty-one states, but were primarily hired in Arizona, Texas, and California. The H-2 program was mostly used by eastern growers to import West Indians, primarily Jamaicans (Portes and Bach 1985: 61–62; Ueda 1994: 33). The number of braceros increased from 32,000 in 1946 to 448,000 in 1959, while the number of H-2 workers increased from 12,000 in 1952 to 17,000 in 1959 (Portes and Bach 1985: 63).

42. California farmers employed about 90 percent of those hired in 1945 (Wells 1996: 57) and about 50 percent of those hired in 1947 (Ueda 1994: 33).

43. Pfeffer 1986: 264.

44. Before July 1951, when Public Law 78 was passed, the bracero program was extended temporarily through several interim agreements. Even after the passage of Public Law 78, the agreements between the United States and Mexico had to be renewed every few years and Congress had to periodically reauthorize funds for the program (Galarza 1977: 32).

45. Lipshultz 1971: 20–29, 60; Stevens 1969: 22.

46. American Farm Bureau Federation 1955c; 1959d; 1959a, b, c.

47. American Farm Bureau Federation 1954a, b, c, d. Farmers' associations

feared that the Mexican government might make costly demands on growers because Mexico was the main source of foreign labor supply for U.S. farmers. For that reason, they sought and established other sources of foreign labor. For example, California growers discussed reopening the Japanese labor market in 1953 and got authorization to do this in 1956. They also negotiated for labor recruitment from Hawaii in 1950, and the Philippines in 1956 (Galarza 1964: 247–49).

48. Massey et al. 1987: 288; Pfeffer 1986: 278; Portes and Bach 1985: 64; Ueda 1994: 34.

49. Street 1957: 204.

50. American Farm Bureau Federation 1954c, 1956a, 1959b.

51. Bartley 1969: 104–18, 314.

52. Abramovitz 1989; W. Bell 1965; Reese 2001; Solinger 1992.

53. John Martin 1979: 68; Piven and Cloward 1977: 198; Ashmore 1994: 31–86; Key 1949: 334–42; John Martin 1979: 69–72; Piven and Cloward 1977: 208–11.

54. Bartley 1969. In 1960, 60 percent of blacks still lived in the South (U.S. Bureau of the Census, cited in Himes 1971: 361).

55. Key 1949: 330–42. Fifty-four years later, Senator Trent Lott's continuing support for Thurmond, and his claim that the country would have been better off had Thurmond won the presidency in 1948, created such a stir that he resigned under fire from his position as Senate Majority Leader.

56. John Martin 1979: 133–34.

57. Civil Rights Congress 1970.

58. Belknap 1987: 28–54.

59. The first Citizens' Council was founded in Indianola, Mississippi, by plantation owner Robert Patterson, within two months of the Brown decision. He later helped to create the Association of Citizen Councils, comprised of more than thirty councils in Mississippi (Bartley 1969: 84–99, 121–22; John Martin 1979: 12–135).

60. Bartley 1969: 82–83; Chalmers 1965: 354; John Martin 1979: 28.

61. Bartley 1969: 32–34; Piven and Cloward 1977: 199.

62. Cited in Bartley 1969: 241.

63. Chalmers 1965: 340.

64. Hawkins 1973: 148.

65. McAdam 1999: 80; U.S. Bureau of Census 1969, p. 4, cited in Himes 1971: 361.

66. Shapiro 1988: 376–82.

67. Coontz 1997: 44.

68. Ayala 1996: 63; Bean and Tienda 1987: 23–24; Senior 1965: 39.

69. New York City's share of Puerto Ricans in the United States declined from 88 percent in 1940 to 83 percent in 1950, and 69 percent in 1960 (Senior 1965: 88; Portes and Grosfoguel 1994: 54; Wagenheim 1975: 71, 74).

70. This transformation of the country's economy was stimulated by Operation Bootstrap, the government's industrialization program. Although manu-

facturing employment rose dramatically in the 1950s, it did not keep pace with the decline in agricultural and garment employment (Ayala 1996; Gann and Duignan 1986: 75).

71. Senior 1965: 40, 87; Portes and Grosfoguel 1994: 54; Bean and Tienda 1987: 23–25; Hedda 1994: 100; Gann and Duignan 1986: 75.

72. Cited in Senior 1965: 37, 43.

73. Senior 1965: 40, 91; Bean and Tienda 1987: 24–25.

74. Senior 1965: 41–42; Gann and Duignan 1986: 83; Hedda 1994: 101–2; Ortiz 1996: 86.

75. Leo Grebler, Joan W. Moore, and Ralph C. Guzman, *The Mexican-American People* (New York: Free Press, 1970), p. 68, cited in Portes and Bach 1985: 63; Samora and Simon 1977: 140.

76. Samora and Simon 1977: 139. The rising number of immigrants deported after World War II supports this claim. About 12,000 undocumented immigrants were deported each year between 1934 and 1943. The number rose abruptly to 31,179 in 1944 and doubled in 1945, continuing upward to 1,089,583 in 1954 (Gann and Duignan 1986: 58–59).

77. Gann and Duignan 1986: 56, 64; Guerin-Gonzales 1996: 66.

78. Bullock 1972: 92.

79. Samora and Simon 1977: 157; Machado 1978: 81–84; Stevens 1969: 17–18; Tuck 1974 [1946]: 217.

80. By 1960, the mean index of residential dissimilarity for 35 southwestern cities was 80.1 for blacks and whites and 54.5 for Latinos and whites. Black-white residential segregation was greater than Latino-white segregation in each of these cities (Moore and Mittelbach 1972: 81, 84).

81. Camarillo 1990: 80; Machado 1978: 80; Tuck 1974.

82. Tuck 1974: 184, 188, 200–1; see also G. Sanchez 1972: 41–42.

83. Cuellar 1972: 197–202; Machado 1978: 85–91; Samora and Simon 1977: 193–94; Stevens 1969: 18; Tuck 1974: 198–9.

84. Stevens 1969: 19; Samora and Simon 1977: 193.

85. Allard and Danziger 2000; Schram, Nitz, and Krueger 1998.

86. Davis 1993: 77.

87. Other scholars mistakenly date the emergence of racialized images of poverty and welfare later, in the 1960s (Quadagno 1994; and Gilens 1999).

88. For a good discussion of the history of stereotypes of blacks within the United States and Europe, see P. Collins (1990: 77), Gilman (1985), Hall (1984), Hooks (1992), Jordan (1974), and Solinger (1992: 187).

89. Gordon 2001: 19.

90. Family experts and psychologists were more likely to recommend counseling than punishment for white unwed mothers, whom they believed suffered from neuroses (Solinger 1992: 187; Gordon 2001: 19). In the early 1950s, social scientists began to claim that the absence of fathers led to personality disorders among the lower class, including the inability to defer gratification, foreshadowing the "culture of poverty" argument that emerged at the end of the decade (A. O'Connor 2001: 109).

91. Friedan 1983: 18, Michel 1999; Rupp and Taylor 1987: 14–16; A. O'Connor 2001: 99.

92. Cherlin 1992: 36; U.S. Children's Bureau 1953: 6.

93. Gerson 1985: 4; Coontz 1997; Honey 1984; Milkman 1987.

94. Cherlin 1992: 35; Coltrane and Collins 2001: 136–142; Coontz 1997: 33–50.

95. Coltrane and Collins 2001: 130–37.

96. Some women left their wartime jobs voluntarily. Others were forced to do so because of managerial prerogatives (Milkman 1987).

97. U.S. Bureau of the Census 1973: 222–23.

98. Gerson 1985; Daniel 1987; Milkman 1987.

99. L. Gordon 2001: 16; Roberts 1997; Handler and Hasenfeld 1991.

100. Jones 1985: 262, 269. At the same time, black mothers who worked were often accused of neglecting their children, or causing personality disorders among them (Roberts 1997: 14; O'Connor 2001).

101. Cherlin 1992: 91–119; W. Wilson 1996.

102. Slightly more than one quarter of all black women who ever married were separated, divorced, or widowed in 1950, compared to 10 percent of their white counterparts. The separation rates for married black women (16 percent) was also four times higher than it was for white women who had previously married. The national rate of out-of-wedlock childbearing experienced the most rapid increase in history when it tripled between 1940 and 1958, rising from 7.1 to 21.0 births per 1,000 unwed women (National Office of Vital Statistics 1960; Jones 1985: 263–306).

103. National Office of Vital Statistics 1960.

104. Jones 1985: 263, 305–6.

105. Levenstein 2000: 21.

106. Solinger 1992.

107. Cited in Solinger 1992: 49.

108. Komisar 1977: 76.

109. Cited in Kentucky Legislative Research Commission 1961: 41–42.

110. Lansdale 1942.

111. Cited in W. Bell 1965: 68.

112. Cited in Solinger 1992: 41.

113. California Farm Bureau Federation 1950a.

114. Cited in St. John 1952b.

115. Cited in Malloy 1951.

116. Georgia Department of Public Welfare 1944: 32.

117. Atlanta Constitution 1949.

118. California Farm Bureau Federation 1950b.

119. Cited in Molloy 1951.

120. Cited in W. Bell 1965: 64.

121. Chang 1994; Handler and Hasenfeld 1991; Mink 1998a.

122. McDuffie County Grand Jury 1952, cited in W. Bell 1965: 64–68, my italics.

123. Cited in Katz 1996: 261.

124. Brown 1999: 176.

125. Jones 1985: 256–57.

126. Cited in W. Bell 1965: 63.

127. Sara J. Hill, Sara J. 1968 Deposition, pp. 8–19, 53; Mary Louise Maxwell, 1966 Deposition, pp. 55–56; Josephine Boulinean Craig, 1967 Deposition, pp. 24–25, in Records of Civil Action Number 10443.

128. Gallup 1972: 1731.

129. U.S. Bureau of the Census 1973: 222–23.

130. Zylan 2000.

131. Georgia Department of Public Welfare 1953a: 27.

132. Eliot 1952: 8. Oettinger 1957: 22.The bureau advocated government-subsidized day care as a child welfare measure that should be made available only to poor mothers (Zylan 2000).

133. Oettinger 1957: 5.

134. Oettinger 1958: 10. At the beginning of the century, maternalist reformers had promoted "suitable home" policies because they believed they could be used to protect neglected and abused children and maintain the image of mothers' pensions and ADC as primarily helping worthy widows. They later opposed them because they prevented poor mothers and their children from receiving financial support (Machtinger 1995).

135. Eliot 1955:14.

136. This is consistent with Pierson (1996: 176–78) and Hicks and Misra (1993).

137. U.S. Bureau of the Census 1956.

138. U.S. Department of Commerce 1958.

139. Alling and Leisy 1950.

140. Incomplete information on the timing of policy changes for a number of states (see Appendix 1), as well as the lack of annual data for key variables, precluded the use of more dynamic time-series or event-history models for this analysis.

141. See appendix and Reese (2001) for details on this quantitative analysis and measures used.

142. U.S. Bureau of the Census 1961.

CHAPTER 5

1. These were the main industries in terms of the value of production and number of employees. The main crops grown were cotton, corn, peaches, pecans, peanuts, and tobacco (Dudley and Smith 1952: 285; Council of State Governments 1950: 536; U.S. Bureau of the Census 1952).

2. Representation in the state assembly was allocated by the following constitutional formula: three representatives to each of the eight most populous counties; two to each of the next thirty; and one to each of the remaining 121 counties, for a total of 205 seats.

3. The overrepresentation of rural counties was also found in elections for

state executive and judicial officers because each county was allotted twice the number of votes as it had representatives in the legislative assembly (Baker 1955: 16, 22).

4. U.S. Bureau of the Census 1954.

5. U.S. Bureau of the Census 1952; Dudley and Smith 1952: 389.

6. Kentucky Committee's Midcentury White House Conference on Children and Youth 1950: 10.

7. U.S. Bureau of the Census 1952, 1954; Dudley and Smith 1952: 389.

8. Georgia Department of Public Welfare 1945–50, *Official Reports*; Source Table 4, Piven and Cloward 1993.

9. Georgia Department of Public Welfare 1945–50, *Official Reports*.

10. Georgia Department of Public Welfare 1949–50: 36.

11. They also adopted new rules for Old Age Assistance, including a requirement that children support parents when financially able and a limit on the value of property they owned. Husbands and wives were required to combine their income when claiming aid for old age benefits (Atlanta Constitution 1949).

12. Atlanta Constitution 1949.

13. The State Board of Social Security was composed of a director and ten members who were appointed by the governor and confirmed by the Senate (Georgia Department of Public Welfare 1944: 1).

14. Georgia Department of Public Welfare, cited in W. Bell 1965.

15. The Social Security Board surprisingly did not contest this provision even though it had declared unconstitutional a similar 1951 Georgia law prohibiting additional aid to mothers who had repeated births out of wedlock (W. Bell 1965: 82, 94).

16. Of the 5,749 cases that were declined that year, 5,053 of them were attributed to the implementation of the new regulations (Georgia Department of Public Welfare 1953b).

17. W. Bell 1965: 82–83.

18. C. A. Doolittle, 1966 Deposition, p. 106, in Records of Civil Action Number 10443.

19. Alan Kemper, 1967 Deposition, p. 13, in Records of Civil Action Number 10443.

20. Harold Parker, 1967 Deposition, p. 37, in Records of Civil Action Number 10443.

21. Key 1949: 106–18.

22. Holmes 1975: 10–29, 15. Rivers's gubernatorial campaign was supported by those who wanted Georgia to participate in federal welfare programs, organized labor who were antagonized by Talmadge's use of militia to break strikes, and blacks who opposed the governor's anti-black ravings. After his election, Rivers rallied support among state legislators for the creation of the state's welfare programs. Yet, the success of this movement proved to be short-lived as the Talmadge faction came back into power soon after (Key 1949; Holmes 1975).

23. Phil R. Cawthon, 1966 Deposition, p. 6 in Records of Civil Action Number 10443.

24. Alan Kemper, 1967 Deposition, p. 11 in Records of Civil Action Number 10443.

25. Georgia Laws, Regular Session 1951: 848–49.

26. Atlanta Constitution 1951a.

27. Alan Kemper, 1967 Deposition, p. 11 in Records of Civil Action Number 10443.

28. In the late 1930s, Georgia's welfare officials used a racial quota system to allocate welfare benefits, until federal welfare officials forced them to get rid of the policy (W. Bell 1965: 35).

29. Between 1945 and 1950, civil rights activists recorded at least thirty-nine racially motivated murders in Georgia, the highest number recorded for any state during that period (Civil Rights Congress 1970).

30. U.S. Bureau of the Census 1952: 11–301–2.

31. Georgia General Assembly House of Representatives 1951; see also Atlanta Constitution 1951d.

32. Sibley 1951.

33. Atlanta Constitution 1951c.

34. Sibley 1951.

35. Alan Kemper, 1967 Deposition, pp. 41–42 in Records of Civil Action Number 10443.

36. Atlanta Constitution 1951c.

37. W. Bell 1965: 71–72.

38. *Georgia Laws, Regular Session 1952*: 1224.

39. W. Bell 1965: 81. The federal government's crackdown on the legislature's 1951 law probably inhibited legislators from creating too many other eligibility rules. As an administrative body, the state welfare board was in a better position to negotiate directly with federal officials about state welfare policies, which it did to replace the contested 1951 law. Nevertheless, the state legislature did adopt a property limit for welfare receipt and passed a law making it a felony to abandon a child (*Georgia Laws, Regular Session 1952*: 173–74).

40. *Georgia Laws, Regular Session 1951*: 6–7.

41. Atlanta Constitution 1951f, 1951g.

42. Davenport 1951.

43. Calhoun County Department of Public Welfare 1952.

44. Mary Louise Maxwell, 1966 Deposition, pp. 38–39 in Records of Civil Action Number 10443.

45. Atlanta Constitution 1951e.

46. St. John 1952a.

47. St. John 1952a.

48. Atlanta Constitution 1952b.

49. St John 1952a.

50. St. John 1952b.

51. Atlanta Constitution 1952b.

52. St. John 1952a.

53. Atlanta Constitution 1952a. Similarly, Kemper released a list of thirty-

one Old Age Assistance cases involving recipients whose children were capable of supporting them to major newspapers in the state "in order to demonstrate the need for tightening welfare regulations" (Atlanta Constitution 1951b).

54. Sibley 1951.

55. Phil R. Cawthon, 1966 Deposition, p. 18 in Records of Civil Action Number 10443.

56. C. A. Doolittle, 1966 Deposition, pp. 106–8; Alan Kemper, 1967 Deposition, p. 16 in Records of Civil Action Number 10443.

57. Georgia Department of Public Welfare 1952: 2

58. Atlanta Constitution 1951a.

59. Trizonis 1951.

60. Holmes 1975: 213–26.

61. Holmes 1975: 86.

62. Holmes 1975: 75–76, 100.

63. Mary Louise Maxwell, 1966 Deposition, pp. 14–15 in Records of Civil Action Number 10443.

64. Georgia Department of Public Welfare 1953a: 22.

65. Depositions of Margaret Butler and Ossie Thomas, 1966–7, in Records of Civil Action Number 10443; Georgia Department of Public Welfare 1953a.

66. Loretha Sadler, 1967 Deposition, p. 35; Johnny Mae Williams, 1967 Deposition, p. 40 in Records of Civil Action Number 10443.

67. Mary Louise Maxwell, 1966 Interrogatories, p. 5 in Records of Civil Action Number 10443; Alto Sellars, 1967 Deposition, pp. 8, 27; B. M. Lee, 1967 Deposition, pp. 4, 14 in Records of Civil Action Number 10443.

68. Mary Louise Maxwell, 1966 Interrogatories, pp. 8, 41–49 in Records of Civil Action Number 10443.

69. Mary Louise Maxwell, 1966 Deposition, pp. 21–27 in Records of Civil Action Number 10443. The testimonies of agricultural workers and those who transported farmworkers in Georgia also indicate that there were very few white women doing seasonal farm work on large farms during the 1950s (see Depositions of Tildon Wheeler, Elton Sanders, Lizzie King, Ozel Jackson, Roberta Richardson, Ora Lee Mathis, Mrs. Lucy Hudson, Mrs. Johnnie Mae Horton, Mary Lee Pressley, and Loretha Sadler, 1966–67, Records of Civil Action Number 10443).

70. Transcript of proceedings had before the Honorable Griffin Bell et al., 1967, Records of Civil Action Number 10443.

71. B. M. Lee, 1967 Deposition, p. 15 in Records of Civil Action Number 10443.

72. Assistant Director of the Georgia Department of Welfare, cited in W. Bell 1965: 95.

73. W. Bell 1965: 95.

74. W. Bell 1965: 84.

75. League of Women Voters of Georgia 1951.

76. Calhoun County Department of Public Welfare 1952.

77. Dade County Department of Public Welfare 1953.

78. Gilmer County Department of Public Welfare 1952.

79. Calhoun County Department of Public Welfare 1952.

80. Georgia Department of Public Welfare 1953a: 27.

81. Smith May 1951; Atlanta Constitution 1951h.

82. The Townsend movement was founded by Dr. Francis Townsend in the 1930s. The movement campaigned for a generous, flat ($200) monthly pension for the elderly, to be financed from taxes on all business transactions, with the dual purpose of aiding the elderly and stimulating the economy by increasing their purchasing power (Pinner, Jacobs, and Selznick 1959: 4).

83. A club was "active" if it ordered 30 or more prepaid membership applications in a contest spanning two years (Holtzman 1975: 51).

84. Kentucky Assembly 1948–60; Kentucky Senate 1948–60.

85. Kentucky Legislative Research Commission 1961.

86. Barnes 1949.

87. Kentucky Department of Economic Security 1950b: 7.

88. Kentucky Department of Economic Security 1949.

89. Kentucky Legislative Research Commission 1950: 151–55. This rule could be waived "if a bastardy proceeding cannot be had or would be futile, or would not be to the best interests of such child, or its mother or of the state" (Kentucky General Assembly 1950, ch. 110).

90. Kentucky Department of Economic Security 1950a: 1.

91. Kentucky Legislative Research Commission 1950: 151–55.

92. Governor's Committee for the 1960 Golden Anniversary White House Conference on Children and Youth 1960: 47.

93. Heinicke 1991; U.S. Bureau of the Census 1962.

94. Kentucky Legislative Research Commission 1952: 22.

95. Kentucky Legislative Research Commission 1952.

96. Kentucky Senate 1952: 1397.

97. Kentucky Legislative Research Commission 1952: 25.

98. Kentucky Legislative Research Commission 1961: 26.

99. Kentucky Legislative Research Commission 1961: ii.

100. Kentucky Legislative Research Commission 1961: 40.

101. These were Christian, Daviess, Floyd, Franklin, Henderson, Madison, Scott, and Harlan counties (Governor's Committee for the 1960 Golden Anniversary White House Conference on Children and Youth 1960).

102. Governor's Committee for the 1960 Golden Anniversary White House Conference on Children and Youth 1960: 34.

103. Governor's Committee for the 1960 Golden Anniversary White House Conference on Children and Youth 1960: 37–38.

104. Governor's Committee for the 1960 Golden Anniversary White House Conference on Children and Youth 1960: 140.

105. Kentucky Legislative Research Commission 1961: 43.

106. Kentucky Legislative Research Commission 1961: 41.

107. The federal agency had declared illegal a similar law enacted in Geor-

gia in 1952 and in 1960 challenged the legality of Louisiana's "suitable home" law that restricted aid to children born out of wedlock.

108. Kentucky Assembly 1960: 1518–19.

109. Kentucky Legislative Research Commission 1961: 51.

110. Kentucky Legislative Research Commission 1961: 30, 41–43.

111. Kentucky Legislative Research Commission 1961: 51.

112. Kentucky Senate 1962: 145.

113. Fenton 1957: 12–41. In 1950, miners made up about 16 percent of Kentucky's labor force (Dudley and Smith 1952: 388).

114. Jewell and Cunningham 1968: 7, 267; Fenton 1957: 12.

115. Blakey 1986: 170. Eastern coal miners, who were highly unionized, were the biggest supporters of the New Deal. It had less support in the Inner Bluegrass area, dominated by a largely nonunionized urban workforce, a significant suburban population, and large farmers. Poor farmers in the Southcentral Knobs region believed that New Deal programs mainly benefited the urban working class and large farmers (Fenton 1957: 66–76).

116. J. Pearce 1987: 48; Syversten 1985: 158.

117. Kavanaugh 1947–50; J. Pearce 1987: 61–70.

118. Alling and Leisy 1950: 33; U.S. Bureau of the Census 1954.

119. J. Pearce 1987: 48; Syversten 1985: 158–60.

120. J. Pearce 1987: 54.

121. Fenton 1957: 62; Jewell and Cunningham 1968: 270.

CHAPTER 6

1. U.S. Bureau of the Census 1952.

2. "California leads all the states of the Union in cash income derived from agriculture and in terms of cash returns, produces more than a third of the nation's commercial fruits, a fourth of the commercial vegetables, and nearly two thirds of the commercial tree nut output" (Dudley and Smith 1952: 100).

3. Dudley and Smith 1952: 100.

4. Baker 1955: 16.

5. CISW was originally called Citizens' Committee for Old Age Pensions.

6. Between 1935 and 1950, 1,073 Townsend clubs were organized in California, more than any other state.

7. Pinner, Jacobs, and Selznick 1959: 4–5; Holtzman 1975: 50–51.

8. McLain became politically active after his family's company went out of business during the depression. While participating in a public works program, he organized the Los Angeles Unemployed Voters Association in 1931. He later worked for the "Ham and Eggs" movement and unsuccessfully ran for various local government offices (Pinner, Jacobs, and Selznick 1959: 25–33).

9. Delaplane 1949a; Pinner, Jacobs, and Selznick 1959.

10. Supporters included the American Federation of Labor, the Congress of Industrial Organizations, the California State Federation of Labor, and the

Brotherhood of Railway Trainmen (San Francisco Chronicle 1949g, Behrens 1949c; Pinner, Jacobs, and Selznick 1959: 52–58, 94).

11. It reduced the age of eligibility to sixty-three for persons with ten years of residence in California and sixty-five for those with five years of residence, increased the amount of property a pensioner could own, and eliminated "relative responsibility" laws that required children to financially support their aged parents. To ensure that enough state funds were allocated to cover the increased cost of the programs for old age and the blind, Proposition 4 required that these programs be given a first lien against the state treasury (San Francisco Chronicle 1948a, 1948c, Behrens 1948a, 1948b, 1948c).

12. Proposition 2 kept the pension increases intact, but eliminated the administrative changes in the program and new eligibility rules created by Proposition 4, dropping an estimated forty thousand pensioners from the rolls (San Francisco Chronicle 1949j). Business groups that campaigned against Proposition 4 included the California County Supervisors' Association (led by an Orange County banker), the San Francisco Chamber of Commerce, and the California Taxpayers' Association (San Francisco Chronicle 1948b). Social welfare agencies, such as the California Council for the Blind and the California Association for Social Welfare, also opposed Proposition 4 (San Francisco Chronicle 1948b, 1948d, 1948e; California Taxpayers' Association 1949: 295). Women's organizations joined the campaign for Proposition 2, including Parent-Teacher Associations, the League of Women Voters, and the California Federation of Business and Professional Women's Clubs (San Francisco Chronicle 1949f, 1949c; Behrens 1949b; see also Pinner, Jacobs, and Selznick 1959: 228).

13. Shortly after its creation, five members of the new Social Welfare Advisory Board quit in order to register their opposition to the new pension program and its administration (San Francisco Chronicle 1949a, 1949b, 1949d, 1949e). They claimed that Myrtle Williams (a retired real estate agent with no previous experience in social work) relied too heavily on McLain's advice when making policy decisions and failed to consult them on key decisions (Pinner, Jacobs, and Selznick 1959: 228, 243–44).

14. McLain 1951: 54–56; Behrens 1949a; Delaplane 1949b.

15. The CISW won each of these cases (San Francisco Chronicle 1949h, 1949i, 1949l, 1949m; Pinner, Jacobs, and Selznick 1959: 234).

16. The vote for Proposition 2 was 1,516,299, while 1,123,723 voted against it (McLain 1951: 2; San Francisco Chronicle 1949k).

17. This bill passed the 1947 legislature but the governor vetoed it because it would have raised state expenditures beyond expected revenues (California Department of Social Welfare 1950b). Prior to 1949, the state disqualified children whose fathers were absent for less than three years, whose mother was absent, or whose parents were ill but not permanently or totally disabled. Children born out of wedlock were disqualified if the alleged father admitted or did not deny paternity even if he did not support the child (Anderson 1949).

18. These included several members of the State Board of Social Welfare, the executive secretary of the Community Welfare Council of Sacramento County,

the Welfare Council of Metropolitan Los Angeles, the executive secretary of the Sacramento Community Welfare Council, the Southwest District Welfare Council, the superintendent of charities of the County of Los Angeles, and the American Association of Social Workers.

19. Supporters included the Los Angeles County Grand Jury for 1949, Los Angeles journalists (such as the editors of the Los Angeles *Daily News*) as well as prominent county officials from Contra Costa, Los Angeles, and San Diego.

20. Governor's Chaptered Bill Files, California State Archive.

21. The bill received fifty ayes and twenty-one nays in the Assembly and unanimous approval in the Senate (California State Legislature 1949).

22. During World War II, only seven children per thousand under eighteen years of age received aid. Prior to the war this rate was twenty-two per thousand. By June 1949 this rate had risen to eighteen per thousand. This rise was primarily due to various demographic changes, including increases in the state's rates of marriages, births, in-migrations, divorces, illegitimacy, and widowhood, which increased the number of female-headed households. Meanwhile, women's employment opportunities declined as war industries collapsed or shrunk (California Department of Social Welfare 1950b). The year after the 1949 law became effective, monthly expenditures nearly doubled, while the number of recipients increased from 87,900 to 184,200 (California Department of Social Welfare 1950a).

23. MacLatchie 1950.

24. California Farm Bureau Federation 1950c: 3; Jelinek 1976.

25. California Farm Bureau Federation 1950a.

26. California Farm Bureau Federation 1950a.

27. California Farm Bureau Federation 1950a.

28. The potato-digging machine was just being tested in 1951. Use of the harvester machine for beets was not used much until 1952. In 1950, only 35 percent of cotton was picked mechanically. Tomato harvesting machines were still being tested in 1951. Grape production was not mechanized until the 1960s (Galarza 1977: 67–69).

29. Pfeffer 1986: 264.

30. There was a three-year strike at the DiGiorgio farm in Kern County, the cotton strike of 1949, and the Tracy tomato strike in 1950. Mexican workers' three-year-long strike on DiGiorgio's farm was broken through the use of native-born workers (Galarza 1977: 110–60).

31. California Farm Bureau Federation 1950a.

32. California Farm Bureau Federation 1950b.

33. Cited in California Senate Interim Committee on State and Local Taxation 1951: 60.

34. McLain 1951: 21.

35. In 1951, the Real Estate Association lobbied for a three-month time limit on eligibility for cases of separation and desertion, clarification that the intent of ADC was to encourage employment and self-maintenance, and a bill denying welfare to parents refusing to work or participate in rehabilitative training

(Governor's Chaptered Bill Files 1951, for Bills 945, 946, and 951; W. Smith 1950).

36. Webber 1951: 121–23.

37. These industries included banking, real estate, railroads, oil and gas, timber, publishing, hotels, cement, aircraft, insurance, and motion pictures (California Taxpayers' Association 1950; California Taxpayers' Association 1951).

38. W. Smith 1950: 268; Will 1952: 127.

39. Hanson 1950: 115, 138.

40. Will, Wyman, and Douglas 1951: 12–14.

41. J. L. Rosenberg 1949: 333.

42. Sly 1950: 136.

43. Shelton 1949: 358.

44. California State Chamber of Commerce 1950.

45. California Taxpayers' Association 1950; California Taxpayers' Association 1951; California State Chamber of Commerce 1950.

46. Some state legislators criticized the use of tax money to pay private lobbyists. Assemblyman Hawkins introduced Assembly Bill 3430 to stop this practice and Assemblyman Ernest Geddes introduced a resolution to investigate the matter. Neither bill passed the legislature (McLain 1951: 22–23).

47. The Senate Interim Committee on Social Welfare also launched a costly investigation of the CISW and tried, unsuccessfully, to prevent the CISW from testifying to legislative committees (California State Legislature 1951a, 1951b; McLain 1951: 54–56).

48. McLain 1951: 10.

49. California Senate Interim Committee on State and Local Taxation 1951: 10.

50. California State Legislature 1951a.

51. California Senate Interim Committee on State and Local Taxation 1951: 10.

52. Beginning in 1931, federal agents and local welfare officials deported, threatened to deport, and urged Mexicans and Mexican-Americans to leave the country voluntarily, even if they were legal residents or citizens of the United States, and subsidized their trip to Mexico. Between 1930 and 1934, well over 400,000 Mexican immigrants and Mexican Americans left the United States for Mexico, and by 1940, the U.S. Mexican population was about half as large as it was in 1930. While these programs supposedly targeted male migrants, entire families were repatriated, and women made up as many as two-thirds of deportees between 1931 and 1933 (Guerin-Gonzales 1996: 77–114; Gann and Duignan 1986: 51; Hondagneu-Sotelo 1995: 174–76; Samora and Simon 1977: 137).

53. Brasher, Springer, and Hanlan 1966: 1.

54. California State Social Welfare Board 1949. Cotton plantings rose rapidly in California in the 1940s, from 341,000 in 1941 to 948,000 in 1949. By 1949, California was one of the principal cotton-producing states in the nation (Galarza 1977: 75).

55. W. Bell 1965: 42–43.

56. U.S. Bureau of the Census 1943: 519; U.S. Bureau of the Census 1954.

57. Bullock 1972: 92.

58. Unfortunately, there is no estimate of the hispanic population for 1950. The census did not use a single indicator of "hispanic" prior to 1970. The 1960 estimates were constructed by combining information from various indicators (Bean and Tienda 1987: 404–9).

59. Douglas 1951: 14; California Farm Bureau Federation 1950a.

60. California Senate Interim Committee on State and Local Taxation 1951; California State Legislature 1951a, AB 3059.

61. Pfeffer 1986: 264; U.S. Bureau of the Census 1952: 5–360–1.

62. Only about 3 percent of ADC recipients were reported to be both non-black and nonwhite in 1948. Hispanic women could have been recorded as white, however (Alling and Leisy 1950: 33).

63. Eliot 1951: 4.

64. Brasher, Springer, and Hanlan 1966: 2, 70.

65. Irwin 1950.

66. Guerin-Gonzales 1996; Tuck 1974: 189, 197–98.

67. McLain 1951: 19.

68. California State Legislature 1951a, b.

69. Governor's Chaptered Bill Files 1951.

70. California Department of Social Welfare 1951–53.

71. Governor's Chaptered Bill Files 1951, chs. 884 and 952.

72. McLain 1951: 30.

73. California State Legislature 1951a, 1951b.

74. McLain 1951: 33.

75. McLain 1951.

76. California State Legislature 1951a.

77. Alameda County Welfare Rights Committee 1964.

78. Alameda County Welfare Rights Committee 1964.

79. New York State Department of Social Welfare 1964.

80. Herwitz 1947.

81. New York Times 1950s; Freeman 1950d.

82. New York Times 1950r; New York Times 1951f; Freeman 1952a.

83. New York Times 1951c; Egan 1951; Greenberg 1950; New York Times 1950y. The Congress of Industrial Organizations ended their affiliation with several leftwing unions because of their procommunist tendencies, while the welfare department crossed them off their list of recognized staff organizations (New York Times 1951p). Two years later, the CIO established a special committee to "oust left-wing unions from the social service field" in New York City (New York Times 1952b).

84. Dales 1949.

85. New York Times 1952i.

86. New York Times 1950d, 1950n, 1951o, 1951a; Egan 1951; Seigal 1950; Dales 1951b, 1951c.

87. New York Times 1952h.

88. New York State Legislature 1951. New York Times 1951g, 1951h, 1951i. The attorney general partially overruled the latter law, claiming that the State Liquor Authority could not revoke or suspend the license of a dealer convicted of cashing a public assistance check for a second time (New York Times 1951j).

89. Dales 1949; New York Times 1951q, 1953a, 1953d.

90. Organized labor and New York City's politicians strongly opposed work-fare programs, which became permanent in 1959, claiming they were punitive and displaced permanent workers. In New York City, tens of thousands of relief recipients were put to work in city jobs. By 1959, twenty-four upstate counties had set up work relief projects (New York Times 1950r, 1951f, 1952j, 1956b, 1958e, 1959w, 1959x; Freeman 1952a; Kihs 1954).

91. New York Times 1954b, 1953c, 1953b.

92. In New York City alone, the Federation of Protestant Welfare Agencies represented 193 agencies, while Catholic Charities had 189 agencies (New York Times 1954b, 1954d).

93. New York Times 1951m, 1951k, 1952c, 1952e, 1952f; W. Weaver 1953.

94. Freeman 1952b.

95. New York Times 1952a; Freeman 1952c.

96. New York Times 1952f.

97. W. Weaver 1953; New York Times 1953d.

98. New York Times 1954d.

99. Dales 1951a.

100. Dales 1951a, 1951c; New York Times 1951a.

101. New York Times 1951n, 1951l.

102. Moscow 1967: 43–49; New York State Legislature 1950–60.

103. Freeman 1950b; Ronan 1950; New York Times 1950c, 1950d, 1950n.

104. New York Times 1949; Dales 1949.

105. These labor leaders included Local 1, United Public Workers of America, the Central Trades and Labor Council and the CIO Labor Council (New York Times 1950b, 1950m). The American Labor Party (ALP), was a leftwing party formed in New York in 1936 and active until 1954. Until 1950, it claimed an average of 175,000 members and usually twice as many votes. Its best known leaders were Congressman Vito Marcantonio and Dr. W. E. B. DuBois (Carter 1969). In 1950, ALP organized several sit-in demonstrations demanding that welfare offices take action on emergency cases (New York Times 1950p, 1950q). Despite protests on the participants' behalf, ranging in size from thirty to two hundred people, they were found guilty. Nine of the twenty people arrested were sentenced to spend thirty days in the workhouse (New York Times 1950z, 1950zi, 1950t, 1950v, 1950w, 1950x, 1950y). Welfare organizations included the New York City Welfare Council and the New York City chapters of the American Association of Social Workers (New York Times 1950m).

106. New York Times 1950c.

107. New York Times 1950c; Freeman 1950c.

108. New York Times 1950n; Freeman 1950e.

109. New York City Department of Public Welfare 1952.

110. Not only was the amount reduced, but checks were issued twice a month. Because relief recipients had to use their first check to pay their rent, they had nothing left for food (New York Times 1950j, 1950k, 1950g, 1950d, 1950h, 1950l, 1950m).

111. New York Times 1950i.

112. New York Times 1950o, 1951b, 1951d.

113. New York State Department of Social Welfare 1964.

114. W. Weaver 1958b.

115. W. Weaver 1960a.

116. Egan 1950; W. Weaver 1958b; Dales 1958a; W. Weaver 1959; New York Times 1959f; Phillips 1959b; New York Times 1960c; W. Weaver 1957.

117. Phillips 1959b; see also Egan 1958: 8. Between 1950 and 1960, New York City's Puerto Rican population rose almost 150 percent, from 246,000 to 613,000, the black population nearly doubled (from 776,000 to 1,141,000), while the white population declined nearly 7 percent, from 7,116,000 to 6,641,000 (U.S. Bureau of the Census, cited in Rodriguez 1974: 185; see also Wagenheim 1975: 103).

118. W. Weaver 1957.

119. Senior 1965: 47.

120. Senior 1952: 18; Adalberto Gilberto Lopez, cited in Hedda 1994: 103; Kihs 1957.

121. Senior 1965: 40–41.

122. Dales 1949.

123. Ortiz 1996: 60–67; Ortiz 1998: 45.

124. Unemployment rates for Puerto Ricans were 11 percent in 1950 and 10 percent in 1960. For blacks in these same years, these figures were 8 and 7 percent respectively (U.S. Bureau of the Census, cited in Rodriguez 1974: 110).

125. Bose 1986: 151; Senior 1965: 93, 100; Portes and Grosfoguel 1994: 54; Bean and Tienda 1987: 26; Gann and Duignan 1986: 78; Ortiz 1996: 60; Ortiz 1998: 45.

126. New York Times 1956a.

127. New York Times 1952g.

128. New York Times 1954a.

129. The first study, released in 1959, found that almost 52 percent of Puerto Ricans and 43 percent of blacks on relief were already employed (compared to only 20 percent for all other welfare cases). The second one, released in 1956, found that among nonresident recipients, the average length of time they resided in the state before receiving assistance was 5.4 months for Puerto Ricans, 4.4 months for southerners, and 4.2 months for all other migrants (Senior 1965: 48).

130. A wide variety of Puerto Rican organizations formed in the 1940s and 1950s, including educational, social service, neighborhood, professional, religious, and cultural organizations. More than half of all Puerto Rican workers belonged to unions in the 1950s (Senior 1965: 101). These groups helped mobilize Puerto Rican voters. As a result, the Puerto Rican vote increased from

35,000 in 1954 to 85,000 in 1956. Even so, in 1958 only two assemblymen in the state of New York were Puerto Rican, and only a handful of Puerto Ricans held elected or appointed positions in New York City (Baver 1984: 44; Senior 1965: 99–111).

131. New York Times 1959x, 1959y; Kihs 1959b.

132. These include the Community Council of Greater New York, the State Association of Councils and Chests, the New York State Catholic Welfare Committee, the (Protestant) State Council of Churches, the Travelers' Aid Society of Albany, the State Committee on Children and Public Welfare, the State Charities Aid Association, the New York Federation of Jewish Philanthropies (New York Times 1958a, 1958b; Egan 1958; New York Times 1958g; Folsom 1958; W. Weaver 1959; New York Times 1959o, 1959p, 1960e, 1960g).

133. New York Times 1958a.

134. New York Times 1959n.

135. Dales 1958a, 1958b; New York Times 1960b.

136. New York Times 1960i, 1959m, 1958d.

137. In addition, welfare advocates also celebrated a legal victory in 1957, when a municipal court judge ruled that affidavits of support for immigrants were a moral rather than a legal duty, prohibiting the welfare department from collecting money when immigrants received welfare (New York Times 1957).

138. Egan 1958: 8; W. Weaver 1958a: 20.

139. Moscow 1967: 43–49; New York State Legislature 1950–60.

140. New York Times 1960j: 32; see also New York Times 1960m: 1.

141. New York Times 1960h: 32.

142. Robinson 1960a: 1.

143. Robinson 1960a: 1.

144. Dales 1960b: 1.

145. Binn 1958.

146. W. Weaver 1960b.

147. New York Times 1961a.

148. Cited in Misra, Moller, and Karides 2003: 494.

149. W. Weaver 1961a.

150. W. Weaver 1961a, 1961b.

151. The Citizens' Committee for Children, the Community Council, the Community Service Society, the New York City Junior League, the Protestant Council, United Neighborhood Houses, and the Women's City Club urged the governor to veto the measure (New York Times 1961b, 1961c, 1961d).

152. Dales 1961; Robinson 1961a; Robinson 1961b.

153. Those approved for return were given plane fare by the city, as well as help with job placement, training, and social assistance from the Commonwealth's Migration Division (Perlmutter 1961; New York Times 1961e, 1961f).

154. Allard 1998; Davis 1993: 80.

155. New York Times 1958h.

156. New York Times 1959z.

157. New York Times 1960m: 25:
158. New York Times 1959o: 31.
159. Robinson 1960b.
160. Kihs 1959a; Robinson 1960b; New York Times 1960a; Phillips 1959a, 1959b; Dales 1960a.
161. New York Times 1960h.
162. New York State Department of Social Welfare 1963.
163. New York City Department of Public Welfare 1958.
164. New York City Department of Public Welfare 1960.
165. New York Times 1958f: 37; C. Bennet 1958; New York Times 1958i.
166. McCaffrey 1958.
167. Kihs 1958a.
168. Kihs 1958b.
169. New York Times 1959k.
170. New York Times 1959q.
171. Phillips 1959a; New York Times 1959s: 12.
172. New York Times 1959l.
173. New York Times 1960d.
174. New York Times 1959r.
175. Kaplan 1960.
176. Kihs 1959a.
177. McCaffrey 1959; New York Times 1960c.
178. Fowle 1959.
179. New York Times 1959i; Kihs 1958b: 79; New York Times 1959g; Crowell 1959.
180. New York Times 1959h.
181. Furman 1959, 22:7.
182. New York Times 1959t: 24.
183. New York Times 1960l: 16.
184. Levenstein 2000.

CHAPTER 7

Epigraph: Cited in Moynihan 1973: 15.
1. Rose 1995: 88. Caseload growth was also linked to rising numbers of female-headed households, labor market inequalities, and urban decline (Durman 1973; Loewenberg 1981).
2. Steensland 2002: 2.
3. Brown 1999: 210, 223, 227; Rose 1995: 83; Katz 1996: 259, 263; Quadagno 1994: 67.
4. Whereas Frances Fox Piven and Richard Cloward argue that Kennedy adopted the service approach in order to maintain black support for the Democratic Party while it moved slowly on civil rights issues, Margaret Weir claims that he did so to demonstrate the originality of his administration (Quadagno

1994: 28). Michael Brown argues that Kennedy first adopted the service approach as a way to evade the question of race but then used it to quell dissent among civil rights activists (Brown 1999: 210, 216).

5. Chappell 2003.

6. Patterson 1986: 131; Komisar 1977: 89; Katz 1996: 270. Because CWT was optional and federal funds only covered 50 percent of administrative costs for most projects, only eleven states participated in the program before it was replaced in 1964 (Rose 1995: 90).

7. Katz 1996: 265; Quadagno 1994: 30.

8. Rose 1995: 81; Brown 1999: 207, 216–22; Quadagno 1990: 15–16.

9. Rose 1995: 82.

10. Katz 1996: 281.

11. Quadagno 1994: 67.

12. Brown 1999: 226; Quadagno 1994: 33–59.

13. Rose 1995: 91.

14. Rose 1995: 80; Brown 1999: 215.

15. Katz 1996: 281; Quadagno 1994: 44–45, 69; Rose 1995: 79–80.

16. Brown 1999: 367; Chappell 2003; Edsall and Edsall 1991: 53; Moynihan cited in Quadagno 1994: 124.

17. Rose 1995: 91.

18. Brown 1999: 215; Gilens 1999: 117.

19. As a 1965 survey revealed, about 35 percent of low-income women reported unwanted births, compared to 15 percent of other women (Luker 1996: 58).

20. The rate of births per 1,000 unmarried women aged 15–44 rose from 21.6 in 1960 to 26.4 in 1970 for all women. The rate of births per 1,000 unmarried women aged 15–44 was 11.6 for white women, compared to 97.6 for black women in 1965 (U.S. Bureau of the Census 1975: 52; U.S. Committee on Ways and Means, House of Representatives 2000: 17).

21. Office of Economic Opportunity (1965), cited in Steensland 2002: 67.

22. Steensland 2002: 69.

23. Steensland 2002: 38–46, 66, 72–73.

24. Steensland 2002: 70–71, 95–96.

25. Steensland 2002: 83–87.

26. Steensland 2002: 70–71.

27. Moynihan 1973: 58; Quadagno 1990: 16.

28. Brown 1999: 247; Quadagno 1994: 105, 145.

29. Brown 1999: 227–62; Katz 1996: 259.

30. Katz 1996: 266.

31. Brown 1999: 227–62.

32. Steensland 2002: 111.

33. Moynihan 1973: 58, 61.

34. Katz 1996: 262–63. When the War on Poverty was implemented, official poverty rates declined from 17.3 percent in 1965 to 11.9 percent in 1972 (U.S. Bureau of the Census 2003). Relative poverty, measured in terms of the percent

of families with incomes below half the median income did not fall, however. In 1965, 12.4 percent of families were relatively poor, compared to 12.5 percent in 1972 (Katz 1996: 278–79).

35. In 1964, there were only seventy elected black officials at any level of government. Five years later, there were 1,500 (Quadagno 1994: 58).

36. Katz 1996: 266.

37. "Counties that shifted from surplus commodity distribution to food stamps experienced a 40 percent decline in participation" (Brown 1999: 255).

38. Rose 1995: 88.

39. Cited in Steiner 1971: 49.

40. Brown 1999: 255.

41. Katz 1996: 272, 276.

42. Piven and Cloward 1977: 293; West 1981: 22.

43. Kotz and Kotz 1977: 182–83; Piven and Cloward 1977.

44. Poverty/Rights Action Center 1966.

45. Kotz and Kotz 1977: 200–1.

46. George Wiley, cited in Burch 1970; Wiley 1972: 2.

47. Cited in Burch 1971: 16.

48. George Wiley Papers.

49. American Association of University Women 1970: 122.

50. This belief reflected Saul Alinsky's influence among community organizers, including Wiley and other key NWRO staff (Kotz and Kotz 1977: 169, 182, 230). Alinsky, a well-known community organizer, spread his method of organizing through training programs and books. On Alinsky's method, see Pruger and Specht (1969) and Stall and Stoecker (1998).

51. American Child 1966.

52. U.S. Bureau of the Census 1975: 63–74.

53. Muro cited in Chappell 2003: 7.

54. West 1981: 23, 53, 145–232; Piven and Cloward 1977: 276; 290–93.

55. West 1981: 210–69.

56. Piven and Cloward 1977; West 1981: 5.

57. Kotz and Kotz 1977: 199, 208; Piven and Cloward 1977: 272; Roach and Roach 1978: 162.

58. Katz 1996: 276.

59. Piven and Cloward 1977: 272; Katz 1996: 272, 276.

60. Katz 1996: 276.

61. Piven and Cloward 1977: 274–75, see also Loewenberg 1981.

62. Isaac and Kelly (1981) found strong support for the hypothesized riot-expenditure relationship in a time series analysis of national level data. Hicks and Swank (1983) also found support using time series analyses of national level data for Piven and Cloward's argument that AFDC caseload growth was due to rioting and Community Action Agencies' legal aid and counseling activities.

63. Piven and Cloward 1977: 294–305; Pope 1990: 63–67.

64. Piven and Cloward 1977: 294–305; Davis 1993: 42.

65. Kornbluh 1997; Pope 1990: 67–68; National Welfare Rights Organization 1972.

66. Abramovitz 1989: 334–35; Davis 1993: 68; Piven and Cloward 1977: 272.

67. Chappell 2003: 1–2.

68. During agenda-setting sessions, NWRO members expressed their desire for better choices regarding maternal employment. They criticized the lack of childcare, job opportunities, and job training for poor mothers (West 1981: 86–92).

69. Piven and Cloward 1977: 305–7.

70. Neubeck and Cazenave 2001: 98; Gilens 1999: 115.

71. Cited in Neubeck and Cazenave 2001: 99.

72. Neubeck and Cazenave 2001: 89; see also Levenstein 2000.

73. Gilens 1999: 105.

74. McAdam 1999.

75. Cited in Edsall and Edsall 1991: 52.

76. Edsall and Edsall 1991: 57.

77. Quadagno 1994: 30.

78. Edsall and Edsall 1991: 4, 11, 17.

79. Gilens 1999: 45–50; Teles 1996: 43–45; Weaver, Shapiro, and Jacobs 1995: 618.

80. Misra, Moller, and Karides 2003: 499.

81. Moynihan 1973: 87.

82. Gilens 1999: 106.

83. Brown 1999: 334.

84. Gilens 1999: 114.

85. Gilens 1999: 109–18.

86. Moynihan 1973: 25.

87. Misra, Moller, and Karides 2003: 496.

88. Moynihan 1973: 88.

89. African Americans made up 47 percent of Neighborhood Youth Corps participants, 81 percent of Concentrated Employment Program participants, and 59 percent of the Job Corps participants.

90. Brown 1999: 281–84; Quadagno 1994: 66–77.

91. Edsall and Edsall 1991: 66–67.

92. Brown 1999; Gordon 2001; Handler 1995: 10–31; Mink 1998a; Walters 1998.

93. Levenstein 2000.

94. Cited in Quadagno 1994: 128.

95. The other two states to adopt these policies in the 1960s were Oregon and Louisiana (Soule and Zylan 1997: 739).

96. They also urged Congress to give states wide discretion in terms of implementing child care and job training (Chase 1967; Hardy 1967).

97. Henkel 1967: 1268.

98. Cobb 1967: A43.

99. The law exempted certain recipients from participation, such as disabled and incapacitated recipients and family members caring for the disabled and incapacitated (Handler 1995: 58; Rose 1995: 92–93; Katz 1996: 270; K. Weaver 2000: 56).

100. Kotz and Kotz 1977: 218.

101. Kotz and Kotz 1977: 251.

102. Kotz and Kotz 1977: 251

103. U.S. Senate Committee on Finance 1967: 35–37.

104. Kotz and Kotz 1977: 257; Weaver 2000: 56; Steiner 1971: 44–50, 80, 329.

105. Bell, Morgan, and Smith 1968: 3–10.

106. Bell, Morgan, and Smith 1968: 7.

107. Handler 1995: 58; Rose 1995: 92–93.

108. Cited in Quadagno 1994: 128.

109. Edsall and Edsall 1991: 35, 55–56, 64.

110. Edsall and Edsall 1991: 63.

111. Edsall and Edsall 1991: 48–52.

112. Edsall and Edsall 1991: 77.

113. Edsall and Edsall 1991: 74–76.

114. Edsall and Edsall 1991: 82–89. According to Quadagno (1994: 79), Nixon adopted these policies because of criticism of his racial conservativism and to reduce racial violence. In 1969, protests for jobs in Chicago, Pittsburgh, and Seattle ended in violent clashes between demonstrators and white construction workers.

115. Moynihan 1973: 53.

116. Edsall and Edsall 1991: 23, 96; Quadagno 1994: 79.

117. Brown 1999: 299; Quadagno 1990: 21; see also Steensland 2002: 32.

118. Brown 1999: 304–5.

119. Katz 1996: 277; Quadagno 1994: 118; Steensland 2002: 199.

120. The inclusion of work requirements in FAP represented a victory for Nixon's advisors, such as Arthur Burns, who claimed that FAP would be opposed by white workers and the business community if it provided income to people who refused to work (Steensland 2002: 140, 176–77, 202, 262; Quadagno 1990: 24).

121. Steensland 2002: 1, 236.

122. Brown 1999: 295–97; Moynihan 1973: 102; Steensland 2002: 125, 198–99. FAP would "triple the number of families receiving government assistance in the south and sixty percent of additional families would be white" (Steensland 2002: 210).

123. Moynihan 1973: 63–65, 102–4.

124. Steensland 2002: 257, 268, 285–86.

125. Steensland 2002: 196–200.

126. Quadagno 1990: 15.

127. Moynihan 1973: 79–81; Quadagno 1990: 17–19.

128. Steensland 2002: 32, 96–99, 227–229; Brown 1999: 299.

129. Quadagno 1990: 16; Steensland 2002: 107–9.
130. Quadagno 1990: 19–20.
131. Steensland 2002: 162, 182–83, 221–25.
132. Steensland 2002.: 106.
133. Quadagno 1990: 21–22; Steensland 2002: 111, 226–27, 257.
134. Brown 1999: 277–78.
135. Steensland 2002: 208–10.
136. Quadagno 1990: 23–24; see also Steensland 2002: 212–13.
137. Steensland 2002: 212–13.
138. Quadagno 1990: 24.
139. Quadagno 1990: 20; Steensland 2002: 217–20.
140. Cited in Quadagno 1994: 133.
141. Steensland 2002: 214.
142. Chappell 2003: 10; Misra, Moller, and Karides 2003: 498; Quadagno 1990: 15–25; West 1981: 310–25.
143. Steensland 2002: 258–59.
144. Steensland 2002: 111, 212–14, 229.
145. Steensland 2002: 158, 238.
146. Steensland 2002: 241–42, 250.
147. Quadagno 1990: 25.
148. Steensland 2002: 260.
149. National Association of Manufacturers Government Operations Subcommittee 1969: 9.
150. Handler 1995: 58–59; Komisar 1977: 101–2.
151. Handler 1995: 58–60.
152. Steensland 2002: 262–64.
153. Steensland 2002: 267–68.
154. Steensland 2002: 283.
155. Moynihan 1973: 500; Steensland 2002: 284–85.
156. Steensland 2002: 271, 283, 287, 289.
157. Steensland 2002: 271, 283, 287, 289–92.
158. Katz 1996: 274; Steensland 2002: 290–301.
159. King 1996: 346–47; Steensland 2002: 342–44.
160. Cited in Steensland 2002: 348.
161. Steensland 2002: 355.
162. Steensland 2002: 358–59.
163. Steensland 2002: 363; King 1996: 350, 357.
164. King 1996: 359.
165. Steensland 2002: 373.
166. Steensland 2002: 360.
167. King 1996: 362.
168. Steensland 2002: 372; King 1996: 362.
169. Katz 1996: 266.
170. West 1981.

CHAPTER 8

1. The campaign reform laws of the early 1970s limited the amount individuals could donate to political campaigns. Instead of reducing the power of big business over the political process, these laws increased it by encouraging greater coordination among corporate heads (Himmelstein 1990: 141).

2. Himmelstein 1990: 141.

3. Clawson, Neustadtl, and Weller 1998: 12–13.

4. Manza and Brooks 1999: 27–28.

5. Vogel 1996: 5–6; 266–88; 304; Ferguson and Rogers 1986: 104–5; Himmelstein 1990: 141–50.

6. Himmelstein 1990: 132, 139; Noble 1997: 107–8; Piven and Cloward 1987: 51.

7. I am borrowing these terms from Domhoff 2002: 70.

8. Himmelstein 1990: 129–64.

9. Clawson, Neustadtl, and Weller 1998.

10. Himmelstein 1990: 130; Ferguson and Rogers 1986; Domhoff 1988; Navarro 1985.

11. Clawson, Neustadtl, and Weller 1998: 154–61.

12. Ferguson and Rogers 1986: 78; Himmelstein 1990: 130–32, 145–51.

13. Vogel 1996: 269; Himmelstein 1990: 130–37.

14. Edsall and Edsall 1991: 167.

15. Block 1996; Plotkin and Scheuerman 1994: 89.

16. Clawson, Neustadtl, and Weller 1998: 162; Johnston 2002.

17. Ferguson and Rogers 1986:11; Derber 1998: 36–37; Sanger and Greenhouse 2002; New York Times 2003.

18. Plotkin and Scheuerman 1994: 14–28, 62–63, 235.

19. Block 1996, ch. 18; Plotkin and Scheuerman 1994: 14.

20. Clawson, Neustadtl, and Weller 1998: 166; Derber 1998: 23; Texeira and Rogers 2000: 71; and Lamis 1999: 35.

21. Times Union 2004.

22. Edsall and Edsall 1991.

23. Texeira and Rogers 2000: 31–32.

24. Manza and Brooks 1999: 213, see also pp. 80, 162.

25. Abramson, Aldrich, and Rohde 2002: 98–103, 113–15, 163; Manza and Brooks 1999.

26. Cassell 1977; Edsall and Edsall 1991; Texeira and Rogers 2000: 32; Schreckhise and Shields 2003: 604; Manza and Brooks 1999: 159–75.

27. Moore, Preimesberger, and Tarr 2001: 1569–77.

28. Himmelstein 1990: 172, 174, 178–79.

29. Edsall and Edsall 1991: 210–11.

30. Denitch 1982; Domhoff 1988: 596; Boggs 2000; McAdam 1999; Klatch 1999. The labor movement was particularly weak. In 1995, less than 15 percent of the nonagricultural labor force belonged to a union, compared to its peak of

35 percent in 1954. This decline was linked to the rise in aggressive union-busting activities by employers, legal obstacles to union militancy, and the failure of unions to invest in organizing (M. Goldfield 1987).

31. Lakoff 1996: 33.

32. Lakoff 1996: 19.

33. Lakoff 1996.

34. Lakoff 1996.

35. Himmelstein 1990: 176; Manza and Brooks 1999: 78, 162; Texeira and Rogers 2000: 31–32.

36. Edsall and Edsall 1991: 101–8; Texeira and Rogers 2000: 9–15.

37. Texeira and Rogers 2000: 6–7, 19, 48–49.

38. Plotkin and Scheuerman 1994: 30, 86, 121–27, 145.

39. Bureau of Labor Statistics 2001.

40. Collins and Yeskel 2000: 16, 23, 42, 115.

41. Real family income declined 5 percent for the bottom fifth, and increased a mere 3 percent among the second quintile between 1979 and 1988. There were a number of reasons for this, including international wage competition, economic restructuring, and the decline of organized labor. The real value of the minimum wage also declined. In 1979, the minimum wage was 80 percent of the amount needed to bring a family of four up to the federal poverty line. By 1998, the minimum wage was only 64 percent of this amount (Collins and Yeskel 2000).

42. Abramson, Aldrich, and Rohde 2002: 75.

43. Boggs 2000: 30–31; Manza and Brooks 1999: 27, 50; Abramson, Aldrich, and Rohde 2002: 82.

44. Texeira and Rogers 2000; Manza and Brooks 1999: 196–97.

45. Lamis 1999: 42–48.

46. Texeira and Rogers 2000: 123–24.

47. Abramson, Aldrich, and Rohde 2002: 103; Texeira and Rogers 2000: 96–116.

48. Although Democrats and Republicans each had fifty seats in the Senate in 2000, Republican vice president Dick Cheney had the tie-breaking vote (Abramson, Aldrich, and Rohde 2002: xiii).

49. Abramson, Aldrich, and Rohde 2002: 98–103, 163.

50. Cassell 1977; Edsall and Edsall 1991.

51. Cited in Lamis 1999: 6.

52. Schreckhise and Shields 2003: 608.

53. Edsall and Edsall 1991: 186.

54. Graham 1994: 31; Edsall and Edsall 1991: 259.

55. Abramson, Aldrich, and Rohde 2002: 2.

56. This victory can be partly attributed to the measure's misleading title, which portrayed it as a "civil rights initiative," and to proponents' aggressive and well-funded advertising campaigns (Taylor 1999). Opposition to affirmative action appealed to white anxiety about diminishing opportunities for employment and higher education that was exacerbated by the state's economic and fis-

cal crisis in the 1980s and early 1990s and the rising number of college admission applications (Duster 1996: 53; Walker 1996).

57. Edsall and Edsall 1991: 138–39, 142–46, 173–87.

58. Edsall and Edsall 1991: 164.

59. Manza and Brooks 1999: 80, 162, 212; Edsall and Edsall 1991; Texeira and Rogers 2000: 19, 43; Lamis 1999: 7–8.

60. Like his Republican predecessors, President Clinton signed into law a wave of "tough on crime" legislation. Under all three administrations, Congress increased the penalties for a wide variety of crimes and raised funding for law enforcement, topping off the effort with the passage of a $30 billion federal crime bill in 1994. Antidrug spending increased from $200 million in the 1970s to $13 billion in 1992, most of which was spent on law enforcement (Parenti 1999; Roberts 1997: 155; Walker 1996: 170).

61. Parenti 1999; Glassner 1999.

62. U.S. Department of Justice 2003, tables 7.1 and 7.10.

63. The Anti-Drug Abuse Act of 1986 imposed a five-year mandatory minimum sentence for offenses involving 100 grams of heroin, 500 grams of cocaine, or 5 grams of crack (Parenti 1999: 57).

64. Roberts 1997: 153, 172, 175.

65. U.S. Bureau of Census 2001a.

66. Lapinski et al. 1997: 360–63. In fact, roughly 800,000 legal immigrants and refugees enter the country each year, while an estimated 300,000 enter the country as undocumented immigrants (Kilty and de Haymes 2000: 14).

67. Lapinski et al. 1997: 365. Nativism is more common among whites, but not confined to them. For example, a 1992 Business Week/Harris Poll found that 69 percent of nonblacks and 53 percent of blacks thought that present-day immigration was bad for the country. Racial and ethnic minorities often fear immigrants will increase competition for unskilled or semiskilled jobs, or resent "middle-man minorities" who do employers' dirty work (Brugge 1995: 6; Sanchez 1997; Jaret 1999: 14; Bonacich and Appelbaum 2000).

68. Armbruster, Geron, and Bonacich 1995; Brugge 1995: 1–11; Calavita 1996; Campus Coalition for Human Rights and Social Justice 1995; Hondagneu-Sotelo 1995; Mehan 1997: 263; Roschell 1995; Schneider 2000; Sanchez 1997; Smith and Tarallo 1995.

69. McDonnell 1996b.

70. Takacs 1999.

71. Kilty and de Haymes 2000: 18–20; Lio 2003; Santoro 1999: 890–91.

72. Brugge 1995: 4; M. Shapiro 1997: 2. A British immigrant, Brimelow claims his Anglo heritage is closely connected to American national culture (Takacs 1999: 597).

73. Cited in Neubeck and Cazenave 2001: 149.

74. Brugge 1995: 4, 7; Diamond 1996: 156–59; Another scholar claims FAIR received $1 million from the Pioneer Fund in 1984 (Walker 1996: 171).

75. Brownstein 1995.

76. McDonnell 1996a.

77. Diamond 1996; Unz, 1994.

78. The Immigration Reform and Control Act of 1986 established sanctions against employers who hired illegal immigrants. This act also provided legal status to some undocumented workers already in the United States and created a "guest worker" program for employers (Brugge 1995; Walker 1996: 173).

79. McBride 1999: 298–99; Parenti 1999; Kilty and de Haymes 2000: 11–12; Fragomen 1997.

80. Diamond 1996: 165; McDonnell 1996b.

81. Brownstein 2002; Chen and Peterson 2001; Stevenson and Greenhouse 2004; Wilgoren 1997.

82. Manza and Brooks 1999: 131.

83. Cited in Coontz 1997: 5.

84. Diamond 1995: 296.

85. Abramson, Aldrich, and Rohde 2002: 2.

86. Coontz 1997; Smith 2001.

87. Luker 1996; Joffe 1998: 294. Ironically, concerns about teen mothers first gained prominence in the early 1970s, when teen birth rates were still falling from their high levels in the 1950s. Despite this decline, concerns about teen mothers increased as they became less likely to get and stay married. Liberal family planning advocates emphasized these concerns, linking teen motherhood to welfare dependency, to persuade public officials to fund contraception for teens in the early 1970s. It was not until the early 1980s that conservatives entered public debates on the issue, and used it to build support for restrictions on women's abortion rights and, later, welfare cutbacks (Luker 1996: 8, 11, 59–76, 83–107).

88. Kellstadt et al. 1994.

89. Diamond 1995: 246.

90. In the 1990s, between one-fourth and one-third of Americans identified as "born again" evangelicals (Diamond 1995: 44; Himmelstein 1990: 115).

91. Wilcox 1994: 249; Himmelstein 1990: 98; see also Diamond 1995.

92. Diamond 1995: 170–76.

93. Diamond 1995: 166; Himmelstein 1990: 106; Hixson 1992: 185–209.

94. Himmelstein 1990: 98; Diamond 1995: 233.

95. An ABC poll showed about 17 percent fewer white Protestants voted for Carter in 1980 than in 1976 (Diamond 1995: 233).

96. Manza and Brooks 1999: 123.

97. Diamond 1995: 233–34, 175; Wilcox 1994: 246.

98. Diamond 1995: 234.

99. Manza and Brooks 1999: 196.

100. Many scoffed when Oral Roberts opportunistically told his viewing audience that "God would call him home" if he did not raise $8 million in donations in three months, and other Christian viewers were shocked by revelations of Jim Bakker's and Jimmy Swaggart's extramarital affairs. The damaged reputations of these preachers led to considerable financial losses for the religious broadcasting industry (Diamond 1995: 244–45).

101. The Republican Party strategically courted this vote, hiring Robertson's campaign manager as a consultant for Bush's campaign.

102. Diamond 1995: 245–49; Green and Guth 1988; Wilcox, Rozell, and Gunn 1996: 543–46.

103. For example, in 1992 undisclosed Christian Right activists won seats on local school boards, city councils, and the water district board in the "San Diego surprise" (Diamond 1995: 244, 255).

104. Diamond 1996; Wilcox 1994; Wilcox, Rozell, and Gunn 1996: 546; Moen 1995: 22.

105. Penning 1994: 337; Diamond 1995: 249–50.

106. Diamond 1995: 243–50; Wilcox, Rozell, and Gunn 1996: 553.

107. The study was based on interviews with GOP officials, campaign activists, political consultants, news reporters, and university professors from all fifty states (Persinos 1994).

108. Diamond 1995: 245.

109. Penning 1994: 340.

110. Diamond 1995: 296.

111. Penning 1994: 340.

112. Kellstedt et al. 1994; Moen 1995: 23–24; Penning 1994: 342; Wilcox 1994: 249; Diamond 1995: 312; Rozell, Wilcox, and Green 1998; Wilcox, Rozell, and Gunn 1996: 547–56.

113. Manza and Brooks 1999: 96.

114. Knuckey 1999: 486–87.

115. Green et al. 2001.

116. Brownstein 2003.

117. Manza and Brooks 1999: 131–52; Schreckhise and Shields 2003.

CHAPTER 9

Second epigraph: Interview with 9to5 staff (August 2001, Milwaukee, WI).

1. Cited in Derber 1998: 20.

2. Derber 1998.

3. Joseph 1995: 1706–7.

4. Joseph 1995.

5. Sparks 2003: 184.

6. Ferguson and Rogers 1986: 78; Himmelstein 1990: 130–37, 145–51; Vogel 1996: 269.

7. I borrow the distinctions between "ultraconservative" and "moderate-conservative" think tanks from Domhoff (2002: 69–98).

8. Domhoff 2002.

9. The twelve foundations were the Lynde and Harry Bradley Corporations, the Carthage Foundation, the Earhart Foundation, the Charles G. Koch, David H. Koch and Claude R. Lambe charitable foundations, the Phillip M. McKenna Foundation, the J. M. Foundation, the John M. Olin Foundation, the Henry Salvatori Foundation, the Sarah Scaife Foundation, and the Smith Richardson

Foundation. Of these, the most active were the Mellon-Scaife, Olin, and Smith Richardson foundations (Callahan 1999).

10. Domhoff 2002: 94.

11. Domhoff 2002: 83–84.

12. For example, eighteen AEI staff joined Reagan's new administration in the early 1980s (Covington 1997: 15; Himmelstein 1990; Stoesz 1988: 147–48; Post 1997: 10; American Enterprise Institute 2001, 2002).

13. Callahan 1999; Media Transparency 2002.

14. Coltrane 2001; see also Domhoff 2002: 70.

15. Weicher 2001. Top officials of conservative think tanks are generously rewarded for their services. In 1996, for example, Heritage Foundation's president was paid $406,052 in salary and another $55,788 in benefits (Soley 1998).

16. Callahan 1999: 19.

17. Callahan 1999.

18. Domhoff 2002: 81.

19. Stefancic and Delgado 1996: 53; Cato Institute 2002a, 2002b, 2002c.

20. Stefancic and Delgado 1996; Callahan 1999.

21. P. Wilson 1995.

22. Stefancic and Delgado 1996: 94.

23. Callahan 1999; Edwards 1998; Quintero 2002; Soloman 1996.

24. Dolny 1998, 2000, 2001.

25. S. Ackerman 1999.

26. Flanders, Jackson, and Shadoan 1996.

27. Derber 1998: 25–26; Gans 1995; Hardisty and Williams 2002; O'Connor 2001: 242–83.

28. Lakoff 1996: 33.

29. Media Transparency 2002; Domhoff 2002: 82.

30. Domhoff 2002: 82–84; Weicher 2001.

31. Cato Institute 2001.

32. Cato Institute 2002e; Tanner 1995.

33. Cited in Cato Institute 2001. According to Tanner, government funds would corrupt charity, raise serious legal questions about the separation between church and state that would invite litigation, burden churches with government red tape, and substitute "coercive government tax financing for compassion-based voluntary giving" (Tanner 2001).

34. Karen Rothmeyer, "Citizen Scaife," *Columbia Journalism Review* (July/August 1981), 48–50, cited in Media Transparency 2002.

35. AEI's funders included Bethlehem Steel, Exxon, J.C. Penney, and Chase Manhattan Bank, the Lilly Endowment, the Smith Richardson Foundation, the Rockefeller Brothers Trust, and the Earhart Foundation (Covington 1997; Domhoff 2002: 82; Stoesz and Policy America 1987: 7).

36. Cited in Covington 1997: 16.

37. Wilayto 1997.

38. Heritage Foundation 2001.

39. Edwards 1998.

40. Stefancic and Delgado 1996.
41. Soloman 1996: 3; Heritage Foundation 1996.
42. Heritage Foundation 2002.
43. Soloman 1996.
44. Stefancic and Delgado 1996: 74–75.
45. O'Connor 2001: 251.
46. Diamond 1995; Stefancic and Delgado 1996.
47. National Committee for Responsive Philanthropy 1991: 12; Scott 1997; Manhattan Institute 2002a; Robins 1998.
48. Business representatives were from Tamko Asphalt Productions, Sandefer Capital Partners, the Windquest Group, Inc., America's Home Place, Tennessee Capital Markets, HBR Capital, Ltd., and Pulsar International (Acton Institute 2002).
49. Acton Institute 2002.
50. Its former director, Gerald P. Regier, was a welfare official, while his successor, Gary L. Bauer, was a domestic policy advisor under the Reagan administration.
51. Connor 2001.
52. Coltrane 2001; Family Research Council 2002.
53. Grant data is from www.mediatransparency.org; Institute for American Values 2002a, 2002b; Coltrane 2001.
54. Cato Institute 2002a, 2002b, 2002c.
55. Dolny 2000, 2001.
56. Chaves 2001; Traditional Values Coalition 2002d.
57. Cited in Coltrane 2001: 401.
58. W. Bennett 1995.
59. Coltrane 2001; Glassner 1999: 87–105.
60. Cited in Weinberg 1998: 62–63.
61. O'Connor 2001: 250; Stefancic and Delgado 1996: 58. Heritage also promoted the book through a well-publicized symposium (Stoesz and Policy America 1987: 14–15).
62. The Pioneer Fund was created in the 1930s and promoted research supporting eugenics and population control (Brugge 1995: 7; Neubeck and Cazenave 2001: 155–56; Jaret 1999: 15).
63. Cited in Brugge 1995: 7.
64. Post 1997: 11–12.
65. C. Murray 1998.
66. Rector 1995a: 69–70; Rector 1995c.
67. Besharov 1995: 3–4.
68. Besharov 1995: 19.
69. Green 2003.
70. Stefancic and Delgado 1996: 54, 85, 94.
71. W. Bennett 1995: 165; Stenfacic and Delgado 1996: 94.
72. Stefancic and Delgado 1996: 92–93.
73. Horowitz 1995.

74. R. Novak 1995; Kolbert 1995; Weaver 2000: 214–15.

75. Haskins and Bevan 1997: 3. By contrast, AEI's fellows claimed in 1995 that abstinence education was "not realistic," but afterward became more favorable toward it (Besharov and Gardiner 1997).

76. Coltrane 2001; Folse 2001; Curran and Abrams 2000: 670–75; National Organization for Women Legal Defense and Education Fund 2001c: 2.

77. Rector 2001a.

78. Rector 2000.

79. National Organization for Women Legal Defense and Education Fund 1999: 3; De Lollis 2001.

80. Fagan 2001a, 2001b, 1995.

81. Bennett 2002.

82. Horn and Bush 1997.

83. Coltrane 2001.

84. Lawrence Mead, currently a professor at New York University, participated in projects and events organized by number of corporate-sponsored think-tanks, including the Urban Institute, the Hoover Institute, the American Enterprise Institute, the Brookings Institution, RAND, and the Wisconsin Policy Research Institute. Conservative foundations—Smith Richardson and Olin Foundations—also sponsored Mead's research (Mead 2001; Media Transparency 2002).

85. O'Connor 2001: 252.

86. Mead 1992: 148; see also Neubeck and Cazenave 2001: 141.

87. Mead 1992: 147–55; see also Weinberg 1998: 66.

88. Sirico 1995b.

89. While Besharov said these could either be public or private sector work assignments, Karl Zinmeister, editor-in-chief of AEI's journal, *American Enterprise,* claimed that they should be made only in the private sector because, "government-supervised workplaces exhibit little discipline" (cited in Post 1997: 12–13).

90. Rector 1995b: 6. Then, Rector urged Congress to first focus on "the most employable recipients," such as fathers in two-parent families, "rather than single mothers with infant children" (Rector 1995a: 70).

91. Besharov 2002.

92. Rector 2000; Rector 2001a.

93. Wilayto 1997; Hudson Institute 2002.

94. Manhattan Institute for Policy Research 2002b.

95. Stefancic and Delgado 1996; Cato Institute 2002d.

96. Quoted in Robins 1998.

97. Cato Institute 2002c, 2002d; Tanner 1995.

98. Stoesz 1988.

99. American Enterprise Institute 1996; Novak 1996.

100. Utt 1995; Stefancic and Delgado 1996: 89.

101. Olasky later served as a fellow with the Acton Institute (Acton Institute 1995; Olasky 1996).

102. Olasky 1996.

103. Sirico 1995a; Sirico called for tax credits for donations to private charities rather than "charitable choice" policies in order to minimize religious organizations' reliance on government funds (Acton Institute 2002; Sirico 2000).

104. Tanner 1995.

105. Cato Institute 2002c, 2002d; see also Tanner 1996.

106. Payne 1997; Sherman 2002a.

107. Cited in Cato Institute 2001.

108. For example, see Hein 2002a, 2002b; Sherman 2002b, 2002c.

109. Manhattan Institute 2002b.

110. Horowitz 1995; Rector 1995a; Tanner 1995.

111. Brown 2003; Piven 2003.

112. Rector 1995a.

113. Brown 2003; Piven 2003.

114. Post 1997: 28–29; Husseini 1998; Domhoff 2002: 79; Domhoff, personal communication, July 22, 2004. In 2002, Strobe Talbot, former deputy secretary of state under President Clinton, became Brookings' president.

115. These include Bell Atlantic, Citibank, J.P. Morgan, Nations Bank, Exxon, Chevron, Toyota, Johnson & Johnson, Dupont, Mobil, and Lockheed Martin.

116. Stefancic and Delgado 1996: 100; Brookings Institution 2002a, 2002b; Husseini 1998.

117. Brookings Institution 2002c.

118. Post 1997: 30–31.

119. Haskins and Blank 2001.

120. Haskins 2001b.

121. Haskins 2001a, 2001b.

122. Bloom and Winstead 2002; Haskins 2001a

123. Fix and Haskins 2002.

124. On the one hand, Isabell Sawhill (2002a, 2002b) urged Congress to focus greater attention on preventing teen pregnancy rather than diverting welfare money into "marriage promotion" or "responsible fatherhood" programs. On the other hand, Ron Haskins urged Congress to encourage states to adopt "innovative programs to promote marriage" and reward states that show "high levels of activity aimed at reducing illegitimacy" (Haskins 2001a).

125. Post 1997.

126. Post 1997; Joseph 1995.

127. Domhoff 2002: 70.

128. M. Schwartz 1998; Plotkin and Scheuerman 1994. This agenda deflected criticism from bloated military spending, which most corporate elites viewed as necessary for safeguarding American business interests (Plotkin and Scheuerman 1994: 63).

129. For example, many consider Lockheed's attempts to develop a statewide computer system to collect child support in California a fiscal nightmare. As one assemblywoman commented, "Even after six years of development and $82

million in state expenditures," Lockheed's system was "slow, overly compli-
cated, and unable to perform even basic accounting functions," and an independent contractor found 1,400 problems with the system (Alquist 1997). In Wisconsin, the nonpartisan Legislative Audit Bureau's recent investigation of
another welfare contractor, Maximus, found more than $400,000 in question-
able or improper expenses (Schultze 2000).

130. Berkowitz 2002; Hartung and Washburn 1998; B. Murray 1999.

131. Esping-Andersen 1996: 16; Moody 1997.

132. Myles and Pierson 1997.

133. Peck and Theodore 1999: 2.

134. Peck and Theodore 1999: 6; see also Peck 2001.

135. Carroll 2001b.

136. Carroll 2001a.

137. Cook 1998.

138. Heuler-Williams 1998.

139. Bernstein 2000.

140. Falcocchio 2001.

141. Carroll 2001a, 2001b. Reviewing the effects of Work Incentive programs during the 1980s, when unemployment was high, Handler and Hasenfeld
found that they were highly ineffective in increasing welfare mothers' labor
force participation. They claim that "under the best scenario WIN was able to
remove less than two percent of AFDC recipients from the rolls" (Handler and
Hasenfeld 1991: 156).

142. Pear 2002d.

143. Handler 1995; Handler and Hasenfeld 1991: 40.

144. Post 1997: 35; Tilly 1996.

145. Cited in Post 1997: 11.

146. Cited in Post 1997: 25.

147. Deparle 1997.

148. Post 1997: 27.

149. Rector 1997.

150. M. Wilson 1999.

151. Blumenberg and Ong 1994; Golden and Appelbaum 1992; Reich 1991.

152. Levy 1994: 23; Tilly 1991.

153. Block 1987: 132–39; Esping-Andersen 1996; Fligstein 1998; Huber and
Stephens 1998; Reich 1991.

154. Esping-Andersen 1996: 27.

155. Block 1987: 132.

156. Block 1996: 122–23.

157. Block 1996; Swank 1998.

158. Offe 1985: 151.

159. Piven 1998: 27.

160. Fligstein 1998; Hicks 1999: 194–229; Huber and Stephens 2001: 226;
Iversen 2001; Swank 1998: 7–16; Swank 2001: 205. Hicks (1999: 229) suggests

that the globalization of trade may have "compensatory effects," because it spurs governments to protect their citizens from the economic risks associated with international trade.

161. Huber and Stephens 2001: 226.

162. Research indicates that only high levels of foreign direct investment spur welfare retrenchment among affluent democracies (Hicks 1999: 194–229). Among coordinated market economies, Huber and Stephens found that financial globalization was more significant than foreign direct investment in constraining welfare spending. They claim that internationalization of capital markets and financial deregulation, along with prior public debt, contributed to growth in real interest rates among affluent democracies, which made deficit spending more difficult to finance in the 1980s and 1990s (Huber and Stephens 2001: 227–30).

163. Fligstein 1998; Huber and Stephens 2001; Swank 1998: 7–16.

164. Huber and Stephens 2001: 227.

165. Swank 1998, 2001.

CHAPTER 10

Epigraph: Ashcroft 1995.

1. Garin, Molyneux, and DiVall 1994; Gilens 1999: 95.

2. Piven 1998.

3. Pierson 1994: 115–19; Rose 1995: 129.

4. Handler 1995: 76–77; Pierson 1994: 122–25; Orloff 2002.

5. Neubeck and Cazenave 2001: 139.

6. Gilens 2003: 122; Gilens (1999: 114) found that an average of 57 percent of poor people portrayed by three major national news magazines between 1967 and 1992 were black.

7. Misra, Moller, and Karides 2003: 493.

8. Handler 1995: 93–106; Teles 1996: 122–43; Fording 2003: 77.

9. Lieberman 2003: 45; Weaver 2000. As Weaver (2000: 129) points out, polls show that "only two percent of voters supporting Clinton just before the election said that the main reason was his position on welfare reform or because he would help the poor." Other polls, however, indicate that welfare reform was ranked third in importance among Clinton's campaign promises (Weaver 2000: 225).

10. Weaver 2000: 127–28.

11. U.S. Committee on Ways and Means, House of Representatives 2000; see also Weaver 2000: 146.

12. Most commonly, states simply failed to adjust these benefits to meet the rising cost of living (Weaver 2000: 14–15; Pierson 1994: 118–19). As a result, "between 1972 and 1990, median adjusted AFDC benefits for a family of four declined from $761 per month to $435 per month" (Myles 1996: 127).

13. U.S. House of Representatives Committee on Ways and Means 1998: tables 7–19 and 7–20.

14. Gilens 1999.

15. Cited in Neubeck and Cazenave 2001: 156–57.

16. Neubeck and Cazenave 2001: 156.

17. Gilens 2003: 122.

18. Pear 2002a.

19. Bruner 1997.

20. Once refugee and elderly immigrants are excluded, working-age legal immigrants are about 27 percent less likely to use welfare than native-born residents (Fix and Passel 1994).

21. M. Schwartz 1998: 10; Piven 1998: 21; Piven 2003: 333; Walters 1998:44–46.

22. Handler 1995: 93–106; Teles 1996: 122–43; Fording 2003: 77; Weaver 2000: 259–60, 308.

23. Rogers-Dillon 2001: 8.

24. Handler 1995: 93–106; Teles 1996: 122–43.

25. Fording 2003: 81–88.

26. Weaver 2000: 119, 266, 291.

27. Weaver 2000: 236, 255, 266.

28. Weaver 2000: 7, 206–7, 229.

29. Weaver 2000: 239–40, 320; On public opposition to family caps and bans on benefits for teen mothers, see Weaver 2000: 180; and Shaw and Shapiro 2002.

30. Weaver 2000: 239–40, 286, 308, 312.

31. Cited in Avery and Peffley 2003: 136.

32. States were significantly more likely to adopt tougher sanctions when a higher share of their caseload was black but not Latino.

33. Soss et al. 2001.

34. Gilens 1999: 45–50; Pierson 1994; Teles 1996: 43–45; Weaver, Shapiro, and Jacobs 1995: 618.

35. Weaver 2000: 171–72.

36. Misra, Moller, and Karides 2003: 492, 497–500.

37. Plotkin and Scheuerman 1994.

38. American public opinion on welfare spending is greatly affected by word choice. For example, a 1993 public opinion poll found that 60 percent of those surveyed believed that the government was spending too much on "welfare." By contrast, only 25 percent believed the government was spending too much on "the poor," while only 9 percent believed the government was spending too much on "poor children" (General Social Survey, cited in Weaver, Shapiro, and Jacobs 1995: 618–9).

39. Lakoff 1996.

40. Orloff 2002; Misra, Moller, and Karides 2003: 492, 501.

41. U.S. Bureau of the Census 2001b: tables 576, 577, p. 373; Mink 1998a: 118; Gornick and Meyers 2003: 46.

42. Mink 1998a.

43. Gilens 1999: 45–50; Pierson 1994; Teles 1996: 43–45; Weaver, Shapiro, and Jacobs 1995: 618.

44. American Broadcast Company/Washington Post surveys, cited in Weaver, Shapiro, and Jacobs 1995: 611.

45. Gilens 1999: 37.

46. Columbia Broadcasting System/New York Times poll, cited in Weaver, Shapiro, and Jacobs 1995: 613.

47. Weaver 2000; see also Shaw and Shapiro 2002: 106.

48. Shaw and Shapiro 2002: 107; Weaver 2000: 181–84.

49. Shaw and Shapiro 2002: 107; Weaver 2000: 177–84.

50. Garin et al. 1994; Gilens 1999: 95. As Gilens (1999: 54) points out, "The same high-income Americans who oppose welfare do not oppose other means-tested anti-poverty programs," suggesting that their opposition to welfare spending does not simply reflect self-interested opposition to paying for targeted social programs (Garin et al. 1994; Gilens 1999: 95).

51. Gilens 1999: 68–72.

52. W. Wilson 1996: 162.

53. Johnson 2003: 157.

54. Harris 2002.

55. Soss et al. 2003: 237–42.

56. Mink 1998a.

57. Weaver 2000: 336.

58. Weaver 2000: 193.

59. Support for these measures varies, depending on the wording of the survey, and may have declined over time as they were debated in Congress. A 1995 poll suggests that most, or 55 percent, of the public supported policies denying public assistance to legal immigrants (Shaw and Shapiro 2002: 118–19). A 1996 General Social Survey poll also found that 62 percent of respondents opposed legal immigrants' eligibility for public assistance during their first year in the country (Question 530).

60. A 1999 national poll by Hickman-Brown Research Inc. found that "seven out of ten Americans oppose the provision of federal funds for education promoting abstinence-only until marriage that prohibits teaching about the use of condoms and contraception for the prevention of unintended pregnancy" (Advocates for Youth 1999).

61. Polls taken in 1993 and 1994 show that most respondents believed that recipients should be allowed to receive benefits at the end of their time limit if they worked for them. A 1993 survey found that more than 70 percent of voters were willing to make exceptions for the two-year consecutive time limit for mothers with preschool children and for those working part-time at low wages. About 60 percent of respondents did not think that work requirements should be applied to mothers of infants (Weaver 2000: 181–84; Garin et al. 1994).

62. Weaver 2000: 181; Weaver, Shapiro, and Jacobs 1995: 620.

63. Polls taken between 1993 and 1995 showed that between 85 and 92 percent of respondents favored providing child care to parents on welfare who could work or look for work. A 1994 survey found that 66 percent supported paying the transportation and commuting costs for welfare recipients to get to their

jobs (Weaver 2000: 181). Another survey showed that 81 percent of the public supported publicly subsidized health insurance for those whose jobs do not provide it (Draut 2001: 13).

64. Weaver, Shapiro, and Jacobs 1995: 614; Shaw and Shapiro 2002: 119.

65. U.S. Congress, Joint Committee on Printing 1996: 367.

66. Weaver 2000: 142.

67. Weaver 2000.

68. Lindsley 2002; Hondagneu-Sotelo 1995.

69. Lindsley 2002: 182.

70. Walker 1996: 171; Roschelle 1995: 443.

71. Blau 1984; Chang 2000: 21–32; Jensen 1988; Kposowa 1998: 147–59; Sanchez 1997: 1021; Tienda and Jensen 1986. One exception to this is the higher rate of Supplemental Security Income usage in 1989 among immigrants, especially Asian refugees (Bean, Van Hook, and Glick 1997: 448).

72. Brugge 1995: 9; Diamond 1996: 159.

73. Mehan 1997: 263.

74. Armbruster, Geron, and Bonacich 1995: 661; Roschelle 1995: 445; Walker 1996: 171; Smith and Tarallo 1995: 665–68; Sanchez 1997: 1012.

75. Mehan 1997: 259–61; Takacs 1999: 605–6.

76. Polls taken in 1993 and 1994 by the Field Institute found that most respondents believed that the children of undocumented immigrants should not be eligible to attend public schools or receive welfare (Lapinski et al. 1997: 381–82).

77. Cimons 1997.

78. Lesher 1996.

79. Polls show that about 63 percent of whites supported the measure, while 77 percent of Latinos opposed it. African-Americans and Asian-Americans were split, with about 53 percent from each group voting against the measure. About 78 percent of Republicans voted for the measure, compared to 64 percent of Democrats who opposed it (Armbruster, Geron, and Bonacich 1995: 661).

80. Armbruster, Geron, and Bonacich 1995: 662; Walker 1996: 178.

81. M. McBride 1999: 298.

82. Cited in Takacs 1999: 602.

83. M. McBride 1999: 298.

84. Weaver 2000: 231.

85. Chang 2000: 61.

86. Chang 2000.

87. Brugge 1995.

88. Mead 1992: 154–55; see also Weinberg 1998: 66.

89. Yoo 2001: 57.

90. Fujiwara 1999: 164.

91. Fujiwara 1999: 135.

92. Lapinski et al. 1997: 372–373.

93. National Research Council 1997: 349.

94. Lapinski et al. 1997: 360–63. In fact, roughly 800,000 legal immigrants

and refugees enter the country each year, while an estimated 300,000 enter the country as undocumented immigrants (Kilty and de Haymes 2000: 14).

95. Shaw and Shapiro 2002: 118–19.

96. Rector and Lauber 1995.

97. Rojas 1997.

98. Stein 1995.

99. M. Shapiro 1997: 1.

100. Shogren 1994b.

101. Brownstein 1995.

102. Shogren 1994a.

103. Fix and Passel 1994.

104. Unz 1994.

105. Reese and Ramirez 2003, 2002.

106. Chang 2000: 61; Fragomen 1997: 441; M. McBride 1999: 299; Parenti 1999.

107. Weaver 2000: 226.

108. Weaver 2000: 246, 291.

109. "Qualified" immigrants included (1) lawful permanent residents, (2) refugees, asylees, and persons granted withholding of deportation or removal, (3) Cuban and Haitian immigrants, (4) those with INS parole for at least one year, (5) conditional entrants, and (6) those identified as victims of domestic violence and their dependents. Other legal immigrants and those who entered the country on or after August 22, 1996 (the day PRWORA passed) were considered "unqualified" to receive federal welfare assistance. Legal immigrants are ineligible for the first five years they are in the United States, unless they are (1) veterans, (2) refugees, or (3) have worked in the United States for ten years or more (National Immigration Law Center 2002).

110. Shogren 1994b.

111. Zimmerman and Tumlin 1999: 11.

112. Weaver 2000: 336.

113. Reese and Ramirez 2003, 2002.

114. Hixson 1992: xxvii.

115. Rodger 2000: 21–23.

116. For example, see Piven and Cloward 1977; Katz 1996.

117. Moen 1995: 28–29, 32.

118. Moen 1995: 27–28.

119. Cited in Watson 1997: 146.

120. Weaver 2000: 211–15.

121. Weaver 2000: 211–15.

122. Young 1995.

123. Shogren 1995b. Founded in 1980 by California-based minister Louis Sheldon, TVC aims to restore the "values needed to maintain strong, unified families." In 2002, it represented 500,000 pastors and church members in 43,000 churches (Traditional Values Coalition 2002a, 2002b).

124. Dr. James Dobson, a former pediatrics professor, formed Focus on the

Family in 1977 to strengthen the "American family." By 2001, it claimed 3.5 million members. The group mobilizes voters around family issues through Dobson's radio show (now broadcast by over three thousand radio stations in the United States), its magazine, and "pro-family" events and conferences (Coltrane 2001; Diamond 1995: 250; Weaver 2000: 215).

125. Eagle Forum 2002a, 2002b.

126. Schlafly 1996b.

127. Schlafly 1996a.

128. Banzhaf 1999.

129. Sparks 2003: 178–79.

130. Schram 2003: 218.

131. Cited in A. Smith 2001: 314.

132. The bonus, $20–25 million, is given annually to the five states that best reduced their out-of-wedlock births without increasing their abortion rates (Banzhaf 1999; Mink 1998a: 70).

133. Education Reporter 1996; Weaver 2000; R. Novak 1995; Young 1995.

134. As of 1999, all states except California authorized state and federal funds for abstinence-only education. Some states even excluded representatives of reproductive rights groups from task forces addressing abstinence issues. States are required to match three state dollars for every four federal dollars for this program (Banzhaf 1999; National Organization for Women Legal Defense and Education Fund 1999: 1, 2–3).

135. National Family Planning and Reproductive Health Association 2003; National Organization for Women Legal Defense and Education Fund 2001a, 2001b, 2001c.

136. National Organization for Women Legal Defense and Education Fund 2001a: 3; 2001b: 2; 2001c.

137. Chaves 2001; see ch. 9. Faith-based organizations with these contracts cannot require their clients to participate in religious activities unless they voluntarily chose the organization through a voucher system (Ackerman 2002: 5–12).

138. Wright and Wong 2002.

139. On the role of right-wing think tanks in pushing for these policies, see chapter 9. On the role of the Eagle Forum, see Education Reporter 1996; Weaver 2000; Novak 1995. On the role of Focus on the Family and TVC, see Weaver 2000: 211; and DeParle 1995. On the role of the Christian Coalition, see Shogren 1995a, 1995b. On the role of the CWA, see Young 1995. See also Stefancic and Delgado 1996: 95; Weaver 2000: 211–15; Diamond 1995: 312; Novak 1995; DeParle 1995; Scheer 1996.

140. Young 1995.

141. Mink 1998a; Weaver 2000.

142. Kammer 1995; M. Nelson 1995.

143. Joffe 1998: 297; Weaver 2000: 265.

144. Mink 1998a: 65.

145. Edin 2000: 114; Lichter, McLaughlin, and Ribar 1997. The rise in out-of-

wedlock childbearing in the United States is due to various factors, including a decline in the stigma attached to it, women's rising labor force participation and age of first marriage, as well as social responses to poverty. Research suggests that the likelihood of marriage increases with the availability of men who earn above poverty wages and have higher educational attainment (Blau, Kahn, and Waldfogel 2000; Edin 2000; Lichter, McLaughlin, and Ribar 2002). Research suggests that poor labor market conditions for black males, as well as cultural differences, explain the particularly high incidence of unwed motherhood among blacks (Bulcroft and Bulcroft 1993; Lichter et al. 1992; Stier and Tienda 1997).

146. Data from the National Survey of Families and Households, 1987–88 and 1992–94, show that unwed mothers are ten times more likely to be on welfare and 70 percent less likely to be working fulltime than mothers who marry at some point in their lives (Alan Guttmacher Institute 1999).

147. Weaver 2000: 211–15.

148. Cited in Weaver 2000: 216.

149. DeParle 1995.

150. Since 1968, welfare mothers were required to cooperate in paternity establishment and child support proceedings, and these requirements were stiffened through a series of laws in 1974, 1984, and 1988. In the 1970s, women's organizations such as the National Organization for Women expressed concerns about federal requirements that poor mothers establish paternity, which were contained in the 1974 child support law (Mink 1998a: 80–83).

151. PRWORA required states to establish paternity and collect payments for a greater share of their welfare cases, reduce TANF benefits 25 percent if a mother refused to identify her child's father without good cause, and subject delinquent fathers to automatic wage withholding and work requirements. At the same time, PRWORA eliminated federal rules requiring states to allow welfare mothers to keep the first $50 of child support, after which two-thirds of states eliminated the policy. Congress also stiffened penalties for noncompliance with child support orders through the 1998 Deadbeat Parents Punishment Act. As a result, parents who owed more than $5,000 in child support who travel across state or country borders to evade their payments, or who willfully owe more than $10,000 for more than two years, could now be charged with a federal felony (Mink 1998a: 72–74; Folse 2001: 146; Curran and Abrams 2000: 666–67).

152. Curran and Abrams 2000: 670–75; National Organization for Women Legal Defense and Education Fund 2001c: 2.

153. Shaw and Shapiro 2002.

154. Shaw and Shapiro 2002: 118; National Public Radio/Kaiser Family Foundation/Kennedy School of Government 2001: 21.

155. Green et al. 2001.

156. D. Ackerman 2002; Coltrane 2001: 389.

157. D. Ackerman 2002: 2.

158. The coalition included representatives from conservative think tanks, such as the Institute for American Values, Family Research Council, Acton Insti-

tute, and Free Congress Foundation, and Christian right organizations, such as Eagle Forum, Concerned Women for America, the Traditional Values Coalition, and National Association of Evangelicals, and conservative organizations, such as the American Conservative Union and Fund for a Conservative Majority (Free Congress Foundation 2001).

159. D. Ackerman 2002: 1–10.

160. Bossom 2002; Diamond 1998: 111; Schlafly 2000; Traditional Values Coalition 2002c, 2002d; Miville 2001 a, 2001b; Ditmer 2002; Winn 2002; Marriage Savers 2002; McManus and McManus 2001.

161. Los Angeles Times 2002; Toner 2002b; MarriageMovement.org 2004.

162. Coltrane 2001.

163. Toner and Pear 2002; Pear 2002f.

164. Because of exceptions to work requirements, only 34 percent of welfare recipients were actually working. George W. Bush sought to minimize these exemptions (Pear 2002d; Fuller 2002; Peterson 2002b).

165. Hilfiker 2002.

166. Lake, Snell, Perry, and Associates. 2002.

167. Hilfiker 2002.

168. Stevenson 2003.

169. Becker 2002.

170. Pear 2002a. FAIR has even urged Congress to revise "public charge" regulations so that immigrants using public assistance could be deported (Federation for American Immigration Reform 2002).

171. Toner and Pear 2002; Pear 2002e; Bennett and Kemp 2002.

172. In response to state officials' criticism, House Republicans decided not to abolish the provision lowering work requirements when states reduced their caseloads, as the George W. Bush administration initially proposed. Yet, their plan would give credit for caseload reductions only for the previous three years, not for reductions since 1995 (Pear and Toner 2002; Pear 2002e).

173. Pear 2002g.

174. Pear 2002c; Pear and Toner 2002; Toner 2002c.

175. Toner 2002a.

176. Pear and Toner 2002.

177. Pear 2002b; Toner 2002a.

178. Pear 2002f.

179. Star Tribune 2003.

180. Pear 2002c.

181. Toner 2002a; Peterson 2002c; Stevenson 2003; Center for Community Change 2004.

182. Pear 2002h; Zedlewski and Loprest 2003.

183. Chen 2002.

184. Clymer 2002.

185. U.S. House of Representatives Committee on Ways and Means 2003; U.S. Senate Committee on Finance 2003.

186. Shaw and Shapiro 2002: 118–19.
187. Peterson 2002c; Pear 2004a, 2004b.
188. Zedlewski and Loprest 2003; Marino 2003; Fremstad and Parrott 2004.
189. Center for Community Change 2004.

CHAPTER 11

Epigraphs: Testimony, Town Hall meeting on welfare reform organized by the Los Angeles Coalition to End Hunger and Homelessness (June 15, 2002, Los Angeles, CA). Slogan used for a press conference organized by the Los Angeles Coalition to End Hunger and Homelessness, May 10, 2002. Interview, HOSEA member (June 2001, Milwaukee, WI). Interview, member of ACORN's Child Care Providers for Action (April 2002, Los Angeles, CA).

1. These figures are for 2003 (U.S. Bureau of the Census 2004).
2. Official poverty rates are calculated by multiplying the price of a minimally sufficient diet for a given family size times three. This measure was based on family budget research conducted in the 1950s that found that on average, families spent about one-third of their budget on food. Using more contemporary family needs budgets, researchers at the Economic Policy Institute estimated that actual poverty rates in the late 1990s were about three times higher among families with children (Gornick and Meyers 2003: 54–55; see also D. Pearce 2002).
3. Center on Budget and Public Policy Priorities 2003.
4. U.S. Conference of Mayors 2003; Witte 2004.
5. International measures of the poverty rate are based on the percentage of the population that earns 50 percent or less of the country's median income (Gornick and Meyers 2003: 75; Annie E. Casey Foundation 2002: 12). Cross-national research indicates that American low wages and lack of public assistance, not the country's higher incidence of single motherhood, explain why the poverty rate for women is so much higher in the United States compared to other affluent nations (Christopher 2002). Other research shows that maternal poverty rates are significantly lower in countries that provide subsidized child care and paid family leave (Misra and Moller 2004).
6. Esping-Anderson 1990.
7. Boggs 2000; Clawson, Neustadtl, and Weller 1998: 12–13.
8. Piven 1998: 27.
9. Lakoff 1996.
10. For example, see Orloff 2002.
11. Gornick and Meyers 2003: 46.
12. Weaver 2000: 181–84; Garin et al. 1994.
13. Gilens 1999: 216.
14. Lake, Snell, Perry, and Associates 2002: 4.
15. Gornick and Meyers 2003: 289–90.
16. On this latter point, see Gornick and Meyers 2003: 5.

17. Piven and Cloward 1977.

18. East, 2000; Mandell and Withorn, 1993; McCrate and Smith, 1998; Reese 2002; Reese and Newcombe 2003; Reese and Ramirez 2002, 2003.

19. Six months afterward, twenty-eight states adopted policies to take advantage of this option, and several other states adopted similar measures (National Organization for Women's Legal Defense and Education Fund 1997).

20. Reese and Ramirez 2002, 2003.

21. Deparle 1997; Enforcing this policy has been difficult, however (Association of Community Organizations for Reform Now 1998).

22. Collins and Yeskell 2000.

23. Labor Research Association 2004; Leondar-Wright 2004.

24. Pearce 2003.

25. Mulder 2004; DeNavas-Walt, Proctor, and Mills 2004.

26. Gornick and Meyers 2003: 32, 59, 179–80; on the rise in overtime, see Moody 1997.

27. See Ehrenreich 2002, and chapter 1.

28. Gornick and Meyers 2003: 277; Hays 2003: 54. By 2000, only 50 percent of people eligible for TANF were receiving it (Marks 2003). The Internal Revenue Service estimates that about one-quarter of EITC benefits available for low-income families are unclaimed (Elguea-Keating 2004).

29. Gornick and Meyers (2003) advocate these policies as crucial to the "earner-carer" citizenship model.

30. Gornick and Meyers 2003: 179–80.

31. Gornick and Meyers 2003: 156–63.

32. Gornick and Meyers 2003: 157–61.

33. Gornick and Meyers 2003: 114–29.

34. Gornick and Meyers 2003: 192.

35. Gornick and Meyers 2003: 198.

36. Gornick and Meyers 2003: 41–42.

37. This estimate is based on a line-by-line analysis by the War Resisters' League of projected expenditures contained in the *Budget of the United States Government, Fiscal Year 2005.* They exclude trust funds, such as Social Security, and estimate that about 80 percent of the interest on the debt is due to military spending (War Resisters' League 2004).

38. See Plotkin and Scheuerman 1994.

39. Gornick and Meyers 2003: 284–85.

40. Longer leaves may lower women's employment, however. Gornick and Meyers 2003: 198–99; 240–45; Misra and Moller 2004.

41. Eisenbrey 2004; Hulse 2004; Kamin, Krogan, and Greenstein 2004; Stewart 2004; Stolberg 2004.

42. Abate 2004.

References

Abate, Tom. 2004. "Kerry's Clintonian Economic Plan: Presidential Challenger Emphasizes Investment, Deficit Reduction." *San Francisco Chronicle*, June 20, J1.

Abramovitz, Mimi. 1989. *Regulating the Lives of Women: Social Policy from Colonial Times to the Present*. Boston, MA: South End Press.

Abramson, Paul R., John H. Aldrich, and David W. Rohde. 2002. *Change and Continuity in the 2000 Elections*. Washington, DC: CQ Press.

Ackerman, David M. 2002. *Public Aid to Faith-based Organizations (Charitable Choice): Background and Selected Legal Issues*. Washington, DC: Congressional Research Service.

Ackerman, Seth. 1999. "The Ever-Present Yet Nonexistent Poor: For Heritage's Poverty Expert, Numbers Mean What He Says They Mean." *Extra!* January/February. Retrieved May 26, 2002 (http://www.fair.org/extra/9901/rector .html).

Acton Institute. 1995. "A Revolution of Compassion." Grand Rapids, MI: Acton Institute. Retrieved May 19, 2002 (http://www.action.org/publicat/randl/ 95sept_oct/olasky.html)

————. 2002. "About the Institute." Grand Rapids, MI: Acton Institute. Retrieved May 19, 2002 (http://www.action.org/about/).

Advocates for Youth. 1999. "Americans Oppose Abstinence-Only Education." Washington, DC: Advocates for Youth. Retrieved December 31, 2003 (http:// www.advocatesforyouth.org/factsfigures/oppabonly.htm).

A Job Is a Right Campaign. 1998. "Community Groups Demand Ban on Winter Evictions." *Newsletter* 3 (6): 1.

Alameda County Welfare Rights Committee. 1964. "Interview with Members of the Welfare Rights Committee." Audiotape, Pacifica Radio Archives.

Alan Guttmacher Institute. 1999. "Married Mothers Fare the Best Economically, Even If They Were Unwed at the Time They Gave Birth." *Family Planning Perspectives* 31 (5): 258–60.

Albelda, Randy. 2001. "Fallacies of Welfare-to-Work Policies." *Annals of the American Academy of Political and Social Science* 577: 66–78.

Albert, Vicky N. and William C. King. 2001. "The Impact of the Economy and Welfare Policy on Welfare Accessions: Implications for Future Reforms." *Journal of Sociology and Social Welfare* 28 (3): 5–27.

Allard, Scott. 1998. "Revisiting 'Shapiro': Welfare Magnets and State Residency Requirements in the 1990s." *Publius* 28 (3): 45–65.

Allard, Scott W., and Sheldon Danziger. 2000. "Welfare Magnets: Myth or Reality?" *Journal of Politics* 62 (2): 350–68.

Alling, Elizabeth, and Agnes Leisy. 1950. *Aid to Dependent Children in a Postwar Year: Characteristics of Families Receiving ADC, June 1948*. Washington, DC: Federal Security Agency, Social Security Administration.

Alquist, Elaine. 1997. "Statement of Assemblywoman Elaine Alquist." Hearing of the California Joint Legislative Audit Committee, May 20. Sacramento: California Legislature.

Altmeyer, Arthur J. 1966. *The Formative Years of Social Security*. Madison, WI: University of Wisconsin Press.

American Association of University Women. 1970. "When Poor People Organize, What Are Their Aims? 'An Adequate Income to Sustain Life.' " *AAUW Journal P.* 122. Box 27 (7). George Wiley Papers. State Historical Society of Wisconsin at Madison.

American Child. 1966. "Strategy of Crisis: A Dialogue." *American Child* 48 (3): 20–32.

American Enterprise Institute. 1996. "Book Summary: *To Empower People: From State to Civil Society*." Washington, DC: American Enterprise Institute. Retrieved February 18, 2002 (http://www.aei.org/bs/bs6105.htm).

———. 2001. *Annual Report 2001*. Washington, DC: American Enterprise Institute. Retrieved May 24, 2002 (http://www.aei.org/annual/finances.htm).

———. 2002. *AEI Scholars*. Washington, DC: American Enterprise Institute. Retrieved May 24, 2002 (http://www.aei.org/scholars/scholars.htm).

American Farm Bureau Federation. 1954a. "Future of Mexican Labor Program Is Uncertain." *American Farm Bureau Federation's Official Newsletter*, January 4, p. 1.

———. 1954b. "New Unilateral Program for Recruiting Mexican Farm Labor Is Planned." *American Farm Bureau Federation's Official Newsletter*, January 18, p. 4.

———. 1954c. "AFBF Urges Congress to Allow Continued Mexican Labor Program." *American Farm Bureau Federation's Official Newsletter*, February 8, p. 1.

———. 1954d. "Here are the Voting Records of the Senate and House on the Mexican Farm Labor Bill." *American Farm Bureau Federation's Official Newsletter*, March 8, p. 2.

———. 1954e. "FB Asks Delay in Expansion of Social Security." *American Farm Bureau Federation's Official Newsletter*, April 12, p.1.

———. 1954f. "Social Security Act Covers Farm Operators." *American Farm Bureau Federation's Official Newsletter*, August 30, p. 3.

———. 1954g. "Farm Labor." *American Farm Bureau Federation's Official Newsletter*, December 20, p. 14.

———. 1955a. "Five Bills Filed to Amend Social Security Legislation." *American Farm Bureau Federation's Official Newsletter*, March 7, p. 39.

———. 1955b. "Measure Would Hike Social Security Coverage, Taxes." *American Farm Bureau Federation's Official Newsletter*, July 18, p. 116.

———. 1955c. "Senate-House Conference Approves 31/2 Year Mexican Labor Program." *American Farm Bureau Federation's Official Newsletter*, August 1, p. 131.

———. 1955d. "Summary." *American Farm Bureau Federation's Official Newsletter*, August 29, p. 140.

———. 1955e. "Policy Resolutions: Social Security." *American Farm Bureau Federation's Official Newsletter*, December 19, p. 211.

———. 1956a. "Senate Bills Would Extend Wage-Hour Law to Cover Farm Workers; FB Protests." *American Farm Bureau Federation's Official Newsletter*, June 4, p. 90.

———. 1956b. "American Farm Bureau Federation Policies for 1957 Adopted at National Convention." *American Farm Bureau Federation's Official Newsletter*, December 17, p. 209.

———. 1957. "American Farm Bureau Federation Policies and Resolutions Adopted for 1958 at National Convention." *American Farm Bureau Federation's Official Newsletter*, December 16, p. 207.

———. 1958. "American Farm Bureau Federation Policies and Resolutions Adopted for 1959 at National Convention: Farm Labor." *American Farm Bureau Federation's Official Newsletter*, December 15, p. 207.

———. 1959a. "Labor Department Proposes Regulation of Farm Workers; Farm Bureau Objects." *American Farm Bureau Federation's Official Newsletter*, February 23, p. 30.

———. 1959b. "FB Says Higher Minimum Wage Would Add to Farmers' Costs." *American Farm Bureau Federation's Official Newsletter*, May 18, p. 77.

———. 1959c. "FB Calls for Withdrawal of Farm Labor Regulations." *American Farm Bureau Federation's Official Newsletter*, September 14, p. 145.

———. 1959d. "Committee Recommends Mexican Program Changes." *American Farm Bureau Federation's Official Newsletter*, November 2, p. 175.

Anderson, Glenn M. 1949. Letter to Governor Warren, July 2. Governors' Bill Files, Assembly Bill 40. California State Archives.

Annie E. Casey Foundation. 2002. *Children at Risk: State Trends 1990–2000.* Baltimore, MD: Annie E. Casey Foundation. Retrieved March 8, 2002 (http://www.aecf.org/kidscount).

Armbruster, Ralph, Kim Geron, and Edna Bonacich. 1995. "The Assault on California's Latino Immigrants: The Politics of Proposition 187." *International Journal of Urban and Regional Research* 19 (4): 655–63.

Ascribe Newswire. 2001. "Homelessness in California Linked to Growing Gap between Rich and Poor, Study Finds: Housing Affordability a Key Factor." *Ascribe Newswire*, October 31. Retrieved September 13, 2003. Available: LEXIS-NEXIS Academic Universe, News Sources.

Ashcroft, John. 1995. "Which Will Survive: The Welfare State or the Republican Revolution? Lecture No. 539." Washington, DC: Heritage Foundation. Retrieved February 11, 2002 (http://www.heritage.org/Research/Welfare/HL539.cfm).

Ashmore, Harry S. 1994. *Civil Rights and Wrongs: A Memoir of Race and Politics, 1944–1994*. New York: Pantheon Books.

Asian Pacific American Legal Center. 2001. "The Impact of Welfare Reform on Asians and Pacific Islanders." Los Angeles: Asian Pacific American Legal Center.

Association of Community Organizations for Reform Now. 1998. "Workfare and Minimum Wage in Los Angeles County." [Pamphlet, October 1998]. Los Angeles: ACORN.

Atlanta Constitution. 1949. "Dependent Children's Aid from State Gets Slash to Meet Federal Rules." *Atlanta Constitution*, June 25, 2:7.

———. 1951a. "The Governor and Relief Rolls." *Atlanta Constitution*, February 5, p. 10.

———. 1951b. "Nauseating Welfare Abuses." *Atlanta Constitution*, February 10, p. 4.

———. 1951c. "Case Histories Listed of Glaring Abuses in State's Old-Age Pension Program." *Atlanta Constitution*, February 11, p. B3.

———. 1951d. "Two Legislative Blows Aimed at Relief Rolls." *Atlanta Constitution*, February 13, p. 7.

———. 1951e. "Two Members Quit Sumter Welfare Unit." *Atlanta Constitution*, February 17, p. 5.

———. 1951f. "Welfare Aide Calls Probe 'Witchhunt.'" *Atlanta Constitution*, March 2, p. 2.

———. 1951g. "Signed FEPC Petition, State Employee Declares." *Atlanta Constitution*, March 29, p. 7.

———. 1951h. "Support-Parents Law Likely to Go Under." *Atlanta Constitution*, July 8, p. B8.

———. 1952a. "69 Child Relief Checks Cashed in Liquor Stores." *Atlanta Constitution*, March 30, p. A12.

———. 1952b. "Children's Aid Abuses Worry County Welfare Boards." *Atlanta Constitution*, April 9, p. 16.

Avery, James M., and Mark Peffley. 2003. "Race Matters: The Impact of News Coverage of Welfare Reform on Public Opinion." In *Race and the Politics of Welfare Reform*, edited by Sanford F. Schram, Joe Soss, and Richard C. Fording, 131–50. Ann Arbor: University of Michigan Press.

Axinn, June, and Herman Levin. 1975. *Social Welfare: A History of the American Response to Need*. New York: Harper and Row.

Ayala, Cesar. 1996. "The Decline of the Plantation Economy and the Puerto Rican Migration of the 1950s." *Latino Studies Journal* 7 (1): 62–90.

Baker, Gordon E. 1955. *Rural Versus Urban Political Power: The Nature and Consequences of Unbalanced Representation*. Garden City, NY: Doubleday and Company.

Banzhaf, Marion. 1999. "Welfare Reform and Reproductive Rights: Talking about Connections." Presentation for the National Network of Abortion Funds on June 11. Seattle, WA: Feminist Women's Health Center. Retrieved on May 23, 2002 (http://www.fwhc.org/tanf.htm).

Barnes, V. E. 1949. Letter to Miss Anne E. Geddes. February 24. Kentucky Department of Libraries and Archives, Department of Economic Security Records, Division: Research and Statistics, Loc: C-70-E-8-F.

Bartley, Numan V. 1969. *The Rise of Massive Resistance: Race and Politics in the South in the 1950s*. Baton Rouge: Louisiana State University Press.

Bashevkin, Sylvia. 2000. "Rethinking Retrenchment: North American Social Policy During the Early Clinton and Chretien Years." *Canadian Journal of Political Science* 33 (1): 7–36.

Baver, Sherrie. 1984. "Puerto Rican Politics in New York City: The Post–World War II Period," in *Puerto Rican Politics in Urban America*, edited by Jennings, James and Monte Rivera, 43–59. Westport, CT: Greenwood Press.

Bean, Frank D., and Marta Tienda. 1987. *The Hispanic Population of the United States*. New York: Russell Sage Foundation.

Bean, Frank D., Jennifer. V. W. Van Hook, and Jennifer Glick. 1997. "Country of Origin, Type of Public Assistance, and Patterns of Welfare Recipiency among U.S. Immigrants and Natives." *Social Science Quarterly* 78 (2): 432–51.

Becker, Elizabeth. 2002. "Politics: Farm Compromise." *New York Times*, April 28, p. 4. Retrieved July 24, 2003. Available: LEXIS-NEXIS Academic Universe, News Sources.

Behrens, Earl C. 1948a. "The Results in the State: Late Tally Shows That Pension Plan May Pass." *San Francisco Chronicle*, November 5, pp. 1, 14.

———. 1948b. "Election Aftermaths." *San Francisco Chronicle*, November 6, pp. 1, 6.

———. 1948c. "State Proposition Results." *San Francisco Chronicle*, November 7, p. 16.

———. 1949a. "State Senate Uproar: Tenney Accused of Putting Editor on State Pay Roll: He Lashes Back." *San Francisco Chronicle*, May 17, p. 9.

———. 1949b. "Propositions One and Two: Business Women's Clubs Recommend School Bonds and Pension Law Revision." *San Francisco Chronicle*, October 27, p. 1.

———. 1949c. "Voters Ditch McLain, but Keep Pension Provisions." *San Francisco Chronicle*, November 9, p. 1.

———. 1949d. "Pension Problems." *San Francisco Chronicle*, November 21, p. 2.

Belknap, Michael R. 1987. *Federal Law and Southern Order: Racial Violence and Constitutional Conflict in the Post-Brown South*. Athens: University of Georgia Press.

Bell, Griffin, Lewis R. Morgan, and Sidney O. Smith, Jr. 1968. "Findings of Fact, April 4." Records of Civil Action Number 10443. Georgia Federal Records Center, East Point, GA. Accession Number 69 A 2139, Box 30–31. Location 86559–60.

Bell, Winifred. 1965. *Aid to Dependent Children.* New York: Columbia University Press.

Bennett, Charles. 1958. "Relief Inquiry Calls City Welfare Chief." *New York Times,* November 13, p. 1.

Bennett, William J. 1995. "Testimony for Empower America." In *Contract with America—Welfare Reform. Hearing before the Subcommittee on Human Resources of the Committee on Ways and Means, House of Representatives.* Pp. 156–78. 104th Cong., 1st sess.

———. 2002. "The Index of Leading Cultural Indicators 2001: Executive Summary." Retrieved June 2, 2002 (http://www.empower.org).

Bennett, William J., and Jack Kemp. 2002. "Keep Reforming Welfare." *Wall Street Journal,* August 1, p. A12.

Bergmann, Barbara. 1996. *Saving Our Children from Poverty: What the United States Can Learn from France.* New York: Russell Sage Foundation.

Berkowitz, Bill. 2002. "Chapter 4: Welfare Privatization: Prospecting among the Poor." In *From Poverty to Punishment: How Welfare Reform Punishes the Poor,* edited by Applied Research Center, 73–88. Oakland, CA: Applied Research Center.

Berkowitz, Edward D. 1995. *Mr. Social Security: The Life of Wilbur J. Cohen.* Lawrence: University Press of Kansas.

Berkowitz, Edward, and Kim McQuaid. 1980. "Chapter 8: Backing into the Future: Social Welfare in the 1950s." In *Creating the Welfare State: The Political Economy of the Twentieth Century Reform,* 135–58. New York: Praeger.

Bernstein, Nina. 2000. "Squabble Puts Welfare Deals under Spotlight in New York." *New York Times,* February 22, p. B1: 5. Retrieved August 15, 2002. Available: LEXIS-NEXIS Academic Universe, News Sources.

———. 2002. "Child-Only Cases Grow in Welfare." *New York Times,* August 14, p. A1. Retrieved March 25, 2004. Available: LEXIS-NEXIS Academic Universe, News Sources.

Berry, Steve. 2001. "Shelter to Turn Away Single Women." *Los Angeles Times,* March 21, p. B1. Retrieved May 25, 2003. Available: LEXIS-NEXIS Academic Universe, News Sources.

Besharov, Douglas J. 1995. *Hearing before the Subcommittee on Human Resources of the Committee on Ways and Means, House of Representatives. 104th Cong., 1st sess., Part 2,* February 10. Serial 104–44. Washington, DC: U.S. Government Printing Office.

———. 2002. "Testimony before the Subcommittee on Human Resources: Hearing on Welfare and Marriage Issues." March 7. *Committee on Ways and Means.* Retrieved July 15, 2003 (http://www.house.gov/ways_means/humres).

Besharov, Douglas, and Karen Gardiner. 1997. "Sex Education and Abstinence: Programs and Evaluation." *Children and Youth Services Review* 19 (5/6): 327–39. Retrieved May 22, 2002 (www.aei.org/sw/swbesharov2.htm).

Binn, Sheldon. 1958. "Rockefeller to Study City Plan for Legal Off-Track Gambling." *New York Times,* September 25, p. 23.

Blakey, George T. 1986. *Hard Times and New Deal in Kentucky: 1929–1939.* Lexington: University Press of Kentucky.

Blau, Francine. D. 1984. "The Use of Transfer Payments by Immigrants." *Industrial and Labor Relations Review* 37: 222–39.

Blau, Francine D., Lawrence M. Kahn, and Jane Waldfogel. 2000. "Understanding Young Women's Marriage Decisions: The Role of Labor and Marriage Market Conditions." *Industrial and Labor Relations Review* 53 (4): 624–47.

Block, Fred. 1987. "Rethinking the Political Economy of the Welfare State." In *The Mean Season: The Attack on the Welfare State,* edited by Fred Block, Richard A. Cloward, Barbara Ehrenreich, and Frances Fox Piven. New York: Pantheon Books.

———. 1996. *The Vampire State.* New York: New Press.

Block, Fred, and Margaret Somers. Forthcoming. "From Poverty to Perversity: Ideas, Markets and Institutions over Two Hundred Years of Welfare Debate." *American Sociological Review.*

Bloom, Dan, and Don Winstead. 2002. "Sanctions and Welfare Reform." WR&B Brief No. 12. Washington, DC: Brookings Institution. Retrieved May 25, 2002 (http://www.brook.edu/dybdocrot/wrb/publications/pb/pb12.htm).

Blumenberg, Evelyn, and Paul Ong. 1994. "Labor Squeeze and Ethnic/Racial Recomposition in the U.S. Apparel Industry." In *Global Production: The Apparel Industry in the Pacific Rim,* edited by Edna Bonacich, Lucie Cheng, Norma Chinchilla, Nora Hamilton, and Paul Ong. Philadelphia, PA: Temple University Press.

Boggs, Carl. 2000. *The End of Politics: Corporate Power and the Decline of the Public Sphere.* New York: Guilford Press.

Bonacich, Edna, and Richard P. Appelbaum. 2000. *Behind the Label: Inequality in the Los Angeles Apparel Industry.* Berkeley: University of California Press.

Bose, Christine. 1986. "Puerto Rican Women in the United States: An Overview." In *The Puerto Rican Woman: Perspectives on Culture, History, and Society,* edited by Edna Acosta-Belen, 147–69. 2d ed. New York: Praeger.

Bossom, Elizabeth. 2002. "President Bush Endorses Abstinence and Marriage: Both Programs Vital to Reform of Welfare System." Washington, DC: Concerned Women For America. Retrieved June 5, 2002 (http://cwfa.org/library/family/2002–02–27_welfare-reform.shtml).

Brandwein, Ruth A., and Diana M. Filiano. 2000. "Toward Real Welfare Reform: The Voices of Battered Women." *Affilia* 15 (2): 224–43.

Brasher, Arlene E., Arabella Martinez Springer, and Archie J. Hanlan. 1966. *Mexican-American Recipients' Orientations toward and Modes of Adaptation to the Welfare System.* School of Social Welfare, University of California, Berkeley.

Bresler, Robert J. 1995. "The End of New Deal Liberalism and the Rise of Populism." *Telos* 104: 13–26.

Brockland, Beth. 2002. "Reforming Welfare Reform." *Dollars and Sense* 243:1. Retrieved June 19, 2003 (http://www.dollarsandsense.org/archives/2002/0902brockland.html).

Brody, Jane E. 2004. "Abstinence-Only: Does It Work?" *New York Times,* June 1, p. F7. Retrieved July 3, 2004. Available: LEXIS-NEXIS Academic Universe, News Sources.

Brookings Institution. 2002a. "About Brookings Institution." Washington, DC: Brookings Institution. Retrieved May 26, 2002 (http://www.brook.edu).

———. 2002b. "Statements of Activities, Years Ended June 30, 2001 and 2000." Washington, DC: Brookings Institution. Retrieved May 26, 2002 (http://www.brook.edu/dybdocroot/EA/Trustees.HTM).

———. 2002c. "Brookings Board of Trustees." Washington, DC: Brookings Institution. Retrieved May 26, 2002 (http://www.brook.edu).

Brown, Michael K. 1999. *Race, Money, and the American Welfare State.* Ithaca, NY: Cornell University Press.

———. 2003. "Ghettos, Fiscal Federalism, and Welfare Reform." In *Race and the Politics of Welfare Reform,* edited by Sanford F. Schram, Joe Soss, and Richard C. Fording, 47–71. Ann Arbor: University of Michigan Press.

Brownstein, Ronald. 1995. "Immigration Debate Roils GOP Presidential Contest." *Los Angeles Times,* May 14, p. A1. Retrieved June 14, 2002. Available: LEXIS-NEXIS Academic Universe, News Sources.

———. 2002. "Immigration Reform on House Democrats' Minds." *Los Angeles Times,* July 23, p. A18. Retrieved September 23, 2003. Available: LEXIS-NEXIS Academic Universe, News Sources.

———. 2003. "For 2004, Bush Has Strength in the White Male Numbers." *Los Angeles Times,* December 28, pp. A1, A40.

Brugge, Doug. 1995. "The Anti-immigrant Backlash." *Public Eye Magazine* 9 (2): 1–13.

Bruner, Karla. 1997. "Wanted: Work, not Welfare: Immigrants Find U.S. a Land of Opportunity; Census Report Refutes Notion that Foreign-Born Residents Just Want an Easy Ride." *Fresno Bee,* April 13, p. A1. Retrieved June 14, 2002. Available: LEXIS-NEXIS Academic Universe, News Sources.

Brzuzy, Stephanie, Layne Stromwall, Polly Sharp, Regina Wilson, and Elizabeth Segal. 2000. "The Vulnerability of American Indian Women in the New Welfare State." *Affilia* 15 (20): 193–203.

Bulcroft, Richard A., and Kris A. Bulcroft. 1993. "Race Differences in Attitudinal and Motivational Factors in the Decision to Marry." *Journal of Marriage and the Family* 55 (2): 338–55.

Bullock, Paul. 1972. "Employment Problems of the MX-American." In *The Changing Mexican-American: A Reader,* edited by Rudolph Gomez, 90–105. El Paso: University of Texas, El Paso.

Burch, Hobart A. 1970. "A Conversation with George Wiley." *Journal,* Nov.-Dec., pp. 3–12. Box 36, Folder 5. George Wiley Papers. State Historical Society of Wisconsin at Madison.

———. 1971. "Insights of a Welfare Mother: A Conversation with Johnnie Tillmon." *Journal,* Jan.-Feb., pp. 13–23. Box 36, Folder 5. George Wiley Papers. State Historical Society of Wisconsin at Madison.

Bureau of Labor Statistics. 2001. "Table: Annual Average Unemployment Rate, Civilian Labor Force 16 Years and Over (Percent). Washington, DC; Bureau of Labor Statistics. Retrieved July 15, 2001 (http://www.bls.gov/cps/prev _yrs.htm).

———. 2003. "Employment Characteristics of Families in 2002." Washington, DC: U.S. Department of Labor.

———. 2004. "Table A.1: Employment Status of the Civilian Noninstitutional Population 16 Years and Over, 1969 to Date." Washington, DC: Bureau of Labor Statistics. Retrieved January 12, 2004 (ftp://ftp.bls.gov/pub/suppl/ empsit.cpseea1.txt).

Bureau of Public Assistance. 1957a. *Characteristics of General Assistance in the United States. Public Assistance Report No. 39.* Washington, DC: U.S. Government Printing Office.

———. 1957b. "Factors Underlying Increase in Aid to Dependent Children Caseload, 1954–57, and in Average Number of Children Per Family Receiving Aid to Dependent Children, 1951–57." Box: Department of Economic Security Agency, Division of Research and Statistics. Loc: C-70-E-8-F. Folder: George Narensky, Regional Representative, Correspondence, 1957. Kentucky Department of Archives and History.

Burnham, Linda. 2001. "Welfare Reform, Family Hardship, and Women of Color." *Annals of the American Academy of Political and Social Science* 577: 39–47.

Calavita, Kitty. 1996. The New Politics of Immigration: Balanced-Budget Conservatism and the Symbolism of Proposition 187. *Social Problems* 43 (3): 284–305.

Calhoun County Department of Public Welfare. 1952. "Annual Report. July 1, 1951-June 30, 1952." County Annual Reports for Department of Family and Children's Social Services. Series 24–8–65. Box 1. Georgia Department of Archives and History.

Calhoun County Welfare Department. 1950. "Annual Report. July 1, 1949-July 1, 1950." County Annual Reports for Department of Family and Children's Social Services. Series 24–8–65. Box 1. Georgia Department of Archives and History.

California Department of Social Welfare. 1950a. Office Memorandum. To E. E. Silveira from Jack W. Snow, September 28, Re: Effect of 'AB40' on Size of ANC Caseload by Month and by Fiscal Year. California State Archives.

———. 1950b. "Aid to Needy Children." Department of Social Welfare Collection, 1950–1954, Legislation. California State Archives.

———. 1951–53. *Biennial and Annual Reports of the State Department of Social Welfare.* Sacramento: California Social Welfare Board.

California Farm Bureau Federation. 1950a. "Report of the Research and Legislation Department." In *Minutes of the Thirty-Second Annual Meeting, California Farm Bureau Federation.* November 12–16, Berkeley, CA.

———. 1950b. "Supplement X: Adopted Resolutions." In *Minutes of the Thirty-Second Annual Meeting, California Farm Bureau Federation.* November 12–13, Berkeley, CA.

———. 1950c. "Supplement Z: Membership Statement." In *Minutes of the Thirty-Second Annual Meeting, California Farm Bureau Federation.* November 12–16, Berkeley, CA.

California Senate Interim Committee on State and Local Taxation. 1951. *Report of the Senate Interim Committee on State and Local Taxation. Aid to Needy Children Program of the State of California,* in *Journal of the Senate, Regular Session.* Vol. 2, appendix. Sacramento: California Legislature.

California State Chamber of Commerce. 1950. *Statewide Committee of the California State Chamber of Commerce, Agriculture and Industry.* Sacramento: California State Chamber of Commerce.

California State Legislature. 1949. *Assembly Final History.* Sacramento: California State Printing Press.

———. 1951a. *Assembly Final History.* Sacramento: California State Printing Press.

———. 1951b. *Senate Final History.* Sacramento: California State Printing Press.

California State Social Welfare Board. 1949. "Minutes of Executive Session, 8/26/49." Earl Warren Papers #423. Proposed Legislation. General Social Welfare. California State Archive.

California Taxpayers' Association. 1949. "Vote Yes on Prop. #2: Association Recommends Adoption." *Tax Digest* 9: 295. Los Angeles: California Taxpayers' Association.

———. 1950. *Tax Digest* 28 (2). Los Angeles: California Taxpayers' Association.

———. 1951. *The Tax Digest* 29 (2). Los Angeles: California Taxpayers' Association.

Callahan, David. 1999. *$1 Billion for Ideas: Conservative Think Tanks in the 1990's.* Washington, DC: National Committee for Responsive Philanthropy.

Camarillo, Albert. 1990. *Chicanos in California: A History of Mexican Americans in California.* Sparks, NV: Materials for Today's Learning. (Orig. pub. 1984).

Campus Coalition for Human Rights and Social Justice. 1995. "California at the Crossroads: Social Strife or Social Unity?" *Social Justice* 22 (3): 53–63.

Cancian, Maria, and Daniel R. Meyer. 2000. "Work after Welfare: Women's Work Effort, Occupation, and Well-Being." *Social Work Research* 24 (2): 69–86.

Carroll, Rodney J. 2001a. "Testimony of Mr. Rodney Carroll, President and CEO, the Welfare to Work Partnership." Subcommittee on 21st Century Competitiveness. Hearing on Welfare Reform: Success in Moving toward Work. 107th Cong., October 16.

———. 2001b. Testimony for the Work Requirements on the TANF Cash Welfare Program Hearing before the Subcommittee on Human Resources of the

Committee on Ways and Means, House of Representatives. 107th Cong., 1st sess. April 3. Serial 107–10.

Carter, R. F. 1969. "Pressure from the Left: The American Labor Party, 1936–1954." Ph.D. dissertation, Department of History, Syracuse University, Syracruse, NY.

Cassell, Carol A. 1977. "Cohort Analysis of Party Identification among Southern Whites, 1952–1972." *Public Quarterly* 41 (1): 28–33.

Cates, Jerry R. 1983. *Insuring Inequality: Administrative Leadership in Social Security, 1935–1954.* Ann Arbor: University of Michigan Press.

Cato Institute. 2001. "Government Funding of Faith-Based Initiatives: Compassionate Conservatism or Corrupting Charity?" *CATO Institute Policy Forum*, February 20. Washington, DC: Cato Institute. Retrieved May 1, 2002 (http://www.cato.org/events/010220apf.html).

———. 2002a. "About CATO." Washington, DC: Cato Institute. Retrieved May 26, 2002 (http://www.cato.org/about/about.html).

———. 2002b. "Board of Directors." Washington, DC: Cato Institute. Retrieved May 26, 2002 (http://www.cato.org/people/directors.html).

———. 2002c. "CATO Institute 25th Anniversary." Washington, DC: Cato Institute. Retrieved May 1, 2002 (http://www.cato.org/25th/timeline.html).

———. 2002d. "Health and Welfare Studies." Washington, DC: Cato Institute. Retrieved May 1, 2002 (http://www.cato.org/research/healthandwelfare/welfare.html).

———. 2002e. "Bush's Welfare Reauthorization Plan Boosts Cash Aid, Weakens Work Requirements, and Broadens Government Intervention in Marriage." *News Releases*, February 28. Retrieved May 1, 2002 (http://www.cato.org/cgibin/scripts/printtech.cgi/new/02–02/02–02–28r.html).

Cauthen, Nancy, and Edwin Amenta. 1996. "Not For Widows Only: Institutional Politics and the Formative Years of Aid to Dependent Children." *American Sociological Review* 61: 427–48.

Center for Community Change. 2004. Policy Alert #330, Wednesday June 23. Retrieved July 3, 2004 (http://66.36.240.156/alerts/default.asp).

Center on Budget and Policy Priorities. 2003. "Poverty Increases and Median Income Declines for Second Consecutive Year." Press Release. Retrieved July 1, 2004 (http://www.cpbb.org/9–26–03pov.htm).

Chalmers, David M. 1965. *Hooded Americans: The First Century of the Ku Klux Klan, 1865–1965.* Garden City, NY: Doubleday and Company.

Chang, Grace. 1994. "Undocumented Latinas: The New 'Employable Mothers.' " In *Mothering, Ideology, Experience, Agency*, 259–85. New York: Routledge.

———. 2000. *Disposable Domestics: Immigrant Women Workers in the Global Economy.* Cambridge, MA: South End Press.

Chappell, Marisa. 2003. "The Radical Potential of Conservative Family Values: The Guaranteed Income Campaign, 1964–1972." Paper presented at the 2003 annual meeting of the Social Science History Association conference, Baltimore, MD.

Chase, Henry. 1967. "Statement on Behalf of the Chamber of Commerce of the United States." In *Social Security Amendments of 1967. Hearings Before the Committee on Finance. U.S. Senate Ninetieth Congress First Session on HR 12080. Part II.* Pp. 1455–63. Washington, DC: U.S. Government Printing Office. National Archive.

Chatham County Department of Public Welfare. 1953. "Annual Report. July 1, 1952–July 1, 1953." County Annual Reports for Department of Family and Children's Social Services. Series 24–8–65. Box 2. Georgia Department of Archives and History.

Chaves, Mark. 2001. "Religious Congregations and Welfare Reform." *Society* 38 (2): 21–27.

Chen, Edwin. 2002. "The Nation: Bush Assails Welfare Plan: The President Calls the Senate Reform Measure a 'Retreat from Success.' He Wants Tougher Employment Rules for Recipient." *Los Angeles Times,* July 30, p. A11. Retrieved September 23, 2003. Available: LEXIS-NEXIS Academic Universe, News Sources.

Chen, Edwin, and Jonathan Peterson. 2001. "Bush Hints at Broader Amnesty." *Los Angeles Times,* July 27, p. A1. Retrieved September 23, 2003. Available: LEXIS-NEXIS Academic Universe, News Sources.

Cherlin, Andrew J. 1992. *Marriage, Divorce, Remarriage.* Rev. ed. Cambridge, MA: Harvard University Press.

Christopher, Karen. 2002. "Single Motherhood, Employment, or Social Assistance: Why Are U.S. Women Poorer than Women in Other Affluent Nations?" *Journal of Poverty* 6 (2): 61–80.

Cimons, Marlene. 1997. "GOP Leader Vows Fight on Immigrant Aid." *Los Angeles Times,* February 10, p. A1. Retrieved June 14, 2002. Available: LEXIS-NEXIS Academic Universe, News Sources.

Citizens for Workfare Justice. 1998. *When Work Doesn't Pay: 'Workfare' in Los Angeles County.* Los Angeles: Citizens for Workfare Justice.

Civil Rights Congress. 1970. *We Charge Genocide: The Historic Petition to the United Nations for Relief from a Crime of the United States Government against the Negro People,* edited by William L. Patterson. New York: International Publishers. (Orig. pub. 1951)

Clawson, Dan, Alan Neustadtl, and Mark Weller. 1998. *Dollars and Votes: How Business Campaign Contributions Subvert Democracy.* Philadelphia, PA: Temple University Press.

Clymer, Adam. 2002. "Republicans Have Edge, But Passing Bush's Plans May Require Compromise." *New York Times,* November 7, p. B5. Retrieved May 11, 2003. Available: LEXIS-NEXIS Academic Universe, News Sources.

Cobb, Tyn. 1967. "Letter to Senator Long from Tyn Cobb, Congressional Action Committee, Winter Park Chamber of Commerce." August 30. In *Social Security Amendments of 1967. Hearings Before the Committee on Finance. U.S. Senate. HR 12080. Part II.* Pp. A43. 90th Cong., 1st sess. Washington, DC: U.S. Government Printing Office. National Archive.

Collins, Chuck, and Felice Yeskel (with United for a Fair Economy). 2000. *Eco-*

nomic Apartheid in America: A Primer on Economic Inequality and Insecurity. New York: New Press.

Collins, Patricia Hill. 1990. *Black Feminist Thought: Knowledge, Consciousness, and the Politics of Empowerment.* New York: Routledge.

Coltrane, Scott. 2001. "Marketing the Marriage 'Solution': Misplaced Simplicity in the Politics of Fatherhood." *Sociological Perspectives* 44 (4): 387–418.

Coltrane, Scott, and Randall Collins. 2001. *Gender, Love, and Property.* 5th ed. Belmont, CA: Wadsworth/Thomson Learning. (Orig. pub. 1995)

Congressional Quarterly Service. 1965. *Congress and the Nation, 1945–1964: A Review of Government and Politics in the Postwar Years. Vol. 1, Part 1.* Washington, DC: Congressional Quarterly Service.

Connor, Kenneth L. 2001. "Fathers Have a Place in Today's Families." Washington, DC: Family Research Council. Retrieved June 7, 2002 (http://www.frc/org/get/aro1i11.cfm).

Conrad, James H. 1989. "Aid to Families with Dependent Children in Texas, 1941–1981." In *For the General Welfare: Essays in Honor of Robert H. Bremner,* edited by Frank Annunziata, Patrick D. Reagan, and Roy T. Wortman, 337–60. New York: Peter Lang.

Cook, Christopher D. 1998. "Plucking Workers: Tyson Foods Looks to the Welfare Rolls for a Captive Labor Force." *Progressive* (August), pp. 28–31.

Coontz, Stephanie. 1997. *The Way We Really Are: Coming to Terms with America's Changing Families.* New York: Basic Books.

Council of State Governments. 1950. *The Book of the States, 1950–51.* Vol. 8. Chicago, IL: Council of State Governments.

Covington, Sally. 1997. "Moving a Public Policy Agenda: The Strategic Philanthropy of Conservative Foundations." Washington: National Committee for Responsive Philanthropy.

Crowell, Paul. 1959. "Revisions Urged in City Welfare." *New York Times,* October 17, p. 1.

Cuellar, Alfredo. 1972. "Perspective on Politics." In *The Changing Mexican-American: A Reader,* edited by Rudolph Gomez, 188–212. El Paso: University of Texas, El Paso.

Curran, Laura, and Laura S. Abrams. 2000. "Making Men into Dads: Fatherhood, the State, and Welfare Reform." *Gender & Society* 14 (5): 662–78.

Dade County Department of Public Welfare. 1952. "Annual Report. July 1, 1951–June 30, 1952." County Annual Reports for Department of Family and Children's Social Services. Series 24–8–65. Box 2. Georgia Department of Archives and History.

———. 1953. "Annual Report. July 1, 1952-June 30, 1953." County Annual Reports for Department of Family and Children's Social Services. Series 24–8-65. Box 2. Georgia Department of Archives and History.

Dales, Douglas. 1949. "Relief Cost Study Urged at Albany." *New York Times,* December 29, p. 27.

———. 1951a. "State Acts to Get Millions in US AID." *New York Times,* January 11, p. 20.

———. 1951b. "Cut in State's Aid for Welfare Is Hit." *New York Times,* January 12, p. 19.

———. 1951c. "$250,174,608 Slated for City by Dewey." *New York Times,* January 31, p. 1.

———. 1958a. "Relief Plan Fails in Albany Senate. *New York Times,* February 20, p. 18.

———. 1958b. "Albany Senators Vote Relief Curb." *New York Times,* March 5, p. 23.

———. 1960a. "Governor Calls City Tax Protest 'Utterly Unfair.'" *New York Times,* February 13, p. 1.

———. 1960b. "State Relief Bill Voted by Senate." *New York Times,* March 8, p. 1.

———. 1961. "State Relief Bill Passed by Senate." *New York Times,* March 22, p. 28.

Daniel, Robert L. 1987. *American Women in the Twentieth Century: The Festival of Life.* San Diego, CA: Harcourt Brace Jovanovich.

Davenport, Steward. 1951. "Welfare Backlog Eased by Inquiry." *Atlanta Constitution,* April 8, p. 20.

Davis, Martha F. 1993. *Brutal Need: Lawyers and the Welfare Rights Movement, 1960–1973.* New Haven, CT: Yale University Press.

Delaplane, Stanton. 1949a. "Pensions Are My Business: George Henry McLain, the Pensioner's Hero." *San Francisco Chronicle,* July 13, p. 17.

———. 1949b. "Welfare Inquiry: Promoter Runs State's Agency, Former Aide Says: Pensioners Pack Session." *San Francisco Chronicle,* October 25, p. 1.

De Lollis, Barbara. 2001. "Out of Wedlock Births Not Decreasing as Welfare Reformers Had Hoped." *Gannett News Service,* November 21. Retrieved December 22, 2003. Available: LEXIS-NEXIS Academic Universe, News Sources.

DeNavas-Walt, Carmen, Bernadette D. Proctor, and Robert J. Mills. 2004. *Income, Poverty, and Health Insurance Coverage in the United States: 2003. Current Population Reports P60–226.* Washington: U.S. Census Bureau, U.S. Department of Commerce. Retrieved October 8, 2004 (http://www.census.gov/prod/2004pubs/P60–226.pdf).

Denitch, Bogdan. 1982. "Social Movements in the Reagan Era." *Telos* 53: 57–66.

DeParle, Jason. 1995. "Sheila Burke Is the Militant Feminist Commie Peacenik Who's Telling Bob Dole What to Think." *New York Times,* November 12, p. 32. Retrieved June 8, 2002. Available: LEXIS-NEXIS Academic Universe, News Sources.

———. 1997. "White House Calls for Minimum Wage in Workfare Plan." *New York Times,* May 16, p. A1.

Derber, Charles. 1998. *Corporation Nation: How Corporations Are Taking Over Our Lives and What We Can Do About It.* New York: St. Martin's Press.

Diamond, Sara. 1995. *Roads to Dominion: Right-Wing Movements and Political Power in the United States.* New York: Guilford Press.

———. 1996. "Right-Wing Politics and the Anti-Immigrant Cause." *Social Justice* 23 (3): 154–68.

———. 1998. *Not by Politics Alone: The Enduring Influence of the Christian Right.* New York: Guilford Press.

Dillon, Sam. 2003. "Report Finds Deep Poverty on the Rise." *New York Times,* April 30, p. A18. Retrieved October 11, 2003. Available: LEXIS-NEXIS Academic Universe, News Sources.

Ditmer, Bob. 2002. "Study of American Fatherhood Revealing." Colorado Springs, CO: Focus on the Family. Retrieved June 5, 2002 (http://www .family.org).

Dolny, Michael. 1998. "What's in a Label?: Right-Wing Think Tanks Are Often Quoted, Rarely Labeled." *Extra!* (May/June). Retrieved May 26, 2002 (http://www.fair.org/extra/9805/think-tanks.html).

———. 2000. "Think Tanks: The Rich Get Richer." *Extra!* (May/June). Retrieved May 26, 2002 (http://www.fair.org/extra/0005/think-tanks-survey .html).

———. 2001. "Think Tanks Y2K." *Extra!* (July/August). Retrieved May 26, 2002 (http://www.fair.org/extra/0108/think_tanks_y2k.html).

Domhoff, G. William. 1988. "Big Money in American Politics." *Theory and Society* 17: 589–96.

———. 1990. *The Power Elite and the State: How Policy Is Made in America.* New York: Aldine De Gruyter.

———. 2002. *Who Rules America? Power and Politics.* 4th ed. Boston: McGraw Hill.

Douglas, Thomas P. 1951. "The Orange County View." *Tax Digest* (January), 14.

Draut, Tammy. 2001. "New Opportunities? Public Opinion on Poverty, Income Inequality, and Public Policy: 1996–2001." New York: Demos, A Network for Ideas and Action. Retrieved September 21, 2001 (http://www.demos-usa.org).

Dudley, Lavinia P., and John J. Smith. 1952. *The Americana Annual: An Encyclopedia of the Events of 1951.* New York: Americana Corporation.

Duncan, Kevin. 2000. "Incentives and Work Decisions of Welfare Recipients: Evidence from the Panel Survey of Income Dynamics, 1981–1988." *American Journal of Economics and Sociology* 59 (3): 433–49.

Durman, Eugene. 1973. "Have the Poor Been Regulated? Toward a Multivariate Understanding of Welfare Growth." *Social Service Review* 47 (3): 339–59.

Duster, Troy. 1996. "Individual Fairness, Group Preferences, and the California Strategy." *Representations* 55: 41–58.

Dyson, Lowell K. 1986. *Farmers' Organizations: The Greenwood Encyclopedia of American Institutions.* New York: Greenwood Press.

Eagle Forum. 2002a. "Join Eagle Forum So You Will Have a Voice at the U.S. Capitol and at State Capitols." Alton, IL: Eagle Forum. Retrieved June 5, 2002 (http://www.eagleforum.org/misc/descript.html).

———. 2002b. "Phyllis Schlafly Bio." Alton, IL: Eagle Forum. Retrieved June 5, 2002 (http://www.eagleforum.org/mic/bio.html).

Eakins, David W. 1969. "Business Planners and America's Postwar Expansion." In *Corporations and the Cold War,* edited by David Horowitz, 143–71. New York: Monthly Review Press.

East, Jean. F. 2000. Empowerment through Welfare Rights Organizing: A Feminist Perspective. *Affilia* 15: 311–28.

Edin, Kathryn. 2000. "What Do Low-Income Single Mothers Say about Marriage?" *Social Problems* 47 (1): 112–33.

Edin, Kathryn, and Laura Lein. 1997. *Making Ends Meet: How Single Mothers Survive Welfare and Low-Wage Work.* New York: Russell Sage Foundation.

Edsall, Thomas Byrne, and Mary D. Edsall. 1991. *Chain Reaction: The Impact of Race, Rights, and Taxes on American Politics.* New York: W.W. Norton and Company.

Education Reporter. 1996. "Education Briefs." *Eagle Forum.* Retrieved June 5, 2002 (http://www.eagleforum.org/educate/1996/jan96/briefs.html).

Edwards, Lee. 1998. "The Power of Ideas." Washington, DC: Heritage Foundation. Retrieved May 24 (http://www.heritage.org/heritage25/heritagetoday/p8.html).

Egan, Leo. 1950. "Official Defends City Welfare Cut." *New York Times,* February 24, p. 44.

———. 1951. "State Republicans Reject City's Plea for 50 Million Aid." *New York Times,* February 14, p. 1.

———. 1958. "Relief Curbs Beaten in Assembly, 72–69." *New York Times,* March 22, p. 1.

———. 1959. "Republicans Back More State Taxes." *New York Times,* January 9, p. 1.

Ehrenreich, Barbara. 2002. *Nickle and Dimed: On Not Getting By in America.* New York: Metropolitan Books.

Eisenbrey, Ross. 2004. "On the Department of Labor's Final Overtime Regulations: Preliminary Analysis of DOL's Final Rule on Overtime Exemptions." Testimony presented before the Subcommittee on Labor, Health, and Human Services and Education of the United States, Senate Committee on Appropriations on May 4, 2004. Retrieved June 29, 2004 (http://www.epinet.org).

Elguea-Keating, Liz. 2004. Speech made by L.A. Territory Manager, IRS-SPEC at the ACORN national convention in Los Angeles, June 27.

Eliot, Martha M. 1951. Statement on Assuming Office as Chief of Children's Bureau. Press Release, September 4. Record Group 102, Transcripts of Speeches, 1948-July 11, 1960, Box 2. National Archives.

———. 1952. "A Look at Programs for Children Today." Speech at the Southern Regional Conference, Child Welfare League of America. Raleigh, NC, March 13. Record Group 102, Transcripts of Speeches, 1948–July 11, 1960, Box 2. National Archives.

———. 1955. "Putting Fission and Fusion to Work for Children." Speech at the National Conference on the Churches and Social Welfare of the National Council of Churches of Christ in America. Cleveland, OH, November 3.

Record Group 102, Transcripts of Speeches, 1948–July 11, 1960, Box 1. National Archives.

Ernst and Young Kenneth Leventhal Real Estate Group. 1998. *1998 Study of Housing Costs*. New York: Ernst and Young Kenneth Leventhal Real Estate Group. Retrieved September 23, 2003 (http: www.gallen.com/eykl/_derived/ sourcecontrol_HousStdy.htm).

Esping-Andersen, Gosta. 1985. "Power and Distributional Regimes." *Politics and Society* 14: 185–222.

———. 1990. *The Three Worlds of Welfare Capitalism*. Princeton, NJ: Princeton University Press.

———, ed. 1996. *Welfare States in Transition: National Adaptations in Global Economies*. Thousand Oaks, CA: Sage Publications.

Esping-Andersen, Gosta, and Walter Korpi. 1984. "Social Policy as Class Politics in Post-War Capitalism: Scandinavia, Austria, and Germany." In *Order and Conflict in Contemporary Capitalism*, edited by John H. Goldthorpe, 179–208. Oxford: Clarendon Press.

Fagan, Patrick F. 1995. "Why Serious Welfare Reform Must Include Serious Adoption Reform." Backgrounder No. 1045. Washington, DC: Heritage Foundation. Retrieved May 24, 2002 (http://www.heritage.org/library/ categories/healthwel/bg1045.html).

———. 2001a. "Encouraging Marriage and Discouraging Divorce." Washington, DC: Heritage Foundation. Retrieved September 20, 2001 (http:www .heritage.org).

———. 2001b. "The Federal and State Government, Welfare and Marriage Issues." Testimony before the Subcommittee on Human Resources, the Committee on Ways and Means. May 22. Washington, DC: Heritage Foundation. Retrieved September 20, 2001 (http://www.heritage.org).

Falcocchio, Lisa. 2001. "New York City Parks Department, Testimony before the Subcommittee on Human Resources of the Committee on Ways and Means." *Hearing: Work Requirements on the TANF Cash Welfare Program*. House of Representatives. 107th Cong., 1st sess. April 3. Serial 107–10.

Family Research Council. 2002. "Family Research Council: Mission Statement." Washington, DC: Family Research Council. Retrieved June 7, 2002 (http:// www.frc/org/aboutfrc.cfm?CFID = 865494&CFTOKEN = 67586084).

Federal Security Administration. 1952. "Public Assistance Goals, 1953." Washington, DC: U.S. Government Printing Office. Record Group 47, Box 1. National Archives.

Federation for American Immigration Reform. 2002. "Issue Brief: Why Are Immigrants on Welfare?" Washington, DC: Federation for American Immigration Reform. Retrieved July 7, 2003 (http://www.fairus.org/html/ 04168907.htm).

Fenton, John H. 1957. *Politics in the Border States*. New Orleans, LA: Hauser Press.

Ferguson, Thomas, and Joel Rogers. 1986. *Right Turn: The Decline of the Democrats and the Future of American Politics*. New York: Hill and Wang.

Fix, Michael, and Ron Haskins. 2002. "Welfare Benefits for Non-Citizens." *Brookings Institute.* WR&B Brief #15. Washington, DC: Brookings Institution. Retrieved May 26, 2002 (http://www.brook.edu/dybdocrot/wrb/publications/pb/pb15.htm).

Fix, Michael E., and Jeffrey S. Passel (with Maria Enchautegui and Wendy Zimmerman). 1994. *Immigration and Immigrants: Setting the Record Straight.* Washington, DC: Urban Institute. Retrieved March 13, 2001 (http://www.urban.org/url.cfm?ID = 305184).

Fix, Michael E., and Jeffrey S. Passel. 2002. "The Scope and Impact of Welfare Reform's Immigrant Provisions." Discussion Paper. Washington, DC: Urban Institute. Retrieved March 12, 2002 (http://www.urban.org).

Fix, Michael E., and Wendy Zimmermann. 1999. "All under One Roof: Mixed-Status Families in an Era of Reform." Washington, DC: Urban Institute. Retrieved March 20, 2001 (http://www.urban.org/url.cfm?ID = 409100).

Flanders, Laura, and Janine Jackson. 1997. "Reforming Welfare Coverage: Five Issues Reporters Need to Address." *Extra!* (May/June). Retrieved May 26, 2002 (http://www.fair.org/extra/9705/welfare-coverage.html).

Flanders, Laura, Janine Jackson, and Dan Shadoan. 1996. "Media Lies: Media, Public Opinion, and Welfare." In *For Crying Out Loud: Women's Poverty in the United States,* edited by Diane Dujon and Ann Withorn, 29–39. Boston, MA: South End Press.

Fligstein, Neil. 1998. "Is Globalization the Cause of the Crises of Welfare States?" Unpublished Paper. Department of Sociology, University of California, Berkeley.

Folse, Kimberly A. 2001. "Child Support/Deadbeat Dads." In *Extraordinary Behavior: A Case Study Approach to Understanding Social Problems,* edited by Dennis L. Peck and Norman A. Dolch, 144–55. Westport, CT: Praeger.

Folsom, Merril. 1958. "Westchester Hits Curbs for Relief." *New York Times,* March 11, p. 31.

Fording, Richard C. 2003. "'Laboratories of Democracy' or Symbolic Politics? The Racial Origins of Welfare Reform." In *Race and the Politics of Welfare Reform,* edited by Sanford F. Schram, Joe Soss, and Richard C. Fording, 72–97. Ann Arbor: University of Michigan Press.

Fowle, Farnsworth. 1959. "City Tightens Rules for Relief Checks." *New York Times,* September 22, p. 1.

Fragomen, Austin T., Jr. 1997. "The Illegal Immigration Reform and Immigration Responsibility Act of 1996: An Overview." *International Migration Review* 31 (2): 438–60.

Free Congress Foundation. 2001. "FCF's Marshner Chairs New Coalition to Support Faith-Based Initiatives." Press release. Washington, DC: Free Congress Foundation. Retrieved May 26, 2002 (http://www.freecongress.org/press/releases/010412.htm)

Freeman, Lucy. 1950a. "City Relief Cuts Hit Many Children." *New York Times,* January 17, p. 29.

———. 1950b. "City Denies It Cut Relief Grants." *New York Times,* January 18, p. 33.

————. 1950c. "Relief Cut Backed by Welfare Aides." *New York Times,* January 19, p. 29.

————. 1950d. "Recovery Record Made in Welfare." *New York Times,* February 1, p. 23.

————. 1950e. "Hilliard Family Tests Relief Diet: 6 Eat a Month for $96, 'Save' $28." *New York Times,* February 6, p. 1.

————. 1952a. "City Welfare Head Reviews Progress." *New York Times,* January 21, p. 22.

————. 1952b. "City Welfare Head Contradicts State." *New York Times,* January 28, p. 19.

————. 1952c. "Hilliard Defends City Relief Work." *New York Times,* February 5, p. 27.

Fremstad, Shawn, and Sharon Parrott. 2004. "The Senate Finance Committee's TANF Reauthorization Bill." Retrieved June 20, 2004 (http://www.cbpp.org/9-9-03tanf.htm).

Friedan, Betty. 1983. *The Feminine Mystique.* New York: Dell Publishing. (Orig. pub. 1963)

Fujiwara, Lynn H. 1999. "Sanctioning Immigrants: Asian Immigrant and Refugee Women and the Racial Politics of Welfare Reform." Ph.D. dissertation, Department of Sociology, University of California, Santa Cruz.

Fuller, Bruce. 2002. "Commentary: Even Tougher Love for Welfare Moms." *Los Angeles Times,* June 11, p. B13. Retrieved June 30, 2003. Available: LEXIS-NEXIS Academic Universe, News Sources.

Furman, Bess. 1959. "A Central Agency for Relief Urged." *New York Times,* April 2, p. 20.

Galarza, Ernesto. 1964. *Merchants of Labor: The Mexican Bracero Story.* Charlotte, NC: McNally and Loftin Publishers.

————. 1977. *Farm Workers and Agri-Business in California, 1947–1960.* Notre Dame, IN: University of Notre Dame Press.

Gallup, George H. 1972. *The Gallup Poll, Public Opinion 1935–1971.* New York: Random House.

Gann, Lewis.H., and Peter J. Duignan. 1986. *The Hispanics in the United States: A History.* Boulder, CO: Westview Press.

Gans, Herbert J. 1995. *The War against the Poor: The Underclass and Antipoverty Policy.* New York: Basic Books.

Garin, Geoffrey, Guy Molyneux, and Linda DiVall. 1994. "Public Attitudes toward Welfare Reform." *Social Policy* 25 (2): 44–49.

George Wiley Papers. Box 16, Folder 7. State Historical Society of Wisconsin at Madison.

Georgia Department of Public Welfare. 1944. *Manual of Public Welfare Administration.* Georgia Department of Archives and History.

————. 1945–50. *Official Reports.* Georgia Department of Archives and History.

————. 1952. "Study of the Effect of Rescindment of the May 1952 Aid to Dependent Children Regulations on the Agency's Budgetary Position." Georgia Department of Archives and History.

———. 1953a. "Georgia Report of Administrative Review of Complaints and Hearing Requests Disposed of 11/1/52–1/31/53." Georgia Department of Archives and History.

———. 1953b. *Official Report for the Fiscal Year 7/1/52–6/30/53.* Georgia Department of Archives and History.

Georgia General Assembly House of Representatives. 1951. *Journal of the House of Representatives of the State of Georgia.* Decatur, GA: Bowen Press.

Georgia Laws, Regular Session 1951. Acts and Resolutions of the General Assembly of the State of Georgia. Atlanta, GA: Press of Foote and Davies.

Georgia Laws, Regular Session 1952. Acts and Resolutions of the General Assembly of the State of Georgia. Atlanta, GA: Press of Foote and Davies.

Gerson, Kathleen. 1985. *Hard Choices: How Women Decide about Work, Career, and Motherhood.* Berkeley: University of California Press.

Gilens, Martin. 1999. *Why Americans Hate Welfare: Race, Media, and the Politics of Antipoverty Policy.* Chicago: University of Chicago Press.

———. 2003. "How the Poor Became Black: The Racialization of American Poverty in the Mass Media." In *Race and the Politics of Welfare Reform,* edited by Sanford F. Schram, Joe Soss, and Richard C. Fording, 101–30. Ann Arbor: University of Michigan Press.

Gilman, Sander. 1985. *Difference and Pathology: Stereotypes of Sexuality, Race, and Madness.* Ithaca, NY: Cornell University Press.

Gilmer County Department of Public Welfare. 1952. "Annual Report. July 1, 1951–June 30, 1952." County Annual Reports for Department of Family and Children's Social Services. Series 24–8-65, Box 4. Georgia Department of Archives and History.

Glassner, Barry. 1999. *The Culture of Fear: Why Americans Are Afraid of the Wrong Things: Crime, Drugs, Minorities, Teen Moms, Killer Kids, Mutant Microbes, Plane Crashes, Road Rage, and So Much More . . .* New York: Basic Books.

Goldberg, Heidi. 2002. "Improving TANF Program Outcomes for Families with Barriers to Employment." Washington, DC: Center on Budget and Policy Priorities. Retrieved March 23, 2002 (http://wwwcbpp.org).

Golden, Lonnie, and Eileen Appelbaum. 1992. "What Was Driving the 1982–88 Boom in Temporary Employment?" *American Journal of Economics and Sociology* 51 (4): 473–93.

Goldfield, David R. 1982. *Cotton Fields and Skyscrapers: Southern City and Region, 1607–1980.* Baton Rouge: Louisiana State University.

Goldfield, Michael. 1987. *The Decline of Organized Labor in the United States.* Chicago: University of Chicago Press.

Goldstone, Robert. 1973. *The American Nightmare: Senator Joseph R. McCarthy and the Politics of Hate.* Indianapolis, IN: Bobbs-Merrill Company.

Gooden, Susan T. 1995. "Local Discretion and Welfare Policy. The Case of Virginia (1911–1970)." *Southern Studies* 6 (4): 79–110.

Goodwin, Joanne L. 1995. " 'Employable Mothers' and 'Suitable Work': A Reevaluation of Welfare and Wage-Earning for Women in Twentieth Century United States." *Journal of Social History* 29: 253–74.

————. 1997. *Gender and the Politics of Welfare Reform: Mothers' Pensions in Chicago, 1911–1929.* Chicago: University of Chicago Press.

Gordon, Linda. 1990. "The New Feminist Scholarship on the Welfare State." In *Women, the State, and Welfare,* edited by Linda Gordon, 9–35. Madison, WI: The University of Wisconsin Press.

————. 1991. "Social Insurance and Public Assistance: The Influence of Gender in Welfare Thought in the United States, 1890–1935." Discussion Paper No. 960–91, Institute for Research on Poverty, University of Wisconsin, Madison.

————. 1994. *Pitied but Not Entitled: Single Mothers and the History of Welfare.* New York: Free Press.

————. 2001. "Who Deserves Help? Who Must Provide?" *Annals of the American Academy of Political and Social Science* 577: 13–23.

Gordon, Rebecca. 2001. *Cruel and Unusual: How Welfare 'Reform' Punishes Poor People.* Oakland, CA: Applied Research Center.

Gornick, Janet C., and Marcia K. Meyers. 2003. *Families That Work: Policies for Reconciling Parenthood and Employment.* New York: Russell Sage Foundation.

Governor's Chaptered Bill Files. 1943–98. Governor's Records. Legislative Resources. Sacramento: California State Archives.

Governor's Committee for the 1960 Golden Anniversary White House Conference on Children and Youth. 1960. *Kentucky County Reports to the 1960 Golden Anniversary White House Conference on Children and Youth.* Prepared by County Chairmen, Kentucky Department of Libraries and Archives, State Publications Collection.

Graham, Hugh Davis. 1994. "Race, History, and Policy: African Americans and Civil Rights since 1964." *Journal of Policy History* 6 (1): 12–39.

Green, John C., and James L. Guth. 1988. "The Christian Right in the R Party: The Case of Pat Robertson's Supporters." *Journal of Politics* 50: 150–65.

Green, John C., James L. Guth, Lyman A. Kellstedt, and Corwin E. Smidt. 2001. "Faith in the Vote: Religiosity and the Presidential Election." *Public Perspective: A Roper Center Review of Public Opinion and Polling* 12 (2): 33–5.

Green, Joshua. 2003. "The Bookie of Virtue." *Washington Monthly* (June). Retrieved May 25, 2004 (http://www.washingtonmonthly.com/features/2003/0306.green.html).

Greenberg, Doris. 1950. "New Work Relief Is Mapped by City." *New York Times,* May 16, p. 33.

Guerin-Gonzales, Camille. 1996. *Mexican Workers and American Dreams: Immigration, Repatriation, and California Farm Labor, 1900–1939.* New Brunswick, NJ: Rutgers University Press.

Hall, Jacquelyn Dowd. 1984. "'The Mind that Burns in Each Body': Women, Rape, and Racial Violence." In *Desire: The Politics of Sexuality,* edited by Ann Snitow, Christine Stansell, and Sharon Thompson, 339–60. London: Virago Press.

Hancock County Department of Public Welfare. 1953. "Annual Report. July 1, 1952–June 30, 1953. County Annual Reports for Department of Family and Children's Social Services. Series 24–8–65. Box 4. Georgia Department of Archives and History.

Handler, Joel F. 1995. *The Poverty of Welfare Reform*. New Haven, CT: Yale University Press.

Handler, Joel, and Yeheskel Hasenfeld. 1991. *The Moral Construction of Poverty: Welfare Reform in America*. Newbury Park, CA: Sage Publications.

Hanson, Chester G. 1950. "Relief across the Nation: California—The 'Sucker' State." *Tax Digest* (April), p. 115–117, 138–139.

Hardisty, Jean, and Lucy A. Williams. 2002. "The Right's Campaign against Welfare." In *From Poverty to Punishment: How Welfare Reform Punishes the Poor*, edited by Applied Research Center, 53–72. Oakland, CA: Applied Research Center.

Hardy, Eugene J. 1967. "Statement on Behalf of the National Association of Manufacturers." In *Social Security Amendments of 1967. Hearings on HR 12080*. Committee on Finance, U.S. Senate, 90th Congress, 1st sess., Part II, A161–67. Washington, DC: U.S. Government Printing Office. National Archive.

Harrington, Michael. 1962. *The Other America: Poverty in the United States*. New York: Macmillan.

Harris, Cherise A. 2002. "Who Supports Welfare Reform and Why?" *Race, Gender, and Class* 9 (1): 96–121.

Hartung, William D., and Jennifer Washburn. 1998. "Lockheed Martin: From Warfare to Welfare." *Nation*, March 2, pp. 11–16.

Haskins, Ron. 2001a. "Making Ends Meet: Challenges Facing Working Families in America." *House Committee on the Budget*. August 1. Retrieved May 26, 2002 (http://www.brook.edu/views/testimony/haskins/20010801.htm).

———. 2001b. "Welfare Reform: An Examination of Effects." *House Committee on Education and the Workforce*. September 20. Retrieved May 26, 2002 (http://www.brook.edu/views/testimony/haskins/20010920.htm).

Haskins, Ron, and Rebecca Blank. 2001. "Revisiting Welfare." *Washington Post*, February 14. Retrieved May 26, 2002 (http://www.brook.edu/views/op-ed/haskins/20010214.htm).

Haskins, Ron, and Carol Statuto Bevan. 1997. "Abstinence Education under Welfare Reform." *Children and Youth Services Review* 19 (5/6): 465–84. Retrieved May 26, 2002 (http://www.aei.org/sw/swhaskinsbevan.htm).

Hawkins, Homer C. 1973. "Trends in Black Migration from 1863 to 1960." *Phylon* 34 (2): 140–52.

Hays, Sharon. 2003. *Flat Broke with Children: Women in the Age of Welfare Reform*. New York: Oxford University Press.

Hedda, Garza. 1994. "To the Land of Ice and Snow." In *Latinas: Hispanic Women in the United States: The Hispanic Experience in the Americas*, 83–104. New York: Franklin Watts.

Hegar, Rebecca L., and Maria Scannapieco. 2000. "Grandma's Babies: The Problem of Welfare Eligibility for Children Raised by Relatives." *Journal of Sociology and Social Welfare* 27 (3): 153–71.

Hein, Jay F. 2002a. "Churches Help Make Welfare Reform Work." Washington, DC: Hudson Institute. Retrieved March 25, 2002 (http://www.hudson.org/index.cfm?fuseaction = publication_details&id = 63).

———. 2002b. "Faith Works in Wisconsin." Washington, DC: Hudson Institute. Retrieved March 25, 2002 (http://www.hudson.org/index.cfm?fuseaction = publication_details&id = 71).

Heinicke, Craig W. 1991. "Black Migration from the Rural American South and Mechanization in Agriculture, 1940–1960." Ph.D. dissertation, Department of Economics, University of Toronto, Canada.

Henkel, Paul. 1967. "Statement on Behalf of the Council of State Chambers of Commerce." In *Social Security Amendments of 1967. Hearings on HR 12080*. Committee on Finance, U.S. Senate 90th Congress, 1st sess., Part II, pp. 1265–89. Washington, DC: U.S. Government Printing Office. National Archive.

Heritage Foundation. 1996. *1996 Annual Report*. Washington, DC: Heritage Foundation, Retrieved May 24, 2002 (http://www.heritage.org).

———. 2001. "Who We Are." Washington, DC: Heritage Foundation. Retrieved February 18, 2002 (http://www.heritage.org/whoweare/).

———. 2002. "People Are Policy; Complete Staff Listing (as of 5/23/02)." Washington, DC: Heritage Foundation. Retrieved May 24, 2002 (http://www.heritage/org/staff).

Herwitz, Victor J. 1947. *Investigation of the New York City Department of Welfare. Report to the State Board of Welfare*. Box 49. New York State Archives.

Herzog, Elizabeth. 1960. *U.S. Children's Bureau Publication 382: Children of Working Mothers*. Washington, DC: U.S. Government Printing Office.

Heuler-Williams, Lisa. 1998. *Study and Evaluation of W2 Workers and Temporary Employment in Milwaukee, Wisconsin*. Milwaukee, WI: Nine to Five, National Association of Working Women.

Hicks, Alexander. 1986. "Class Influence on Redistributive Policy: The Case of U.S. State Governments, 1951–1961." *Journal of Political and Military Sociology* 14 (1): 91–114.

———. 1999. *Social Democracy and Welfare Capitalism: A Century of Income Security Politics*. Ithaca, NY: Cornell University Press.

Hicks, Alexander, and Joya Misra. 1993. "Political Resources and the Growth of Welfare in Affluent Capitalist Democracies, 1960–1982." *American Journal of Sociology* 99 (3): 668–710.

Hicks, Alexander, and Duane H. Swank. 1983. "Civil Disorder, Relief Mobilization, and AFDC Caseloads: A Reexamination of the Piven and Cloward Thesis." *American Journal of Political Science* 27: 695–716.

Hilfiker, David. 2002 "Welfare Reform: New Rules Would Only Tighten Poverty's Grip." *Los Angeles Times*, September 29, p. M2.

Himes, Joseph. 1971. "Some Characteristics of the Migration of Blacks in the United States." *Social Biology* 18 (4): 359–66.

Himmelstein, Jerome L. 1990. *To the Right: The Transformation of American Conservativism*. Berkeley: University of California Press.

Hixson, William B. 1992. *Search for the American Right Wing: An Analysis of the Social Science Record, 1955–1987*. Princeton, NJ: Princeton University Press.

Hodgson, Godfrey. 1976. *In Our Time: America From World War II to Nixon*. London: MacMillan London.

Hoey, Jane. 1944a. Policy Memo to the Social Security Board: Report on Regional Advisory Group Conferences to the Project on Service in the Administration of Aid to Dependent Children, April 29. Record Group 47, Social Security Board Policy Memorandum, 1938–1944. National Archives.

———. 1944b. Social Security Board Policy Memo. Suggested State Legislation for 1945—Public Assistance, October 14. Record Group 47, Social Security Board Policy Memorandum 1938–1944. National Archives.

———. 1944c. State Letter No. 43, Re: Statement of Purpose of ADC, December 2. Record Group 47, Box 1. National Archives.

———. 1945a. State Letter No. 46. Re: 'Suitable Home' Provision of State Public Assistance Plans, March 5. Record Group 47, Box 1. National Archives.

———. 1945b. State Letter No. 47: Re: Relatives' Responsibility in Public Assistance State Plans, March 5. Record Group 47, Box 1. National Archives.

———. 1946. State Letter No. 70. Re: Federal Statement on Employment of ADC Moms, November 26. Record Group 47, Box 1. National Archives.

Holmes, Michael S. 1975. *The New Deal in Georgia: An Administrative History.* Westport, CT: Greenwood Press.

Holtzman, Abraham. 1975. *The Townsend Movement: A Political Study.* New York: Octagon Books. (Orig. pub. 1963).

Hondagneu-Sotelo, Pierrette. 1995. "Women and Children First: New Directions in Anti-Immigrant Politics." *Socialist Review* 95 (1): 169–90.

Honey, Maureen. 1984. *Creating Rosie the Riveter: Class, Gender, and Propaganda During World War II.* Amherst: University of Massachusetts Press.

Hooks, Bell. 1992. *Black Looks: Race and Representation.* Boston, MA: South End Press.

Horn, Wade, and Andrew Bush. 1997. "Fathers, Marriage, and Welfare Reform." *Welfare Policy Center of the Hudson Institute.* Retrieved February 18, 2002 (http://www.hudson.org).

Horowitz, Michael. 1995. "Statement of Michael Horowitz, Senior Fellow, Hudson Institute." In *Contract with America-Welfare Reform. Hearing Before the Subcommittee on Human Resources of the Committee on Ways and Means, House of Representatives.* 104th Cong., 1st sess. Part 1, pp. 80–82.

Howard, Donald S. 1948. "Public Assistance Returns to Page One." *Social Work Journal* (April), 47–54.

Huber, Evelyne, and John D. Stephens. 1998. "Internationalization and the Social Democratic Model: Crisis and Future Prospects." *Comparative Political Studies* 31 (3): 353–97.

———. 2001. *Development and Crisis of the Welfare State: Parties and Policies in Global Markets.* Chicago: University of Chicago Press.

Hudson Institute. 2002. *Research and Projects.* Washington, DC: Welfare Policy Center of the Hudson Institute. Retrieved February 18, 2002 (http://www.welfarereformer.org).

Hulse, Carl. 2004. "House Approves $447 Billion in Spending for Military." *New York Times,* May 21, p. A1. Available: LEXIS-NEXIS Academic Universe, News Sources.

Husseini, Sam. 1998. "The Establishment's Think Tank." *Extra!* (November/ December). Retrieved May 26, 2002 (http://www.fair.org/extra/9811/ brookings.html).

Illinois Agricultural Association. 1956. "I.A.A. Resolutions." *I.A.A. Record.* 34 (12): 30–32.

Institute for American Values. 2002a. "About the Institute for American Values." New York: Institute for American Values. Retrieved May 27, 2002 (http://www.americanvalues.org/html/institute_at_a_glance.shtml).

———. 2002b. "Board of Directors." New York: Institute for American Values. Retrieved May 27, 2002 (http://www.americanvalues.org/html/personnel .shtml).

Institute for Wisconsin's Future. 1998a. *Transitions to W-2: The First Six Months of Welfare Replacement.* Milwaukee, WI: Institute for Wisconsin's Future.

———. 1998b. *The W-2 Job Path: An Assessment of the Employment Trajectory of W-2 Participants in Milwaukee.* Milwaukee, WI: Institute of Wisconsin's Future.

———. 1999. "Life after Welfare: 'Just Barely Making It.'" *W-2 Connection* 2 (1).

Institute for Women's Policy Research. 1994. "Few Women Fit the Stereotypes." *Research-in-Briefs.* Washington, DC: Institute for Women's Policy Research.

Irwin, Frank H. 1950. "Migrant Relief in Cotton Belt: Non-resident Aid Becomes Problem." *Tax Digest* (March), 77–104.

Isaac, Larry, and William R. Kelly. 1981. "Racial Insurgency, the State, and Welfare Expansion: Local and National Level Evidence from the Postwar United States." *American Journal of Sociology* 86: 1346–86.

Iversen, Torben. 2001. "The Dynamics of Welfare State Expansion: Trade Openness, De-industrialization, and Partisan Politics." In *The New Politics of the Welfare State,* edited by Paul Pierson, 45–79. New York: Oxford University Press.

Jackson, Kenneth T. 1985. *Crabgrass Frontier: The Suburbanization of the United States.* New York: Oxford University Press.

Jaret, Charles. 1999. "Troubled by Newcomers: Anti-Immigrant Attitudes and Action During Two Eras of Mass Immigration to the United States." *Journal of American Ethnic History* (Spring), 9–39.

Jelinek, Lawrence James. 1976. "The California Farm Bureau Federation, 1919– 1964." Ph.D. dissertation, Department of History, University of California, Los Angeles.

Jensen, Leif. 1988. "Patterns of Immigration and Public Assistance Utilization, 1970–1980." *International Migration Review* 22 (1): 51–83.

Jewell, Malcolm Edwin, and Everett W. Cunningham. 1968. *Kentucky Politics.* Lexington: University of Kentucky Press.

Joffe, Carole. 1998. "Welfare Reform and Reproductive Politics on a Collision Course." In *Social Policy and the Conservative Agenda,* edited by Clarence Y. H. Lo and Michael Schwartz, 290–301. Malden, MA: Blackwell Publishers.

Johnson, Daniel M., and Rex R. Campbell. 1981. *Black Migration in America: A Social Demographic History.* Durham, NC: Duke University Press.

Johnson, Martin. 2003. "Racial Context, Public Attitudes, and Welfare Effort in the American States." In *Race and the Politics of Welfare Reform*, edited by Sanford F. Schram, Joe Soss, and Richard C. Fording, 151–67. Ann Arbor: University of Michigan Press.

Johnston, David Cay. 2002. "Tax Analysis Says the Rich Still Win." *New York Times*, July 14, pp. 3, 10. Retrieved October 10, 2003. Available: LEXIS-NEXIS Academic Universe, News Sources.

Jones, Jacqueline. 1985. *Labor of Love, Labor of Sorrow: Black Women, Work, and the Family from Slavery to the Present*. New York: Vintage Books.

Jordan, Winthrop D. 1974. *The White Man's Burden: Historical Origins of Racism in the United States*. New York: Oxford University Press.

Joseph, Jeffrey H. 1995. "Statement for the Record on Welfare Reform before the Subcommittee on Human Resources of the House Committee on Ways and Means for the U.S. Chamber Commerce." In *Hearing before the Subcommittee on Human Resources of the Committee on Ways and Means, House of Representatives. Part 2, February 10, Serial 104–44*. 104th Cong., 1st sess., pp. 1706–708. Washington, DC: U.S. Government Printing Office.

Kamin, David, Richard Kogan, and Robert Greenstein. 2004. "Administrative Memo Confirms Plans for Budget Cuts in Many Discretionary Programs in 2006." Washington, DC: Center on Budget and Policy Priorities. Retrieved June 25, 2004 (http://www.cbpp.org/6-1-04.htm).

Kammer, Fred. 1995. "Statement of Rev. Fred Kammer, S.J., President, Catholic Charities USA, Alexandria, Virginia." In *Contract with America—Welfare Reform. Hearing before the Subcommittee on Human Resources of the Committee on Ways and Means, House of Representatives*, 714–22. 104th Cong., 1st sess.

Kaplan, Morris. 1960. "Wagner Approves Welfare Changes." *New York Times*, January 29, p. 13.

Katz, Michael B. 1996. *In the Shadow of the Poorhouse: A Social History of Welfare in America*. 10th ed. New York: Basic Books. (Orig. pub. 1986)

Kavanaugh, Frank K. 1955–59. *Kentucky Directory*. Frankfort, KY: Roberts Printing Co. Kentucky Department of Libraries and Archives.

Keam, Robert. 1954. Letter to Mr. Roswell B. Perkins, Assistant Secretary of the Department of Health, Education, and Welfare. May 28. Record Group 235, Decimal Series 600. General Circular File, 1/51–12/55. National Archives.

Kellstedt, Lyman, John Green, James Guth, and Corwin Smidt. 1994. "Religious Voting Bias in the 1992 Election: The Year of the Evangelical?" *Sociology of Religion* 55 (3): 307–26.

Kentucky Assembly. 1948–60. *Journal of the Assembly*. Lexington: Kentucky State Printing Press.

Kentucky Committee's Midcentury White House Conference on Children and Youth. 1950. *Report of the Kentucky Committee's Midcentury White House Conference on Children and Youth*. Kentucky Department of Libraries and Archives.

Kentucky Department of Economic Security. 1949–53. *Statistical Journal*. Kentucky Department of Libraries and Archives, State Publications Collection.

———. 1949. "Semi-Annual Statistical Report on Reasons for Closing—Aid to Dependent Children. Report for Half Year Ending 6/30/49." Department of Economic Security Records. Division: Research and Statistics. Discontinued Federal Reports on Public Assistance. Loc: C-70-E-8-F. Kentucky Department of Libraries and Archives.

———. 1950a. "Recent Changes in Kentucky Economic Security Laws." *Statistical Journal* (April). Kentucky Department of Libraries and Archives, State Publications Collection.

———. 1950b. "Eligibility Requirements for Public Assistance." *Statistical Journal* (August). Kentucky Department of Libraries and Archives, State Publications Collection.

Kentucky General Assembly. 1950. *Acts of the General Assembly of the Commonwealth of Kentucky.* Frankfort, KY: Legislative Research Commission.

Kentucky Legislative Research Commission. 1950. *Child Welfare Laws of Kentucky. Information Bulletin #4.* Frankfort: Kentucky Legislative Research Commission. Kentucky Department of Libraries and Archives.

———. 1952. *Welfare: Public Assistance. A Report to the Committee on Functions and Resources of State Government. Research Publication #21.* Frankfort, KY: n.p.

———. 1961. *Illegitimacy in Kentucky. Research Report #4.* Frankfort: Kentucky Department of Archives and History.

Kentucky Senate. 1948–62. *Journal of the Senate.* Lexington: Kentucky State Printing Press.

Key, V. O. 1949. *Southern Politics in State and Nation.* New York: Alfred A. Knopf.

Kihs, Peter. 1954. "Work Relief Here Will Halt June 30." *New York Times,* April 21, p. 1.

———. 1957. "City Relief Roll Held Down Despite Job-Hunter Influx." *New York Times,* June 2, p. 1.

———. 1958a. "11 Slum Inspection Teams Set up in New City Drive." *New York Times,* November 26, p. 1.

———. 1958b. "Relief Fraud Put at 2 Million Here." *New York Times,* December 7, p. 79.

———. 1959a. "Governor Scored on New Policies." *New York Times,* February 4, p. 17.

———. 1959b. "Mayor Bars Plan to Cut Migration." *New York Times,* October 2, p. 1.

Kilty, Keith M., and Vidal de Haymes, Maria. 2000. "Racism, Nativism, and Exclusion: Public Policy, Immigration, and the Latino Experience in the United States." *Journal of Poverty* 4 (1–2): 1–25.

King, Desmond. 1996. "Sectionalism and Policy Formation in the United States: President Carter's Welfare Initiatives." *British Journal of Political Science* 26: 337–67.

Klatch, Rebecca. 1999. *A Generation Divided: The New Left, the New Right, and the 1960s.* Berkeley: University of California Press.

Knox, Robert. 2002. "For Richer and for Poorer: Rising Prices Widens Housing

Gap." *Boston Globe,* August 11, p. 1. Retrieved September 23, 2003. Available: LEXIS-NEXIS Academic Universe, News Sources.

Knuckey, Jonathon. 1999. "Religious Conservatives, the Republican Party, and Evolving Party Coalitions in the United States." *Party Politics* 5 (4): 485–96.

Kolbert, Elizabeth. 1995. "Ideas and Trends: Fantasyland: Whose Family Values are They Anyway?" *New York Times,* August 6, p. 4. Retrieved June 8, 2002. Available: LEXIS-NEXIS Academic Universe, News Sources.

Komisar, Lucy. 1977. *Down and Out in the USA: A History of Public Welfare.* Rev. ed. New York: Franklin Watts.

Kornbluh, Felicia. 1997. "'To Fulfill Their Rightly Needs': Consumerism and the National Welfare Rights Movement." *Radical History Review* 69: 76–113.

Kotz, Nick, and Mary Lynn Kotz. 1977. *A Passion for Equality: George A. Wiley and the Movement.* New York: W.W. Norton and Company.

Kposowa, Augustine J. 1998. *The Impact of Immigration on the United States Economy.* Lanham, MD: University Press of America.

Kraly, Ellen P., and Charles Hirschman. 1990. "Racial and Ethnic Inequality among Children in the United States." *Social Forces* 69 (1): 33–51.

Krinsky, John, and Ellen Reese. 2000. "Contemporary Welfare Rights Activism: A Comparison of Three Cities." Paper presented at the 2000 annual meeting of the Society for the Study of Social Problems, Washington, DC.

Labor Research Association. 2004. "Low-Wage Nation. Economic Notes from Labor Research Association, June 22, 2004." New York: Labor Research Association. Retrieved June 25, 2004 (http://www.laborresearch.org/story2.php/358).

Lake, Snell, Perry, and Associates. 2002. "Public Views on Welfare Reform and Children in the Current Economy." Washington, DC: Lake, Snell, Perry, and Associates. Retrieved July 15, 2003 (http://www.futureofchildren.org/usr_doc/lsp_welfare_survey.PDF).

Lakoff, George. 1996. *Moral Politics: What Conservatives Know That Liberals Don't.* Chicago: University of Chicago Press.

Lamis, Alexander P., ed. 1999. *Southern Politics in the 1990s.* Baton Rouge: Louisiana State University Press.

Lansdale, Robert T. 1942. *The Florida Suitable Home Law: A Statistical Analysis of 17,999 Aid to Dependent Children Cases Affected.* Gainesville: Florida State University.

———. 1961. "The Impact of the Federal Social Security Act on Public Welfare Programs in the South." *Research Reports in Social Science* 4: 28–49.

Lapinski, John S., Pia Peltola, Greg Shaw, and Alan Yang. 1997. "Trends: Immigrants and Immigration." *Public Opinion Quarterly* 61 (2): 356–83.

Lazarowitz, Arlene. 1982. "Years in Exile: The Liberal Democrats, 1950–1959." Ph.D. dissertation, Department of History, University of California, Los Angeles.

League of Women Voters. 1951. *Let's Talk about Public Welfare in Georgia.* Atlanta: League of Women Voters of Georgia.

Leondar-Wright, Betsy. 2004. "Black Job Loss Déjà Vu." *Dollarsand Sense,* no.

253. Retrieved June 25, 2004 (http://www.dollarsandsense.org/0504leondar
.html).

Lesher, Dave. 1996. "Wilson Rescinds Cutbacks in Food Stamps." *Los Angeles
Times,* September 20, p. A1. Retrieved May 18, 2001. Available: LEXIS-
NEXIS Academic Universe, News Sources.

Levenstein, Lisa. 2000. "From Innocent Children to Unwanted Migrants and
Unwed Moms: The Public Discourse on Welfare 1960–1961." *Journal of
Women's History* 11 (4): 10–33.

Levy, Frank. 1994. "Incomes and Income Inequality since 1970." Working Paper
No. 94–001. Industrial Performance Center, Massachusettes Institute of
Technology, Boston.

Lichter, Daniel T., Diane K. McLaughlin, George Kephart, and David J. Landry.
1992. "Race and the Retreat from Marriage: A Shortage of Marriageable
Men?" *American Sociological Review* 57 (6): 781–99.

Lichter, Daniel T., Diane K. McLaughlin, and David C. Ribar. 1997. "Welfare and
the Rise in Female-Headed Families." *American Journal of Sociology* 103 (1):
112–43.

———. 2002. "Economic Restructuring and the Retreat from Marriage." *Social
Science Research* 31 (2): 230–56.

Lieberman, Robert C. 2003. "Race and the Limits of Solidarity." In *Race and the
Politics of Welfare Reform,* edited by Sanford F. Schram, Joe Soss, and
Richard C. Fording, 23–46. Ann Arbor: University of Michigan Press.

Lindhorst, Taryn, Ronald J. Mancoske, and Alice Abel Kemp. 2000. "Is Welfare
Reform Working? A Study of the Effects of Sanctions on Families Receiving
Temporary Aid to Needy Families." *Journal of Sociology and Social Welfare*
27 (4): 185–201.

Lindsley, Syd. 2002. "The Gendered Assault on Immigrants." In *Policing the
National Body: Sex, Race, and Criminalization,* edited by Jael Silliman and
Anannya Bhattacharjee, 175–96. Cambridge, MA: South End Press.

Lio, Shoon. 2003. "Speak American: Language and the Constitution of American National Identity." Master's thesis, Department of Sociology, University
of California, Riverside.

Lipshultz, Robert J. 1971. "American Attitudes towards Mexican Immigration:
A Dissertation." San Francisco: R and E Research Associates. (Orig. pub.
1962)

Loewenberg, Frank M. 1981. "The Destigmatization of Public Dependency."
Social Service Review 55 (3): 434–52.

Loprest, Pamela. 1999. "Families Who Left Welfare: Who Are They and How
Are They Doing?" Discussion Papers. Assessing the New Federalism. Washington, DC: Urban Institute. Retrieved March 12, 2002 (http://www.urban
.org).

———. 2003. "Fewer Welfare Leavers Employed in Weak Economy." Washington, DC: Urban Institute. Retrieved December 15, 2003 (http://www.urban
.org/url.cfm?ID = 310837).

Loprest, Pamela, and Douglas Wissoker. 2002. "Employment and Welfare

Reform in the National Survey of America's Families." Discussion Papers. Assessing the New Federalism. Washington, DC: Urban Institute. Retrieved March 12, 2002 (http://www.urban.org).

Loprest, Pamela, and Sheila R. Zedlewski. 1999. "Current and Former Welfare Recipients: How Do They Differ?" Discussion Papers. Assessing the New Federalism. Washington, DC: Urban Institute. Retrieved March 12, 2002 (http://www.urban.org).

Los Angeles Times. 2002. "Many 'Injured by the Helping Hand.'" Los Angeles Times, February 27, p. A10.

Luker, Kristin. 1996. Dubious Conceptions: The Politics of Teenage Pregnancy. Cambridge, MA: Harvard University Press.

Lund, Chester B. 1953. Memo to Leonard J. Wilbert, August 19. Record Group 235. General Classified Files 1/51–12/55. Decimal Series 600. National Archives.

Machado, Manuel A. 1978. Listen Chicano! An Informal History of the Mexican-American. Chicago: Nelson Hall.

Machtinger, Barbara. 1995. "Shaping the Maternalist Welfare State: Mothers' Pensions and the U.S. Children's Bureau, 1912–1939." Ph.D. dissertation, Department of History, Boston College, Boston, MA.

MacLatchie, Elizabeth B. 1950. Letter to Charles I. Schottland, State Director of the Department of Social Welfare, October 3. Department of Social Welfare 1950–1954, Legislation. California State Archives.

Malloy, Paul. 1951. "The Relief Chiselers Are Stealing Us Blind," Saturday Evening Post, September 8, p. 32.

Mandell, Betty Reid, and Ann Withorn. 1993. "Keep on Keeping On: Organizing Welfare Rights in Massachusetts," Pp. 128–148 in Mobilizing the Community, edited by Robert Fisher and Joseph Kling, 128–48. Newbury Park, CA: Sage.

Manhattan Institute for Policy Research. 2002a. "Manhattan Institute Senior Fellows' Areas of Expertise." New York: Manhattan Institute. Retrieved May 25, 2002 (http://www.manhattan-institute.org/html.scholars.htm).

———. 2002b. "Manhattan Institute Center for Civic Innovation Program Areas." New York: Manhattan Institute. Retrieved May 25, 2002 (http://www.manhattan-institute.org/html/cci.htm).

Manley, John F. 1973. "The Conservative Coalition in Congress." American Behavioral Scientist 17 (2): 223–47.

Mann, Susan Archer. 1990. Agrarian Capitalism in Theory and Practice. Chapel Hill: University of North Carolina Press.

Manza, Jeff, and Clem Brooks. 1999. Social Cleavages and Political Change: Voter Alignments and U.S. Party Coalitions. New York: Oxford University Press.

Marino, Jacqueline. 2003. "How Marriage Has Gone from a Private Matter to a Public Policy." Plain Dealer, Sunday Magazine, September 14, p. 17.

Marks, Alexandra. 2001. "Homeownership vs. Homelessness: Prosperity Yields Two Views of U.S. Housing." Christian Science Monitor, January 22.

Retrieved September 13, 2003 (http://search.csmonitor.com/durable/2001/01/22/p3sl.htm).

———. 2003. "Welfare Reform, in Times of Both Boom and Bust." *Christian Science Monitor,* August 22, p. 1. Retrieved October 19, 2003. Available: LEXIS-NEXIS Academic Universe, News Sources.

MarriageMovement.org. 2004. "Media Coverage of the Administration's Healthy Marriage Initiative, January 14, 2004–February 9, 2004." New York: Institute for American Values. Retrieved on June 26, 2004 (http://www.marriagemovement.org/backgrounder.htm)

Marriage Savers. 2002. "About Marriage Savers." Potomac, MD: Marriage Savers. Retrieved June 8, 2002 (http://www.marriagesavers.org).

Martin, John Frederick. 1979. *Civil Rights and the Crisis of Liberalism: The Democratic Party 1945–1976.* Boulder, CO: Westview Press.

Martin, Joyce A., Melissa M. Park, and Paul D. Sutton. 2002a. Births, Preliminary Data for 2001. *National Vital Statistics Reports* 50 (10). Hyattsville, MD: National Center for Health Statistics.

Massey, Douglas S., Rafael Alarcon, Jorge Durand, Humberto Gonzalez. 1987. *Return to Aztlan: The Social Process of International Migration from Western Mexico.* Berkeley: University of California Press.

McAdam, Doug. 1999. *Political Process and the Development of Black Insurgency, 1930–1970.* 2d ed. Chicago: University of Chicago Press. (Orig. pub. 1982)

McBride, Jessica. 1998. "Disabled Boy Dies in Scalding Tub." *Milwaukee Journal Sentinel,* June 16, p. 1. Retrieved June 23, 2004. Available: LEXIS-NEXIS Academic Universe, News Sources.

McBride, Michael. J. 1999. "Migrants and Asylum Seekers: Policy Responses in the United States to Immigrants and Refugees from Central America and the Caribbean." *International Migration* 37 (1): 289–314.

McCaffrey, James P. 1958. "Jury Here to Study Misuse of Welfare." *New York Times,* October 1, p. 1.

———. 1959. "84 Indicted Here in Relief Frauds." *New York Times,* January 20, p. 37.

McConnell, Grant. 1953. *The Decline of Agrarian Democracy.* Berkeley: University of California Press.

McCrate, E., and J. Smith. 1998. "When Work Doesn't Work: The Failure of Current Welfare Reform." *Gender & Society* 12: 61–80.

McCune, Wesley. 1956. *Who's behind Our Farm Policy?* New York: Frederick A. Praeger.

McDonnell, Patrick J. 1996a. "California's Immigration Hot Button Awaits GOP Candidates." *Los Angeles Times,* March 2, p. A10. Retrieved June 14, 2002. Available: LEXIS-NEXIS Academic Universe, News Sources.

———. 1996b. "Activists See Dire Immigration Threat." *Los Angeles Times,* August 11, p. A3. Retrieved June 14, 2002. Available: LEXIS-NEXIS Academic Universe, News Sources.

McKee, Seth C., and Daron R. Shaw. 2003. "Suburban Voting in Presidential Elections." *Presidential Studies Quarterly* 33 (1): 125–44.

McLain, George. 1951. *The Story of the 1951 California Legislature and Its Effect on the Needy Aged, Blind, and Dependent Children*. Los Angeles: California Institute of Social Welfare. California State Library.

McManus, Michael J., and Harriet McManus. 2001. "Testimony before the Subcommittee on Human Resources of the House Committee on Ways and Means." Hearing on Welfare and Marriage Issues, May 22. Retrieved May 25, 2002 (http://wwws.house.gov/search97cgi/s97_cgi?action=View &VdkVgwKey=http%3A%2F%2F . . .).

Mead, Lawrence. 1992. *The New Politics of Poverty: The Nonworking Poor in America*. New York: Basic Books.

———. 2001. "Curriculum Vitae." Department of Politics, New York University, NY. Retrieved October 1, 2001 (http://www.nyu.edu/gsas/dept/politics/faculty/mead/mead_vitae.pdf).

Media Transparency. 2002. "Search Results for String: Welfare Reform." Minneapolis, MN: Media Transparency. Retrieved May 27, 2002 (http://www.mediatransparency.org/search_results/comment_string_search_results.asp?Message=welfare+reform).

Mehan, Hugh. 1997. "The Discourse of the Illegal Immigration Debate: A Case Study in the Politics of Representation." *Discourse and Society* 8 (2): 249–70.

Mertz, Paul E. 1978. *New Deal Policy and Southern Rural Poverty*. Baton Rouge: Louisiana State University Press.

Mettler, Suzanne Bridget. 1994. "Divided Citizens: State Building, Federalism, and Gender in the New Deal." Ph.D. dissertation, Department of American Government, Cornell University, Ithaca, NY.

———. 2000. "States' Rights, Women's Obligations: Contemporary Welfare Reform in Historical Perspective." *Women and Politics* 21 (1): 1–34.

Michel, Sonya. 1999. *Children's Interests/Mothers' Rights: The Shaping of America's Child Care Policy*. New Haven, CT: Yale University Press.

Milkman, Ruth. 1987. *Gender at Work: The Dynamics of Job Segregation by Sex during World War II*. Urbana: University of Illinois Press.

Miller, Herman P. 1965. "Changes in the Number and Composition of the Poor." In *Poverty in America*, edited by Margaret S. Gordon. San Francisco, CA: Chandler Publishing Company.

Mills, Robert J., and Shilesh Bhandari. 2003. *Health Insurance Coverage in the United States: 2002. Current Population Reports*. P60–223. Washington, DC: U.S. Census Bureau, U.S. Department of Commerce.

Milwaukee Women and Poverty Public Education Initiative. 2000. *The Status of Employment Opportunity for W-2 Participants in Central City Milwaukee*. Milwaukee, WI: Milwaukee Women and Poverty Public Education Initiative.

Mink, Gwendolyn. 1990. "The Lady and the Tramp: Gender, Race, and the Origins of the American Welfare State." In *Women, the State, and Welfare*, edited by Linda Gordon, 92–122. Madison: University of Wisconsin Press.

———. 1995. *The Wages of Motherhood: Inequality in the Welfare State, 1917–1942*. Ithaca, NY: Cornell University Press.

———. 1998a. *Welfare's End*. Ithaca, NY: Cornell University Press.

———. 1998b. "'The Lady and the Tramp' (II): Feminist Welfare Politics, Poor Single Mothers, and the Challenge of Welfare Justice." *Feminist Studies* 24 (1): 55–64.

———. 2001. "Violating Women: Rights and Abuses in the Welfare Police State." *Annals of the American Academy of Political and Social Science* 577: 79–91.

Misra, Joya, and Stephanie Moller. 2004. "Familialism and Welfare Regimes: Poverty, Employment, and Family Policies." Paper presented at the 2004 Casework Conference in San Francisco, CA.

Misra, Joya, Stephanie Moller, and Marina Karides. 2003. "Envisioning Dependency: Changing Media Depictions of Welfare in the 20th Century." *Social Problems* 50 (4): 482–504.

Miville, Charles R. 2001a. "Faith-Based Push Changes Course." Colorado Springs, CO: Focus on the Family. Retrieved June 5, 2002 (http://www .family.org).

———. 2001b. "State Leaders Back Welfare Funds for Marriage." Colorado Springs, CO: Focus on the Family. Retrieved June 5, 2002 (http://www .family.org).

Moen, Matthew C. 1995. "The Fourth Wave of the Evangelical Tide: Religious Conservatives in the Aftermath of the 1994 Elections." *Contention* 5 (1): 19–38.

Molloy, Paul. 1951. "The Relief Chiselers Are Stealing Us Blind." *Saturday Evening Post* 223 (Sept. 8): 32, 143.

Moody, Kim. 1997. *Workers in a Lean World: Unions in the International Economy*. London: Verso.

Moore, Joan W., and Frank G. Mittelbach. 1972. "Measuring Residential Segregation in 35 Cities." In *The Changing Mexican-American: A Reader*, edited by Rudolph Gomez, 80–89. El Paso: University of Texas, El Paso.

Moore, John L., Jon P. Preimesberger, and David R. Tarr, eds. 2001. *Congressional Quarterly's Guide to U.S. Elections*. 4th ed. Vol. 2. Washington, DC: CQ Press.

Moore, Stephen. 1998. *A Fiscal Portrait of the Newest American*. Washington, DC: National Immigration Forum and Cato Institute.

Morris, Pamela A. 2002. "The Effects of Welfare Reform Policies on Children." *Social Policy Report* 16 (1): 4–19.

Moscow, Warren. 1967. *What Have You Done for Me Lately? The Ins and Outs of New York City Politics*. Englewood Cliffs, NJ: Prentice-Hall.

Moynihan, Daniel P. 1973. *The Politics of a Guaranteed Income: The Nixon Administration and the Family Assistance Plan*. New York: Random House.

Mulder, James T. 2004. "Study: Uninsured Exceed Census Estimates; Families USA Report Details the Problems of Those Who Lack Health Insurance." *Post-Standard* (Syracuse, NY), June 17, p. A1. Retrieved July 1, 2004. Available: LEXIS-NEXIS Academic Universe, News Sources.

Murray, Bobbi. 1999. "No Welfare for Lockheed or Maximus." *LA Weekly,* July 23.

Murray, Charles. 1998. "The Underclass Revisited." Washington, DC: American Enterprise Institute. Retrieved February 18, 2002 (http://www.aei.org/ps/psmurray.htm).

Myles, John. 1996. "When Markets Fail: Social Welfare in Canada and the United States." In *Welfare States in Transition: National Adaptations in Global Economies,* edited by Gosta Esping-Andersen. Thousand Oaks, CA: Sage Publications.

Myles, John, and Paul Pierson. 1997. "Friedman's Revenge: The Reform of 'Liberal' Welfare States in Canada and the United States." Working Paper No. RSC 97/30. European University Institute, Florence, Italy.

National Association of Manufacturers Government Operations Subcommittee. 1969. *Incentives and the Welfare Programs: An NAM Position Paper.* New York: National Association of Manufacturers.

National Committee for Responsive Philanthropy. 1991. *Special Report: Burgeoning Conservative Think Tanks.* Washington, DC: National Committee for Responsive Philanthropy.

National Family Planning and Reproductive Health Association. 2003. "Oppose Dangerous, Unproven Abstinence-Unless-Married Education Programs." Washington, DC: National Family Planning and Reproductive Health Association. Retrieved December 31, 2003 (http://www.nfprha.org/pac/factsheets/absunlessmarried.asp).

National Immigration Law Center. 2002. *Guide to Immigrant Eligibility for Federal Programs.* Los Angeles, CA: National Immigration Law Center.

National Low Income Housing Coalition. 2002. "Rental Housing for America's Poor Families: Farther Out of Reach Than Ever." Washington, DC: National Low Income Housing Coalition. Retrieved August 31, 2003 (http://www.nlihc.org/oor2002/introduction.htm).

National Office of Vital Statistics. 1960. "Table 1-U: Ratio of Illegitimate Live Births, by Color: Reporting States: 1940, 1950, 1959, and 1960," in *Vital Statistics of the United States,* vol. 1. Washington: U.S. Government Printing Office.

National Organization for Women Legal Defense and Education Fund. 1997. *Annual Report.* New York: NOW Legal Defense and Education Fund.

———. 1999. *What Congress Didn't Tell You: A State-by-State Guide to the Welfare Law's Hidden Reproductive Rights Agenda.* New York: NOW Legal Defense and Education Fund.

———. 2001a. "TANF Reauthorization: General Overview." New York: NOW Legal Defense and Education Fund.

———. 2001b. "TANF Reauthorization: Marriage, Fatherhood and Family Formation Initiatives." New York: NOW Legal Defense and Education Fund. Retrieved March 31, 2002 (http://www.nowldef.org/html/issues/wel/marriagefamily.html).

———. 2001c. "TANF Reauthorization: State Marriage Initiatives." New York:

NOW Legal Defense and Education Fund. Retrieved March 31, 2002 (http://www.nowldef.org/html/issues/wel/statemarriage.html).

National Public Radio/Kaiser Family Foundation/Kennedy School of Government. 2001. *National Survey on Poverty in America.* Menlo Park, CA: Henry J. Kaiser Family Foundation. Retrieved July 15, 2003 (http://www.kff.org).

National Research Council. 1997. *The New Americans: Economic, Demographic, and Fiscal Effects of Immigration.* Edited by James P. Smith and Barry Edmonston. Washington, DC: National Academy Press.

National Welfare Rights Organization. 1972. "Program: 1972 National Conference: People before Politics." Box 7. Folder 9. George Wiley Papers. State Historical Society of Wisconsin at Madison.

Navarro, Vicente. 1985. "The 1984 Election and the New Deal: An Alternative Interpretation." *Social Policy* 16 (1): 7–17.

Nelson, Barbara J. 1990. "The Origins of the Two-Channel Welfare State: Workmen's Compensation and Mothers' Aid." In *Women, the State, and Welfare,* edited by Linda Gordon, 123–51. Madison: University of Wisconsin Press.

Nelson, Mary. 1995. "Statement of Mary Nelson, Bethel, New Life, Inc., Chicago, Illinois; and Evangelical Lutheran Church of America." In *Contract with America—Welfare Reform. Hearing before the Subcommittee on Human Resources of the Committee on Ways and Means, House of Representatives,* 723–34. 104th Cong., 1st sess.

Neubeck, Kenneth J., and Noel A. Cazenave. 2001. *Welfare Racism: Playing the Race Card against America's Poor.* New York: Routledge.

New York City Department of Public Welfare. 1952. *Annual Report, 1951.* New York: New York City Public Library.

———. 1958. *Annual Report, 1957.* New York: New York City Public Library.

———. 1960. *Annual Report, 1959.* New York: New York City Public Library.

New York State Department of Social Welfare. 1957. Bulletin 159. Box 15. New York State Archive. Albany, New York.

———. 1963. Bulletin 159a. Box 15. New York State Archive. Albany, New York.

———. 1964. *Background Information on Public Assistance Programs in New York State. Special Research and Statistical Reports No. 30.* Office of Social Research and Statistics. Albany, New York.

New York State Legislature. 1950–60. *Record and Index.* Albany: New York Legislature. New York City Public Library.

New York Times. 1949. "Hilliard defends 5% Cuts in Relief." *New York Times,* December 21, p. 34.

———. 1950a. "Union Groups Join to Bar Relief Cut." *New York Times,* January 5, p. 3.

———. 1950b. "Relief Shift Is Charged." *New York Times,* January 6, p. 9.

———. 1950c. "Mayor Asks Study of Relief Grants." *New York Times,* January 11, p. 25.

———. 1950d. "Protest Political Hilliard Declares." *New York Times,* January 12, p. 24.

———. 1950e. "Hillard Reopens Work Relief Plan." *New York Times,* January 16, p. 27.

———. 1950f. "The Welfare Findings." *New York Times,* January 20, p. 24.

———. 1950g. "Relief Cut Brings Appeal for Food." *New York Times,* January 21, p. 15.

———. 1950h. "Letters to the Times: Relief Budgets." *New York Times,* January 25, p. 26.

———. 1950i. "G.O.P. Is Confident on Albany Budget." *New York Times,* February 3, p. 20.

———. 1950j. "Relief Sit-in Is Ended." *New York Times,* February 4, p. 6.

———. 1950k. "Full Relief Demanded." *New York Times,* February 5, p. 53.

———. 1950l. "Mayor Wants State To Bar Relief Cuts." *New York Times,* February 16, p. 4.

———. 1950m. "City Relief Study Assigned To Labor." *New York Times,* February 18, p. 10.

———. 1950n. "Letters to the Times: Relief Proposal Criticized." *New York Times,* February 24, p. 22.

———. 1950o. "Relief Grant Rises Considered by City." *New York Times,* March 16, p. 26.

———. 1950p. "12 Arrested in Sit-in at Welfare Bureau." *New York Times,* April 4, p. 60.

———. 1950q. "20 Paroled Here in Welfare Row." *New York Times,* April 5, p. 42.

———. 1950r. "Diploma Mill Head Sued in Relief Fraud." *New York Times,* April 8, p. 10.

———. 1950s. "City Steps up War on Relief Frauds." *New York Times,* April 18, p. 33.

———. 1950t. "20 Are Convicted in Welfare Case." *New York Times,* April 19, p. 2.

———. 1950u. "20 Are Sentenced for Welfare Row." *New York Times,* April 26, p. 4.

———. 1950v. "Release Denied 13 Men." *New York Times,* April 22, p. 36.

———. 1950w. "Picket Line Set up at Hilliard's Home." *New York Times,* April 24, p. 12.

———. 1950x. "Absent Hilliard Picketed." *New York Times,* April 25, p. 24.

———. 1950y. "Mayor Assails Communists for Frightening City's Needs." *New York Times,* May 19, p. 11.

———. 1950z. "Eleven Found Guilty in Welfare Sit-in." *New York Times,* June 1, p. 12.

———. 1950zi. "Nine Get Jail Terms for Welfare Sit-in." *New York Times,* June 3, p. 30.

———. 1951a. "State War Basis Asked by Dewey." *New York Times,* January 4, p. 17.

———. 1951b. "Relief of Payments to Go up Jan. 16." *New York Times,* January 5, p. 18.

———. 1951c. "Hilliard Weighs Quitting City Job." *New York Times*, January 13, p. 13.

———. 1951d. "Relief Checks on Friday Will Carry Increases." *New York Times*, January 16, p. 26.

———. 1951e. "Democrats to Help in Welfare Post." *New York Times*, January 31, p. 17.

———. 1951f. "Federal Aid Rift Spurs State Study." *New York Times*, February 23, p. 20.

———. 1951g. "Relief Check Bill Voted." *New York Times*, March 16, p. 27.

———. 1951h. "State Funds Plan on Pensions Voted." *New York Times*, March 17, p. 32.

———. 1951i. "State Housing Law Now Covers State." *New York Times*, April 8, p. 94.

———. 1951j. "Liquor Authority Curbed." *New York Times*, June 22, p. 14.

———. 1951k. "Social Aide Warns of Relief Abuses." *New York Times*, November 12, p. 27.

———. 1951l. "State Welfare Plan Held Home Rule Curb." *New York Times*, November 21, p. 15.

———. 1951m. "City Assured on Plan for Relief Publicity." *New York Times*, November 24, p. 9.

———. 1951n. "City Welfare Due to Rise $5,000,000." *New York Times*, November 29, p. 35.

———. 1951o. "Review Advocated for Relief Set Up." *New York Times*, November 30, p. 25.

———. 1951p. "Lewis Union Seeks to Get Social Workers as Recruits to Its District 50." *New York Times*, December 12, p. 44.

———. 1951q. "Would Bare Relief Rolls." *New York Times*, December 31, p. 14.

———. 1952a. "Against Public Welfare." *New York Times*, January 18, p. 26.

———. 1952b. "CIO Opens Drive on Leftist Unions." *New York Times*, January 22, p. 32.

———. 1952c. "Protecting Aid Recipients." *New York Times*, January 23, p. 26.

———. 1952d. "$126,161,211 Asked for City Hospitals." *New York Times*, February 7, p. 18.

———. 1952e. "Council Fights Cut in Service on 'El.'" *New York Times*, March 1, p. 17.

———. 1952f. "Welfare Inquiry Asked: Too Much Is Spent." *New York Times*, March 5, p. 31.

———. 1952g. "TB Drugs Increase Relief Food Costs." *New York Times*, June 7, p. 40.

———. 1952h. "Welfare Studies Asked." *New York Times*, June 18, p. 14.

———. 1952i. "Farmers Ask Dewey for Welfare Study." *New York Times*, December 10, p. 39.

———. 1952j. "End of Cuts Seen in Welfare Rolls." *New York Times*, December 22, p. 26.

————. 1953a. "State Welfare Spending Debated." *New York Times,* February 25, p. 12.

————. 1953b. "Welfare Revision Urged at Albany." *New York Times,* March 10, p. 21.

————. 1953c. "Dewey Signs Bill Increasing TB Aid." *New York Times,* April 10, p. 15.

————. 1953d. "Some Relief Rolls Open." *New York Times,* October 29, p. 33.

————. 1954a. " City Relief Rolls Rise 2% Weekly; State Help Sought in Recession." *New York Times,* March 8, p. 1.

————. 1954b. "Protestant Welfare." *New York Times,* March 9, p. 26.

————. 1954c. "Welfare Goups Lauded." *New York Times,* March 27, p. 19.

————. 1954d. "Welfare Secrecy Scored by Women." *New York Times,* November 11, p. 40.

————. 1956a. "Mayor Assails Bill on Relief Residence." *New York Times,* March 10, p. 18.

————. 1956b. "City Welfare List Reduced in April." *New York Times,* May 28, p. 29.

————. 1957. "Alien-Aid Pledges Ruled Not Binding." *New York Times,* October 12, p. 1.

————. 1958a. "Residence Bill Scored." *New York Times,* January 31, p. 19.

————. 1958b. "A Wall around New York." *New York Times,* February 3, p. 22.

————. 1958c. "City Relief Needs Show Sharp Rise." *New York Times,* February 4, p. 31.

————. 1958d. "Speaker Heck's Voice." *New York Times,* March 25, p. 32.

————. 1958e. "Jobless Total Up: Rise Is Smallest in Last 5 Months." *New York Times,* April 8, p. 1.

————. 1958f. "City Relief Rolls Near 1950 Record." *New York Times,* April 23, p. 37.

————. 1958g. "Harriman Bars Stricter Relief." *New York Times,* September 16, p. 56.

————. 1958h. "Welfare Is Criticized." *New York Times,* October 29, p. 37.

————. 1958i. "Intimidation Denied by Welfare Chief." *New York Times,* November 8, p. 6.

————. 1959a. "Rockefeller Bids State Take Lead." *New York Times,* January 2, p. 16.

————. 1959b. "Liberals Stress Recession Fight." *New York Times,* January 2, p. 17.

————. 1959c. "Few Needy Found to Be Newcomers." *New York Times,* January 2, p. 27.

————. 1959d. "Social Insurance and Public Assistance." *New York Times,* January 8, p. 18.

————. 1959e. "Man Uses Relief to Win in Stocks." *New York Times,* January 9, p. 29.

————. 1959f. "Legislature Sets Inquiry on Relief." *New York Times,* January 17, p. 16.

————. 1959g. "'Difficult' Families to Get Aid." *New York Times,* January 19, p. 27.

————. 1959h. "Welfare Agency Claims Credit for Unearthing Fraud Cases." *New York Times,* January 22, p. 18.

————. 1959i. "City Welfare Unit Got Back 24 Million." *New York Times,* February 2, p. 28.

————. 1959j. "Letters to the Times: Charges of Welfare Abuse." *New York Times,* February 4, p. 32.

————. 1959k. "Relief Crackdown Urged by Leibowitz." *New York Times,* February 10, p. 13.

————. 1959l. "City Answers Jury on Relief Problems." *New York Times,* February 12, p. 19.

————. 1959m. "Residence Test For Relief?" *New York Times,* March 4, p. 30.

————. 1959n. "Letters to the Times: Monopoly in Inflation." *New York Times,* March 9, p. 28.

————. 1959o. "Tightened Rules for Relief Urged." *New York Times,* March 9, p. 31.

————. 1959p. "Relief Bills Scored." *New York Times,* March 10, p. 29.

————. 1959q. "Jury Scores City on Its Childcare." *New York Times,* March 20, p. 22.

————. 1959r. "McCarthy Answers Jury on Childcare." *New York Times,* March 21, p. 22.

————. 1959s. "McCarthy Dismisses Critic of Welfare." *New York Times,* April 10, p. 12.

————. 1959t. "Mayor Urges Charter Revision in Annual Message to Council." *New York Times,* April 15, p. 24.

————. 1959u. "Social Services." *New York Times,* April 15, p. 24.

————. 1959v. "City Schools Get $5,000,000 in Aid." *New York Times,* April 21, p. 47.

————. 1959w. "Rockefeller Acts Past 250 Bills." *New York Times,* April 25, p. 14.

————. 1959x. "Leibowitz Urges Cut in Migration." *New York Times,* September 25, p. 1.

————. 1959y. "Governor Opposes Relief Law Curbs." *New York Times,* September 30, p. 23.

————. 1959z. "Welfare System Hit." *New York Times,* December 22, p. 14.

————. 1960a. "Bill Seeks to Open Welfare Records." *New York Times,* January 10, p. 73.

————. 1960b. "State Senate Votes to Let Towns Oust Transient Welfare Cases." *New York Times,* January 20, p. 23.

————. 1960c. "Letters to the Times: Residence Law Opposed." *New York Times,* January 21, p. 30.

————. 1960d. "Child Aid Policy Upheld by State." *New York Times,* February 2, p. 27.

————. 1960e. "Job Offers Urged as Curb on Relief." *New York Times,* February 9, p. 19.

———. 1960f. "Kings Grand Jury Cites Relief Cuts." *New York Times,* February 10, p. 24.

———. 1960g. "Bills to Tighten Relief Scored as Harmful to Needy Minors." *New York Times,* March 7, p. 21.

———. 1960h. "The Residence Requirement." *New York Times,* March 9, p. 32.

———. 1960i. "For a Veto of Relief Bills." *New York Times,* March 19, p. 20.

———. 1960j. "A Good Rockefeller Veto." *New York Times,* March 24, p. 32.

———. 1960k. "Governor Signed 1,089 New Laws." *New York Times,* May 2, p. 24.

———. 1960l. "State Action Urged on Welfare Groups." *New York Times,* June 15, p. 29.

———. 1960m. "Dumpson Renews Pledge on Inquiry." *New York Times,* November 17, p. 25.

———. 1961a. "Resident Bill Hit by Welfare Chief." *New York Times,* March 6, p. 17.

———. 1961b. "A State Welfare Fence." *New York Times,* March 7, p. 34.

———. 1961c. "Letters to the Times: Residence Issues in Relief." *New York Times,* April 5, p. 36.

———. 1961d. "Welfare Bill Upheld." *New York Times,* April 8, p. 18.

———. 1961e. "Civilized Relief Rules." *New York Times,* September 29, p. 34.

———. 1961f. "San Juan Assists City on Indigents." *New York Times,* November 3, p. 24.

———. 2002. "More People on Welfare after Years of Decline." *New York Times,* December 31, p. A16. Retrieved May 11, 2003. Available: LEXIS-NEXIS Academic Universe, News Sources.

———. 2003. "Time and a Half in the Capital." *New York Times,* October 8, p. A30. Retrieved October 10, 2003. Available: LEXIS-NEXIS Academic Universe, News Sources.

Nichols, Laura, and Barbara Gault. 1999. "The Effects of Welfare Reform on Housing Stability and Homelessness." *Welfare Reform Network News,* 2 (2): 1–13.

9to5. 2000. *Illegal and Unfair Practices: Milwaukee's Temporary Agencies.* Milwaukee, WI: 9to5.

Noble, Charles. 1997. *Welfare As We Knew It: A Political History of the American Welfare State.* New York: Oxford University Press.

North Carolina State Board of Public Welfare. 1952. "Minutes for August 8, 1952." *Minute Books, 1920–1961.* North Carolina State Archive.

Novak, Michael. 1996. "Executive Summary: To Empower People: From State to Civil Society." American Enterprise Institute. Retrieved February 18, 2002 (http://www.aei.org/bs/bs6105.htm).

Novak, Robert. 1995. "Conservatives Riled at Senate 'Queen.'" *Buffalo News,* July 6, *Viewpoints,* p. 3B.

O'Connor, Alice. 2001. *Poverty Knowledge: Social Science, Social Policy, and the Poor in Twentieth Century U.S. History.* Princeton, NJ: Princeton University Press.

O'Connor, James. 1973. *The Fiscal Crisis of the State.* New York: St. Martin's Press.

Oettinger, Katherine Brownwell. 1957. "Maternal Employment of Children." Address at Conference on Work in the Lives of Married Women, Arden House, New York, October 23. Record Group 102, Transcripts of Speeches, 1948–July 11, 1960, Box 1.

———. 1958. "Services to Unmarried Parents." Address before the Florence Crittenton Homes Association, Washington, DC, October 13. RG 102, Transcripts of Speeches, 1948–July 11, 1960, Box 1.

Offe, Claus. 1985. *Contradictions of the Welfare State,* edited by John Keane. Cambridge, MA: MIT Press.

Olasky, Marvin. 1996. "The Right Way to Replace Welfare." *Policy Review* 76: 46–51.

Orloff, Ann Shola. 1991. "Gender in Early U.S. Social Policy," *Journal of Policy History* 3: 249–81.

———. 2002. "Explaining U.S. Welfare Reform: Power, Gender, Race and U.S. Policy Legacy." *Critical Social Policy* 22 (1): 96–118.

Ortiz, Altagracia. 1996. "Puerto Rican Women in the Garment Industry of New York City, 1920–1980." In *Puerto Rican Women and Work: Bridges in Transnational Labor,* edited by Altagracia Ortiz, 55–81. Philadelphia, PA: Temple University Press.

———. 1998. "Puerto Rican Women Workers in the Twentieth Century: A Historical Appraisal of the Literature." In *Puerto Rican Women's History: New Perspectives,* edited by Felix V. Matos Rodriguez and Linda C. Delgado, 38–61. Armonk, NY: M.E. Sharpe.

Parenti, Christian. 1999. *Lockdown America: Police and Prisons in the Age of Crisis.* London: Verso.

Patriquin, Larry. 2001. "The Historical Uniqueness of the Clinton Welfare Reforms: A New Level of Social Misery?" *Journal of Sociology and Social Welfare* 28 (3): 71–94.

Patterson, James T. 1986. *America's Struggle against Poverty: 1900–1985.* Cambridge, MA: Harvard University Press.

Payne, James. 1997. "The Smart Samaritan: Five Habits of Highly Effective Charities." *Policy Review: The Journal of American Citizenship,* no. 83. Washington, DC: Heritage Foundation. Retrieved May 25, 2002 (http://ww .heritage.org/policyreview/may97/thpayne.html).

Pear, Robert. 2002a. "Bush Plans Seeks to Restore Food Stamps for Noncitizens." *New York Times,* January 10, p. A1: 1. Retrieved July 24, 2003. Available: LEXIS-NEXIS Academic Universe, News Sources.

———. 2002b. "House Democrats Propose Making the '96 Welfare Law an Antipoverty Weapon." *New York Times,* January 24, p. A24. Retrieved June 30, 2003. Available: LEXIS-NEXIS Academic Universe, News Sources.

———. 2002c. "Governors Want Congress to Ease Welfare Work Rule." *New York Times,* February 24, p. 1:27. Retrieved June 30, 2003. Available: LEXIS-NEXIS Academic Universe, News Sources.

———. 2002d. "Study by Governors Calls Bush Welfare Plan Unworkable." *New York Times,* April 4, p. A18. Retrieved June 30, 2003. Available: LEXIS-NEXIS Academic Universe, News Sources.

———. 2002e. "House G.O.P. Softens Bush Welfare Plan." *New York Times,* April 10, p. A23. Retrieved June 30, 2003. Available: LEXIS-NEXIS Academic Universe, News Sources.

———. 2002f. "G.O.P. Dispute Delays Vote on Welfare Bill." *New York Times,* May 16, p. A20. Retrieved May 11, 2003. Available: LEXIS-NEXIS Academic Universe, News Sources.

———. 2002g. "House Passes a Welfare Bill with Stricter Rules on Work." *New York Times,* May 17, p. A1. Retrieved May 11, 2003. Available: LEXIS-NEXIS Academic Universe, News Sources.

———. 2002h. "50 Senators Ask Daschle for Debate on Renewing Welfare Law." *New York Times,* September 12, p. A12. Retrieved May 11, 2003. Available: LEXIS-NEXIS Academic Universe, News Sources.

———. 2004a. "Defying Bush, Senate Increases Child Care Funds for the Poor." *New York Times,* March 31, p. A1. Retrieved April 5, 2004. Available: LEXIS-NEXIS Academic Universe, News Sources.

———. 2004b. "Senate, Torn by Minimum Wage, Shelves Major Welfare Bill." *New York Times,* April 2, p. A15. Retrieved April 5, 2004. Available: LEXIS-NEXIS Academic Universe, News Sources.

Pear, Robert, and Robin Toner. 2002. "Republicans Rally behind Welfare Proposals that States Oppose." *New York Times,* April 11, p. A29. Retrieved May 11, 2003. Available: LEXIS-NEXIS Academic Universe, News Sources.

Pearce, Diana M. 2002. "Measuring Welfare Reform Success by a Different Measure." In *From Poverty to Punishment: How Welfare Reform Punishes the Poor,* edited by Applied Research Center, 166–86. Oakland, CA: Applied Research Center.

Pearce, John Ed. 1987. *Divide and Dissent: Kentucky Politics, 1930–1963.* Lexington: University Press of Kentucky.

Peck, Jamie. 2001. *Workfare States.* New York: Guilford Press.

Peck, Jamie, and Nikolas Theodore. 1999. "'Dull Compulsion': Political Economies of Workfare." Working Paper No. 30. Manchester International Centre for Labour Studies, University of Manchester, Great Britain.

Penning, James M. 1994. "Pat Robertson and the GOP: 1988 and Beyond." *Sociology of Religion* 55 (3): 327–44.

Perlmutter, Emanuel. 1961. "City Tells Puerto Rico to Act in 3 Months on Relief Ineligibles." *New York Times,* September 26, p. 1.

Persinos, John F. 1994. "Has the Christian Right Taken Over the Republican Party." *Campaigns and Elections* (September), 21–24.

Peterson, Jonathan. 2001. "The Nation; Poverty Study Puts New Wrinkle in Welfare-to-Work Debate; Services: Families of Single, Employed Women Did Not Fare as Well as Others During Economic Boom, Report Finds." *Los Angeles Times,* August 16, p. A15. Retrieved May 18, 2003. Available: LEXIS-NEXIS Academic Universe, News Sources.

———. 2002a. "The Nation: White House to Try to Restore Food Aid to Legal Immigrants." *Los Angeles Times*, January 10, p. A15. Retrieved July 24, 2003. Available: LEXIS-NEXIS Academic Universe, News Sources.

———. 2002b. "The Nation: Welfare Plan Would Count Family Time." *Los Angeles Times*, March 28, p. A1. Retrieved July 2, 2003. Available: LEXIS-NEXIS Academic Universe, News Sources.

———. 2002c. "The Nation: Child-Care Issue Dominates Debate Over Welfare Bill; Congress: In This House, the Measure Turned into a Polarized Clash over Treatment of the Poor and States' Rights." *Los Angeles Times*, May 2, p. A21. Retrieved June 30, 2003. Available: LEXIS-NEXIS Academic Universe, News Sources.

———. 2002d. "The Nation: Child-care Issue Frames Welfare Reform Debate." *Los Angeles Times*, October 6, p. A22. Retrieved June 30, 2003. Available: LEXIS-NEXIS Academic Universe, News Sources.

Pfeffer, Max J. 1983. "Social Origins of the Three Systems of Farm Production in the United States." *Rural Sociology* 48 (4): 540–62.

———. 1986. "Immigration Policy and Class Relations in California Agriculture." In *Studies in the Transformation of U.S. Agriculture*, edited by A. Eugene Havens, 252–86. Boulder, CO: Westview Press.

Phillips, McCandlish. 1959a. "Welfare Charges Aired in Albany." *New York Times*, February 19, p. 25.

———. 1959b. "Welfare Aid Curb Arouses Dispute." *New York Times*, February 20, p. 12.

Pierson, Paul. 1994. *Dismantling the Welfare State? Reagan, Thatcher, and the Politics of Retrenchment.* New York: Cambridge University Press.

———. 1996. "The New Politics of the Welfare State." *World Politics* 48: 143–79.

———. 2001a. "Introduction: Investigating the Welfare State at Century's End." In *The New Politics of the Welfare State*, edited by Paul Pierson, 1–14. New York: Oxford University Press.

———. 2001b. "Chapter 3: Post-Industrial Pressures on Mature Welfare States." In *The New Politics of the Welfare State*, edited by Paul Pierson, 80–104. New York: Oxford University Press.

Pierson, Paul, ed. 2001c. *The New Politics of the Welfare State.* New York: Oxford University Press.

Pinner, Frank A., Paul Jacobs, and Philip Selznick. 1959. *Old Age and Political Behavior: A Case Study.* Berkeley: University of California Press.

Piven, Frances Fox. 1998. "Welfare and the Transformation of Electoral Politics." In *Social Policy and the Conservative Agenda*, edited by Clarence Y. H. Lo and Michael Schwartz, 21–36. Malden, MA: Blackwell Publishers.

———. 2003. "Why Welfare Is Racist." In *Race and the Politics of Welfare Reform*, edited by Sanford F. Schram, Joe Soss, and Richard C. Fording, 323–35. Ann Arbor: University of Michigan Press.

Piven, Frances Fox, and Richard Cloward. 1977. *Poor People's Movements: Why They Succeed, Why They Fail.* New York: Vintage Books.

———. 1987. "The Historical Sources of the Contemporary Relief Debate." In

The Mean Season: The Attack on the Welfare State, edited by Fred Block, Richard A. Cloward, Barbara Ehrenreich, and Frances Fox Piven, 3–39. New York: Pantheon Books.

———. 1993. *Regulating the Poor: The Functions of Public Welfare.* Updated version. New York: Vintage Books. (Orig. pub. 1971)

Plotkin, Sidney, and William A. Scheuerman. 1994. *Private Interest, Public Spending: Balanced-Budget Conservativism and the Fiscal Crisis.* Boston, MA: South End Press.

Pope, Jackie. 1990. "Women in the Welfare Rights Struggle: The Brooklyn Welfare Action Council." In *Women and Social Protest,* edited by Guida West and Rhoda Lois Blumberg, 57–74. New York: Oxford University Press.

Portes, Alejandro, and Robert L. Bach. 1985. *Latin Journey: Cuban and Mexican Immigrants in the United States.* Berkeley: University of California Press.

Portes, Alejandro, and Ramon Grosfoguel. 1994. "Caribbean Diasporas: Migration and Ethnic Communities." *Annals, American Academy of Political and Social Science* 533: 48–68.

Post, Charles. 1997. "The Capitalist Policy Planning Network and the Welfare Reform Act of 1996." Paper presented at the 1997 annual meeting of the American Sociological Association, Toronto, Canada.

Poverty/Rights Action Center. 1966. "Goals for a National Welfare Rights Movement. The Report of Workshop 2, National Welfare Rights Meeting, Chicago, Illinois, August 6–7, 1966." Box 7, folder 7. George Wiley Papers. State Historical Society of Wisconsin at Madison.

Pruger, Robert, and Harry Specht. 1969. "Assessing Theoretical Models of Community Organization Practice: Alinsky as a Case in Point." *Social Service Review* 43 (2): 123–35.

Quadagno, Jill. 1984. "Welfare Capitalism and the Social Security Act of 1935." *American Sociological Review* 49: 632–47.

———. 1985. "Two Developments of Welfare State Development: Reply to Skocpol and Amenta." *American Sociological Review* 50: 575–78.

———. 1988. "From Old-Age Assistance to Supplemental Security Income: The Political Economy of Relief in the South, 1935–1972." In *The Politics of Social Policy in the United States,* edited by Margaret Weir, Ann Shola Orloff, and Theda Skocpol, 235–63. Princeton, NJ: Princeton University Press.

———. 1990. "Race, Class, and Gender in the U.S. Welfare State: Nixon's Failed Family Assistance Plan." *American Sociological Review* 55: 11–28.

———. 1994. *The Color of Welfare: How Racism Undermined the War on Poverty.* New York: Oxford University Press.

Quintero, Sofia. 2002. "Heritage's Gift Horse: What Will Foundation Gain from Training the Media?" *Extra!* (January/February). Retrieved May 26, 2002 (http://www.fair.org/extra/0201/heritage-training.html).

Quigley, John M., Steven Raphael, Eugene Smolensky, Erin Mansur, and Larry A. Rosenthal. 2001. *Homelessness in California.* San Francisco: Public Policy Institute.

Rector, Robert. 1995a. "Testimony before the Sub-committee on Human Resources. January 13, 1994." In *Contract with America–Welfare Reform. Hearing Before the Subcommittee on Human Resources of the Committee on Ways and Means, House of Representatives.* 104th Cong. 1st sess. Part 1, 65–79.

———. 1995b. "Why Congress Must Reform Welfare." Backgrounder No 1063. Washington, DC: Heritage Foundation. Retrieved September 20, 2001. (http://www.heritage.org/Research/Welfare/BG1063.cfm).

———. 1995c. "The Forgotten Crisis: S. 1120, Welfare Reform, and Illegitimacy." Committee Brief No. 18. Washington, DC: Heritage Foundation. Retrieved September 20, 2001 (http://www.heritage.org/library/categories/regulation/cb18.html).

———. 1997. "Washington's Assault on Welfare Reform." Issue Bulletin No. 244. Washington, DC: Heritage Foundation. Retrieved September 20, 2001 (http://www.heritage.org/library/categories/healthwel/ib244.html).

———. 2000. "Welfare: Broadening the Reform." Issues 2000, Chapter 8. Washington, DC: Heritage Foundation. Retrieved September 20, 2001 (http://www.heritage.org).

———. 2001a. "The Effects of Welfare Reform." Testimony before the Subcommittee on Human Resources, the Committee on Ways and Means. March 15, 2001. Washington, DC: Heritage Foundation. Retrieved September 10, 2001 (http://www.heritage.org/library/testimony/test031501b .html).

———. 2001b. "The Size and Scope of Means-Tested Welfare Spending." Testimony before the Subcommittee/Committee. August 1. Washington, DC: Heritage Foundation. Retrieved September 10, 2001 (http://new.heritage .org/Research/Welfare/Test080101.cfm).

Rector, Robert, and William F. Lauber. 1995. "Elderly Non-Citizens on Welfare Will Cost the American Taxpayer $328 Billion Over the Next Decade." Washington, DC: Heritage Foundation. Retrieved February 11, 2002 (http:// www.heritage.org/library/categories/healthwelf/fyi54.html).

Reese, Ellen. 2001. "The Politics of Motherhood: The Restriction of Poor Mothers' Welfare Rights in the United States, 1949–1960." *Social Politics: International Studies in Gender, State, and Society* 8 (1): 65–112.

———. 2002. "Resisting the Workfare State: ACORN's Campaign to Improve General Relief in Los Angeles." *Race, Gender, and Class* 9 (1): 72–95.

Reese, Ellen, and Garnett Newcombe. 2003. "From Welfare Rights to Workers' Rights: The Transformation of Welfare Rights Activism in the United States." *Social Problems* 50 (2): 294–318.

Reese, Ellen, and Elvia Ramirez. 2002. "The New Ethnic Politics of Welfare: Political Struggles over Immigrants' Rights to Welfare in California." *Journal of Poverty* 6 (3): 29–62.

———. 2003. "The Politics of Welfare Inclusion: Explaining State-Level Restorations of Legal Immigrants' Welfare Rights." Paper presented at the 2003 annual meeting of the American Sociological Association, Atlanta, GA.

Rehner Iverson, Roberta. 2000. "TANF Policy Implementation: The Invisible Barrier." *Journal of Sociology and Social Work* 27 (2): 139–59.

Reich, Robert B. 1991. *The Work of Nations: Preparing Ourselves for 21st Century Capitalism.* New York: Vintage Books.

Rivera, Carla. 1998. "Skid Row's Changing Face." *Los Angeles Times,* July 28, p. A1. Retrieved May 23, 2003. Available: LEXIS-NEXIS Academic Universe, News Sources.

———. 2001. "The Growing Numbers and Problems of Women on Skid Row." *Los Angeles Times,* p. 2: 3. Retrieved May 23, 2003. Available: LEXIS-NEXIS Academic Universe, News Sources.

———. 2002. "Roofless Refuge on Skid Row." *Los Angeles Times.* September 26, p. 2: 3. Retrieved May 23, 2003. Available: LEXIS-NEXIS Academic Universe, News Sources.

Roach, Jack L., and Janet K. Roach. 1978. "Mobilizing the Poor: Road to a Dead End." *Social Problems* 26 (2): 160–71.

Roberts, Dorothy. 1997. *Killing the Black Body: Race, Reproduction, and the Meaning of Liberty.* New York: Pantheon Books.

Robins, Harvey. 1998. "Conservatives Plant a Seed in New York City." *Boston Globe,* February 22. Retrieved May 25, 2002 (http://www.manhattan-institute .org/html/_bglobe-conservatives_plant_a_.htm).

Robinson, Layhmond. 1960a. "Curb on Welfare Passed in Albany." *New York Times,* March 18, p. 1.

———. 1960b. "Governor Agrees to Relief Inquiry." *New York Times,* May 1, p. 68.

———. 1961a. "Legislators Vote to Limit Welfare." *New York Times,* March 24, p. 24.

———. 1961b. "Governor Signs New Relief Law." *New York Times,* April 15, p. 12.

Rodger, John J. 2000. *From a Welfare State to a Welfare Society: The Changing Context of Social Policy in a Postmodern Era.* New York: St. Martin's Press.

Rodriguez, Clara. 1974. *The Ethnic Queue in the U.S.: The Case of Puerto Ricans.* San Francisco: R and E Research Associates.

Rogers-Dillon, Robin H. 2001. "What Do We Really Know about Welfare Reform?" *Society* 38 (2): 7–15.

Rojas, Aurelio. 1997. "Immigrants Worried about Reform: Los Angeles, the New Ellis Island, Braces for Cuts." *San Francisco Chronicle,* February 13, p. A1.

Ronan, Thomas P. 1950. "Mayor Won't Quit but Plans to Cut Outside Activities." *New York Times,* February 14, p. 1.

Roschelle, A. R. 1995. "The Political Mileage of Racism." *Peace Review* 7 (3–4): 443–47.

Rose, Nancy E. 1995. *Workfare or Fair Work: Women, Welfare, and Government Work Programs.* New Brunswick, NJ: Rutgers University Press.

Rosenberg, Alec. 2003. "Bay Area Housing Costs Keep Rising, Census Shows."

Alameda Times-Star, May 31, p.1. Retrieved September 13, 2003. Available: LEXIS-NEXIS Academic Universe, News Sources.

Rosenberg, J. L. 1949. "Struggle Ahead: 'The Issue Is Statism.'" *Tax Digest* (October), 332–33.

Rothstein, Richard. 2002. "Schoolchildren of Welfare Parents." *New York Times,* June 5, p. B8. Retrieved June 30, 2003. Available: LEXIS-NEXIS Academic Universe, News Sources.

Rowe, Joyce Louise. 1993. "The 'Working Poor': Single Mothers and the State, 1911–1950." Ph.D. dissertation, Department of History, Ohio State University, Columbus, OH.

Rozell, Mark J., Clyde Wilcox, John C. Green. 1998. "Religious Constituencies and Support for the Christian Right in the 1990s." *Social Science Quarterly* 79 (4): 815–27.

Rupp, Leila, and Verta Taylor. 1987. *Survival in the Doldrums: The American Women's Rights Movement, 1945 to the 1960s.* New York: Oxford University Press.

Samora, Julian, and Patricia Vandel Simon. 1977. *A History of the Mexican-American People.* Notre Dame, IN: University of Notre Dame Press.

San Francisco Chronicle. 1948a. "Pension Proposal Calls for Radical Changes." *San Francisco Chronicle,* October 11, p. 24.

———. 1948b. "Chamber of Commerce Opposes Aged, Blind Aid Proposition." *San Francisco Chronicle,* October 13, p. 11.

———. 1948c. "Editorial: No. 4 and the Pension Spoilsmen." *San Francisco Chronicle,* October 21, p. 3.

———. 1948d. "Editorial: A Surly Project Appears." *San Francisco Chronicle,* October 21, p. 22.

———. 1948e. "Opposition to Blind, Pension Plan: Welfare Group against Proposition 4." *San Francisco Chronicle,* October 26, p. 3.

———. 1949a. "New State Welfare Adviser Resigns." *San Francisco Chronicle,* March 3, p. 8.

———. 1949b. "Dr. Chickering Quits State Welfare Board." *San Francisco Chronicle,* March 10, p. 2.

———. 1949c. "Opponent of Prop. 4 Quits as Aide to Mrs. Williams." *San Francisco Chronicle,* July 13, p. 17.

———. 1949d. "'McLain the Boss': Welfare Department Aide Tells Why He Walked Out of State Job." *San Francisco Chronicle,* August 24, p. 9.

———. 1949e. "Hazel Hurst Quits State Social Welfare Board." *San Francisco Chronicle,* September 17, p. 2.

———. 1949f. "McEnerney to Head S.F. Sound Pension Committee." *San Francisco Chronicle,* September 20, p. 12.

———. 1949g. "The Blind Accuse Welfare Agency Called Collector For McLain." *San Francisco Chronicle,* October 8, p. 1.

———. 1949h. "Governor Singles Out Assemblyman Evans for Special Attention." *San Francisco Chronicle,* November 4, p. 1.

———. 1949i. "FBI Taking No Part in State Pension Inquiry." *San Francisco Chronicle*, November 9, p. 3.

———. 1949j. "McLain Asks Funds." *San Francisco Chronicle*, November 10, p. 5.

———. 1949k. "How the Balloting Went: McLain Defeat Overwhelming." *San Francisco Chronicle*, November 10, p. 1.

———. 1949l. "Sacramento Jury Maps Lobby Inquiry." *San Francisco Chronicle*, November 18, p. 9.

———. 1949m. "Pension Suit." *San Francisco Chronicle*, November 29, p. 7.

Sanchez, George I. 1972. "History, Culture, and Education." In *The Changing Mexican-American: A Reader*, edited by Rudolph Gomez, 24–52. El Paso: University of Texas, El Paso.

———. 1997. "Face the Nation: Race, Immigration, and the Rise of Nativism in Late Twentieth Century America." *International Migration Review* 31 (4): 1009–30.

Sanchez, Jesus. 2003. "Rising Southern California Rents Are Bucking the National Trend." *Los Angeles Times*, February 6, p. 3:1. Retrieved September 13, 2003. Available: LEXIS-NEXIS Academic Universe, News Sources.

Sanger, David E., and Steven Greenhouse. 2002. "President Invokes Taft-Hartley to Open 29 Ports." *New York Times*, October 8, p. A1. Retrieved September 16, 2003. Available: LEXIS-NEXIS Academic Universe, News Sources.

Santoro, Wayne. A. 1999. "Conventional Politics Takes Center Stage: The Latino Struggle against English-only Laws." *Social Forces* 77 (3): 887–909.

Savner, Steve, Julie Strawn, and Mark Greenberg. 2002. "TANF Reauthorization: Opportunities to Reduce Poverty by Improving Employment Outcomes." Center for Law and Social Policy. Retrieved March 11, 2002 (http://www.clasp.org).

Sawhill, Isabel V. 2002a. "Testimony before the Subcommittee on Human Resources." Committee on Ways and Means. April 11. Washington, DC: Brookings Institution. Retrieved May 26, 2002 (http://www.brook.edu).

———. 2002b. "Issues in TANF Reauthorization: Building Stronger Families." Testimony before the Senate Finance Committee. May 16. Washington, DC: Brookings Institution. Retrieved May 26, 2002 (http://www.brook.edu).

Scheer, Robert. 1996. "Religion's Role Is to Inform, Not Inflame: The Alternative to Tolerance Is the Acceptance of 'Pro-Life' Killing and Other Unsupportable 'Political' Statements." *Los Angeles Times*, March 5, p. B7. Retrieved June 8. 2002. Available: LEXIS-NEXIS Academic Universe, News Sources.

Schlafly, Phyllis. 1996a. "The Fraud and the Failure Called Welfare." Alton, IL: Eagle Forum. Retrieved June 5, 2002 (http://www.eagleforum.org/column/jan96/1–25–96.html).

———. 1996b. "Welfare: Fraud and Failure." Alton, IL: Eagle Forum. Retrieved June 5, 2002 (http://www.eagleforum.org/psr/1996/feb96/welfare.html).

———. 2000. "Sex Education Has Become X-Rated." *Education Reporter*, September 20. Retrieved June 5, 2002 (http://www.eagleforum.org/column/2000/sept00/00–09–20.shtml).

Schneider, Dorothee. 2000. "Symbolic Citizenship, Nationalism, and the Distant State: The United States Congress in the 1996 Debates on Immigration Reform." *Citizenship Studies* 4 (3): 255–73.

Schram, Sanford. 2001. "Written Testimony of Sanford F. Schram before the U.S. House of Representatives, Committee on Education and the Workforce, Subcommittee on 21st Century Competitiveness." September 20. Retrieved November 30, 2001 (http://www.house.gov/ed_workforce/hearings/107th/21st/welfare92001/schram.htm).

———. 2003. "Putting a Black Face on Welfare." In *Race and the Politics of Welfare Reform*, edited by Sanford F. Schram, Joe Soss, and Richard C. Fording, 196–221. Ann Arbor: University of Michigan Press.

Schram, Sanford, Lawrence Nitz, and Gary Krueger. 1998. "Without Cause or Effect: Reconsidering Welfare Migration as a Policy Problem." *American Journal of Political Science* 42 (1): 210–30.

Schrecker, Ellen W. 1989. "The Two Stages of McCarthyism." In *McCarthyism*, edited by Thomas C. Reeves, 98–101. Malabar, FL: Robert E. Krieger Publishing Company.

Schreckhise, William D., and Todd G. Shields. 2003. "Ideological Realignment in the Contemporary U.S. Electorate Revisited." *Social Science Quarterly* 84 (3): 596–612.

Schultze, Steve. 2000. "Maximus to Pay Back $500,000: Firm Also Plans Extra Spending for Poor after Audit." *Milwaukee Journal Sentinel*, October 14, p. B1. Retrieved April 4, 2004. Available: LEXIS-NEXIS Academic Universe, News Sources.

Schwartz, Herman. 2001. "Round Up the Usual Suspects!: Globalization, Domestic Politics, and Welfare State Change." In *The New Politics of the Welfare State*, edited by Paul Pierson, 17–44. New York: Oxford University Press.

Schwartz, Michael. 1998. "Introduction: What Went Right? Why the Clinton Administration Did Not Alter the Conservative Trajectory in Federal Policy." In *Social Policy and the Conservative Agenda*, edited by Clarence Y. H. Lo and Michael Schwartz, 1–18. Malden, MA: Blackwell Publishers.

Scott, Janny. 1997. "Turning Intellect into Influence: Promoting Its Ideas, the Manhattan Institute Has Nudged New York Rightward." *New York Times*, May 12, p. B1. Available: LEXIS-NEXIS Academic Universe, News Sources.

Seavey, Dorie, and Ashley F. Sullivan. 2001. *Household Food Security Study Summaries*. Boston: Food Security Institute, Center on Hunger and Poverty.

Seigal, Kalman. 1950. "Caseload and Cost of Welfare Drop." *New York Times*, June 29, p. 58:2.

Senior, Clarence. 1952. *Strangers and Neighbors: The Story of Our Puerto Rican Citizens*. New York: Anti-Defamation League of B'nai Brith.

———. 1965. *The Puerto Ricans: Strangers—Then Neighbors*. Chicago: Quadrangle Books. (Orig. pub. 1961)

Shapiro, Herbert. 1988. *White Violence and Black Response: From Reconstruction to Montgomery*. Amherst: University of Massachusetts Press.

Shapiro, Michael J. 1997. "Narrating the Nation, Unwelcoming the Stranger: Anti-Immigration Policy in Contemporary 'America.'" *Alternatives* 22 (1): 1–34.

Shaw, Greg M., and Robert Y. Shapiro. 2002. "The Polls—Trends: Poverty and Public Assistance." *Public Opinion Quarterly* 66: 105–28.

Shelton, James E. 1949. "Achievement vs. Stagnation: Creeping Collectivism Threatens Freedom." *Tax Digest* (October), 334–36, 357–59.

Sherman, Amy. 1998. "Churches and Welfare Reform: Can Christians Work with Government to Help the Poor?" Washington, DC: Hudson Institute. Retrieved March 25, 2002 (http://www.hudson.org/index.cfm?fuseaction=publication_details&id = 101).

———. 2002a. "Americans Want Handups . . . Not Handouts." Washington, DC: Hudson Institute. Retrieved March 25, 2002 (http://www.hudson.org/index.cfm?fuseaction = publication_details&id = 84).

———. 2002b. "A New Path Out of Poverty? A Close Look at Mississippi's 'Faith and Families' Program." Washington, DC: Hudson Institute. Retrieved March 25, 2002 (http://www.hudson.org/index.cfm?fuseaction=publication_details&id = 104).

———. 2002c. "Cross Purposes: Will Conservative Welfare Reform Corrupt Religious Charities?" Washington, DC: Hudson Institute. Retrieved March 25, 2002 (http://www.hudson.org/index.cfm?fuseaction=publication_details&id=135).

Sherman, Arloc, Cheryl Amey, Barbara Duffield, Nancy Ebb, and Deborah Weinstein. 1998. *Welfare to What? Early Findings on Family Hardship and Well-Being.* Washington: Children's Defense Fund and National Coalition for the Homeless.

Shogren, Elizabeth. 1994a. "Bill Ties Welfare Reform to Cut in Immigrant Aid." *Los Angeles Times,* May 11, p. A4. Retrieved June 14, 2002. Available: LEXIS-NEXIS Academic Universe, News Sources.

———. 1994b. "Plans to Cut Safety Net Leave Legal Immigrants Dangling." *Los Angeles Times,* November 21, p. A1. Retrieved June 14, 2002. Available: LEXIS-NEXIS Academic Universe, News Sources.

———. 1995a. "Welfare Debate Focusing on Out-Of-Wedlock Births, Reform: Conservative Push to Deny Cash Benefits to Teenagers Who Bear Children: Issue Signals Shape and Intensity of Upcoming Senate Action." *Los Angeles Times,* August 3, p. A14. Retrieved June 8, 2002. Available: LEXIS-NEXIS Academic Universe, News Sources.

———. 1995b. "Senate, House on Own Paths in Welfare Debate: Congress: Upper Chamber's Provision Suggest It Is Not as Attuned to the Conservative Groups Seeking Support for 'Family Values' Legislation." *Los Angeles Times,* September 16, p. A4. Retrieved June 8, 2002. Available: LEXIS-NEXIS Academic Universe, News Sources.

Sibley, Celestine. 1951. "Talmadge Asks Law Limiting Aid to Illegitimate Babies." *The Atlanta Constitution,* January 25, p. 1.

Simon, Stephanie. 2002a. "Homeless, Helpless, Hopeless: A Surge in Evictions across the Country Illustrates the Depth of the Economic Recession." *Los Angeles Times*, January 12, p. A1.

———. 2002b. "Havens for Homeless Facing More Than They Can Handle: As Economy Lags, Cities Report That Demand Is Soaring for Food and Shelter." *Los Angeles Times*, December 22, p. A22. Retrieved September 13, 2003. Available: LEXIS-NEXIS Academic Universe, News Sources.

Sirico, Robert A. 1995a. "Statement of Rev. Robert A. Sirico, President, the Acton Institute for the Study of Religion and Liberty, Grand Rapids, Michigan; and Member, Michigan Civil Rights Commission." In *Contract with America-Welfare Reform. Hearing Before the Subcommittee on Human Resources of the Committee on Ways and Means, House of Representatives.* 104th Cong., 1st sess., Part 1, 209–15.

———. 1995b. "Escape from the Welfare Trap." *Washington Times*, September 1. Retrieved May 19, 2002 (http://www.acton.org/research/editorials/sirico/escapewelfare.html).

———. 2000. "How Can Welfare Reform Improve?" *Detroit News*, May 26. Retrieved May 19, 2002 (http:www.acton.org/research/editorials/sirico/welfarereform.html).

Sklar, Kathryn Kish. 1993. "The Historical Foundations of Women's Power in the Creation of the American Welfare State, 1830–1930." In *Mothers of a New World: Maternalist Politics and the Origins of the Welfare State*, edited by Seth Koven and Sonya Michel. New York: Routledge.

Skocpol, Theda. 1992. *Protecting Soldiers and Wives: The Political Origins of Social Policy in the United States.* Cambridge, MA: Belknap Press of Harvard University Press.

Sly, John F. 1950. "Is There a Way Out? Beginnings of Welfare State Traced: Address at the 24th Annual California Taxpayers' Association Meeting." *Tax Digest* (April), 113–14, 134–37.

Smith, Anna Marie. 2001. "The Politicization of Marriage in Contemporary American Public Policy: The Defense of Marriage Act and the Personal Responsibility Act." *Citizenship Studies* 5 (3): 303–20.

Smith, David M., and Maurice Blanc. 1996. "Citizenship, Nationality, and Ethnic Minorities in Three European Nations." *International Journal of Urban and Regional Research* 20 (1): 66–82.

Smith, Michael Peter, and Bernadette Tarallo. 1995. "Proposition 187: Global Trend or Local Narrative? Explaining Anti-Immigrant Politics in California, Arizona, and Texas." *International Journal of Urban and Regional Research* 19 (4): 655–63.

Smith, Willard. 1950. "Some County Problems: Federal and State Laws Increase Costs." *Tax Digest* (August), 267–69, 284–85.

Smith May, Hoke. 1951. "$5,000 Rule Protects Chiselers, Says Solon." *Atlanta Constitution*, June 15, p. 19:1.

Social Security Administration. 1949. "State Letter #118: State Plans for Old-

Age Assistance, Aid to Dependent Children, and Aid to the Blind—Revised Outline and Instructions—Preliminary Issuance for Review and Testing by State Agencies, 7/5/49." Record Group 47, Box 1. National Archives.

———. 1957. Commissioner's Action Minutes, December 24. Minutes of Meetings. Record Group 47, Box 29. National Archives.

Social Security Administration/Department of Health, Education, and Welfare, Bureau of Public Assistance. 1949–60. *Characteristics of State Public Assistant Plans.* Washington, DC: U.S. Government Printing Office.

Social Security Board. 1945. Board Minutes, December 28. Record Group 47, Social Security Board Minutes of Meetings, 12/45–4/46. National Archives.

Soley, Lawrence. 1998. "Heritage Clones in the Heartland: Local Think Tanks' 'Research' Comes Pre-digested." *Extra!* (September/October). Retrieved May 26, 2002 (http://www.fair.org/extra/9809/local-think-tanks.html).

Solinger, Rickie. 1992. *Wake Up Little Susie: Single Pregnancy and Race before Roe v. Wade.* New York: Routledge.

Soloman, Norman. 1996. "The Media's Favorite Think Tank: How the Heritage Foundation Turns Money into Media." *Extra!* (July/August). Retrieved May 26, 2002 (http://www.fair.org/extra/9607/heritage.html).

Soss, Joe, Sanford F. Schram, Thomas P. Vartanian, and Eric O'Brien. 2001. "Setting the Terms of Relief: Explaining State Policy Choices in the Devolution Revolution." *American Journal of Political Science* 45: 378–403.

———. 2003. "The Hard Line and the Color Line: Race, Welfare, and the Roots of Get-Tough Reform." In *Race and the Politics of Welfare Reform*, edited by Sanford F. Schram, Joe Soss, and Richard C. Fording, 225–53. Ann Arbor: University of Michigan Press.

Soule, Sarah A., and Yvonne Zylan. 1997. "Runaway Train? The Diffusion of State-Level Reform in ADC/AFDC Eligibility Requirements, 1950–1967." *American Journal of Sociology* 103 (3): 733–62.

Southworth, Caleb. 2002. "Aid to Sharecroppers: How Agrarian Class Structure and Tenant-Farmer Politics Influenced Federal Relief in the South, 1933–1935." *Social Science History* 26 (1): 33–70.

Sparks, Holloway. 2003. "Queens, Teens, and Model Mothers: Race, Gender, and the Discourse of Welfare Reform." I *Race and the Politics of Welfare Reform*, edited by Sanford F. Schram, Joe Soss, and Richard C. Fording, 171–95. Ann Arbor: University of Michigan Press.

St. John, M. I. 1952a. "Peach Welfare Head Quits, Says More Children on Relief Than in School." *Atlanta Constitution*, January 9, p. 1.

———. 1952b. "30 Pct. on Relief Rolls in Clark Held Ineligible." *Atlanta Constitution*, January 21, p. 1.

Stall, Susan, and Randy Stoecker. 1998. "Community Organizing or Organizing Community? Gender and the Crafts of Empowerment." *Gender & Society* 12 (6): 729–56.

Star Tribune. 2003. "Welfare Reform II: A Congress Detached from Reality." *Star Tribune* (Minneapolis, MN), September 13, p. A24. Retrieved October 19, 2003. Available: LEXIS-NEXIS Academic Universe, News Sources.

Steensland, Brian. 2002. "The Failed Revolution: Policy, Culture, and the Struggle for Guaranteed Income in the U.S., 1965–1980." Ph.D. dissertation. Department of Sociology, Princeton University, NJ.

Stefancic, Jean, and Richard Delgado. 1996. "The Attack on Welfare." In *No Mercy: How Conservative Think Tanks and Foundations Changed America's Social Agenda*, 82–95. Philadelphia, PA: Temple University Press.

Stein, Dan. 1995. "Testimony of Dan Stein, Federation for American Immigration Reform." In *Contract with America-Welfare Reform. Hearing Before the Subcommittee on Human Resources of the Committee on Ways and Means, House of Representatives.* 104th Cong., 1st sess., Part 1, 446–57.

Steiner, Gilbert Y. 1971. *The State of Welfare*. Washington, DC: Brookings Institution.

Stephens, John D. 1979. *The Transition from Capitalism to Socialism*. London: MacMillan Press.

Stevens, Larry. 1969. *Mexican-Americans in California: A Brief History*. Stockton, CA: Stockton Federation of Teachers.

Stevenson, Richard W. 2003. "Bush Urges Congress to Extend Welfare Law, with Changes." *New York Times*, February 26, p. A23. Retrieved May 11, 2003. Available: LEXIS-NEXIS Academic Universe, News Sources.

Stevenson, Richard W., and Steven Greenhouse. 2004. "Bush on Immigration: The President: Plan for Illegal Immigrant Workers Draws Fire from Two Sides." *New York Times*, January 8, p. A28. Retrieved May 13, 2004. Available: LEXIS-NEXIS Academic Universe, News Sources.

Stewart, Jocelyn. 2004. "U.S. Blamed in Cuts to Rental Aid for Poor: Changes to Housing Program Will Lead to Higher Costs, Canceled Contracts, Critics Say." *Los Angeles Times*, June 3, p. B1. Retrieved June 25, 2004. Available: LEXIS-NEXIS Academic Universe, News Sources.

Stier, Haya, and Marta Tienda. 1997. "Spouses or Babies? Race, Poverty and Pathways to Family Formation in Urban America." *Ethnic and Racial Studies* 20 (1): 91–122.

Stoesz, David. 1988. "Packaging the Conservative Revolution." *Social Epistemology* 2 (2): 145–53.

Stoesz, David, and Policy America. 1987. "Policy Gambit: Conservative Think Tanks Take on the Welfare State." *Journal of Sociology and Social Welfare* 14 (4): 3–20.

Stolberg, Sheryl Gay. 2004. "Senate Pass $447 Billion Pentagon Package." *New York Times*, June 23, p. A4. Retrieved June 29, 2004. Available: LEXIS-NEXIS Academic Universe, News Sources.

Street, James H. 1957. *The New Revolution in the Cotton Economy: Mechanization and Its Consequences*. Chapel Hill: University of North Carolina Press.

Suárez-Orozco, C., and M. Suárez-Orozco. 1995. *Transformations: Migration, Family Life and Achievement*. Stanford, CA: Stanford University Press.

Swank, Duane. 1998. "Global Capital, Democracy, and the Welfare State: Why Political Institutions Are So Important in Shaping the Domestic Response to

Internationalization." Working Paper No. 1.66. Center for German and European Studies, University of California, Berkeley.

———. 2001. "Political Institutions and Welfare State Restructuring: The Impact of Institutions and Social Policy Change in Developed Democracies." In *The New Politics of the Welfare State*, edited by Paul Pierson, 197–237. New York: Oxford University Press.

Swank, Duane H., and Alexander Hicks. 1984. "Militancy, Need and Relief: The Piven and Cloward AFDC Caseload Thesis Revisited." *Research in Social Movements, Conflict, and Change* 6: 1–29.

Syversten, Thomas H. 1985. "Earle Chester Clements, 1947–50." In *Kentucky's Governors, 1792–1985*, edited by Lowell H. Harrison, 157–62. Lexington:The University Press of Kentucky.

Takacs, Stacy. 1999. "Alien-nation: Immigration, National Identity and Transnationalism." *Cultural Studies* 13 (4): 591–620.

Tanner, Michael. 1995. "Welfare Reform: Testimony of Michael Tanner (Director, Health and Welfare Studies, Cato Institute) before the Finance Committee, United States Senate." March 9. Washington, DC: Cato Institute. Retrieved May 1, 2002 (http://www.cato.org/testimony).

———. 1996. "Replacing Welfare." *CATO Policy Report.* Washington, DC: Cato Institute. Retrieved May 1, 2002 (http://www.cato.org/pubs/policy_report/cpr-18n6–1.html).

———. 2001. "Corrupting Charity: Why Government Should Not Fund Faith-Based Charities." Briefing Papers No. 62. Washington, DC: Cato Institute. Retrieved May 1, 2002 (http://www.cato.org/pubs/briefs/bp-062es.html).

Taylor, Ula. 1999. "Proposition 209 and the Affirmative Action Debate on the University of California Campuses." *Feminist Studies* 1: 95–103.

Teles, Steven M. 1996. *Whose Welfare? AFDC and Elite Politics.* Lawrence: University of Kansas Press.

Texeira, Ruy, and Joel Rogers. 2000. *America's Forgotten Majority: Why the White Working Class Still Matters.* New York: Basic Books.

Theoharis, Athan. 1971. *Seeds of Repression: Harry S. Truman and the Origins of McCarthyism.* Chicago: Quadrangle Books.

Tienda, Marta, and L. Jensen. 1986. "Immigration and Public Assistance Participation: Dispelling the Myth of Dependency." *Social Science Research* 15 (4), 372–400.

Tilly, Chris. 1991. "Reasons for the Continuing Growth of Part-time Employment." *Monthly Labor Review* 114 (3): 10–18.

———. 1996. "Workfare's Impact on the New York City Labor Market: Lower Wages and Worker Displacement." Working Paper No. 92. Russell Sage Foundation, New York.

Times Union. 2004. "Spending Sense; Congressional Republicans Appear to Have Gotten the Message on Priorities." *Times Union,* April 1, p. A18.

Toner, Robin. 2002a. "Helping the Poor in the Post-Welfare Era." *New York Times,* March 3, p. 4:1. Retrieved July 2, 2003. Available: LEXIS-NEXIS Academic Universe, News Sources.

————. 2002b. "Bush's Proposal on Welfare Draws Fire from Democrats." *New York Times*, March 12, p. A20. Retrieved July 2, 2003. Available: LEXIS-NEXIS Academic Universe, News Sources.

————. 2002c. "States Worry about Bush Welfare Rules." *New York Times*, April 30, p. A22. Retrieved July 2, 2003. Available: LEXIS-NEXIS Academic Universe, News Sources.

Toner, Robin, and Robert Pear. 2002. "Bush's Plan on Welfare Law Increases Work Requirement." *New York Times*, February 26, p. A23. Retrieved July 2, 2003. Available: LEXIS-NEXIS Academic Universe, News Sources.

Traditional Values Coalition. 2002a. "Why Join TVC's E-Mail." Anaheim, CA: Traditional Values Coalition. Retrieved June 5, 2002 (http://www.traditionalvalues.org).

————. 2002b. "Empowering People of Faith with Truth." Anaheim, CA: Traditional Values Coalition. Retrieved June 5, 2002 (http://traditionalvalues.org/sections.php?op = viewarticle&artid = 1).

————. 2002c. "Welfare Reform Legislation Passes." May 24, 2002. Anaheim, CA: Traditional Values Coalition. Retrieved June 5, 2002 (http://traditionalvalues.org/article.php?sid = 304).

————. 2002d. "White House Faith-Based Initiative Leader Outlines Future." Anaheim, CA: Traditional Values Coalition, May 24, 2002. Retrieved June 5, 2002 (http://traditionalvalues.org/article.php?sid = 303).

Tramburg, John W. 1954. Memo to Mr. Russell R. Larmon, Assistant Secretary, Subject: Mr. Rockefeller's Concern about Criticisms Made of the ADC program, January 25. Record Group 235, GCF 1951–1955, Decimal Series 600. National Archives.

Transcript of Proceedings Had Before the Honorable Griffin B. Bell, the Honorable Lewis R. Morgan, and the Honorable Sidney O. Smith, Jr. in Atlanta, Fulton County, GA on Friday, April 7, 1967. Records of Civil Action Number 10443. Georgia Federal Records Center, East Point, GA. Accession Number 69 A 2139, Box 30–31. Location 86559–60.

Trattner, Walter I. 1974. *From Poor Law to Welfare State: A History of Social Welfare in America*. New York: Free Press.

Trizonis, Chris. 1951. "Judge Flays 'Racket' in Cases of Abandonment." *Valdosta Times*, April 9. County Board Minutes. Folder: Lowdnes County. Series 24–8–34. Box 13A. Georgia Department of Archives and History.

Tuck, Ruth D. 1974. *Not with the Fist*. New York: Harcourt, Brace. (Orig. pub. 1946)

Turner, Jonathan H., and Charles E. Starnes. 1976. *Inequality: Privilege and Poverty in America*. Pacific Palisades, CA: Goodyear Publishing Company.

Ueda, Reed. 1994. *Postwar Immigrant America*. New York: St. Martin's Press.

U.S. Bureau of the Census. 1943. *Sixteenth Census of the United States: 1940. Vol. II: Characteristics of the Population*. Washington, DC: U.S. Government Printing Office.

————. 1952. *1950 Census of the Population, Vol. II: Characteristics of the Population*. Washington, DC: Government Printing Office, Table 30

———. 1954. *Statistical Abstract of the United States, 1954*, Table. no. 29. Washington, DC: U.S. Government Printing Office.

———. 1956. *United States Census of Agriculture: 1954. Vol. II: General Report.* Washington, DC: U.S. Government Printing Office.

———. 1961. *1960 Census of the Population, Vol. I: Characteristics of the Population.* Washington, DC: U.S. Government Printing Office.

———. 1962. *Statistical Abstract of the United States, 1954*, Table. no. 29. Washington, DC: U.S. Government Printing Office.

———. 1973. *Statistical Abstract of the United States: 1973.* Washington, DC: U.S. Government Printing Office, Tables 353 and 355.

———. 1975. *Historical Statistics of the United States, Colonial Times to 1970.* Washington, DC: U.S. Government Printing Office.

———. 2001a. "The Foreign-Born Population in the United States." *Current Population Reports: March 2000.* Washington, DC: U.S. Government Printing Office.

———. 2001b. *Statistical Abstract of the United States.* Washington, DC: U.S. Government Printing Office, Table 68.

———. 2004. "POV1: Age and Sex of All People, Family Members and Unrelated Individuals Iterated by Income-to-Poverty Ratio and Race," and "POV2: People in Families by Family Structure, Age, and Sex, Iterated by Income-to-Poverty Ratio and Race," in *Detailed Poverty Tables: 2003.* Retrieved October 8, 2004 (http://ferret.bls.census.gov/macro/032004/pov/toc.htm).

U.S. Children's Bureau. 1953. *United States Children's Bureau Publication Number 341: Helping Delinquent Children.* Washington, DC: U.S. Government Printing Office.

U.S. Committee on Ways and Means, House of Representatives. 2000. *Background Material and Data on Major Programs within Jurisdiction of the Committee on Ways and Means.* Washington, DC: U.S. Government Printing Office.

U.S. Conference of Mayors. 2003. "U.S. Conference of Mayors-Sodhexho Hunger and Homelessness Survey." Press Release. December 18.

U.S. Congress, Joint Committee on Printing. 1996. *Congressional Directory of the 104th Congress.* Washington, DC: U.S. Government Printing Office.

U.S. Department of Commerce. 1958. *U.S. Income and Output.* Washington, DC: U.S. Government Printing Office.

U.S. Department of Health, Education, and Welfare. 1960. *Illegitimate Births: United States, 1938–1957, Vital Statistics—Special Reports* 33 (5). Washington, DC: U.S. Government Printing Office.

———. 1961a. *Public Assistance under the Social Security Act, Public Assistance Report No. 47.* Washington, DC: U.S. Government Printing Press.

———. 1961b. *Vital Statistics of the United States, 1960. Vol. 1: Natality.* Washington, DC: U.S. Government Printing Office.

U.S. Department of Health and Human Services. 2002. *Annual Report to Congress.* Washington, DC: Government Printing Office.

U.S. Department of Health and Human Services, National Center for Health Statistics. 2001a. *National Vital Statistics Report* 49 (1).

———. 2001b. *National Vital Statistics Report* 49 (5).

———. 2001c. *National Vital Statistics Report* 49 (6).

U.S. Department of Justice. 2003. *Compendium of Federal Justice Statistics, 2001.* Washington, DC: U.S. Government Printing Office.

U.S. House of Representatives Committee on Ways and Means. 1998. *1998 Green Book.* Washington, DC: U.S. Government Printing Office.

———. 2003. "Committee Members." Retrieved November 21, 2003 (http://waysandmeans.house.gov/members.asp?comm=0).

U.S. Senate Committee on Finance. 1967. *Brief Summary of the Major Recommendations Presented in Oral and Written Statements during Public Hearings on H.R. 12080.* Washington D.C.: U.S. Government Printing Office. National Archive.

———. 2003. "Committee Members." Retrieved November 21, 2003 (http://finance.senate.gov/sitepages/committee.htm).

U.S. Student Association. 2002. *2002 Organizing Guide.* Washington, DC U.S. Student Association.

Unz, Ron. K. 1994. "Immigration or the Welfare State: Which Is Our Real Enemy?" *Policy Review* 79: 33–38.

Urban Institute. 2001. "Welfare Reform Turns Five." Press Release. August 21. Washington, DC: Urban Institute. Retrieved March 12, 2002 (http://www.urban.org).

Utt, Ronald D. 1995. "How to Achieve $11 Billion in Savings from Privatization in FY 1996." Heritage Foundation Committee Brief No. 6. A Special Report to the Budget and Appropriations Commitees. February 22. Washington, DC: Heritage Foundation. Retrieved February 2, 2002 (http://www.heritage.org).

Ventura, Stephanie J., and Christine A. Bachrach. 2000. "Nonmarital Childbearing in the United States, 1940–1999." *National Vital Statistics Reports* 48 (16).

Vogel, David. 1996. *Kindred Strangers: The Uneasy Relationship between Politics and Business in America.* Princeton, NJ: Princeton University Press.

Wagenheim, Karl. 1975. *A Survey of Puerto Ricans in the U.S. Mainland in the 1970s.* New York: Praeger Publishers.

Walker, Richard. 1996. "California's Collision with Race and Class." *Representations* 55: 163–83.

Walters, Ronald. 1998. "The Democratic Party and the Politics of Welfare Reform." In *Social Policy and the Conservative Agenda,* edited by Clarence Y. H. Lo and Michael Schwartz, 37–52. Malden, MA: Blackwell Publishers.

War Resisters League. 2004. "Where Your Income Tax Money Really Goes: The United States Federal Budget for Fiscal Year 2005." New York: War Resisters League. Retrieved June 3, 2004 (http://www.warresisters.org/piechart.htm).

Watson, Justin. 1997. *The Christian Coalition: Dreams of Restoration, Demands for Recognition.* New York: St. Martin's Press.

Weaver, Kent. 2000. *Ending Welfare as We Know It.* Washington, DC: Brookings Institution.

Weaver, R. Kent, Robert Y. Shapiro, and Lawrence R. Jacobs. 1995. "The Polls—Trends: Welfare." *Public Opinion Quarterly* 59: 606–27.

Weaver, Warren. 1951. "New Battle Looms over Colored OLEO." *New York Times*, December 28, p. 11.

———. 1953. "State Board Backs Relief Board Bill." *New York Times*, February 26, p. 19.

———. 1957. "Non-resident Aid Heaviest in the City." *New York Times*, February 18, p. 16.

———. 1958a. "Albany Bill to Curb Relief Loses Again: Heck Takes Floor to Help Defeat It." *New York Times*, March 26, p. 20.

———. 1958b. "State G.O.P. Split over Relief Curb." *New York Times*, August 20, p. 28.

———. 1959. "Inquiry on Relief in State Planned by Legislature." *New York Times*, January 12, p. 1.

———. 1960a. "Battle Is Begun on Relief Limit." *New York Times*, January 15, p. 33.

———. 1960b. "Governor Vetoes Year's Residence as a Relief Rule." *New York Times*, March 23, p. 1.

———. 1961a. "Rockefeller Bars Relief Residency." *New York Times*, March 9, p. 19.

———. 1961b. "Relief Bill Eases Residency Issues." *New York Times*, March 17, p. 1.

Webber, Lane D. 1951. "25 Years of Taxpayer Activity: Some Association Contributions Outlined." *Tax Digest* (April), 121–23.

Weicher, John C. 2001. "Reforming Welfare: The Next Policy Debates." *Society* (Jan./Feb.), 16–20.

Weinberg, Sylvia. 1998. "Mexican American Mothers and the Welfare Debate: A History of Exclusion." *Journal of Poverty* 2 (3): 53–75.

Wells, Miriam J. 1996. *Strawberry Fields: Politics, Class, and Work in California Agriculture.* Ithaca, NY: Cornell University Press.

West, Guida. 1981. *The National Welfare Rights Movement: The Social Protest of Poor Women.* New York: Praeger.

Wilayto, Phil. 1997. *The Feeding Trough: The Bradley Foundation, 'The Bell Curve' and the Real Story behind Wisconsin's National Model for Welfare Reform.* Milwaukee, WI: A Job Is a Right Campaign.

Wilcox, Clyde. 1994. "Premillenialists at the Millenium: Some Reflections on the Christian Right in the Twenty-First Century." *Sociology of Religion* 55 (3): 243–61.

Wilcox, Clyde, Mark J. Rozell, and Roland Gunn. 1996. "Religious Coalitions in the New Christian Right." *Social Science Quarterly* 77 (3): 543–58.

Wiley, George. 1972. "Statement at the Children's March for Survival." February 3. George Wiley Papers. State Historical Society of Wisconsin at Madison.

Wilgoren, Jodi. 1997. "Chastised GOP Softens Stance on Immigration." *Los Angeles Times*, November 23, p. A1. Retrieved September 23, 2003. Available: LEXIS-NEXIS Academic Universe, News Sources.

————. 2002. "After Welfare, Working Poor Still Struggle, Report Finds." *New York Times*, April 25, p. A20. Retrieved May 11, 2003. Available: LEXIS-NEXIS Academic Universe, News Sources.

Will, Arthur J. 1952. "Reprint of a Speech made at the 26th Annual Meeting of the California Taxpayers' Association." *Tax Digest* (April), 127–31.

Will, Arthur J., George W. Wyman, and Thomas P. Douglas. 1951. "What About Aid to Needy Children? Three Welfare Directors Tell Problems." *Tax Digest* (January), 12–14.

Wilson, Mark D. 1999. "Successful Welfare Reform Requires State Flexibility on the Minimum Wage." Executive memorandum No. 625. Washington, DC: Heritage Foundation. Retrieved February 11, 2002 (http://www.heritage.org/library/execmemo/em625.html).

Wilson, Pete. 1995. "Kicking America's Welfare Habit: Politics, Illegitimacy, and Personal Responsibility." Lecture and Seminars No. 540. Washington, DC: Heritage Foundation. Retrieved September 20, 2001 (http://www.heritage .org/Research/Welfare/HL540.cfm).

Wilson, William Julius. 1996. *When Work Disappears: The World of the New Urban Poor*. New York: Alfred A. Knopf.

Winn, Pete. 2002. "Abstinence Funding Battle Heats Up." Colorado Springs, CO: Focus on the Family. Retrieved June 5, 2002 (http://www.family.org).

Witte, Griff. 2004. "Nation's Social Safety Net in Tatters as More People Lose Their Jobs." Washington Post, September 26. Retrieved October 1, 2004. Available: LEXIS-NEXUS Academic Universe, News Sources.

Wright, Gavin. 1986. *Old South, New South: Revolutions in the Southern Economy since the Civil War*. New York: Basic Books.

Wright, Wendy, and Pamela P. Wong. 2002. "A Charitable Option." Washington, DC: Concerned Women of America. Retrieved March 31, 2002 (http://cwfa .org/library/_familyvoice/2000–03/06–11_12.shtml).

Yoo, Grace. 2001. "Shaping Public Perceptions on Immigrants on Welfare: The Role of Editorial Pages of Major U.S. Newspapers." *International Journal of Sociology and Social Policy* 21: 47–62.

Young, Penny. 1995. "Statement of Penny Young, Legislative Director, Concerned Women of America." In *Contract with America—Welfare Reform. Hearing before the Subcommittee on Human Resources of the Committee on Ways and Means, House of Representatives*, 823–28. 104th Cong., 1st sess.

Zedlewski, Sheila R., and Pamela Loprest. 2003. "Welfare Reform: One Size Does Not Fit All." *Christian Science Monitor*, August 25, p. 9. Retrieved August 25, 2003. Available: LEXIS-NEXIS Academic Universe, News Sources.

Zieger, Robert H. 1994. *American Workers, American Unions*. Baltimore, MD: Johns Hopkins University Press.

Zimmerman, Wendy, and Karen C. Tumlin. 1999. "Patchwork Policies: State Assistance for Immigrants under Welfare Reform." Occasional paper No. 24. Washington, DC: Urban Institute. Retrieved November 23, 2001 (http:// www.urban.org).

Zylan, Yvonne. 1995. "The Divided Female State: Gender, Citizenship, and U.S. Social Policy Development, 1945–1990." Ph.D. dissertation, Department of Sociology, New York University, NY.

———. 2000. "Maternalism Redefined: Gender, the State, and the Politics of Day Care, 1945–1962." *Gender & Society* 14 (5): 608–29.

Index

Text: 10/13 Aldus
Display: Aldus
Indexer: Kevin Millham
Cartographer: Bill Nelson
Compositor: BookMatters, Berkeley
Printer and Binder: Maple-Vail Manufacturing Group